Literary Theory and the New Testament

THE ANCHOR YALE BIBLE REFERENCE LIBRARY is a project of international and interfaith scope in which Protestant, Catholic, and Jewish scholars from many countries contribute individual volumes. The project is not sponsored by any ecclesiastical organization and is not intended to reflect any particular theological doctrine.

The series is committed to producing volumes in the tradition established half a century ago by the founders of the Anchor Bible, William Foxwell Albright and David Noel Freedman. It aims to present the best contemporary scholarship in a way that is accessible not only to scholars but also to the educated nonspecialist. It is committed to work of sound philological and historical scholarship, supplemented by insight from modern methods, such as sociological and literary criticism.

John J. Collins
General Editor

THE ANCHOR YALE BIBLE REFERENCE LIBRARY

Literary Theory and the New Testament

MICHAL BETH DINKLER

YALE
AYBRL

Yale
UNIVERSITY
PRESS

NEW HAVEN
AND
LONDON

Yale University Press books may be purchased in quantity for educational, business, or promotional use. For information, please e-mail sales.press@yale .edu (U.S. office) or sales@yaleup.co.uk (U.K. office).

Set in Adobe Caslon and Bauer Bodoni type by Newgen North America.
Printed in the United States of America.

Library of Congress Control Number: 2019937180
ISBN 978-0-300-21991-3 (hardcover : alk. paper)

A catalogue record for this book is available from the British Library.
This paper meets the requirements of ANSI/NISO Z39.48-1992 (Permanence of Paper).

10 9 8 7 6 5 4 3 2 1

Contents

Acknowledgments

The lone writer is one of the most resilient and long-standing literary tropes. I'm sure you can picture it: the writer writes, alone in a bare room and barely aware of passersby. Still, no book is born straight from the mind of one solitary scribbler. This book certainly wasn't.

This book arose out of a montage of moments, most of which I could never have anticipated or orchestrated, and many of which blend together in my memory. *Literary Theory and the New Testament* exists because my family nurtured in me a lifelong love for narrative and a deep thirst for the intellectual life; because mentors like François Bovon and John Darr encourage(d) me to draw on my training in literary theory when interpreting the New Testament and gave invaluable feedback in my earliest attempts to do so; because my New Testament colleagues at Yale Divinity School—Harry Attridge, Adela Collins, JanJan Lin, Judy Gundry, and Dean Gregory Sterling—have shown unfailing good cheer and consistent interest in my work. This book is the direct result of countless interactions with others: a long conversation with Scott Elliott, feedback from good friends and top-notch Lukan scholars Brittany Wilson and Daniel Lynwood Smith, generative dialogue with my deeply engaged students at Yale (notably, the 2014 Literary Criticism and the NT seminar), and Timothy Gannett's and Zachary Smith's remarkably thorough research assistance.

Certain parts of the book began as conference papers and thus benefited from ensuing discussions with colleagues at the Annual Meeting of the Studiorum Novi Testamenti Societas at the University of Pretoria (2017); the "Verstehen und Interpretieren: Zum Basisvokabular von Hermeneutik und Interpretationstheorie" Conference at the University of Zurich (2016); the Society of Biblical Literature's Gospel of Luke and Book of Acts units' session on characterization at the 2016 annual meeting; the "The Fact of Value? 'Normativity' in the Humanities" Conference at Yale University (2016); the "Jesus, quo vadis? Entwicklungen und Perspektiven der aktuellen Jesus-forschung" Symposion at Johannes Gutenberg University (2016); and the Columbia Seminar for the Study of the New Testament at Columbia University (2016 and 2019).

You quite literally would not be reading this were it not for John Collins, who championed the project from the start; Zachary Smith, who devoted countless hours both to meticulous research and to formatting; or Heather Gold and the rest of the Yale University Press editorial team, who so ably assisted in the production of the manuscript. I am grateful, too, for Dean Gregory Sterling's generous support and a yearlong research leave funded by Yale University.

If *Literary Theory and the New Testament* does what it is meant to do, it will be in large part because Stephen Moore, Jerry Camery-Hoggatt, and an anonymous reviewer read the entire manuscript, offering incisive questions and wise suggestions. Adele Reinhartz, who read the whole book more than once, was a particularly thoughtful and judicious editor. My thinking about the literariness of the New Testament has been ineluctably shaped by the scholarship of Moore, Camery-Hoggatt, and Reinhartz; that they would engage with my work so rigorously and charitably continues to humble and astonish me.

A writer's thoughts will never become a book without the generosity and effort of so many others. And yet, the trope of the solitary writer is a trope for a reason. The greatest gift a writer can ask for, ultimately, is a room of her own to write. I dedicate this book to John, Alethea, and Daelen, with deep gratitude for giving me that gift, time and again, when they would rather have had their wife and mama off the computer, out of her head, and fully in the mix, and to my fiercely brilliant sister, Brynn, who—since the day she was born—has been reminding me that even when I'm alone in a room of my own, I'm never truly alone.

Introduction

> A large tanker sits off "Author's Point" in the bay of Biblical Stud-
> ies. . . . Her decks remain crowded with those who energetically
> cast their lines out into the water, fishing for meaning. . . . Yet this
> tanker, once master of the bay, is no longer the sole craft upon the
> waters.
> *George Guthrie*

So begins George Guthrie's brief but entertaining allegorical account of
biblical scholarship's "uses of various literary criticisms and linguistics."
Boats of interpreters move about the bay, seeking the "fish" of meaning—
casting their lines off the coast of "Author's Point," in or below the "Tides
of the Text," or from various "Reader Reefs." The proliferation of publications in New Testament (NT) studies that refer to "literary criticisms
and linguistics" has given rise to a massive and unwieldy body of scholarly
literature. "The bay has gotten crowded," Guthrie concludes, "and we must
ask what we are to do about it."[1]

Before we get to the question of "what we are to do about it," I propose
that we extend Guthrie's act of imagination. What if, in addition to a Bay
of Biblical Studies, we picture a Lake of Literary Studies where boats of
literary critics are also fishing for meaning using various literary criticisms
and linguistics, just in different (non-biblical) corpora? *Literary criticism*
concerns the techniques and strategies employed by specific literary works
and the responses they evoke—the approaches, that is, that various critics take when interpreting a text. One way to organize this book, then,
might be to describe how NT scholars have invited literary critics to serve
as navigators as they search for good spots to fish in sometimes turbulent
interpretive currents. How, for example, have biblical scholars appropriated
postcolonial literary criticism in Gospel interpretation? How have biblical
scholars applied the interpretive techniques they've learned from feminist
literary critics to the Pauline corpus, or to Johannine literature?

Certainly, such scholarship (scholars'-*ships*?) can be found in the Bay of Biblical Studies, and they will be discussed throughout the book. But the picture this paints is too pristine. If we take a closer look at the Bay of Biblical Studies, we find an intriguing state of affairs: The bay is not just crowded. It's chaotic. We don't find boats of different kinds of criticisms floating about looking for a calm corner in which to cast their nets. Instead, as Guthrie puts it, we find a "cacophony of voices clamoring for the collective ear of the discipline," all apparently competing for the role of Master of the Bay.[2] Scholars in various boats chide others for catching nothing but "their own bait minnows," for "seeing boots where others see fish," or for fishing "in the wrong location all along." Meanwhile, deconstructionists "sit laughing in the middle of the bay simply throwing sticks of dynamite at the other boats. For them fish cannot be caught and all fishing expeditions are fool's errands."[3] These disciplinary crosscurrents in the Bay of Biblical Studies deserve attention. Why the stark divisions? And in the midst of these arguments over fishing for meaning, what has happened to *the literary*?

A common critique that has been levied at literary-minded NT scholars is that they have fallen victim to what Stephen Moore and Yvonne Sherwood dub the "time warp factor."[4] Biblical scholars are often described as hopelessly old-fashioned, always lagging behind the literary critics. A. K. M. Adam, for one, says that biblical scholars "usually draw on modes and methods that have flourished outside the biblical-interpretation industry ... after a delay of from five to twenty years."[5] The implication, of course, is that NT scholars' engagements with literary criticism are passé before they even go to print. This assessment rings true in some respects. However, I contend that there is a far more fundamental and debilitating difference between the Bay of Biblical Studies and the Lake of Literary Studies than a simple time lag.

The difference is not primarily about the various forms of criticism employed—what we might think of as the fishing strategies employed by various boats of critics—but about the *theories* on which our approaches are predicated and our interpretive decisions made. As literary critic Jonathan Culler explains, theory is the "discursive space *within which* literary and cultural studies now occur, even if we manage to forget it, as we forget the air we breathe. We are ineluctably *in theory*."[6] Specific acts of criticism (literary and otherwise) are always based on theories (literary and otherwise) about how language works, what communication entails, and the complicated relationship between reality and representation.

Critical Theory (sometimes, simply Theory) is a term that has evolved over time and still engenders confusion. At first, "Critical Theory" referred to a technical form of philosophy that was developed by the so-called Frankfurt School in early twentieth-century Germany. Eventually, though, "Critical Theory" became more fluid and capacious, encompassing a whole congeries of theoretical discourses and intellectual movements (including, but not only, the literary). When I use "Critical Theory" or "Theory" (note the capital *C* and *T*) in this book, I'm *not* referring to any intellectual theory that might be deemed critical (that is, "critical theory" without capital letters), but rather to this conglomeration of interconnected boundary-crossing intellectual discussions that developed throughout the twentieth century. Culler defines Critical Theory as "discourses that come to exercise influence outside their apparent disciplinary realm because they offer new and persuasive characterizations of problems or phenomena of general interest: *language, consciousness, meaning, nature and culture, the functioning of the psyche, the relations of individual experience to larger structures, and so on.*"[7]

The fog of Theory settled over the academy in the twentieth century, at times giving rise to major navigational challenges in multiple academic disciplines, including not just literature and philosophy, but also psychology, sociology, engineering, and biology, *inter alia*. The scholar who ignores Theory is, to borrow some imagery from Benjamin Franklin, "like a man travelling in foggy weather;—those at some distance before him on the road he sees wrapped up in the fog, as well as those behind him, and also the people in the fields on each side; but near him all appear clear, though in truth *he is as much in the fog as any of them.*"[8] When it comes to interpreting literature, each of us is "as much in the fog" as any other, whether or not we acknowledge it. As Terry Eagleton famously wrote, "An opposition to [T]heory usually means an opposition to other people's theories and an ignorance of one's own."[9]

In contrast to biblical scholars, contemporary literary scholars have been far more likely to engage with and seek out the benefits of Critical Theory. Literary critics have discovered that, just as fog provides a vital source of moisture in certain ecosystems, so can the broader discourses of Critical Theory serve as sources of nourishment for scholars of literature. Attending to questions about "language, consciousness, meaning, nature and culture, the functioning of the psyche, the relations of individual experience to larger structures, and so on" has provided literary critics a rich repository of intellectual resources on which to draw as they seek to understand and assess literary texts.[10]

Biblical scholars, meanwhile, have been caught up in debates about whether Critical Theory is necessary, useful, or even relevant to the interpretive enterprise. Some are intrepid Theory-ophiles, convinced that the concerns and questions raised by Theory are inescapable for biblical scholarship. These scholars consider it irresponsible not to attend closely to one's own theoretical commitments; to them, refusing to engage with Theory can be ethically dubious and even dangerous. Other biblical interpreters try ardently to avoid Theory. Nebulous and formless, Theory for them does not lead to clarity, but to interpretive anarchy and confusion. But there's more. For some, the fog of Theory is not just murky, but malevolent, perhaps best compared to a London "pea-souper" of Dickensian fame: a canopy that provides criminals cover, bewilders hapless boatmen, and leaves lost travelers stranded. "The fog," Dickens writes, "filled every nook and corner with a thick dense cloud.... Every object was obscured.... The warning lights and fires upon the river were powerless beneath this pall."[11] Yet still elsewhere, we find biblical scholars who simply ignore Theory altogether. They continue to fish as they always have, imagining that the skies are always clear and the sun always bright on the Bay of Biblical Studies.

Why, when contemplating the intersections of Theory and biblical studies, do *some* tell a tale of "traditionally minded biblical scholars marooned in a small rowing boat" in a bay that has been "thoroughly colonized by Theory," while *others* recount a "saga of latter-day redemption in which the (literary-)Theoretical arrives, however belatedly, to save us from a sclerotic history-obsessed legacy"?[12] How, moreover, do those perspectives—both of which assume that Theory has been influential in biblical studies—cohere with Moore and Sherwood's claim that amongst biblical scholars, "Theory has had too little impact, all told, to merit much attention"?[13] Why do some NT scholars find Theory useful for understanding biblical literature, while others insist that Theory obscures the way to interpretive clarity? Again, we might ask, What, in the midst of all of this fog, has happened to the *literary*? In what sense(s) is the Bible *literary*? And if the fog of Theory *already* sits over the Bay of Biblical Studies, then why should we look to the Lake of Literary Studies at all?

To address these questions, we first must get our bearings.

Some Definitions

What do we mean by the terms "literature" and "the literary"? Such a deceptively simple question is highly problematic. For one thing, what constitutes literature can seem self-evident—almost a matter of intuition. Still, Stephen Greenblatt and Giles Gunn rightly observe that "there are no transcendent or absolute rules about what belongs in the zone of the literary and in the zone of the nonliterary."[14] It's exceedingly common in books of literary theory for the critic to raise the question, shrug her proverbial shoulders, and resignedly resort to the old cliché: We know it when we see it.[15]

Nevertheless, we need at least a working definition. On a most basic level, I define literature as *written poetry or prose that communicates through the use of specific linguistic techniques, and that is taken by society to be meaningful beyond its immediate context of origin.* With this definition, I'm intentionally drawing together two distinct approaches to answering the question, What is literature?

The first approach is epitomized by René Wellek and Austin Warren's *Theory of Literature* (1949), in which they declare, "The simplest way of solving the question is by distinguishing the particular use made of language in literature."[16] By this, they mean that in contrast to everyday and scientific uses of language, literature uses connotative, ambiguous language such as metaphor, rhythm, symbolism, and the like. Their definition therefore *ex*cludes texts that are denotative, transparent, and aimed at persuading readers to do a specific action (examples would include research reports, personal correspondence, propaganda, and policy memos). This came to be known as a *poetics of deviation*—that is, the assumption that "literary" poetic language deviates from "everyday" prosaic language in its use of literary techniques. The problem with a poetics of deviation, of course, is that everyday and scientific language often *do* employ so-called literary language, and literature often *does* persuade readers to immediate action. Furthermore, Wellek and Warren do not give adequate attention to contexts of reception. For example, Dostoyevsky's *Prestuplenie i nakazanie* (*Crime and Punishment*) is obviously considered literature in Russia, but untranslated, it communicates nothing at all to someone who does not know Russian.

The second approach to defining literature is represented by John Ellis's well-known discussion in *The Theory of Literary Criticism* (1974). Ellis defines literature as texts "that are used by society in such a way that the text is not taken as specifically relevant to the immediate context of its origin."[17] Ellis's definition therefore *ex*cludes texts like journalistic articles, legal contracts, advertisements, tweets, and status updates on social media, all of which are relevant for their immediate originary contexts and then (typically) cease to be so. Ellis's phrase "used by society" recognizes that people can *choose* to take such texts as relevant or meaningful beyond the immediate circumstances to which they refer. That is, a text can be perceived as literature even if its author did not intend for it to be so read. This is the case, for example, with the letters of Paul, which—as NT scholars are fond of pointing out—are occasional documents, written to specific people on specific occasions. Though Paul certainly intended for his epistles to be "specifically relevant to the immediate context of [their] origin," centuries of societies after him have taken them as meaningful beyond their original contexts.[18]

I draw together elements of both approaches in order to define literature as *written poetry or prose that communicates through the use of specific linguistic techniques, and that is taken by society to be meaningful beyond its immediate context of origin.* I should note that by defining literature so broadly, I'm intentionally running beyond the narrower definition that would restrict literary study to fiction and poetry; while literature frequently portrays fictive or imaginary worlds, it does not always do so, and the modern fact/fiction dichotomy is rarely helpful when considering ancient literature that operates by different generic conventions. At the same time, I don't wish to adopt so broad a definition that anything at all "counts" as literature. A number of disciplines, including literary studies' close intellectual cousin cultural studies, adopt virtually boundless conceptions of texts and literature (for example, some *do* read tweets and receipts as literature). Still, we need some way to delimit our focus. For our purposes here, we'll *ex*clude unwritten forms of communication (such as dance, visual arts, and speaking), and written communication that is *not* poetry or prose (for example, shopping lists, inscriptions, labels, or recipes).[19] Even if nonliterary acts and practices like these have literary elements, they're not always *best* understood under the category of *literature.*

This is also why simply engaging Critical Theory alone won't suffice. We want to keep the *literary* in theory. The theories of figures like Marx, Freud, Foucault, and Althusser consider cultures and societies broadly, not just literature. To cite Culler again, Critical Theory is "an unbounded corpus of writings" about "problems or phenomena of general interest: *language, consciousness, meaning, nature and culture, the functioning of the psyche, the relations of individual experience to larger structures, and so on.*"[20] To these "problems and phenomena," I would add concepts like body, gender, power, race, community, identity, trauma, and more. These, too, cut across disciplinary lines; they can be operative in and relevant for literary *and* nonliterary modes of communication. Certainly, literary theorists have gained nuance and sophistication from their ongoing dialogues with Critical Theory, but literary theory itself has narrower parameters than the "unbounded corpus" of Theory.

Literary theory, then, *investigates the means by which humans make meaning through written poetry and prose.* As such, literary theory includes the history and evolution of literary genres (epic, narrative, and so on), as well as *all* aspects of literary communication (that is, author, work, reader, world). For as long as humans have been writing and thinking about literature, three sets of interrelated concerns have driven the discussions:

- Hermeneutical concerns (such as how language functions, where textual meaning resides)
- Evaluative concerns (how we assess the literary, aesthetic, and practical value of a text)
- Metadisciplinary concerns (what critics ought to be doing vis-à-vis the literary, including which works are worthy of canonical status)

I'll say more about each of these areas in the next chapter. For now, though, I wish to underscore two points. First, no discourse about the literary has ever been static or universal. Literary criticisms and theories span over 2,500 years of time and space, stretching—as one recent literary handbook is titled—"from Plato to postcolonialism," and now, on into *post*-poststructuralism (Moore calls the latter term "inelegant but necessary").[21] Throughout this long arc of literary study, the hermeneutical, evaluative, and metadisciplinary dimensions of literature have been debated constantly and vigorously contested. As Greenblatt and Gunn say of literary studies, "Not only is the canon of literary works in any genre fashioned by a simultaneous perambulation and transgression of boundaries but *the very concept of the literary is itself continually renegotiated.*"[22]

This has always been the case. Writers as far back as Aristophanes, Aeschylus, Euripides, and Aristotle not only composed great literature but theorized—and disagreed—about its nature and purpose. Yun Lee Too makes the point in *The Idea of Ancient Literary Criticism:*

> Ancient literary criticism is not a discourse to be taken for granted; nor is it a self-obvious or self-evident discipline. . . . As modern readers, we might be deceived into assuming that the texts constituting ancient criticism have always served the purposes that we now perceive them to fulfil—amongst these, attesting to and presenting an origin for a tradition of writing about how to produce and evaluate literary texts. . . . [Yet we] forget or to fail to notice that this discourse and its texts are no less the result of often arbitrary authorizations which manifest themselves as debates, quarrels, or serious questionings.[23]

Even in antiquity, the boundaries around the space that we call "the literary" were based on competing claims about language and literature, authority and authorship, art and aesthetics, community and communication. Literary theory, in other words, is and always has been in flux.

Second, we shouldn't shy away from or try to erase the complexities. They arise from the nature of the subject itself: we are studying literature, after all. This is why I disagree with Markus Bockmuehl, who predicted in 2006,

> The study of the New Testament primarily as literature, narrative, or rhetoric will . . . inevitably turn out to be a somewhat impoverished exercise on at least two fronts. First, judged by any broad-based esthetic standard, the New Testament documents never invite, and rarely reward, interpretation from a primarily literary point of view. They represent second-rate literature in often third-rate linguistic forms. . . . Second and more important, the texts in any case do not present themselves as concerned with either literature or rhetoric. To view them primarily (rather than *en passant*) in this fashion is rather like using a stethoscope to examine a light bulb: it can be done and does produce unfamiliar results, but it offers an analysis that does justice neither to the object nor to the instrument.[24]

Bockmuehl's assessment that NT texts represent "second-rate literature in often third-rate linguistic forms" depends entirely on his own *evaluative* definition of what constitutes literature—a definition he leaves unspecified. His light bulb metaphor is also misguided. Employing literary theory is exactly like using a stethoscope to examine a beating human heart: it allows us to listen more carefully to what's going on beneath the text's surface, to discern its peculiar rhythms and intonations, to understand its inner workings.

Literary theory is necessary because written human communication will always (albeit to varying degrees) be ambiguous, unstable, multilayered—whence comes its enduring power. All reading is interpretive, even when a text seems self-evident and clear. Literary theory helps us judge the validity of such impressions of clarity. Interpreters make competing claims even about texts that, to some, seem perfectly straightforward. Literary theory helps us decide between these competing claims. Moreover, the normative assumptions underlying competing interpretations typically remain unspoken, taken for granted as though they are universally known and shared. Literary theory helps us expose these unspoken assumptions and thereby make space for difference, correct misunderstandings, and carefully consider the implications of our interpretations.

"At its best," writes Eagleton, literary theory "poses questions to [other] pursuits, rather than meekly coexisting with them as one option among others. Rather than simply providing new methods for the study of literary works, it asks about the nature and function of literature and the literary institution. . . . Properly understood, then, literary theory is a kind of meta-discourse."[25] And yet there is a delicate balance to be struck here between meta-discursive theorizing and attending to actual texts. F. Scott Spencer is not alone in finding it "frustrating to wade through some heavy discussion of literary methodology to arrive at a few pages of application to biblical study which reveal nothing that could not have also been deduced by more conventional means."[26]

I agree with Irene de Jong, who insists that theoretical concepts are

> *not* to be introduced for their own sake or to be nit-picked endlessly, but to be applied to texts. They should sharpen and enrich our interpretation of texts. At the same time, theory should never become a straightjacket. Inevitably, as in grammar, there will be passages that are difficult to label as device A or B or perhaps as both. In such cases the function of theory is to highlight textual complexity, not to straighten it out.[27]

This book, therefore, proceeds in the following way.

The Plan of the Book

Chapter 1 provides an introductory overview of literary studies and its early intersections with NT studies, with special attention to the problematic ways those intersections are typically portrayed in NT scholarship. Chapters 2–4 trace the three major paradigm shifts in literary theory of the modern period: formalism, structuralism, and poststructuralism. With this shared foundation of knowledge firmly in place, chapters 5–6 then present illustrative case studies, one from each of the two major literary genres of the NT (chapter 5, narrative, and chapter 6, epistle).[28] Here's a more in-depth glimpse of where we're headed:

In chapter 1, I seek to correct several unhelpful misconceptions about literary theory and literary criticism that unfortunately continue to typify descriptions of NT scholarship's so-called literary paradigm shift. I also return to the cloudy canopy of Critical Theory in order to highlight two interrelated themes that can enrich our engagements with the literature of the NT: the power of normativity and the necessity of critical reflexivity.

Like every academic discipline, the field of literary studies underwent a number of major paradigm shifts over the twentieth and early twenty-first centuries. Chapters 2–4 are organized around three especially pivotal literary paradigm shifts: chapter 2 focuses on literary approaches that look to a text's formal features to determine meaning; chapter 3 concerns literary criticisms that assume that deep universal structures of language and thought determine meaning; and chapter 4 discusses the rise of poststructuralism, which assumes that social and linguistic contexts wed meaning to particularities to such an extent that a text's meaning can never be finalized or fixed. In each of these chapters, I introduce the given paradigm's major hermeneutical, evaluative, and metadisciplinary principles, summarize several representative forms of literary criticism within that paradigm, and assess NT scholars' engagements with those literary approaches to date.

What becomes clearer in retrospect is the extent to which the paradigms discussed in chapters 2–4 are born of their own particular locations and moments in time: "Modes of literary criticism . . . are expressions of cultural history. The definitions of literature they assume, the thematic and formal strategies they favor, and the genres and individual works they canonize are each responses to particular situations and reflect particular ideological concerns."[29] Each paradigmatic development responds to aspects of earlier paradigms, sometimes challenging and other times incorporating them. This should serve as a salutary reminder that categorizing currents of literary theory or criticism is merely a heuristic move. In many ways, they are inseparable, running together like currents of water in a stream. Critics converse and ideas converge. Discourses intersect and inspire new discourses.

For reasons that will be discussed later in the book, the critical shifts occasioned by poststructuralism were so cataclysmic and unprecedented that they changed the nature of literary studies itself. In fact, as the poststructuralist paradigm gained prominence amongst literary critics, "the literary" began to drift out of the center of the lake it had long called home. As Simon During puts it, in the wake of poststructuralism, language and literature became "vehicle[s] of cultural-political identities," rather than legitimate objects of study in their own right.[30] Today, many would prefer to rename the lake entirely, calling it either the Lake of Literary *and* Cultural Studies or even simply the Lake of *Cultural* Studies. Among many other examples, we could look to *The Encyclopedia of Literary and Cultural Theory*, published in 2011, which is made up of three volumes: I. *Literary Theory from 1900 to 1966*; II. *Literary Theory from 1966 to the Present*; and III. *Cultural Theory*. Regarding the choice to devote the third volume solely to cultural theory, Michael Ryan explains, "An entirely new field (adjacent yet connected to the study of literature), cultural studies comprises many of the themes, issues, and concerns that can be found in literary studies, from gender and politics to history and economics. Yet it also represents a remarkable broadening of concerns to include visual studies, popular music, advertising and magazines, subcultures, and the media."[31]

Here—without diminishing the significance of the critical turn toward cultural studies—I wish to keep the discussion firmly within the realm of the *literary*. Therefore, the final two chapters draw together aspects of some of the most recent literary approaches in order to proffer fresh literary interpretations of specific NT texts. Chapter 5 asks how insights from literary theory's New Formalism and New Historicism might inform our approaches to the character of Jesus as a literary figure. Taking the intercalated Synoptic stories about Jesus, Jairus's daughter, and the hemorrhaging woman (Mark 5.21–43//Luke 8.40–56//Matthew 9.18–26) as the textual focus, I pair New Historicism's historically contextualized approach to literary characters with New Formalism's attention to the "critically interventive power" of form.[32] I argue that rethinking our notions of literary characterization and narrative form in dialogue with these literary discourses reveals a richly textured *and* widely contextualized literary Jesus.

Chapter 6 brings literary theorists' engagements with affect theory and ecocriticism to bear on Paul's Corinthian correspondence, focusing especially on the purported divide between Paul's epistolary and corporeal forms of self-presentation. I argue that Pauline scholars too often replicate the dichotomizing epistolary rhetoric in the letters themselves, either by reinscribing the argument of Paul's opponents in 2 Corinthians 10.10 (thereby pitting Paul's powerful epistolary voice *over and against* his weak body), or conversely, by assuming that letters constitute a less powerful substitute for Paul's (obviously preferable) bodily presence (thereby privileging corporeal presence *over and against* epistolary presence). Drawing on recent developments in literary theory, I propose that we can do better justice to ancient views about bodies, texts, authors, and agency if we consider the Corinthian corpus as engendering an alternative but equally powerful form of presence (epistolary embodiment).

Each of these latter two chapters presents its own discrete argument. More important than the details of either case study, however, is the fact that together, they point to the *wide* array of interpretive possibilities that can emerge when one engages with contemporary literary theory. Like Mieke Bal, in her introduction to *Travelling Concepts in the Humanities*, I view these case studies as "showcases of practices" that "will open up venues for differentiated but specific uses of [literary] concepts, as sites of both methodological openness and reflection and, hence, without the loss of accountability and intersubjective communication that so often accompanies such openness."[33]

Presenting "showcases of practices" reminds us that there are many fish in the sea of biblical literature; the very diversity of "catches" attests to the depth and beauty of all that the bay has to offer. I know that some will hear this and fear that literary theory sets interpreters adrift to float, unmoored and anchorless, like poet Edward Pollock's "phantom fleets from a shoreless and unsounded sea."[34] One of my goals with this book is to show that literary theory is not, in fact, about riding the currents of whatever interpretive fad is most . . . well, current.

It's important to state clearly what this book is not. It's not an exhaustive demonstration of all interpretive options, nor is it a how-to manual for specific methods of literary interpretation. It's not a glossary of literary terms and concepts, nor a concordance of literary tropes and images used in the NT. These kinds of resources are available elsewhere. Neither is this book an apology for one kind of literary criticism or literary theory over another. In other words, I will not claim, as John Ashton does of NT narrative critics, that those who adopt a particular methodology or approach "put out to sea in a very leaky vessel."[35] There are many productive ways for NT scholars to work with, learn from, and contribute to literary theory; indeed, my own bookshelves are lined with fine examples.

Moreover, while this book engages critically with others' literary treatments of NT texts, my aim is not to attack those biblical scholars who did the crucial pioneering work of engaging literary theory in the first place. My own perspective is poststructuralist insofar as I believe that language is contextually determined, and always presents multiple interpretive possibilities, but I would never go so far as Guthrie's deconstructionists, who say that "all fishing expeditions are fool's errands." It's true that *some* pro-Theory scholars would well fit Guthrie's description of deconstructionists "throwing sticks of dynamite at the other boats."[36] My goal, however, is at once less explosive and more basic.

Literary concerns are central to the New Testament, but they are hardly simple. I've written this book for NT interpreters who recognize that this is so, but who—for any number of reasons—are not familiar with contemporary critical scholarship on literature and literary theory. Perhaps you're like a colleague of mine who, upon reading an early draft of this introduction, observed that he simply never looked to literary theory because it's hard enough to stay up to date with his "*real* work"—exegeting biblical texts. Or perhaps you're like the many who *have* ventured into literary theory, only to find themselves frustrated by the perplexing prose of a Jacques Derrida or Julia Kristeva. Other reasons for NT interpreters' reticence to explore literary studies will emerge in due course. For now, I'll simply insist that literary matters aren't peripheral to the work of biblical studies; they are constitutive of it. Interpreters of NT literature need the significant intellectual resources that literary theory has to offer.

1 Biblical Studies and Literary Studies: Finding Common Ground in Critical Chaos

> A good deal of our impatience with the diversity and seeming chaos is rooted in a demand from criticism for something it cannot do, at the cost of overlooking many of its genuine powers.
> *Meyer H. Abrams*

Biblical studies "has gotten crowded," says George Guthrie, "and we must ask what we are to do about it." One way of "doing something about it" has been to provide disciplinary overviews of the various critical methodologies in biblical scholarship. Students of biblical studies could drown in all the encyclopedia entries, exegetical handbooks, methodological guidebooks, and historical retrospectives tracing the trends and trajectories of modern biblical scholarship. The problem is that, for several reasons (not least, limited space), when it comes to NT studies' so-called literary paradigm shift, the very accounts that are meant to clarify the state of the field and thereby create common ground have instead given rise to a number of confusions.[1]

Presumably, everyone would acknowledge that literary methods are significant for studying biblical texts. And yet, the import of this insight is not always so clear. As the *Handbook of Biblical Criticism* attests, literary criticism is "one of the most potentially ambiguous terms in the field of biblical studies."[2] Recognizing the confusions in and deficiencies of biblical scholars' customary claims about literary criticisms and literary theory is the necessary first step toward reading the NT in light of contemporary advancements in literary studies. Thus, we begin with a very basic overview of the mid-twentieth-century "literary paradigm shift" in biblical studies, and then we'll consider three claims about NT literary criticism that—despite the frequency with which they appear—simply do not stand up to scrutiny. NT scholars need a better way of conceptualizing the interdisciplinary interactions between biblical studies and literary studies.

The rest of the chapter consists of three movements toward that end. First, we'll consider a simple but useful schema for categorizing various forms of literary criticism; next, we'll use that framework as a means of orienting ourselves to the many kinds of literary inquiry that can be useful for biblical studies. Still, orientation is not enough if we want to understand and be able to adjudicate between the various literary approaches in NT scholarship. The third move therefore turns toward Critical Theory, a "paradoxically expansive yet selective body of work" that encompasses literary matters, but also far exceeds them.[3] As I said in the introduction, literary critics have been far more willing than biblical scholars to acknowledge and engage with Critical Theory. While many *biblical* critics prefer to pretend that biblical studies is *not* immersed in "a sea of gray, like any other academic association," *literary* critics have found that "within the vast monochrome expanse, unique forms of intellectual life do flourish."[4] We'll get to those flourishing life forms soon enough. Before that, we need to reconsider the standard account of modern biblical scholarship's "literary paradigm shift."

Literary Criticisms Enter Biblical Studies: A Basic Overview

Retrospectives on modern biblical scholarship tend to tell a similar tale. They typically explain that for centuries, readers viewed the New Testament as uniquely mysterious—a text written by authors whose "pens were in the firm grip of the Holy Spirit."[5] For all the tortuous hermeneutical twisting and turning occasioned by heresiological debates, interpreters throughout the late antique and medieval periods, and on into the Reformation, shared a fundamentally God-centered worldview. As Peter Hawkins observes, the Bible's aesthetic value was simply assumed as a natural consequence of its divine provenance: "For centuries, appreciation for Scripture's artistry sprang from the devout conviction that its divine Author would offer nothing less than perfection."[6]

In the nineteenth century, cultural developments sparked by scientists like Charles Darwin (who sought to identify evolutionary origins and development) and fueled by philosophers like Friedrich Schleiermacher (who collapsed the distinction between *hermeneutica profana* and *hermeneutica sacra*) contributed to fundamental shifts in biblical interpretation.[7] During the Enlightenment period, modernist commitments to positivism and scientific rationalism replaced religion-based worldviews; accordingly, previously normative conceptions of meaning, language, value, and critical inquiry were seriously challenged, and in some cases, decisively rejected.[8]

Stephen Moore and Yvonne Sherwood's "critical manifesto," *The Invention of the Biblical Scholar,* traces how Enlightenment challenges to ecclesial and scriptural authority led to the "invention of a particular and peculiar academic entity—the professional biblical scholar," and to critical biblical scholarship as a new kind of historically oriented academic discipline.[9] This newly created professional biblical scholar typically considered literary criticism to be just another form of historical criticism—another "tool" in the interpreter's exegetical "toolbelt." In 1978, for example, Norman Petersen marveled that "for most historical critics, 'literary criticism' refers to *source* criticism!"[10] Indeed, most twentieth-century biblical scholars considered literary criticism to be textual analysis that begins "from the standpoint of lack of continuity, duplications, inconsistencies and different linguistic usage, with the object of discovering what the individual writers and redactors contributed to a text, and also its time and place of origin."[11] In spite of major theoretical shifts during the latter half of the twentieth century, this modernist view of literary criticism still stubbornly circulates in scholarly publications.[12]

Throughout the 1960s and 1970s, postmodernism's famous "incredulity toward metanarratives" began to destabilize historical criticism's modernist foundations. In the face of these larger cultural shifts, some biblical scholars pivoted to literary studies for fresh inspiration. With remarkable regularity, descriptions of biblical scholarship point to James Muilenburg's presidential address at the 1968 Society of Biblical Literature (SBL) annual meeting as the inauguration of literary approaches to biblical texts. Muilenburg called biblical scholars to move beyond *dia*chronic analyses (considering biblical texts as they've developed over time) toward *syn*chronic analyses (looking at a text as it is at a single moment in time). Muilenburg labeled the latter "rhetorical criticism":

> The aspect of all these works which seems to me most fruitful and rewarding I should prefer to designate by a term other than stylistics. What I am interested in, above all, is in understanding the nature of Hebrew literary

composition, in exhibiting the structural patterns that are employed for the fashioning of a literary unit, whether in poetry or in prose, and in discerning the many and various devices by which the predications are formulated and ordered into a unified whole. Such an enterprise I should describe as rhetoric and the methodology as rhetorical criticism.[13]

Muilenburg had precursors, of course, but it wasn't until the time just after his address that the field saw a true upsurge in synchronic approaches to NT literature.[14] Volumes reflecting this shift, like William Beardslee's *Literary Criticism of the New Testament* (1970) and Norman Petersen's *Literary Criticism for New Testament Critics* (1978), appeared after 1968.[15]

One of the primary concerns in this so-called literary paradigm shift was the issue of genre. NT scholars are constantly arguing about the literary genres we find in the NT. Are the Gospels Hellenistic historiography, Jewish apologetic history, Greco-Roman *bioi*, a mix of genres, or something else entirely? Is the Letter to the Hebrews an epistle, or "the greatest Christian sermon ever preached or written"? Is the book of Revelation a letter, a prophecy, or an apocalypse? Specifics aside, on a very basic level, the books of the NT can be divided into two main prose genres: narratives and epistles.[16]

Let me offer a quick explanatory note about this book's focus on prose as opposed to poetry. Certainly, we find poetry *in* the literature of the NT. Psalms, hymns, and lyrical language are embedded in the NT narratives and epistles. Strictly speaking, however, no one book of the NT is considered poetry. We find nothing in the NT comparable to the book of Psalms, for example. The poetic passages in the NT are relatively few, and their identification as such remains problematically dependent on (often fairly arbitrary) editorial decisions such as versification and indentations.[17] For this reason, and because poetry functions according to its own distinct linguistic rules, I've chosen to focus the discussions in this book on the broader *prose* genres of narratives and epistles.

When NT scholars began to adopt synchronic literary approaches, they did so in quite different ways with respect to epistolary versus narrative texts.[18] NT critics interested in the synchronic literary dimensions of the *epistles* didn't turn immediately to literary studies. Most of them turned to the technical art (Greek, *technē;* Latin *ars*) of Greco-Roman rhetoric (Greek, *rhētorikē*), found in ancient progymnasmata and rhetorical handbooks. Unsurprisingly, Pauline scholars were among the first to begin using this form of literary analysis. Paul's epistles had always been seen as attempts at persuasion; so-called classical rhetorical criticism simply provided a new means of exploring an already accepted view of the epistles' literary nature. The official entry of classical rhetoric into NT studies is typically credited to Hans Dieter Betz, who proposed that Galatians is an *apologetic* letter (a type of forensic or judicial rhetoric), though George Kennedy also had an enormous influence on this development.[19] Betz and Kennedy paved the way for later scholars to embark on a kind of literary mining expedition, seeking to identify and classify specific rhetorical techniques in NT literature; indeed, classical rhetorical criticism remains a prominent literary approach to New Testament texts today.

When NT scholars interested in *narrative* first began to interpret in a synchronic way, they turned to what they saw as "the *more valid* contributions of formalism or new criticism in secular literary studies" for inspiration. Early inquiries in this vein focused on Jesus's parables—short stories that were easily seen as "aesthetic objects, that is, carefully organized, self-contained, coherent literary compositions." This form of parable scholarship was epitomized by the collaboration of the Groupe d'Entrevernes in France and the work of scholars like Robert Funk, John Dominic Crossan, and Dan Via in the United States.[20] Over the course of the 1980s, literary-minded NT critics also began to follow the lead of Hebrew Bible scholars like Robert Alter (whose *The Art of Biblical Narrative* appeared in 1981) and Meir Sternberg (who published *The Poetics of Biblical Narrative* in 1985), who were appropriating insights from the literary subfield of structuralist narratology. A flurry of narrative-critical studies appeared in quick succession, including volumes by David Rhoads and Donald Michie (Mark), Jack Dean Kingsbury (Matthew), R. Alan Culpepper (John), and Robert Tannehill (Luke-Acts).[21]

Three Misconceptions about Literary Theory and Literary Criticisms

Publication dates and trends like those above can hardly be contested. But, as we'll see, the conventional accounts of NT studies' "literary paradigm shift" tell only partial truths, and have perpetuated unhelpful misconceptions about literary studies. When it comes to descriptions of NT literary criticism, three claims have pounded again and again, like drumbeats through the decades, and really ought to be abandoned. To begin, I'll lay out these repeated claims and why they continue to hold sway in our collective imagination, and then we'll look at the reasons that they're misleading.

First, biblical scholars regularly declare that literary approaches were adopted as *a rejection* of "the endless stream of seemingly unanswerable questions posited by historical criticism, or the lack of regard for the text in its final form except as it points to its earlier stages of production."[22] Inspired by the mode of literary formalism known as the New Criticism (discussed in the next chapter), early NT literary critics were concerned, as the saying goes, with just "the words on the page." If meaning lies in the text itself, they held, then, "when the scholar uses these texts as sources of information about historical events, persons, or views which lie behind them, he is forcing concerns which are subordinate in the text into a dominant position. . . . The scholar and the text are working at cross-purposes, and the information must be extracted in spite of the stubborn efforts of the text to speak in its own way."[23]

Understandably, many saw this shift toward literary approaches as a direct assault on historical criticism. In 1980, for example, Norman Petersen observed, "The historical critical paradigm is in a process of potentially revolutionary change. . . . The future of the historical critical paradigm is a lively question." Even the organization of the well-known 1993 collection *To Each Its Own Meaning: An Introduction to Biblical Criticisms and Their Application* reflects this view. The first two sections concern "Traditional Methods" (for example, form and redaction criticisms) and "Expanding the Tradition" (such as social-scientific criticism). The final category, "Overturning the Tradition," is where one finds literary approaches like structuralism and reader-response criticism. And at the turn of the twenty-first century, Karl Möller explained,

> An increasing number of scholars have declared the historical-critical approach bankrupt, impracticable and unhelpful given the tasks the biblical interpreter faces. Thus . . . the whole surge of recent alternative methods (such as New Criticism, poetics or narratology, reader-response theory or reception aesthetics, structuralist criticism and deconstruction as well as "ideological criticisms," such as feminist or Marxist criticism or liberation hermeneutics) are characterized, by and large, by such an attitude.[24]

Now, two decades into the twenty-first century, literary criticism hasn't usurped historical criticism in the "revolutionary" way that Petersen augured, but the perception that literary criticisms are *anti-* or *a*historical remains strong.

A second refrain in overviews of biblical scholarship has been the claim that NT literary critics approach the text *syn*chronically (as opposed to form, source, and redaction critics, who approach the text *dia*chronically), and that they do so because they value the text in its unified "final" form. This drumbeat began as early as 1932, when Muilenburg declared that for biblical scholars, "*the chief end should be* the perception of the literary unity in which one gains a sense of form, a central purpose, and, if possible, the occasion which inspired the narrative." Twenty-five years later, in 1957, Northrop Frye repeated the familiar refrain, writing that "a purely literary criticism would see the Bible, not as the scrapbook of corruptions, glosses, redactions, insertions, conflations, misplacings, and misunderstandings revealed by the analytic critic, but as a typological unity." In 1971, Amos Wilder declared that a "plea for the properly autonomous creation of the artist" stands as "a persuasive protest against that kind of criticism which *obscures the unity of the work* either by preoccupation with isolated elements or by some didactic concern." And in 1987, Tremper Longman called literary criticism "an entirely new approach to interpretation" because of "the contention that biblical texts should be studied as wholes."[25] Literary critics like these, David Aune explains, took "a synchronic approach to the biblical text" *because* they privileged textual unity and deemed a text "an artistic success" if "all the elements" could be integrated "into an overall construal of the whole."[26]

Rhetorical treatments of NT epistles also appeared to defend the literary unity of individual letters.[27] Within the historical-critical paradigm, partition theories had so dominated the discourse that, in 1977, Harry Gamble declared, "The unity of every one of the authentic letters of Paul has been disputed, with the single exception of the small letter to Philemon. . . . There appears to be a far-reaching consensus of critical judgment *against* the integrity of several letters." Gamble, still relying on the older historical-critical definition of literary criticism, called this "far-reaching consensus" a "literary-critical principle."[28] Rhetorical critics took an opposite approach. Margaret Mitchell, for example, describes her influential rhetorical analysis of 1 Corinthians, *Paul and the Rhetoric of Reconciliation*, as "a sustained defense of the *unity* of 1 Corinthians on the basis of a *literary rhetorical* analysis," which, she insists, is "the appropriate primary methodology for addressing this question."[29]

Third, retrospectives repeatedly state that NT scholars turned toward literary theory because they wanted to recover the value of NT literature *qua* literature, and they wanted to affirm the biblical authors' literary sophistication. Put differently, literary scholars' perceived attack on historical criticism was, in their view, a defensive move, meant to rescue the NT from historical critics who approached the text with "a dissecting knife" in hand.[30] So, for example, we find NT narrative critics like David Rhoads, co-author of the classic early formalist reading of a Gospel, *Mark as Story,* saying that he "brackets" historical concerns "and looks at the closed universe of the story-world" because "we know how to take the text apart to analyze it; adding narrative criticism to our study is an opportunity to *reaffirm the original achievement* of Mark in creating a unified story."[31] Similarly, advocates of rhetorical criticism like Ben Witherington are effusive in their praise for Paul's "considerable skill with rhetoric" and his "penchant for using even its most complex devices and techniques."[32] Such assertions contribute to the perception that NT scholars adopted literary criticism because they wished to "show that the biblical writings *were not inferior* to their classical counterparts, by illustrating that the Bible had many of the same classical forms."[33]

To sum up thus far, accounts of the field of NT scholarship regularly claim that NT literary critics (1) are anti- or ahistorical, locating meaning in the text alone; (2) take a synchronic approach because they value the so-called final form of the text as a unified, "accomplished piece of artistry";[34] and (3) wish to defend the literariness of NT texts and the literary prowess of NT authors. Biblical scholars then respond to, and often reject, this composite picture of literary approaches.

But if NT literary criticism is anti- or ahistorical, how is it that *some* NT scholars—who, importantly, *also* draw inspiration from literary studies—can call it "a singularly painless extension" of the historical-critical approaches against which it purportedly rebelled?[35] Why does Scott Elliott, for one, argue that NT literary critics created an entirely unique brand of inquiry—"narrative criticism"—which has "no clear parallel in the larger sphere of literary theory outside of biblical studies, much less in narratology specifically"? How can he say that it actually constitutes a "new quest for history"?[36] If NT literary critics defend the literary beauty of NT texts, then what should we make of the fact that Norman Petersen, author of *Literary Criticism for New Testament Critics,* calls the New Testament "*nonliterary writings*"?[37] If NT literary critics define a literary work as a unified whole, then how are we to understand Amos Wilder's declaration at the start of *Early Christian Rhetoric* that "'meaning' is related *not* to the literary work as

object, even when taken as a whole"?[38] And if unity and literary sophistication are inextricably linked, then why does Raj Nadella say that "the presence of *contradictory* voices [testifies to] the evangelist's superior artistic
skills," such that Luke's Gospel "emerges as a sophisticated literary work,"
typified by "*divergence* in perspectives"?[39]

In my view, such differences arise from an unaddressed underlying tendency in NT scholarship: we tend to describe and relate to literary scholarship as though it's a cohesive monolithic discourse. In reality, as Vincent
Leitch observes, "The modes and conventions of academic critical reading
have proliferated during the contemporary period, *prompting continuous fu-
sions and flexibilizations.*"[40] This may seem obvious, but it's worth underscoring: literary scholarship is hardly homogenous. Much like biblical scholars,
literary critics sometimes cross one another, and mutually exclusive convictions collide. Other times, literary criticisms coalesce under eclectic poly-
hyphenated flags (like Leitch's example, "Marxist feminist deconstructive
postcolonial cultural criticism").[41] Add to this the fact that various biblical scholars interact with *different* literary-critical blendings—in different
ways, for different reasons—and biblical scholars' conflicting claims about
literary criticism are less surprising.

Literary critic Meyer Abrams's description of his field as it stood in the
mid-twentieth century might just as well be a description of references to
"the literary" in biblical studies today:

> Many theories of art cannot readily be compared at all, because they *lack a
> common ground* on which to meet and clash. They seem incommensurable
> because stated in diverse terms, or in identical terms with diverse significa-
> tion, or because they are an integral part of larger systems of thought which
> differ in assumptions and procedure. As a result it is hard to find where they
> agree, where they disagree, or even, what the points at issue are.[42]

The three normative claims about biblical literary criticism outlined
above obscure how literary approaches in biblical scholarship "cannot readily be compared" to one another because "they lack a common ground on
which to meet and clash." We need a means of ordering our critical discussions of the literary and the New Testament.

Literary Studies: A Fresh Look

In some ways, the situation in literary studies has paralleled that in biblical studies. In 1925, I. A. Richards characterized literary studies as marked

by "inexhaustible confusion, a sufficiency of dogma, no small stock of pre-judices, whimsies and crotchets, a profusion of mysticism, a little genuine speculation, sundry stray inspirations, pregnant hints and random *aper-çus.*"[43] Richards's denunciation in his essay "The Chaos of Critical Theories" reverberated in the literary field for decades. This is evident, not least, in the surge of works published around the turn of the century with titles like *After Theory* (Terry Eagleton's well-known book of 2003 and its 1996 pre-decessor by Thomas Docherty).[44]

Still, Abrams insists in his classic work of literary criticism, *The Mirror and the Lamp,* that the "seeming chaos" and the conversations it engenders "are not to be deplored." Though he recognizes Richards's famous polemic, Abrams argues that methodological diversity itself can be enriching:

> If our critics had not disagreed so violently, our artistic inheritance would doubtless have been less rich and various. . . . The very fact that any well-grounded critical theory in some degree alters the aesthetic perceptions it purports to discover is a source of its value . . . for it may open [the inter-preter's] senses to aspects of a work which other theories, with a different fo-cus and different categories of discrimination, have on principle overlooked, underestimated, or obscured.[45]

The danger posed by diverse critical methodologies—and the divergent vocabularies and theoretical assumptions undergirding them—is that some literary critics may be tempted to adopt as normative the approach that seems best to them, and in the process, subordinate or reject as invalid the concerns of other critics. We see this all the time. But while each form of literary criticism may be valid within its own frame of reference, none on its own can account for the full range of interpretive horizons engendered by a given literary text. Abrams thus implores literary critics to take off their methodological blinders and take a look around.

To make the complexities more manageable and thus take full advan-tage of the enriching effects of methodological diversity, Abrams proposes a basic taxonomy of literary approaches. The scheme is organized around four poles of interpretive prioritization: An *author* composes a *text* for a *reader* about the *universe.* Every comprehensive hermeneutical theory should ac-count for how these dimensions relate to one other, but in point of fact, nearly every critical approach to literature leans more heavily toward one orientation or another. For convenience, and to emphasize the artificiality of these categories, Abrams offers a diagram (see fig. 1).

UNIVERSE
Mimetic Approaches
TEXT
Objective Approaches

ARTIST   AUDIENCE
Expressive Approaches   Pragmatic Approaches

Figure 1. *Interpretive prioritization. Adapted from Abrams,* Mirror and the Lamp, *6.*

Mimetic, Universe-Oriented Approaches

Mimetic, universe-oriented approaches reflect the core dictum already well established by the time of Socrates: "Art imitates reality." That is, a literary text imitates the world it portrays. Aristotle took this view, for example, when discussing the six elements of tragedy: "Not a few tragedians *do in fact use these* as qualitative elements; indeed, virtually every play has spectacle, the *mimēsis* of character, plot, verbal expression, song, and the *mimēsis* of intellect" (*Poet.* 1450a).

A referential view of language broadly, and of literary art more narrowly, dominated literary criticism for centuries. Abrams detected a shift in the nineteenth century, when, he states, literary criticism became "primarily oriented, not from work to universe, but from work to audience."[46] Nevertheless, mimetic forms of criticism were powerful even up through the twentieth century, as literary critics like Erich Auerbach, E. D. Hirsch, and W. J. Harvey remained resolutely committed to realism in literature.

Expressive, Author-Oriented Approaches

Expressive, author-oriented approaches are characterized by the view that "a work of art is essentially the internal made external, resulting from a creative process operating under the impulse of feeling, and embodying the combined product of the poet's perceptions, thoughts, and feelings."[47] The profound power of poetic genius has appeared as a trope again and again in literary theory, from pseudo-Longinus's *On the Sublime* in the first century CE, to the Romanticist William Wordsworth's famous declaration that "all good poetry is the spontaneous overflow of powerful feelings" at the end of the eighteenth.[48] The frequent use of "poet" in such discussions reflects a special preoccupation with poetic literature, but prose has been discussed similarly for centuries, as well.

The concept from the expressive theoretical orientation that has proven most durable—and most debated in the modern age—is that of authorial intent. Expressive forms of criticism locate the meaning of a literary text in the message that its author intended to convey. Hirsch put the matter forcefully in his essay "In Defense of the Author": "If the best meaning were not the author's, then it would be the critic's—in which case the critic would be the author of the best meaning. Whenever meaning is attached to a sequence of words it is impossible to escape an author."[49] Notably, expressive approaches border on the mimetic, except that the emphasis is not on what the text reports about its world, but rather on the effects of extratextual milieux in shaping the author's values, and—more narrowly—on the intellectual and historical circumstances that prompted and informed the production of a given text.

Work-Oriented, Objective Approaches

Work-oriented, objective approaches deal with the literary text as an object of study in its own right. Abrams calls these forms of criticism "objective" not because they are without presupposition or bias, but because they consider the meaning of a work to be independent of its relation to reality, independent of its author's intent, and independent of its audience's responses: "The 'objective orientation' . . . on principle regards the work of art in isolation from all these external points of reference, analyzes it as a self-sufficient entity constituted by its parts in their internal relations, and sets out to judge it solely by criteria intrinsic to its own mode of being."[50]

Aristotle, though he takes a mimetic approach to literature generally, adopts a work-oriented approach in practice when, in the *Poetics,* he discusses genres as static, ontologically distinct literary units: "Epic poetry, then, and the poetry of tragic drama, and moreover, comedy and dithyrambic poetry . . . differ one from another in three respects: the media, the objects, and the mode of *mimēsis*" (*Poet.* 1447a). From an objective theoretical perspective, a literary text once shared has been "cut free" to enjoy what Paul Ricoeur calls a "threefold semantic autonomy"—an autonomy, that is, "in relation to the speaker's intention, to its reception by its original audience, and to the economic, social, and cultural circumstances of its production."[51]

Pragmatic, Audience-Oriented Approaches

Pragmatic, audience-oriented approaches take as their main focus the literary text's effects upon its audience(s). Abrams designates this orientation "pragmatic" because "it looks upon the work of art chiefly as a means to an end, an instrument for getting something done, and tends to judge its value according to its success in achieving that aim."[52] Traditionally, that ultimate aim has been described by invoking Sir Philip Sidney, who (following Horace) famously wrote that poetry, properly written, works to "this end, *to teach and delight.*"[53]

Classical Greco-Roman rhetoric also leans toward the pragmatic view of literary art to the extent that it concerns the systematic, reasoned oratorical methods by which a *rhētor* could persuade an audience. Ancient dramatic arts served a moral function, Aristotle taught, insofar as they could create cathartic relief for an audience, "effecting through pity and fear the purification of such emotions" (*Poet.* 1449b).[54] The distinction between *mimetic* and *pragmatic* literary approaches is that the former sees literature as representing what *is,* while the latter sees it as representing what *ought to be.*

Not all pragmatic literary criticism considers literary art to be a vehicle of moral suasion, however. Some audience-based literary approaches, known variously as reception aesthetics, reader-response criticism, or affective stylistics, seek to understand all of the effects a text might have on its audience. From this perspective, the meaning of a work, as Leitch summarizes, "is to be encountered in the experience of it, not in the detritus left after the experience. Literature is process, not product."[55]

It should be obvious that Abrams's taxonomy simplifies what is in fact a complex critical landscape. But remember: this was by design. Abrams himself recognized that "it would be possible, of course, to devise more complex methods of analysis which, even in a preliminary classification, would make more subtle distinctions. By multiplying differentiae, however, we sharpen our capacity to discriminate at the expense both of easy manageability and the ability to make broad initial generalizations." The better approach, Abrams avers, is to adopt "an analytic scheme which avoids imposing its own philosophy, by utilizing those key distinctions which are already common to the largest possible number of the theories to be compared, and then to apply the scheme warily, in constant readiness to introduce such further distinctions as seem to be needed for the purpose in hand."[56]

Abrams's analytic scheme offers a clear, simple framework for categorizing hermeneutical postures toward literary texts, even as it remains flexible enough to represent multiple interpretive orientations at once. This is why I suggest that we use Abrams's taxonomy as an entrée into the perplexing plurality of perspectives on "the literary" in biblical studies.

Before providing a few examples of how this hermeneutical wayfinding might work, I wish to address some potential concerns. Given that ancient literary texts were typically read aloud to hearers, some biblical scholars might be concerned about Abrams's use of the term "reader." Others, perhaps, noting that ancient literary composition and reception were more fluid and communal than modern practices, will worry that Abrams's use of singular nouns (such as "author" or "text") occludes ancient practices of forgery and pseudonymity, or sidesteps the realia of manuscript variations, textual corruptions, and scribal intercalations. Scholarly contestations about such topics are ongoing, and for good reason.

Recall, though, that Abrams qualifies his taxonomy by commending a "readiness to introduce such further distinctions as seem to be needed for the purpose in hand."[57] There's nothing to keep us from expanding or adjusting the four categories to make them more historically applicable to the purpose we have in hand. We might, for example, consider the term "Author" as signifying the ancient person(s) responsible for creating or composing a text, including redactors who collected, edited, and incorporated various sources into the "texts" that we interpret today. Similarly, we can think of Abrams's mentions of a "Text" as more general references to that which has been expressed and received, in whatever form. And we might conceive of the term "Reader" broadly as a reference to the various audiences that receive, hear, and/or interpret texts. Recognizing the significance of such conceptual adjustments, surely we can affirm with Abrams that these four elements (again, broadly construed)—Author, Text, Reader, Universe—adequately encompass the phenomena involved in human literary communication.

"A good deal of our impatience with the diversity and seeming chaos" in literary studies, Abrams declared, is "rooted in a demand from criticism for something it cannot do, *at the cost of overlooking many of its genuine powers*."[58] We want to recover the "genuine powers" of literary criticisms—and the theories on which they are based—for NT scholarship, as well. Abrams's categories can help us do so.

Considering "the Literary" and the NT with Meyer Abrams

One of the most influential twentieth-century works concerning literary style and biblical narrative was philologist Eric Auerbach's 1946 volume, *Mimesis: The Representation of Reality in Western Literature*. As its title suggests, *Mimesis* provides a ready example of Abrams's *mimetic* orientations toward literature. In *Mimesis*, Auerbach contrasts the literary sophistication of Homeric epic with the sparse narration he finds in the Bible, concluding that the Bible's literary style reflects "an effective version" of a deeper truth: God is incomprehensible.[59] Another classic example of the mimetic mode is Amos Wilder's *Early Christian Rhetoric*, published in 1971. Wilder argues that the New Testament's simple literary style reflects Christ's humility. For Wilder, the language of the NT reflects the kerygmatic nature of reality, representing "the way things are and the way things happen."[60]

Expressive, author-oriented literary approaches to the NT are exemplified by those who look to literary aspects of a text in order to discern its ancient author's (or final redactor's) original intentions. This goal sometimes appears under different labels. Certain NT scholars, for example, use rhetorical criticism "to achieve a better understanding of the movement of the author's thought, intent, and message," while others look to specific literary phenomena (such as irony or intertextuality) for clues about an author's communicative agenda. An example of the latter can be found in Richard Hays's influential book *Reading Backwards: Figural Christology and the Fourfold Gospel Witness*, in which Hays contends that "we will learn to read Scripture rightly only if our minds and imaginations are opened by seeing the scriptural text—and therefore the world—through the Evangelists' eyes."[61]

Other NT scholars employ *work-oriented, objective* forms of literary criticism. Typically drawing on the literary subfield of narratology to interpret the Gospels, these scholars have developed what is now known in NT studies as "narrative criticism." This approach focuses mainly on the world of the story, and presupposes what Petri Merenlahti calls an "indissociable triune alliance" between the "unity of the gospels, their literary value, and the usefulness of a literary approach."[62] David Rhoads, for instance, in his programmatic article "Narrative Criticism and the Gospel of Mark" (1982), describes his own evolution as a scholar in terms of "a shift from fragmentation to wholeness."[63]

NT scholars who utilize forms of reader-response criticism fit well under the rubric of Abrams's *pragmatic, audience-oriented* approaches. As Robert Fowler observes, "in antiquity virtually all 'criticism' was reader oriented, because all literature was reader oriented." In the ancient world, words were not innocuous; there was a general "fascination with, and fear of, the power of words to form character." Reader-response critic Wolfgang Iser's concept of the *implied reader* is useful for considering the texts' original audiences because we can only reconstruct those original audiences based on what is "implied" in and by the text. Jerry Camery-Hoggatt explains that an implied reader "possesses specific competencies—skills and bodies of knowledge—against which the details of the narrative work out their rhetorical play. Those competencies can only be understood within the social and linguistic matrix which the author or redactor assumes." The hermeneutical conviction underlying this approach is that the study of ancient literature "demands that the modern reader have the historical information that the text assumes of its implied reader."[64]

NT scholars like Fowler consider reader-oriented theories to be particularly "well suited to deal with a text that takes aim at the reader at every step." NT texts "take aim," in part, by inviting audience participation in the meaning-making process. Kathy Maxwell, for instance, argues that missing information in the Gospel of Luke "impels the audience to do more than merely receive the story. . . . The silence of intentional gaps invites the audience to speak, to engage the unfolding rhetoric, and to become part of the story themselves."[65] Others, though, would not say that a text "takes aim" or "impels" an audience. Drawing on reader-response critics like Stanley Fish, these interpreters place greater emphasis on the audience's constitutive role in meaning-making as a social construction. Such distinctions notwithstanding, reader-response criticisms belong in Abrams's category of *pragmatic* approaches.

Abrams's categories also provide a way of situating diametrically opposed claims *about* NT literary approaches. Here's an example. When narrative critics began to shift their attention to the elements of story, certain historically oriented scholars mounted vociferous defenses of traditional author-oriented interpretive guidelines. Mark Alan Powell has traced five objections that appear repeatedly in such critiques. Historical critics often complain that narrative criticism (1) treats the Gospels as coherent narratives when they are actually collections of disparate material; (2) imposes on ancient literature concepts drawn from the study of modern literature; (3) seeks to interpret the Gospels through methods that were devised for the study of fiction; (4) lacks objective criteria for the analysis of texts; and (5) rejects or ignores the historical witness of the Gospels. Yet, at the very same time, Elliott laments "the extent to which narrative critics *uphold* many of the fundamental conclusions of historical critics, even while positioning themselves over against the historical critical method itself." So which is it? Are literary and historical critics "perpetual sparring partners," as Moore and Sherwood put it, or is NT narrative criticism actually incurably *historical*?[66]

Setting aside for now the relative validity of such assessments (we'll get to that later), one way to understand the discrepancy between them is to recognize, first, that the objections that Powell identifies reflect the incorrect perception that as a *work-oriented* approach, narrative criticism necessarily excludes all extratextual matters; and second, that Elliott is identifying narrative critics' persistent propensity in practice—their own rhetoric notwithstanding—to (re)turn to *expressive, author-oriented* concerns (which Elliott labels "historical").

Stephen Moore's critique of James Resseguie's oft-cited *JAAR* article "Reader-Response Criticism and the Synoptic Gospels" provides another illustration of the heuristic value of Abrams's taxonomy. Resseguie makes his theoretical orientation clear in his article: "The reader-response critic is concerned not with what the text *says* or *shows*, but with what the text *does* to the reader."[67] But according to Moore, Resseguie's theoretical tenets are in "deep contradiction" with his actual readings.[68] Moore sees a vast difference between Resseguie's *theoretical* "implied reader" (who is "free" to interpret the text in his or her own idiosyncratic ways) and his *practical* "implied reader" (who is governed by the strictures of the text, which are governed by its author). The crux of the problem, for Moore, is this: "The 'several . . . even infinite realizations' of the given text, affirmed in [Resseguie's] theoretical sections, swiftly reduce to the definitive realization (what its author might have intended) in actual practice."[69] Does NT reader-response criticism focus on the interactions between text and reader, or does it use novel concepts to mask not-so-novel goals like recovering authorial intent?

Again, without assessing the relative merits of these claims, we can draw on Abrams's categories to reframe the discrepancy. Resseguie's focus is *audience-oriented* in a very particular way: he wants to identify the ancient readerly competencies and conventions assumed by the text because he believes that "the reader can interact with a text *only to the extent that conventions are shared by both text and reader*."[70] Moore does not share that assumption. He suggests, instead, that we ought to measure "the adequacy of competing approaches to the Gospels . . . by the respective degrees of awareness they exhibit of the Gospels' ineluctable rhetoricity."[71] Moore argues that Resseguie's version of reader-response criticism remains inattentive to the text's attempts to persuade readers *and* to readers' freedom to refuse the text's overtures; thus, Moore insists, Resseguie's interpretations are *over*determined by the text and its (imagined) author. In other words, Moore and Resseguie are both interested in *pragmatic, audience-oriented* issues, but they construe the relationships between author, text, and audience differently.[72]

Even as we can identify distinct analytical emphases (for example, work-oriented or audience-oriented approaches), we have to remember that critics regularly meld two or more of these interpretive orientations. For instance, according to Powell, it is "accepted as axiomatic in literary circles that the meaning of literature transcends the historical intentions of the author."[73] Yet at the same time, many who employ narrative criticism (a purportedly *work-oriented* approach) remain concerned with *expressive* questions. Tannehill, one of the earliest NT scholars to employ narrative criticism, asks repeatedly how the *author* of Mark's Gospel has intentionally "undertaken the more subtle task of speaking through story to his friends."[74] This focus appears in more recent literary-inspired works, as well. Elizabeth Shively's 2012 treatment of Mark's Gospel, for example, recognizes that Mark 3.22–30 "can be viewed analytically as a composite discourse," but concludes that "literary features verify the conclusion that Mark *intentionally* crafted it as a unified discourse."[75] Similarly, the classical rhetorical methodology described earlier can be understood as *mimetic* insofar as it treats rhetoric as "a universal phenomenon which is conditioned by basic workings of the human mind and heart and by the nature of all human society," and texts as reflections of an unchanging external universe.[76] But this *mimetic* orientation is hardly incompatible with Kennedy's definition of rhetoric as "that quality in discourse by which a speaker or writer seeks to accomplish his purposes" (a more *expressive* orientation). Rhetorical criticism also consistently returns to *pragmatic* issues, seeking, as Kennedy puts it, to read the text "as it would be read by an early Christian."[77]

As these examples attest, NT scholars have appropriated literary concepts and methodologies in diverse and complicated ways. Treating "literary studies" and/or biblical scholars' engagements with literary issues as though any of them is univocal trivializes the distinctions *and* the similarities between them.

I just described how Abrams's taxonomy might work as a kind of compass, a way of orienting oneself when venturing into the "critical chaos" of biblical scholars' varying engagements with literary studies. Still, orientation alone is not enough. We need to be able not only to *explain* differing approaches to literary matters (such as Moore's construal of readers *versus* Resseguie's), but also to be able to *adjudicate between* them. The best way to do that, in my view, is to do what many *literary* critics have done: to engage with Critical Theory, the "discourses that come to exercise influence outside their apparent disciplinary realm because they offer new and persuasive characterizations of problems or phenomena of general interest."[78]

Critical Theory

It's worth remembering that the origins of the English word "theory" can be found in the Greek *theōria*, "vision," or "sight." A "theory" suggests a way of seeing things. There's no denying the fact, however, that Critical Theory, as a diffuse body of sometimes conflictual theories, can be disorienting. Moore's delineation of Theory, for example, reads like the table of contents of an anthology of literary criticisms with various kinds of other intellectual discourses interspersed throughout:

> Russian formalism, French structuralism, semiotics, poststructuralism, deconstruction, Lacanian and post-Lacanian psychoanalytic theory, assorted Marxisms and neo-Marxisms, reader-response criticism and *Rezeptionsäs-thetik*, "French feminist theory," "third-wave" feminist theory, gender studies, queer theory, New Historicism, cultural materialism, cultural studies, postcolonial studies, and (academic) postmodernism tout court, along with carefully selected slices of what is known (often polemically) as "continental philosophy."[79]

We'll return to Critical Theory's complexities later (see especially chapter 3's discussion of normativity as negative). The goal here is simply to bring some clarity—an interval of visibility, if you like—to Theory, and to consider where *the literary* lies within it. In the previous chapter, I cited Culler's description of Critical Theory as the "discursive space *within which* literary and cultural studies now occur, even if we manage to forget it, as we forget the air we breathe."[80] As I said in the introduction, Critical Theory has created atmospheric shifts that have fundamentally altered previous ways of approaching language, texts, and contexts; these changes now constitute part of the critical air that scholars breathe, even as the winds of intellectual inquiry continue to blow in new directions. We are all, Culler insists, "ineluctably *in theory*."[81]

What does that mean, exactly? The complex vortex of discourses that constitute Critical Theory share a number of characteristics. At the risk of oversimplifying, I wish to highlight just two. Theory, in all its iterations, pushes us to recognize, first, the *power of normativity*, and second, the *necessity of critical reflexivity*. Some terminological clarifications are in order. By *normativity* (from the Latin *normalis*, "made according to a carpenter's square," or "in conformity with rule"), I mean the claim, made implicitly or explicitly, that one's interpretation is definitive, and therefore the standard (the *norm*) against which all other interpretations are to be measured and judged. *Reflexivity*, as its etymology suggests (from the Latin *reflexivus*, or to *re*, "again" + *flectere*, "to bend"), is a turning or bending back on oneself. By *critical reflexivity*, then, I mean the willingness to recognize that none of us is neutral; every reader's cultural and social location conditions her or his perspective, which then influences the reader's critical questions, presuppositions, frames of reference, methods of research, and so on. Reflexivity suggests, consequently, that none of our interpretations should be considered definitive, and that we are ethically responsible to turn a reflexive critical eye on our own work as well as others.' Reflexivity is a form of intellectual honesty.

Critical Theory foregrounds the various ways that normativities—ideological belief systems, taken-for-granted norms—constantly evolve out of and revolve around socially constructed, individually assimilated conceptions of reality. Theory on the whole draws critical attention to the fact that as humans make sense of the world, we inevitably obscure certain aspects of reality and highlight others. We don't always intend to do so; it happens simply by virtue of the epistemological structures through which we perceive and interpret reality. Theory assumes that everyone interprets from a particular, limited, *normative* position.

Put differently, in biblical studies, there is no *one*, objective, positionless point from which to discern meaning. Such a position never existed. Consider Yii-Jan Lin's penetrating Theory-informed meta-analysis of NT text criticism. Traditional text critics would say that they "do not presume to dictate what an interpretation should be; they only offer others the tools by which interpretation can be conducted. . . . Lower criticism is supposed to provide the foundation upon which higher criticism—interpretation, exegesis, hermeneutics—is built." NT text critics might claim that they simply establish the foundation on which interpretation is built, but Lin, inspired by Michel Foucault, challenges that claim: "The tools provided for interpretation presume the type of interpretation that should be produced. When it is stated that scribal errors disfigure or modify the meaning carried by a text, the meaning, as a static, recoverable entity, becomes the assumed desideratum of the interpreter. . . . Textual critics' beliefs regarding language and meaning are *as significant* as the exegesis of interpreters using their editions."[82] Even if text critics are not self-consciously interpreting, but instead "offering others tools" with which to interpret, they still must do so from a particular *position*; establishing foundations is also a constructive activity, and depends upon certain normative judgments.

The text critics to whom Lin refers are but one set of biblical scholars who continue to behave as though Critical Theory doesn't exist. John Barton provides another example; referring to postmodernism, which he equates with Theory, Barton declares, "I do not believe in it for a moment."[83] But Theory is not a mythical thing in which one chooses to believe or not to believe, like a unicorn or a dragon. In the postmodern age, Critical Theory is in the air like a fog. Even as "the procession of . . . life was still rolling," wrote Robert Louis Stevenson, "the fog still slept on the wing."[84]

Theory's insistence on the power of normativity is one reason that I tend to chafe at standard descriptions of literary approaches. Often, scholars compare literary discourses (Marxist, feminist, deconstructionist, and so on) to tools, as though an interpreter, looking into a theoretical toolbox, simply chooses, uses, and replaces a particular criticism, just as one would a hammer. But some literary discourses (like deconstruction) are not *methods* at all; they're theories about language and literature. Another prevalent analogy is that literary criticisms are like glasses—lenses through which an interpreter reads a text. Readers try on a pair of glasses, then take them off and return them to their case. Often, the default assumption underlying these toolbox and glasses analogies is that an interpreter chooses a tool to use, or a pair of glasses to wear, from a place of neutrality, a *non*-position. However, the nature of human communication and comprehension means that everyone *already* reads from a particular *limited* vantage point. We can't always put on and take off critical glasses at will; certain lenses are welded to our faces. Normative assumptions and judgments about interpretive strategies are themselves *positionalities*, and as such, they are inescapable aspects of all interpretation. As Simon Goldhill observes, "Implying that methodology is a supplement to reading rather than what makes reading possible" is one of "the greatest of all critical fictions." The "claim of 'no methodology,'" Goldhill continues, "may be naïve but is never innocent."[85]

This is why Critical Theory calls for critical reflexivity. If every critic's perceptions are ineluctably shaped by her particular contexts and are therefore not neutral, then "research texts like any others, are to be read and re-read, not as representations (accurate or flawed) of the world, but as contested claims to speak 'the truth' about the world, constituted in the play of disciplines of the social."[86] Theory challenges us to recognize, interrogate, alter, and justify our own claims to knowledge and truth with the same critical rigor we bring to the ancient literature we read. Moore and Sherwood are right: "Theory's most important contribution is the self-reflexive and metacritical moves it makes possible."[87]

Certain biblical scholars (especially feminist critics) have been articulating the need for rigorous critical reflection in NT scholarship for quite some time.[88] In 1987, Elisabeth Schüssler Fiorenza's presidential address at the annual SBL conference recognized that biblical studies had "adopted insights and methods derived from literary studies and philosophical hermeneutics," but lamented that biblical scholars had still "refused to relinquish its rhetorical stance of value-free objectivism and scientific methodism." Schüssler Fiorenza then proclaimed the inauguration of a new "rhetorical-ethical" phase of biblical scholarship, which would be marked by "self-understanding of scholarship as communicative praxis."[89] Still, decades later, the prescient "rhetorical-ethical" phase that Schüssler Fiorenza heralded remains less of a phase than a set of preoccupations shared by a select group of NT critics.

Why is this the case? Why are so many NT scholars averse to Critical Theory? Why will so many admit to Rudolf Bultmann's well-known principle that there is no presuppositionless exegesis, while refusing to consider Critical Theory's emphases on normativity and critical reflexivity? Perhaps it's as simple as Guthrie's observation: "We do not care for people messing with our paradigms." But we can delve more deeply yet. I believe that Critical Theory suffers from an image problem among biblical scholars. You'll recall from the quote above that Barton denounces Theory (which he equates with postmodernism) in no uncertain terms: "As 'a theory' (sometimes, with staggering imperialism, just 'theory,' with no article!) claiming to explain or expose culture, art, meaning, and truth, I find postmodernism absurd, rather despicable in its delight in debunking all serious beliefs, decadent and corrupt in its indifference to questions of truth; I do not believe in it for a moment." Totalizing descriptors like "absurd," "despicable," "decadent," and "corrupt" portray Theory as an enemy to all that (Barton implies) is good about biblical scholarship.[90] Barton's assessment of Critical Theory is by no means unique: unfortunately, many biblical scholars turn away from Theory based on incorrect stereotypes.

Theory is hardly "indifferent to questions of truth." The point, rather, is that it enables critical reflexivity—namely, the "self-understanding of scholarship as communicative praxis" to which Schüssler Fiorenza appeals—and thus, can usefully expose NT scholars' habitual blind spots, a necessary step without which we cannot revise or improve our work. Far too often, unacknowledged normativities function to legitimate critics' own normative views. Critical Theory, Moore and Sherwood write, calls biblical scholars to "unpick the locks of the disciplinary mechanism itself and expose its inner operations; to probe the discomfort zones that mark the edges of acceptable and normative practice in our guild; to examine the system of exclusions that constitute our professional identities as biblical scholars; and to reflect on how this system relates to that order of knowledge we call 'modern.'"[91] Nuanced, intellectually robust discussions of the literary dimensions of NT texts require that we "unpick the locks" and "expose our inner operations." They require careful attention to the normative theoretical assumptions on which our own and others' conceptions of literature and literariness are based. Normativity and reflexivity simultaneously sustain and (re)shape one another. Reflexivity is, in a sense, the *yang* to normativity's *yin*.

The Literary in Theory

This brings us back to a key question: Where is the *literary* in Critical Theory? In the introductory chapter, I said that *literary theory* focuses on *the means by which humans make meaning through written poetry and prose*. I also said that, while fluid and diverse, literary theory generally concerns three interconnected sets of issues:

- Hermeneutical matters (how language functions, where textual meaning resides)
- Evaluative concerns (how we assess the literary value of a text)
- Metadisciplinary views (what critics ought to be reading and doing vis-à-vis the literary)

Let's consider each in turn.

Hermeneutical Concerns

Like "literary," the term "hermeneutics" has always been difficult to define. In a narrow sense, "hermeneutics" refers to the modern philosophical discipline pioneered by Friedrich Schleiermacher. Schleiermacher defined hermeneutics as "the art of understanding," and differentiated between *subtilitas explicandi* (exactness of explication) and *subtilitas intelligendi* (exactness of understanding).[92] Later, Hans-Georg Gadamer, following his mentor Martin Heidegger, advanced the more expansive view that hermeneutics concerns the conditions of possibility that enable or hinder understanding; for Gadamer, hermeneutics properly aims "not to develop a procedure of understanding, but to clarify the conditions in which understanding takes place."[93] Another giant in the modern hermeneutical tradition, Paul Ricoeur, defines hermeneutics as "the theory of the rules that preside over an exegesis—that is, over the interpretation of a particular text, or of a group of signs that may be viewed as a text."[94]

When I use terms like *hermeneutics* and *hermeneutical* in this book, I'm *not* referring to the technical philosophical discourse. Rather, like Clifford Geertz, I use these terms broadly to refer to "the systematic study of meaning, the vehicles of meaning, and the understanding of meaning," that is, the whole nexus of issues related to human understanding, including languages and messages, (mis)understanding and meaning, (mis)interpretation and perception, (mis)representation and translation.[95] To borrow Eagleton's explanation: "All reading involves interpretation; but hermeneutics inquires into what goes on when we interpret."[96] How does language work? How does form relate to content? Where does textual meaning reside (is meaning contingent on authorial intent, or "just the words on the page," or readerly perceptions)? Frye sees a predictable pendulum swing with respect to the latter question: "Throughout literary history, there has been a recurrent dialectical movement between Aristotelian, mimetic views of *art as product* and Longinian views of *art as process*."[97] In this book, *hermeneutical* will refer to theories about how literature works as a form of communication between human beings—as product, process, or otherwise.

Evaluative Concerns

In addition to hermeneutical convictions about how language functions and where meaning lies, literary theory has always concerned itself with questions of literary *value*. Literary theorists ask, What makes literature important? Does its value lie in its power to inspire change? In its aesthetic beauty? Its intellectual profundity? Or, perhaps, in its accurate representation of the world? Frye observed, "Every deliberately constructed hierarchy of values in literature known to me is based on a concealed social, moral, or intellectual analogy."[98] What are the social, moral, and intellectual underpinnings of our evaluative decisions? How do variables like sex and gender, class and social status, race and ethnicity, nations and cultures shape aesthetic decisions? Are there universal standards by which we should judge the merit of a work of literary art?

When the literature in question is considered by many to be holy Scripture, do (or should) we judge it by different standards? Should we attend more closely to the ethical implications of such literature than to its aesthetics, or are ethics and aesthetics inextricably intertwined? Is Crossan correct when he claims that it's *because* parables "articulate a referent so new and so alien to consciousness that the referent can only be grasped within the metaphor itself"?[99] Or, contrarily, is Robert Stein right to say that "the greatest reverence we can give to the parables of Jesus is *not* to treat them as literary accounts"?[100] Does a literary-critical approach to NT texts divorce the person of Jesus from the Christian Church's doctrinal propositions, and consequently threaten the authority of both the Church and the Bible? And if so, should biblical scholars care? Richard Hays, for one, insists that "the real work of interpretation is to *hear* the text, . . . to read and teach Scripture in a way that opens up its message, a way that both models and fosters trust in God."[101] Wilder similarly values "that ultimate Real or Being itself which discloses itself in the work, in the language *event* of which the work is only the vehicle."[102] But Stein lists "existentialism's language event" as one of many regrettable "modern-day fads or trends."[103] Who's right? Where is the value in NT literature?

This relates to a complaint I often hear NT scholars make about literary theory: It doesn't provide an interpretive "payout." In the last chapter, I referred to the frustration felt by Spencer and others upon encountering long-winded explanations of literary theory that don't then illuminate the text. Spencer goes on to explain: "Modern literary theory has its own complex jargon and method of argumentation which can quickly weary even the most diligent student in search of practical aids to understanding the biblical text. The burden is on the biblical critic informed by secular literary theory to demonstrate clearly and succinctly how such theory enhances comprehension of the biblical message."[104] Regrettably, it is true that literary theorists' language can often impede rather than facilitate understanding (an ironic reality, given their hermeneutical interests in the effectiveness of language). I agree with Spencer that biblical critics ought to demonstrate the relevance and usefulness of a given theory, concept, or discourse to their interests and the questions at hand.

However, I'd also insist that unspoken evaluative assumptions undergird these claims, and that they ought to be stated explicitly, since they're not always shared. For example, how does one define "enhanced comprehension of the biblical message"? There are different kinds of comprehension and illumination. One interpreter might experience a subjective feeling of resonance with a passage and consider that to be "increased understanding," whereas another might evaluate the extent to which an interpretation aligns with ancient intellectual views and consider that "enhanced comprehension." Moreover, Spencer's statement suggests that there is one ("the") biblical message. But as we'll explore in coming chapters, literature always communicates more than one message; there are always multiple levels of meaning. We have to stipulate what kind of biblical messages we're hoping to understand, and how we'll evaluate that understanding. Literary theory helps us recognize these various kinds of evaluative concerns so that we can articulate the register on which we're discussing a given text and the criteria by which we're judging it.

Metadisciplinary Concerns

Integrally related to hermeneutical and evaluative concerns are field-related questions about the critic's ultimate goal(s), the proper procedures by which to meet those goals, and whose role it is to decide such matters. How do our critical questions and reading strategies shape the outcomes of our inquiries? How do new interpretive strategies relate to the old? We must always remember that biblical critics are themselves situated in institutions (academic, ecclesial, and/or others) that shape the acceptable interpretive parameters. Importantly, such parameters typically include ideas about the corpus of works that we should study. At various times in both literary and biblical studies, canonicity has been at the center of critical controversy. Which texts are worthy of study, and why? Which are excluded from study, and why? What is the canon of texts that forms the minimal level of professional competence?

There is a dialogical dimension to metadisciplinary discussions in the field of literary theory, as well. Literary critics talk to and about one another, sometimes in acrimonious and polemical terms. Frank Lentricchia, for instance, caused a major stir with his 1996 essay "Last Will and Testament of an Ex-Literary Critic," in which he denounces literary theory as ruining his personal, "ravishingly pleasurable" experience of literature.[105] Vincent Leitch fired back that those who proclaim "the sacred antitheory oath 'I love literature'" are engaging in "othering, scapegoating, and politicizing" what they wrongly perceive to be "a grandiose homogenized allegorical figure: the Big Bad 'T'heory."[106] The point here is not to determine who's right or wrong in such altercations, but to notice the rhetorically loaded language of the disciplinary debate itself. It's important to ask not only about how a critic goes about doing literary analysis, but also about how she represents her work vis-à-vis the work of others. Is one literary approach defined *over and against* another? What are the charges levied against other approaches? How do proponents of the latter respond?

This brings us back to the question I bracketed earlier: How do we judge the *validity* of NT scholars' claims about literary theory? Is there a *critical* dimension to literary theory?

Criticism in Literary Theory

The English word "criticism" derives from the Greek word *krisis,* "to judge." How should we judge statements that don't merely reflect different interpretive orientations or emphases (think of Abrams's poles of author-based, audience-based priorities, and so forth), but actually reject literary theory altogether? What about those like Holly Carey, who describes contemporary literary theory as "*antithetical* to the enterprise of biblical studies"? Is John Van Seters right or wrong when he says that postmodern literary scholars read "the final form of the text in a completely fanciful manner without any concern for its historical context"? Is Thomas Hatina correct to say that literary treatments of intertextuality are "*inimical* to current historical-critical inquiry," that for poststructuralist literary critics, "all interpretation is viewed as misinterpretation," and that literary theorists hope "authors perish so that readers may reign"?[107]

I contend that, like those who dismiss Critical Theory more broadly, these scholars base their descriptions of contemporary literary theory on caricatures of what literary theory is and does. Think back to our earlier discussion of the three normative claims that routinely appear in accounts of NT studies' "literary paradigm shift." Such reports declare that NT literary critics (1) are anti- or ahistorical; (2) privilege a text's "final" unified form; and (3) wish to defend the literary sophistication of NT texts and their authors. We're now in a position to see how these claims are unhelpfully reductionistic when it comes to hermeneutical, evaluative, and metadisciplinary matters.

Here's what I mean. To say that NT literary critics are anti- or ahistorical is to make a statement about their *hermeneutics*. But NT literary critics do not all share the same hermeneutical convictions. They don't all agree, for example, about the functions of *koine* Greek constructions, or about how the Gospel of Matthew's narrative form relates to its content, or about how the book of Revelation's earliest audience would have understood its apocalyptic imagery. NT scholars who employ literary approaches don't all agree about the degree to which Paul's sociohistorical contexts (should) shape our understandings of his epistles, nor is there a consensus about whether or how historical Jesus research should impact treatments of Jesus's literary characterization in the Gospels.

Meanwhile, the claim that literary-leaning NT scholars privilege a text's extant unified form concerns their *evaluative* views. Yet again, it's inaccurate to imply that NT literary critics value NT texts in the same ways or for the same reasons. Some, for instance, value Revelation's powerful apocalyptic symbolism, others laud the book of Hebrews's use of rhetorical tropes to theological ends, others praise the so-called Christ Hymn of Philippians 2 for its lyricism, and others view Mary's Magnificat in the Gospel of Luke as some of the most sublime language in the whole of literature. Textual unity is but one of many possible evaluative considerations relevant for NT literature.

Finally, to say that literary critics wish to defend the sophistication of NT texts and their authors is to make a statement about their *metadisciplinary*, or field-related aims. Here too, though, we find variety and multiplicity instead of uniformity. Certain NT literary critics, for example, consider the author of Mark to be a relatively mediocre storyteller. *Their* aim when studying Mark's Gospel is not to defend his literary prowess; they think he has none. Some NT scholars employ literary criticism, to use Powell's words, "with the goal of determining the effects the stories are expected to have on their audiences."[108] Defending the stylistic beauty of NT literature is only one possible aim for those who employ literary criticism.

Holding in tension the varying perspectives we find within and between these heuristic categories—namely, the hermeneutical, evaluative, and metadisciplinary dimensions of the literary—facilitates more precise assessments of biblical scholars' claims about literary approaches. John Ashton's strong denunciation of NT narrative criticism is a case in point. Ashton says that synchronic approaches are legitimate in theory, but he specifically questions the utility of NT narrative criticism for three reasons. First, he says, a Gospel "has a history" and thus "should not be assumed to be a single, fully integrated composition"; second, narrative criticism is theoretically clumsy and unnecessarily complicated, like "using a combine harvester to mow the garden lawn"; and third, it ignores the difference between fiction and reality, an oversight that Ashton dubs "sheer obscurantism." Ashton considers NT narrative criticism to be "more of a fad than a fashion" because it "misconceives the *true nature* of the Gospels."[109]

Note that Ashton's reference to the Gospels' "true nature" reveals a particular *hermeneutical* position: a Gospel cannot communicate as a unified story because it is not *by nature* an "integrally conceived unitary" text. Of course, this weds the "true nature" of a text to the person or people who originally "conceived" it, and implies that one cannot understand a narrative as it stands in a particular moment in time. Based on his underlying presuppositions, Ashton dismisses the results of narrative criticism as "trifling, if not altogether illusory."[110]

There are several problems with this assessment, however. For one, Ashton overlooks the fact that some NT narrative critics hold the very same hermeneutical views that he does; they simply come to a different conclusion because they *do* perceive the Gospels as "integrally conceived unitary" narratives. Meanwhile, other NT narrative critics might respond that their emphasis on textual unity is an *evaluative* decision (unity is one criterion by which they judge the text as it is now), not a *hermeneutical* one (they do not believe that a story must have been originally composed as unified in order to communicate). Ashton's dismissal of NT narrative criticism is regrettably based on a false image of theoretical uniformity amongst NT narrative critics. Ashton's assessment reflects the larger problematic trend that I've already mentioned, and that I hope this book will help to temper: when discussing literary studies, NT scholars often homogenize literary methods and movements that are in fact heterogeneous, and then criticize or reject them wholesale.

Finding Common Ground in Critical Chaos:
Concluding Thoughts

I began this chapter by noting that many retrospectives and "state-of-the-art" introductions depict biblical scholarship's "literary paradigm shift" in misleading and unhelpful terms. The very phrase "literary paradigm shift" is telling in its singularity, as though "literary" represents but one paradigm. Instead, I suggested that a better way to conceive of literary approaches would be to use Meyer Abrams's taxonomy of mimetic, expressive, objective, and pragmatic modes of literary analysis. Seeing these different interpretive positionalities puts us in a better place to understand why Critical Theory insists on the power of normativity and the necessity of critical reflexivity; it also helps us sort through contestations over *hermeneutical, evaluative,* and *metadisciplinary* literary concerns. In the next chapter, we'll focus on the literary theorists from whom the first wave of NT literary critics drew their inspiration: the literary formalists.

2 What Makes the Stone Stony: The Formalist Literary Paradigm

Art exists that one may recover the sensation of life; it exists to make one feel things, to make the stone stony.
Viktor Shklovsky

There are as many formalisms as there are formalists.
Pavel Medvedev

At the outset of this book, I imagined biblical studies as a bay and literary studies as a lake, both crowded with critics "fishing" for meaning in different places and in various ways. In this chapter, instead of the watery images of bay and lake, we turn to the *terra firma* of literary form. Put simply, the *formalist literary paradigm* focuses on the autonomous final form of the text as it stands. Unlike those who search for meaning in the intention or cause that gave rise to a text (Abrams's author-oriented, expressive approaches from the previous chapter), and unlike those who look to the effects that a text produces in readers (Abrams's audience-oriented, pragmatic approaches), *literary formalists* hold that meaning cannot be perceived apart from the form of the work itself (Abrams's work-oriented, objective approaches).[1]

Put differently, formalists focus on the features of a text in the same way that a tourist might look to the craggy outcroppings of a mountain range and discover in its unique construction a discernible shape. Nathaniel Hawthorne, for instance, writes of a "Great Stone Face" that "formed on the perpendicular side of a mountain by some immense rocks, which had been thrown together in such a position as . . . to resemble the features of the human countenance."

44

Although matters of form have never been entirely missing from biblical studies, the mid-twentieth century saw a new kind of attention to form, as biblical scholars began to adopt the insights of literary formalists. The formalist conviction "that literature, like all other arts, is best studied by the detailed observation of what is taken to constitute the formal structure of individual works" fit quite naturally with many aspects of biblical studies at the time.[2] Formalist biblical interpretation gained currency throughout the 1980s, especially amongst those studying the Gospel narratives, and eventually became widely accepted in the guild as a legitimate and useful way to analyze NT texts.

Fast-forward several decades, and the situation is quite nearly the opposite. The Literary Aspects of the Gospels and Acts (LAGA) unit of the Society of Biblical Literature (SBL), which for years had warmly welcomed formalist pursuits, is no longer active. Moreover, despite many publishers' and editors' concerted efforts to expand the methodological and theoretical perspectives represented in their pages, few recent monographs or top journal articles in biblical studies could properly be considered formalist in orientation. Today, it appears that Lynn Poland's assessment is still widely shared: "[Formalism's] weaknesses as a program for literary study [are] that it ignores the historical dimensions of interpretation and fails to explicate that complex process by which texts can transform our experience of the world and our structures of belief."[3] In part, formalism fell out of favor due to the enormously destabilizing effects of poststructuralism (discussed in later chapters).

In *literary studies*, formalism struggled, but it never disappeared. At the turn of the twenty-first century, Richard Strier declared that formalism had become a "dirty word" amongst literary critics. And yet, Strier also insisted, literary scholarship "can't do without it."[4] Formalism comes and goes in literary studies in what Paul de Man sees as a never-ending cycle: "It is a fact that this sort of thing happens, again and again, in literary studies. . . . The structural moment of concentration on the code for its own sake cannot be avoided, and literature necessarily breeds its own formalism. . . . Formalism, it seems, is an all-absorbing and tyrannical muse."[5] Unwilling (unable?) to abandon the formalist muse entirely, formalists in the literary field have engaged with and learned from their critics. Consequently, literary formalisms have continued to mature over the years, giving rise to rich new interdisciplinary discourses like New Formalism and postclassical narratology.

NT scholars' general abandonment of literary-formalist approaches cuts us off from an entire realm of useful and relevant intellectual resources. The good news is that formalism's disappearance from biblical scholarship was and remains entirely unnecessary. So that we might see what we're missing when we assume that literary formalism is "*at odds with*, or at least *insufficient for*, the full task of biblical interpretation," we first need to answer some prior questions.[6] What happened to literary formalism in biblical studies? Why, when formalist concepts were so eagerly adopted at first, are they now virtually absent from biblical scholars' critical discussions? And why do NT scholars continue to ignore the formalist literary paradigm when it has proven so resilient in the field of literary studies?

In this chapter, I argue that the rejection of formalism in multiple corners of NT scholarship is the direct result of a common but misleading account of our discipline's development. Recognizing the deficiencies of that history opens the door for reconsideration of the NT texts' formal features in light of contemporary advancements in literary formalism. I contend that NT scholars fail to take full advantage of literary formalism in part because in accounts of the discipline's development, we tend to (1) uncritically merge what are in fact separate strands of formalism in literary studies, and (2) distinguish so strongly between formalism and historicism that they become widely *but falsely* perceived as opposites. We'll consider each tendency in turn. Along the way, we'll come back to the three sets of interrelated issues in literary theory: how language functions and where textual meaning resides (hermeneutical issues); how we assess the value of literature (evaluative concerns); and what we ought to be reading and doing when we study literature (metadisciplinary matters).[7]

The Landscape of Literary Form

Strictly speaking, literary formalism is better conceived in the plural, as literary formalism*s*. Indeed, in literary circles, it is "a recurrent theoretical principle in critical debate" that formalism "is not . . . a coherent critical or artistic 'movement' . . . nor a widely endorsed slogan."[8] Rather, formalism itself comes in many forms, including Russian formalism, New Criticism, Chicago School criticism, and Neo-Aristotelianism.

In order to highlight the crucial differences *between* formalists and *within* formalisms, I'll describe two of the most influential strands of the formalist literary paradigm in broad strokes: first, we'll consider Russian formalism, typically cited as literary formalism's starting point, and then we'll turn to the so-called New Criticism, which rose to prominence mainly in Britain and the United States.

Russian Formalism

A few years prior to the Bolshevik Revolution of 1917, several young Russian scholars—in St. Petersburg and in Moscow—began gathering together to discuss literary matters. What started as a tight-knit group of upstart young professors quickly gained momentum and spread beyond Russia. Recognizing with Peter Steiner that the school labeled "Russian formalism" is "resistant to synthesis," we can still say that on the whole, Russian formalism was markedly shaped by two major social forces of that time period—revolution and evolution—both of which were typified in their own ways by a struggle for survival.[9]

In an age of great social and political upheaval, Russian formalists sought to enact a revolution of their own in the literary realm. They were driven by an overarching *metadisciplinary* aim—one that cut to the very core of the literary-critical enterprise. Counteracting "the methodological confusion prevailing in traditional literary studies," Russian formalists sought to claim the legitimacy and status of a "science."[10] Boris Eichenbaum, leader of the influential Russian Society for the Study of Poetic Language, wrote that their aim was to reconceive literary study as its own "independent science of literature."[11] And in 1928, Viktor Žirmunskij, reflecting on Russian formalism as a whole, observed, "It would be more correct to speak not of a new *method* but rather of the new *tasks* of scholarship, of a new sphere of scholarly *problems*."[12]

Russian formalists shifted the focus of literary scholarship as a discipline. In 1921, Roman Jakobson famously wrote that "the object of study in literary science is not literature but 'literariness' (*literaturnost*)."[13] In other words, the *disciplinary* desire to "systematize literary scholarship as a distinct and integrated field of intellectual endeavor" led the Russian formalists to pose a foundational *evaluative* question: What makes literary art *literary*? Or, as Eichenbaum's co-leader Viktor Shklovsky famously framed the question: What makes "the stone *stony*"?[14]

Early on, the Russian formalists' answer to this evaluative question reflected their *hermeneutical* stance. They defined *literaturnost* by distinguishing between "literary" and "everyday" language. This so-called *poetics of deviation* assumes that poetic language deviates from prosaic language in its use of specific literary techniques, which they called "devices" (meter, repetition, irony, plot, and so forth). "If the study of literature wants to become a science," taught Jakobson, "it must recognize the device as its only hero."[15] Importantly, the Russian formalists insisted that devices shouldn't be abstracted from a text and discussed as separate literary features; they always function in relationship to one another, thereby uniting form and content.

Evolution worked its way into Russian formalist hermeneutical theorizing through the class struggle highlighted in Marxism and the struggle for genealogical dominance emphasized in Darwinism. In any given text, Jakobson's "hero" of literary study—the literary device or technique—will always be a hero under siege. Jakobson held that literary structure is comprised of a hierarchy of devices; "the dominant" device "foregrounds" certain linguistic elements, "rules, determines, and transforms the remaining components," rendering those remaining components marginal.[16] So in poetry, the dominant device might be rhyme and meter, whereas a novel might be marked predominantly by its pyramidal plot structure (though such characteristic features hardly exhaust the nature or function of either form).

But as Russian formalism developed, the consensus shifted. Russian formalists came to see evaluative ascriptions of "dominant" and "marginalized" or "literary" and "everyday" language as not fixed but relative; they realized that definitions and evaluations of literariness are contingent, changing over time as they interface with variegated social and historical forces. Yury Tynyanov concluded, "All fixed, static definitions of [literature] are swept away by the fact of evolution."[17] This, of course, renders the early poetics of deviation problematic, since it depends on a stable form of "everyday" language from which "literary" language deviates. Eventually, Russian formalists came to conceive of literary value judgments as dependent on the varied conceptions and uses of language that always operate differently in particular sociocultural contexts. Their ultimate answer, then, to the question of what makes literary art *literary* is that literariness depends on the *use* to which a given linguistic utterance is put—that is, its function.

This gave rise to a new *evaluative* question: Does a truly literary work function to *facilitate* comprehension, or to *unsettle* prior understandings? While a pragmatist would say that language should *enable* comprehension, Shklovsky argued the opposite. Shklovsky evaluated literature based on its capacity to render the normative unfamiliar. His concept of *ostranenie*—

typically translated *defamiliarization,* but sometimes *estrangement*—refers to literature's capacity to draw attention in fresh, unfamiliar ways to what has become habitual and expected in ordinary perception. The problem, as Shklovsky saw it, is that over time, such literary techniques become automatized. Old literary forms become routine, failing to defamiliarize as they once had. Still, for Russian formalists like Shklovsky, the value of literary art lies in its ability to rend the veil of familiarity from our eyes, and thereby create the possibility of individual and social transformation.

Most NT scholars today would say that this is precisely the value of Jesus's parables: these short stories defamiliarize what has become standard, challenge views that their listeners take for granted, and thus engender change. C. H. Dodd's well-known definition of the parable from 1935 is still widely cited today: "At its simplest the parable is a metaphor or simile drawn from nature or common life, arresting the hearer by its vividness or strangeness and leaving the mind in sufficient doubt about its precise application to tease it into active thought."[18] In short, the contemporary scholarly consensus is that "Jesus consistently used this form of teaching to challenge conventional beliefs of his day."[19]

NT interpreters did not always see the parables this way. Modern historical-critical parable research began around the turn of the twentieth century with the publication of Adolf Jülicher's programmatic two-volume work, *Die Gleichnisreden Jesu.* Jülicher argued, against earlier allegorical interpretations, that parables communicate one central moral message using one single point of comparison (*tertium comparationis*)—an assessment based on his *a priori* dogmatic conviction that the historical Jesus would only have used language to clarify, never to confuse (compare Mark 4.11–12).[20] Note Jülicher's evaluative choice; he values clarity over confusion.

Dodd, along with his German contemporary Joachim Jeremias and Glasgow professor A. T. Cadoux, challenged Jülicher's parable theory, and thus paved the way for the so-called literary turn in parable scholarship in the mid-twentieth century.[21] The new generation of parable scholars, most notably Robert Funk and Dan Via, found the formalist literary paradigm compelling, and began to approach Jesus's parables as "genuine works of art, real aesthetic objects."[22] Ruben Zimmermann summarizes: "The hermeneutical principle here is that a parable can be appropriately understood *if one understands its linguistic structure.*"[23] Like the Russian formalists, these parable scholars held that language is always moving toward ossification and conventionality—what Funk labeled "sedimentation in language."[24] The need then arises for *ostranenie*, the disruption of the mundane.

Mikhail Bakhtin

Not technically considered a Russian formalist, Mikhail Bakhtin was heavily influenced by Russian formalist thinkers. Beginning in 1918, he met regularly in the Belorussian towns of Vitebsk and Nevel with a group that eventually came to be called the Bakhtin Circle. Bakhtin developed and recorded his anti-authoritarian ideas throughout the 1920s and 1930s, but they remained unpublished for decades because Stalin strictly regulated intellectuals' ability to speak into the public square. In fact, the Bakhtin Circle was forcibly disbanded in the late 1920s, when several of its members were arrested. Let's look briefly at the reasons that Bakhtin posed such a threat to the constricting social forces at work in Stalin's Soviet Union.

Hermeneutically, Bakhtin was ahead of his time. His now-classic essay "Discourse in the Novel" seeks to overcome the separation between abstract formal linguistics on the one hand and sociological analysis on the other. The ultimate site of ideological struggle, Bakhtin insists, is language. Moreover, as later poststructuralists also insisted, language is fundamentally a social phenomenon, encoding multiple perspectives simultaneously. In Bakhtinian terms, language is *polyphonic* or *dialogic,* inherently marked by *heteroglossia,* or multivocality (from the Greek *hetero,* "other, different," and *glossia,* "language"). Bakhtin's conclusion was that society's constant attempts to limit the meaning of an utterance or discourse (that is, to make it *monologic*) are always in some way distortive.

In his classic work *Problems of Dostoevsky's Poetics,* Bakhtin draws out the implications of his hermeneutical views with respect to the novel. Bakhtin contrasts Tolstoy's novels, which he views as negatively authoritarian, with Dostoevsky's, which celebrate multiple perspectives without attempting to control them or subordinate them to the author's view. Using the Tolstoy-Dostoevsky comparison as his case study, Bakhtin argues that even if a writer like Tolstoy attempts to communicate one authoritative, unified message, the true nature of novelistic discourse is dialogical. It will always entail a clash of viewpoints; it will always resist unification. Considering Bakhtin's topsy-turvy perspectives and the fact that he celebrates the chaos precipitated by colliding dialogic points of view, we can hardly marvel that the Soviet regime found him threatening.

NT scholars have discovered in Bakhtin a fruitful interlocutor in a number of ways, but the Bakhtinian notion of *carnival* has proven particularly popular.[25] Inspired by medieval carnivals, which were themselves associated with the unrestrained festivals of Saturnalia, Bakhtin suggests that on both ideological and literary levels, "*Carnival* celebrate[s] temporary liberation from the prevailing truth and from the established order; it mark[s] the suspension of all hierarchical rank, privileges, norms."[26] The "carnivalization of literature" thus refers to the suspension of "official" systems and structures of inequality, in favor of freely and intentionally violating and satirizing dominant normativities in and through literature. Literary texts do so partly by juxtaposing and complicating antitheses (what Bakhtin calls *syncrises*) like death and rebirth, fasting and feasting, and wealth and poverty, in such a way as to enable and enact alternatives to the established order. Gospel scholars like Raj Nadella, for example, turn to the carnivalesque as a means of explaining the "heterogeneity and inconsistency that characterize the Gospel [of Luke's] portrayals of wealth." Nadella suggests that "the third Gospel is more interested in accommodating disparate perspectives than in ... offering a coherent portrayal of wealth or a consistent set of instructions on the issue."[27] Depicting the "polyphony of perspectives" is, for Bakhtin, the true value of literary art; it has become, for scholars like Nadella, the value of NT literature, as well.

NT scholars' common claim that formalism is an ahistorical, synchronic approach to literature actually mirrors the charge of Russian formalism's Soviet detractors. In fact, the label "formalism" initially was intended as a pejorative term, meant to suggest that Russian formalists were stuck in their own insular intellectual circles. Supposedly disconnected from the real world, they were perceived as privileging literary form above more important social concerns like the common good.[28] However, as Eichenbaum insists, that never reflected the actual work that Russian formalists were doing: "It is difficult to recall who coined this name, but it was not a very felicitous coinage. It might have been convenient as a simplified battle cry but it fails, as an objective term, to delimit the activities of the 'Society for the Study of Poetic Language.'"[29] These critical activities included—and as time went on, became increasingly predicated upon—extratextual diachronic concerns. As we saw above, in Russian formalist thought, "the prime significance of major social factors is *not at all* discarded."[30]

Soviet detractors like Leon Trotsky may have denigrated Russian formalists for being out of touch with society, but the very fact that Stalin's regime forcibly suppressed Bakhtin and the Russian formalists bespeaks a fear of the power and increasing influence of their ideas *on* society. In the end, Russian formalism was a casualty of Social Realism, the official, state-mandated guidelines for artistic work in the communist Soviet Union. The Union of Soviet Writers (1932–1934) expressly condemned avant-garde modernist writing and its focus on the alienation of modern life, instead advancing Stalin's call for writers to work as "engineers of the human soul."[31]

Many handbooks of literary theory state that, after the death of Russian formalism itself, the questions and aims that animated the formalists lived on through the New Criticism. These overlapping branches of formalism share some of the same proclivities and even some of the same contributing figures (such as Jakobson), but there are also significant geographic, chronological, and conceptual differences between them.[32] The following sketch explains why Russian formalism and New Criticism should not be seen as simply synonymous.

The New Criticism

Unlike Russian formalism and Bakhtinian dialogism, New Criticism has no specific theoretical or national point of origin. The phrase itself was first used by Joel E. Spingarn in "The New Criticism: A Lecture Delivered at Columbia University, March 9, 1910." "Every poet," Spingarn declared, "re-expresses the universe in his own way, and every poem is a new and independent expression."[33] T. S. Eliot, William Empson, and I. A. Richards were influential in the development of New Criticism in England in the 1920s, though its popularity really rose following the American John Crowe Ransom's book *The New Criticism*, published in 1941.[34] As we saw above, Russian formalism was not a methodology. In contrast, many today describe New Criticism as exactly that: "an empirical methodology." Some, in fact, consider the description "New Criticism" itself to be a misnomer, because in their view, it is essentially "a reading practice."[35]

The New Critics' "close reading" is certainly formalism's most significant and long-lasting contribution to the literary field. Much like the French pedagogical *explication de texte*, close reading entails slow, scrupulous, intentional reading that attends to the text's rhyme and rhythm, meter and metrics, tropes and techniques in isolation from the circumstances in which the text originated. Close reading was especially influential during the 1930s–1960s and, in the United States, had a lasting impact beyond that time due to widespread adoption in university courses of Cleanth Brooks and Robert Penn Warren's textbook anthologies, *Understanding Poetry* (1938) and *Understanding Fiction* (1943).[36] New Criticism's undergirding assumptions persisted even after New Criticism had supposedly become passé in literary studies.[37]

Yet New Criticism was not *only* a reading practice; it was—like all reading—practice predicated upon theory. One of the New Critics' seminal hermeneutical convictions is epitomized in the enduring titular image of Brooks's well-known work *The Well-Wrought Urn* (alluding to two famous poems: John Keats's "Ode on a Grecian Urn" and John Donne's "The Canonization"). That is, a poem (and a text more generally), as a "well-wrought urn," is *a self-contained, unified, autonomous artifact.* As modernist poet and critic T. S. Eliot had earlier declared, "Poetry is poetry and not another thing."[38] In other words, the New Critics employed close reading strategies because of their hermeneutical conviction that meaning resides in the poem itself. In this sense, they were like the Russian formalists, insisting on the inseparability of form and content.

As I said in the introductory chapter, a discipline or movement can often be described by what its practitioners define themselves *against*. This is especially evident in a number of New Critical texts, which, though written relatively late, typify what came to be New Critical orthodoxy. One axiomatic New Critical heresy can be traced to Brooks's eleventh chapter of *The Well-Wrought Urn*, titled "The Heresy of Paraphrase." There, Brooks expresses a New Critical truism regarding the literary critic's object of study: *the focus of literary criticism should be on literature itself, unrestrained by matters that, even if closely related, are not about literature.* Because they prized the autonomy and legitimacy of "the poem itself" as an aesthetic object, New Critics tended to eschew much of what literary critics had seen as necessary elements of their analytical work (identification of allusions, philological genealogies, generic comparanda, paraphrases, plot synopses, and so forth). For the New Critic, these should never be the central concerns of a literary critic.

Two other foundational New Critical texts are "The Intentional Fallacy" (1946) and "The Affective Fallacy" (1949), both co-written by literary critic William Wimsatt and philosopher Monroe Beardsley. First, like the Russian formalists, Wimsatt and Beardsley reject any appeal to authorial intention as determinative of meaning, labeling such an appeal "the intentional fallacy." Second, but *unlike* the Russian formalists, Wimsatt and

Beardsley dismiss appeals to readerly response as an interpretive key, labeling this "the affective fallacy."[39] While the intentional fallacy confuses "the poem and its origins," they write, the affective fallacy confuses "the poem and its *results*"; the consequence of both is that "the poem itself, as an object of specifically critical judgment, tends to disappear."[40] New Criticism's hermeneutical views are summarily expressed in a famous line from Archibald MacLeish: "A poem should not mean / But be."[41]

We should be careful to note that the New Critical emphasis on "the poem itself" is often exaggerated in caricatures of the supposedly "strong anti-historical bias in the New Criticism."[42] However, as Jonathan Culler rightly clarifies, "Formalism does not involve a denial of history, as is sometimes claimed. What it rejects is historical interpretation that makes the work a symptom, whose causes are to be found in historical reality."[43] In truth, some of the most prominent New Critical thinkers, including Wimsatt and Beardsley, Brooks, R. P. Warren, Eliot, Wellek, and A. Warren, were concerned with extrinsic influences on both production and interpretation of texts.[44] Wellek, for instance, explicitly called for a recovery of history, and answered his own call by writing a multivolume *History of Modern Criticism*. Wimsatt and Beardsley, while denouncing the "intentional fallacy," also readily recognize that "a poem does not come into existence by accident," and even as they reject the "affective fallacy," they don't deny that a poem has "emotive import" for readers.[45] Wellek insists that "the New Critic who supposedly denies that a work can be illuminated by historical knowledge at all" is nothing but a "straw man."[46] Instead, the key hermeneutical point for the New Critics is a matter of prioritization: external dimensions of a text are not *un*important, but neither should they be equated with textual meaning.

In addition to these *hermeneutical* views, New Critical interpretive fallacies are also fueled by an *evaluative* principle: no longer can authorial intent be the sole or primary criterion by which we determine meaning. Wimsatt and Beardsley insisted that authorial intent "is neither available nor desirable *as a standard for judging* the success of a work of literary art." This means that *poetry is not answerable to, or validated by, anything other than its own existence as an aesthetic object.* So Wimsatt and Beardsley: "The poem is not the critic's own and not the author's (it is detached from the author at birth and goes about the world beyond his power to control it)."[47] No longer governed by its author, a literary text can only be evaluated based on the extent to which it is grounded in universally shared human experience.[48] Note the presumption of universality here. As we'll see in chapter 3, this is crucial for the structuralist literary paradigm, as well.

Again, parable scholars were some of the first NT critics to adopt the tenets of New Criticism, probably because parables were *already* being treated as distinct stories, and can easily be separated from the Gospel contexts in which they are embedded. Dan Via, one of the most prominent parable scholars to draw on the New Criticism, insisted that, "while the parables have an existential-theological dimension they are, nevertheless, genuine aesthetic objects."[49] As genuine aesthetic objects, moreover, parables should never be reduced to an explanation or a didactic "main message." Bernard Brandon Scott, for example, appropriates the New Critical heresy of the paraphrase when he writes, "We cannot state what a parable means, for it has no meaning separate from itself."[50] And Elizabeth Struthers Malbon observes that for parable scholars Robert Tannehill, Robert Funk, Dan Via, and John Dominic Crossan, "'A poem should not mean / But be'—and a parable should not refer but impel."[51]

Wimsatt and Beardsley's evaluative emphasis on universally shared human experience and their claim that "the poem belongs to the public" might sound democratizing, akin to more contemporary deconstructions of the concept of "canon."[52] But while the latter seek to broaden the scope of literary works considered canonical (read: "valuable") in Western society, and have had slow but equalizing effects, New Critical views, perhaps counterintuitively, served an opposite purpose. When it came to the field of literary studies—that is, *metadisciplinary* issues—New Criticism helped to legitimate and further codify a normative Western canon of traditionally "successful" literary works.[53] This is partly because the New Critical *evaluative* emphasis on universal human experience was so strongly wedded to the conviction that as an academic *discipline*, literary criticism must be governed by detached, regulable objective principles.

Much as the Enlightenment gave rise to the modern professional biblical scholar, the institutionalization of literature as an academic discipline gave rise to a new brand of (uniquely qualified) expert: the literature professor.[54] According to Ransom, the correct sphere for such "specially trained critics" is an institution of higher learning: "It is from the professors of literature . . . that I should hope eventually for the erection of intelligent standards of criticism. It is their business. Criticism must become more scientific, or precise and systematic, and this means that it must be developed by the collective and sustained effort of learned persons—which means that its proper seat is in the universities."[55] Like Russian formalists, New Critics insisted on the disinterested expertise of the specially trained critic who could employ standardized, systematic interpretive principles.

Despite their similar conceptions of the critic as neutral observer, there is a subtle distinction to be made here regarding the ultimate *telos* of the Russian formalists and that of the New Critics. As Eichenbaum had put it, Russian formalists sought to establish an "independent science of literature."[56] New Critics, on the other hand, responded to modernity's increasing scientism by defending literature's aesthetics as an alternative and valid epistemological mode in and of itself. I. A. Richards established a practical distinction, picked up and developed by later New Critics, between the language of science, which is *referential,* and the language of literary art, which is *poetic.*[57] For the New Critics, poetic language functions metaphorically—indeed, according to Ransom, "miraculously"—to illuminate truth.[58]

Further, the practices and processes of each school evolved according to that subtle difference: Russian formalist thought led to a *de*-emphasis on specific texts and close readings. Even if some Russian theorists did discuss specific writings in their work, their critical objectives were not *hermeneutical* with respect to *individual* texts. That is, they didn't aim primarily to determine the meaning of a given text. Rather, their goal as literary scientists was to identify and describe the literary devices of which all literary art is constructed. The New Critics, in contrast, held that the underlying goal of all critical reading was "the problem of *making out the meaning*" of individual literary texts.[59] New Critics held that a text's grammar, syntax, and other formal elements are constitutive of meaning, and thus, close readings of specific texts are the best way to attain the critic's main goal: understanding "the text itself." Put crudely, the main distinction here is that Russian formalists were concerned with literature writ large, while New Critics were concerned with analyzing specific literary works.

To sum up, various strands of formalist thought are not the same, but neither are they mutually exclusive. Biblical scholars commonly conflate them due to certain overlaps between them. In terms of *hermeneutics,* formalists of different kinds agree that textual meaning cannot be perceived apart from form, and it cannot be found in the causes that gave rise to a text (whether those causes are an author's biography, psychology, or original intention). When it comes to *metadisciplinary* questions, most formalists share the view that the critic's role is to analyze "the text itself" objectively (as opposed to subjective, eclectic, or personal modes of literary analysis).

Despite these commonalities, however, formalist approaches are distinct and multilayered. Portraying them as one monolithic movement creates a false and flattened picture that prohibits NT scholars from taking full advantage of the formalist literary paradigm.

We turn now to the second problematic tendency that leads NT scholars to miss formalism's value. While scholarly discussions of the role of literary criticism in biblical studies tend to conflate distinct formalist theories, they often mischaracterize NT scholars' early appropriations of formalism as a stark rejection of the historical-critical method. Although pioneering NT literary scholars ostensibly rejected the historical-critical paradigm, literary formalism and the historical-critical method actually overlapped significantly.

Reconsidering Literary Formalism in Biblical Studies

It is true, of course, that obvious differences exist between literary formalist and historical-critical approaches to NT literature. Consider the subdiscipline of NT form criticism (*Formgeschichte*), which Norman Petersen dubs "the principal contributor to the historical-critical theory."[60] Despite the eponymous similarity between NT *form criticism* and *formalism*, the referent of "form" in form criticism differs markedly from its referent in literary formalism. Form critics are interested in the *earliest forms* of NT texts and traditions, while literary formalists focus on a text's *extant form* (from any given point in time).

Notice that this distinction reflects different *hermeneutical* postures toward NT texts. NT form critics like Martin Dibelius, Karl L. Schmidt, and Rudolf Bultmann considered NT texts to be collections of disparate oral traditions that circulated prior to being recorded and redacted. NT writers, Dibelius asserted, were actually "collectors, transmitters, editors"— in other words, they were *not* authors.[61] The form-critical *metadisciplinary* aim, then, is to remove editorial elements in order to identify the earliest elements of a particular form (such as a miracle story, parable, aphorism, or creed).[62] Working hand in hand with other historical-critical scholars such as source critics (who identify prior written sources on which a text draws) and redaction critics (who identify editorial interpolations and other textual amendations), form critics seek to trace the developments that an orally transmitted *Ur*-form underwent before being incorporated into a written source like Mark's Gospel.[63]

Contrast that with the literary formalist views discussed above. Literary formalists seek to identify and explicate how literary devices can create what Brooks and Warren call the text's "total poetic effect" as it stands in any given moment.[64] NT scholars drawing on literary formalism are therefore *not primarily* concerned with an "original" *Ur*-form and its subsequent developments, but with any given version of a literary form as constitutive of meaning. This was Muilenburg's point when he pushed biblical scholars to move "beyond" form criticism: each literary unit, he insisted, ought to be approached as "an indissoluble whole, an artistic and creative unity, a unique formulation."[65]

We wouldn't want to efface these hermeneutical and disciplinary distinctions. Still, accounts of biblical studies often overstate the differences, depicting NT literary criticism and historical criticism as polarized opposites. The common explanation is that NT scholars (especially those interested in narrative) took up formalism as *a rejection* of their historically oriented colleagues. Indeed, first-wave NT literary critics made such claims themselves. Malbon, for instance, explains that narrative criticism "grew up *in reaction against* certain excesses of historical criticism."[66] The received story, then, is that NT scholars turned to formalism because they were "frustrated" with historical criticism; it's *because* they were dissatisfied with "piecemeal and fragmentizing" historical-critical approaches that they chose to employ "holistic *over against* atomistic analyses."[67]

Rarely is it sufficient simply to assert that approaches are different; we ought to delineate exactly *how* they differ. Situating literary formalism and historical criticism *over against* one another masks the significant convergences between them, and thereby distorts our comprehension of both discourses. The following section offers a corrective to the standard storyline's disproportionate emphasis on the disjunctures between literary and historical criticisms. Recognizing the affinities also allows us to discern the differences more precisely. In addition to providing a more accurate account of NT scholars' engagements with literary theory, I'd like to highlight two other reasons that this corrective is necessary.

The first is that, as you'll remember from the previous chapter, three misleading claims appear regularly in accounts of NT studies' literary paradigm shift, each of which corresponds to one of literary theory's three main domains (hermeneutical, evaluative, and metadisciplinary). It is often said that NT literary criticism (1) is anti- or ahistorical (*hermeneutical*); (2) privileges a text as a unified whole (*evaluative*); and (3) defends the literary sophistication of NT texts and their authors (*metadisciplinary*). The shared assumptions between NT historical critics, first-wave NT literary critics, and literary formalists that I'm about to outline will demonstrate why the claims above are misleading. Second, as we'll discuss in chapter 4, these shared assumptions form a set of hermeneutical, evaluative, and metadisciplinary principles to which *post*structuralists eventually objected. Seeing where these areas overlap thus helps to explain why poststructuralism created such a sea change in biblical studies. But we're getting ahead of ourselves.

Despite accounts that define historical-critical approaches *against* literary approaches like formalism, the reality is that NT historical critics, first-wave NT literary critics, and literary formalists *shared* the following assumptions, which reflect the three main sets of literary concerns: (1) literary forms evolve out of and develop in response to life circumstances (*hermeneutical*); (2) a work of art stands autonomously as "an object of knowledge *sui generis* which has a special ontological status," and aesthetic sophistication is defined by textual unity (*evaluative*);[68] and (3) a critical approach to texts necessarily entails making objective, scientific value judgments about their literariness (*metadisciplinary*). We'll look at each in turn.

Hermeneutical

Russian formalists, NT form critics, and first-wave NT literary scholars alike conceived of literary history as a dynamic evolutionary struggle, in which a particular setting in life (*Sitz im Leben*) gives rise to unique literary forms. As I mentioned previously, Russian formalists were strongly influenced by scientific discourses regarding evolution. In one of nine famous formalist theses published in 1928, Jakobson and Tynyanov summarize: "A disclosure of the immanent laws of the history of literature (and language) allows us to determine the character of each specific change in literary (and linguistic) systems. However, these laws do not allow us to explain the tempo of evolution or the chosen path of evolution when several theoretically possible evolutionary paths are given."[69] Anticipating later theorizing about intertextuality, Russian formalists thought of literary forms as constantly adopting and adapting previous texts, such that literature itself is ever evolving and dissolving.[70]

Like the Russian formalists, NT form critics held that literary forms evolve out of and develop in response to life circumstances.[71] Franz

Overbeck's 1882 dictum provided a kind of motto for form criticism: "A literature has its history in its forms; every history of literature (*Literaturge-schichte*) will be a history of forms (*Formengeschichte*)."[72] Petersen considers this central to the historical-critical project: "Essential to the historical-critical theory of biblical literature is the evolutionary model upon which it is constructed."[73] For NT form critics like Bultmann, the early church's unprecedented circumstances, coupled with the unique kerygmatic content of the gospel message, gave rise to the written Gospel as its own *sui generis* literary form. According to Bultmann, this new literary form, produced through the transmission of tradition and various source materials, represented "the union of the Hellenistic *kerygma about Christ* . . . with the *tradition of the story of Jesus*."[74]

It's important to note that for many scholars who employ historical-critical methods, conceiving of literary history in evolutionary terms did *not* imply that literary forms became increasingly *superior*. In fact, for some, the opposite is true: some envision a kind of *de*volution from authentic original materials to contaminated or derivative later accounts.[75] A devolutionary conception of literary history is predicated upon several Enlightenment-based assumptions about history more broadly. One such assumption is that historical data decay over time such that the longer the chronological distance between now and then, the more is lost and the harder it is to recover a given historical reality. What's more, a traditional principle of modern historiography is that gaps in the data (what is lost as time goes on) can be filled by the so-called *analogy of history*, which itself depends on the assumption that reality remains consistent over time. Based on that presupposition, historical-critical NT scholars reject the *historicity* of stories about miracles *prima facie* since miracles are, by definition, without analogy in human experience. Many conclude that miracle stories were invented by later Christian communities and retroactively attributed to Jesus.[76] Graham Twelftree considers this approach to be "fundamentally flawed" because in this case, he writes, scholars "confuse form with content."[77]

Evolutionary concepts of literary development proved to be especially persistent in twentieth-century parable scholarship. As I noted above, modern historical-critical parable research began with Jülicher's *Die Gleichnisreden Jesu*. According to Hans-Josef Klauck, Jülicher "resisted being included in the gallery of ancestors of form criticism," but Jülicher's most famous student was Bultmann, whose form-critical study *par excellence, History of the Synoptic Tradition*, explicitly drew on his teacher's categories.[78] Adopting and adapting Jülicher's views, form critics like Bultmann regularly identified the parables as the products of very early Christian communities, uniquely tied to the first-century CE *Sitz im Leben*. It's no surprise that when Dodd famously challenged Jülicher's claim that parables are unambiguous, an evolutionary view of literary history remained largely intact. Even when a new generation of literary-leaning parable scholars disavowed historical-critical approaches like form criticism, they still sought to situate a parable in its original *Sitz im Leben* in order to discern its evolutionary development.[79] The majority of NT scholars at the time agreed with Jeremias's view that "the retranslation of the parables into the mother-tongue of Jesus" was "the most important aid to the recovery of their original meaning."[80]

By the mid-1970s, poststructuralists had already been challenging the idea that language is a closed, discrete system that develops evolutionarily.[81] Nevertheless, the older views remained prevalent amongst literary-leaning parable scholars, who followed a procedure that was "closely related to the analytical (form-critical) method of Bultmann."[82] Funk, for example, conceived of parabolic language through a Bultmannian, evolutionary hermeneutical lens, while Crossan maintained the goal of searching for a parabolic *Ur*-text.[83] As Shawn Kelley has written, these scholars' work with the parables can be seen as "the American offspring of Bultmannian demythologizing, as the parable acts as another version of the demythologized kerygma."[84]

Within this hermeneutical perspective, language is always inevitably moving toward ossification, conventionality, and ultimately, inauthenticity; this is why the need arises for a disruption of Funk's "sedimentation in language."[85] This need can be conceived in terms of one of the main concepts that the early parable scholars shared with the Russian formalists: defamiliarization, or *ostranenie*. It might be helpful now to reread Dodd's oft-cited definition of the parable in light of Shklovsky's view that poetic language defamiliarizes standard norms: "At its simplest the parable is a metaphor or simile drawn from nature or common life, arresting the hearer by its vividness or strangeness and leaving the mind in sufficient doubt about its precise application to tease it into active thought."[86] For literarily attuned parable scholars, Jesus's poetic parables represent one way to disrupt the mundane.[87]

The point of this section has been to show how, far from being entirely opposed to historical-critical modes, early advocates of literary formalism in NT studies held similar *hermeneutical* views: they agreed that language (d)evolves, and that, given accretions of time and convention, the "unedited" versions of a literary form are most authentically connected to the earliest communities and, often, to Jesus himself. This also meant that parable scholars as different as Jülicher, Jeremias, and (early) Crossan all held that the critic's *metadisciplinary* goal was a historical one: to reconstruct the original form(s) and setting(s) of the parabolic materials.

Evaluative

A work of art stands autonomously as "an object of knowledge *sui generis* which has a special ontological status," and aesthetic sophistication is defined by textual unity. The first part of this axiom—that a text is ontologically unique and inherently autonomous—is most readily recognizable in the classic form-critical argument mentioned above that the Christian Gospel represents a *sui generis* literary genre.[88] Bultmann famously proposed that "there develops out of the kerygma *the literary form: Gospel*." Consequently, any ancient literary comparanda to which one might point "serve only to throw the uniqueness of the Gospel into still stronger relief. . . . It is thus an original creation of Christianity."[89] These are Bultmann's final words in his enormously influential *History of the Synoptic Tradition;* as Richard Burridge points out, "they are also the last words on the question of the genre of the gospels for nearly half a century."[90] The distinctive combination of each individual pericope (*die einzelne Perikope*), Jesus's teachings, and the proclamation of the gospel message (the *kerygma*), together render the written Gospel, in New Critical terms, "an object of knowledge *sui generis* which has a special ontological status."[91]

This view of the Gospel as autonomous object raises a tension that is exacerbated when we contrast formalism too sharply with historical-critical approaches to NT literature. Consider again the example of parable scholarship. The formalist emphasis on a text's autonomy might seem to contradict the parable's (purported) purpose to "impel," since the latter function is contextually determined and thus depends on a particular *Sitz im Leben*.[92] This is the reason that Poland critiques literary formalists, whom she charges with "a central internal inconsistency": "While on the one hand they wish to uphold the autonomy and self-sufficiency of literary art, and to maintain its discontinuity with extrinsic spheres of meaning, on the other hand they argue that literature provides a kind of 'experiential' knowledge which can extend and transform our perceptions of human experience in the world—surely an extrinsic aim."[93]

Yet, Mogens Kjärgaard correctly counters that this "apparently paradoxical tension" is not so paradoxical when one recognizes "that the poles of the condition of tension are to be found on two different levels." One level, the aesthetic autonomy of the parable, concerns its "linguistic infrastructure," while the other, its potential to create change in the world, relates instead to its "function as a performative" speech act.[94] When it comes to the level of a text's "linguistic infrastructure," historically oriented NT critics and literarily oriented NT scholars tend to agree with the formalist view that a literary unit (whether parable, pericope, passage, or an entire work) can stand alone—indeed, can be *meaningful*—as an autonomous artifact. Roland Frye's 1971 article "A Literary Perspective for the Criticism of the Gospels" is predicated on this very assumption: "A literary work is its own meaning, and its meaning cannot be univocally abstracted from it. This is the one literary principle upon which all competent literary critics now agree."[95]

Another area of NT studies that drew explicitly on literary formalism was narrative criticism. R. Alan Culpepper, for example, in his groundbreaking narrative-critical work *Anatomy of the Fourth Gospel*, says he "owes a great deal" to Roman Jakobson.[96] But early narrative critics like Culpepper didn't entirely differ from historical-critical scholars in their approach to narrative. As Adele Reinhartz has pointed out, for example, the content of NT form critics' work "does not differ substantially from the sorts of close readings advocated by the so-called 'new criticism.'" Reinhartz illustrates with reference to Johannine scholarship: "Bultmann's analysis of John 9, for example, goes through the story sequentially and in great detail, indicating how the narrative proceeds and what response may be created in the reader by each new detail or plot element.... As with Bultmann, [redaction critic] Fortna's actual analysis of the Gospel narrative could easily have been undertaken using the approach that Culpepper describes, but his study responded to a completely different set of questions—the literary strata of the Gospel and its history of composition." In a section of the chapter tellingly titled "Literary Criticism as an Implicit Foundation for Historical Criticism," Reinhartz recognizes that although none of the major historical-critical Johannine scholars "betrays any direct knowledge of literary theory and criticism," their actual interpretations demonstrate "sensitivity to the workings of the narrative, language and symbolism."[97] In sum, traditional historical-critical biblical scholars, pioneers of literary approaches to the NT, and the literary formalists shared the evaluative conviction that a work of art stands autonomously as "an object of knowledge *sui generis* which has a special ontological status."

The second part of this evaluative axiom—that textual unity is a mark of literary sophistication—is shared even by scholars whose final aesthetic assessments of NT literature diametrically oppose one another. On the one hand, we have NT literary scholars (especially in Gospel scholarship) who quite consciously assume textual unity *a priori* and laud the texts' literary sophistication. This is perhaps most evident in discussions of the Gospel of Luke and the Acts of the Apostles.[98] Robert Tannehill's narrative-critical commentary on the Lukan corpus begins, "Luke-Acts is the longest and most complex narrative in the New Testament. It was written by an author of literary skill and rich imagination who had a complex vision of the significance of Jesus Christ and of the mission in which he is the central figure. This complex vision is presented in a unified literary work of two volumes."[99] Tannehill clearly assumes that literary complexity, authorial skill, and textual unity are indissolubly linked. More recently, Carl Holladay's commentary on Acts praises its "sophisticated literary style," which Holladay locates "toward the higher registers of Hellenistic Koine."[100] He also emphasizes the continuity between Acts and the Gospel: "Acts is not a sequel conceived by Luke after completing his Gospel but a part of Luke's original literary vision. It was not an afterthought: Luke anticipates Acts, which presupposes Luke."[101]

Associating textual unity with literary sophistication is common outside Lukan scholarship as well. We find this in Kelli O'Brien's recent explanation that, in contrast to the oft-repeated description of Mark's Gospel as "pearls on a string" (preexisting traditional materials haphazardly strung together), "the Gospel of Mark is now considered a work of considerable story-telling skill and theological insight." O'Brien suggests that this trend began with William Wrede, but she explicitly credits narrative critics for the decisive evaluative shift: "In the last 30 years or so, literary critics have sought and found connections between pericopes with literary devices such as setting, characterization, and use of symbols."[102] Certainly, a long list of examples could support O'Brien's claim. James Williams, for instance, prioritized the whole Gospel of Mark over its constituent parts in *Gospel against Parable*, while earlier, Austin Farrer had analyzed "the element of artificial symbolism [that makes] visible the oneness of that factual enigma which is gradually unfolded as the Gospel proceeds."[103]

We also have NT scholars, however, who assess NT writings as literarily *un*sophisticated based on the very same view—namely, that literary sophistication is marked by textual unity. In fact, many of the earliest proponents of literary approaches in NT studies considered early Christian literature to be *Kleinliteratur* ("low" or "folk" literature, produced collectively), as opposed to *Hochliteratur* ("high" or "cultivated" literature, produced by educated individuals, which demonstrates authorial consciousness through aesthetic style and organization).[104] Because NT texts were written in the *koine* (common) Greek of the ancient Mediterranean, and because they were seen as disorganized, they struck many as unsophisticated. This is why Amos Wilder, for example, held that comparing "existing Greek literary forms" to Christian writings led down "a blind alley": early Christian literature, he declared, "belonged to a different world."[105]

Accounts that *oppose* NT literary criticism to historical criticism obscure the fact that NT form critics, at least, defined literary sophistication in the very same way. Some scholars say that the form critics' *sui generis* argument discussed above *precludes* aesthetic evaluation of the Gospels. Stanley Porter, for example, declares, "The form critical conclusion was that [the Gospels] were unique, neither the *Hoch-* nor *Kleinliteratur* of the ancient world."[106] Turning to the form critics themselves, however, we find that they made such evaluative judgments freely and frequently. Dibelius, Schmidt, and Bultmann all explicitly referred to the Gospels as *Kleinliteratur;* all three concluded that the Gospels were *un*literary.[107]

Dibelius asserted more generally that early Christian folk communities (*Volksgemeinden*) "gave no place to the artistic device and tendencies of literary and polished writing. The products of *Kleinliteratur* found their readers in circles not touched by *Hochliteratur.*"[108] Overbeck, among others, concluded that Paul's letters also represent "a literary *non*-form."[109] Indeed, for most form critics and early NT literary scholars, NT writings are decidedly *not* literary creations.[110] In this instance, then, the real difference between formalists in literary studies and those in biblical studies is that the former studied literature they found to be literarily sophisticated, while the latter studied texts they deemed to be literarily unrefined.

Strier rightly recognizes that "the question of literary value is built into the [formalist] approach."[111] Still, we have to remember that the criteria by which we judge literary value are always products of their time. This is the problem with Bockmuehl's claim, cited in the introduction to this book, that NT texts "represent second-rate literature in often third-rate linguistic forms."[112] Today, most scholars recognize that the categories of *Kleinliteratur* and *Hochliteratur* have always "owed more to romantic notions of primitivity than to insights into comparative literature."[113] Clearly, NT literature is not as linguistically or aesthetically complex as other literature from the ancient world, but few critics today would accept Adolf Deissmann's judgment that NT texts are unliterary "folklore" produced by "simple unlearned folk of the Roman Imperial period."[114] The upshot here is that when disciplinary accounts directly contrast NT literary approaches to historical-critical approaches, they miss an underlying point of connection between them—namely, the shared assumption that true aesthetic sophistication requires a singular author who intentionally composes an integrated, intricately organized literary text. Dibelius's assessment that the Gospel writers were authors "only in the smallest degree," early literary critics' labelling of NT texts as *Kleinliteratur, and* narrative critics' claim that the Gospels are sophisticated stories are all predicated on the *very same* conceptions of literary sophistication.[115] For all of them, an episodic collection of preexisting, discrete oral and written traditions without determinable authorial intent or provenance *cannot* be evaluated as truly *literary*. For all of them, a true work of art stands alone as an autonomous meaningful object, and literary sophistication is defined by textual unity.

Metadisciplinary

In addition to the above views—which focus on language and the object of study—literary formalists, NT historical critics, and early NT literary scholars shared a *metadisciplinary* goal, as well: they all sought to legitimate their work as autonomous and scientific academic disciplines.[116] They held in common the view that a critical approach to texts necessarily entails making objective, scientific value judgments about their literariness. When we oppose historical criticism to literary formalism, we obscure the fact that modern biblical scholarship and Russian formalism, which arose around the same time (the first few decades of the twentieth century), faced similar challenges (grappling with the implications of post-Enlightenment modernity for interpreting texts). The specter of Kant still loomed large, constricting conceptions of critique to "a pure judgment of taste" that is "not influenced by charm or emotion" but rather informed solely by "the purposiveness of the form."[117]

The metadisciplinary overlap between NT historical criticism and literary formalism becomes clearer if we compare the inimitable historical critic Adolf von Harnack's definition of NT research (*Wissenschaft*) with the Russian formalist agenda. So Harnack: "If the *person* of Jesus stands at the center of the Gospel, how can the foundation for a reliable and generally accepted knowledge of that person be gained except through historical-critical research? . . . And who can carry on this research *unless he pursues it as scientific theology?*"[118] Now consider Eichenbaum again: "What is at stake are not the methods of literary study but the principles upon which literary science should be constructed—its content, the basic object of study, and the problems that organize it as a specific science."[119] For Harnack as for Eichenbaum, true scholarly work must be seen as *wissenschaftlich*, scientific inquiry. Consequently, as a specialized form of knowledge, the discipline must also be rigorously and resolutely regulated if it is not to be contaminated.

In sum, around the start of the twentieth century, NT scholars and formalist literary scholars were confronting the very same challenges, and many responded in the same ways: by demarcating their discipline as a scrupulous and disinterested science, by claiming informed objectivity and unbiased neutrality as the ideal posture toward their object of study, and by considering it their critical duty to render authoritative judgment on a text's aesthetic merit. None of these goals changed when literary NT scholars first began adopting formalist approaches.

The problem is that situating the historical *over and against* the literary trades on simplistic stereotypes and reduces the complexities involved in all of the respective discourses. To illustrate, the shared evaluative definition of literary sophistication discussed above problematizes the common claim that NT literary critics adopted formalist approaches with the metadisciplinary aim of *defending* the aesthetic sophistication of NT texts against historical-critical scholars. That particular strand of the standard plot is misleading in at least two ways: first, it conveys the impression that form critics are unconcerned with aesthetic evaluation; second, and conversely, it implies that a formalist approach either presupposes or necessarily concludes that NT texts are literarily sophisticated. But as we just saw, neither adequately reflects reality. Poland's summary of the "central doctrines of formalist theory" would apply just as well to historical-critical and early literary approaches to the NT: they *all* generally presuppose "the autonomy and inutility of art, the impersonality of the artist, and the disinterestedness of criticism."[120]

Clarifying the Real Distinctions between Formalists, NT Historical Critics, and First-Wave NT Literary Critics

Understanding the convergences outlined above illuminates the real divergences between the three interpretive traditions. One such difference can be seen if we look more closely at the conclusions that historical-critical NT scholars and early literary NT scholars drew from their shared premises regarding form and content. As we saw above, NT historical critics and NT literary critics shared a formalistic purpose vis-à-vis the field of NT scholarship: authorizing each NT text as "an object of knowledge."[121] They went about fulfilling that purpose in different ways, however.

NT form critics, for their part, promoted the value of NT texts *not* by arguing for their aesthetic sophistication, but by shifting the locus of valuation altogether. For example, they insisted that, though the Gospel *form* was literarily lacking, the existential and theological *content* renders such formal features inconsequential.[122] While NT form critics were interested in form in one sense (especially formal categorization), they effectively subordinated what they viewed as literary deficiencies to other concerns. In this way, they could preserve the truth value of the content of the Christian Gospel, despite their devaluation of its literary construction.

In contrast, early NT literary scholars agreed with formalists in the literary field that form and content can never be separated in the search for meaning. Early NT literary critic William Beardslee faulted Bultmannian hermeneutics for "thrust[ing] literary form into the background as secondary and separable from the existential stance which the form expresses."[123] Wilder, too, charged form critics with cheapening the "whole story of man and salvation as the Bible presents it." This is why Wilder, while agreeing with Bultmann that NT writings cannot compare with "sophisticated and artistic" Greek literature, nevertheless cautioned that "the impulse to dignify the Gospels in the eyes of the cultured" is fundamentally misguided.[124]

Early literary NT critics like Wilder did attempt to "dignify" NT literature, but from a different direction than historically oriented critics.[125] Because they held the *evaluative* assessment that NT texts were unliterary, but also held the formalist *hermeneutical* view that form and content are inseparable, they faced a conundrum: they needed to find another way to value the form. They did so by adopting a mimetic perspective. They argued that the elliptical, ambiguous literary style of biblical writers accurately reflects the unadorned theological truth of its content.[126] Wilder held that NT texts give rise to a unique "language event," the form of which mirrors "the law of the Gospel and of Christ himself: humiliation and incognito." In other words, Wilder concurs with the form-critical evaluative judgment that the early Christian literary form is *Kleinliteratur*, but his aesthetic devaluation of NT writings serves rhetorically to bolster his case that early Christian literature is *true* art. "In the case of *true works of art*," he writes, "our attention is not usually drawn to form apart from matter. . . . In all genuine artifacts, including language-forms, shape and substance are inseparable and mutually determinative."[127] In contrast, according to Wilder, the Greek poets' literary sophistication reflects the artifice and falsity of their worldviews. Essentially, for first-wave NT literary critics, the value of biblical literature lies not in its formal literary sophistication, but in the very lack thereof; the text's artlessness is proof of its truthfulness.

My intention with this chapter has been to dispel some of the misunderstandings that have led NT scholars to neglect literary formalism today. Literary scholars have revived the formalist literary paradigm through the relatively new movement dubbed (helpfully, if unimaginatively) "New Formalism."[128] New Formalists object to what they consider to be the literary field's uncritical turn toward cultural studies at the expense of form and literary aesthetics; they seek to offer instead a "myriad of answers and kaleidoscopically fragmented visions of how to hone form (back) into a viable theoretical shape and to (re)assign it a critically interventive power."[129] In chapter 5, I'll draw on this and other recent developments in literary theory to offer just one of these "myriad of answers" regarding the form of Synoptic stories.

What Makes the Stone Stony: Concluding Thoughts

I began this chapter with the contention that NT scholars unnecessarily limit our conceptual resources when we fail to engage with the formalist literary paradigm. I argued that in order to understand why biblical scholars are so reticent to embrace formalist approaches, we have to recognize two major problems with the common account of biblical scholarship's development: first, when discussing the literary paradigm shift in NT studies, we often conflate what are in fact distinct kinds of literary formalism. To counter this tendency, I spent some time introducing the convergences and divergences between Russian formalism and the New Criticism.

Second, accounts of biblical scholarship typically overstate the conceptual rift between literary formalism and historical-critical approaches like form criticism. As a corrective to this tendency, I pointed out that actually, historical-critical NT scholars, first-wave NT literary critics, and literary formalists shared a number of key assumptions: (1) *hermeneutical:* literary forms evolve out of and develop in response to life circumstances (a text's *Sitz im Leben*); (2) *evaluative:* a work of art stands autonomously as an object of knowledge, and aesthetic sophistication is defined by textual unity; and (3) *metadisciplinary:* literary critics must make objective, scientific value judgments about the literariness of texts. We'll encounter these shared assumptions again when we discuss poststructuralists' refusal to take any of them for granted in chapter 4. First, though, we need to consider the paradigm to which that "post" was appended: structuralism.

3 Searching for Signs in the Stars: The Structuralist Literary Paradigm

It is my delight to . . . spend my life touring the boundless skies, learning of the constellations and the contrary motions of the planets. But this knowledge alone is not enough. A more fervent delight is it to know thoroughly the very heart of the mighty sky, to mark how it controls the birth of all living beings through its signs.
Manilius, Astronomica

Without language, thought is a vague, uncharted nebula. There are no pre-existing ideas, and nothing is distinct before the appearance of language.
Ferdinand de Saussure

The previous chapter considered the first major literary paradigm on which early NT literary scholars drew: literary formalism. Drawing a comparison there to what viewers might discern in the form of a mountain range, we saw that, for literary formalists, close readings of the "text itself" reveal its meaning. In this chapter, we turn to a second major paradigm in literary studies, which assumes that universal principles structure human communication. Because the latter set of approaches are epitomized by the movement labeled *structuralism*, I refer to this as the *structuralist* paradigm.

As we shift our paradigmatic focus, I suggest that we also shift our act of imagination from the great stone faces of the mountains to celestial bodies of the night sky. Let me say a word about why I think the imagery of constellations provides a helpful metaphorical entrée into literary approaches that consider deep underlying structures of language to be the source of meaning. The first-century Roman author of an early treatise on astrology, Marcus Manilius, wrote that the sky "controls the birth of all living beings through its signs" (*Astronomica* 1.13–19). For Manilius, the signs of the sky control creation. "By hidden laws," he declares, "the stars wield sovereign power" (*Astronomica* 1.66–67).[1] Similarly, the father of structuralism, Ferdinand de Saussure, held that it is by signs—indeed, by "hidden laws"—that language has the power to create. "Without language," wrote Saussure, "thought is a vague, uncharted nebula. There are no pre-existing ideas, and nothing is distinct before the appearance of language."[2] Much as Manilius sought to understand how the sky "controls . . . through its signs," Saussure sought to understand how language controls meaning through fixed linguistic signs. Language corrals the chaos of the cosmos into something comprehensible.

Structuralism is the quintessential example of approaches that seek to reveal transcultural principles undergirding a text, but other strands of literary theory make such positivist assumptions, as well. In this chapter, we'll look at narratology, genre theory, Marxism, psychoanalysis, and early feminism. There is certainly much to distinguish these discourses from one another. I don't mean to suggest that they're always mutually compatible or even that we should combine them in practice, necessarily. On that count, I prefer to heed Terry Eagleton's warning: "However generously liberal-minded we aim to be, trying to combine structuralism, phenomenology and psychoanalysis is more likely to lead to a nervous breakdown than to a brilliant literary career."[3] Still, I discuss these diverse approaches together because when it comes to studying literature, they all share the paradigmatic *hermeneutical* view that deep underlying systems of signification produce meaning. They all seek to draw literary conclusions that will hold true across time, space, and culture, regardless of location, perspective, or context. As products of the modernist moment, these totalizing literary approaches exist in the same closed universe; their "stars," that is, appear to remain stable.

One might think this would lead NT scholars to embrace such approaches unequivocally, since NT interpretation has for so long sought to make stable universal objective claims (whether of the historical-critical, Christian apologetic, or some other variety). In reality, though, NT scholars' responses to the structuralist literary paradigm have been nothing but equivocal. In 1976, when surveying "recent literary structuralist approaches" in biblical studies, John Rogerson warned that "there could be an irrational landslide towards structuralist interpretations," which in his view, "could only be bad for biblical studies."[4] In contrast, the very same year, Daniel Patte, an early and ardent advocate of structuralist exegesis, declared in no uncertain terms that introducing structuralism into "traditional" biblical scholarship was "neither a luxury nor a fad but a 'must' if one wants to carry out the exegetical task."[5]

One decade later, few NT scholars would have described structuralism as a "must" for exegesis. Tremper Longman predicted that "the vast majority of biblical scholars" would never do so.[6] In 1995, Stanley Porter published a chapter titled "Literary Approaches to the New Testament" that appears to confirm Longman's hunch. Porter doesn't even discuss structuralism, explaining in a footnote that it is "a *moribund* subdiscipline of NT studies" and "only tangentially related to literary criticism."[7] Then again, if Longman's prediction came true, if Porter was right that structuralism was "moribund" by 1995, how could Mark Bailey say that structuralism "dominated" biblical scholarship in 1998, *three years after* Porter dismissed it?[8] Was structuralism "moribund" by the mid-1990s, or did it in fact "dominate" late twentieth-century biblical scholarship?

Porter's and Bailey's conflicting claims are symptomatic of a broader ambivalence amongst biblical scholars regarding structuralism. Also in 1995, a group of ten biblical scholars called the Bible and Culture Collective published *The Postmodern Bible*, the result of over four years of collaborative work. They report that when asking their guiding questions—"How are biblical structuralism and narratology related to the radical currents in literary criticism? Are these approaches part of the problem or part of the solution?"—they could not come to a consensus: "Some of us perceive structuralism as indeed locked into positivist paradigms, as needing to be, along with other positivisms, the *object* of the radical critique we intend. Others of us . . . would suggest that the structuralist turn was *the* turn in recent critical consciousness, and that [structuralism] must . . . be the *subject* as well as the object of critique."[9] Not much has changed in this regard. Today, despite more familiarity in NT scholarship with poststructuralism and postmodern resistance toward "grand narratives," the structuralist literary paradigm continues to confound consensus.

By way of illustration, consider NT scholars' apparently incommensurate complaints about different literary criticisms' search for meaning in deep universal structures. Some NT critics claim that discourses like narratology take the quest for universality too far; as Longman put it, structuralist approaches offer "very limited help toward understanding the text" because they're "ahistorical," that is, not grounded *enough* in contextual particularities.[10] Yet, often the very same NT critics disparage approaches like feminist literary criticism for being "ideological," by which they mean *overly* focused on particular issues or contexts, or not concerned *enough* with universally applicable claims. Neil Elliott observes that so-called "'contextualized' or 'perspectival' approaches" like Marxism "have most often been met with a studied silence or marginalization."[11] Anyone who is unacquainted with literary theory will understandably wonder at these strange vicissitudes.

Who was right about structuralism? Should we consider it a "must" à la Patte, or worth only a castaway footnote à la Porter? Moreover—and more importantly—if we're interested in the literary dimensions of NT texts, then do structuralist forms of literary inquiry have anything at all to offer NT interpreters today? Much as I argued in the previous chapter with respect to formalism (but for different reasons), I contend that NT scholars' marginalization of these approaches unnecessarily confines us as we seek to address the complex questions to which the study of NT literature gives rise.

In this chapter, after briefly introducing structuralism, I'll outline the following strands of literary theory, all of which look in their own ways for deep underlying universal structures in human communication: narratology, genre theory, Marxism, psychoanalysis, and early feminism. Of course, the modern forms of these literary discourses have fallen out of favor in today's postmodern landscape; none actually functions any longer according to the terms in which I'm about to discuss them. Nevertheless, it's worth spending time to understand them for (at least) two reasons: first, their hermeneutical, evaluative, and metadisciplinary views formed the "condition of possibility" (Kant's *Bedingungen der Möglichkeit*) in which the current chaos of literary criticisms arose; second, NT scholars' misunderstandings or misrepresentations of literary approaches too often lead to their desuetude today. My goal with this chapter is to clear the way for NT interpreters' future engagements with the *contemporary* iterations of literary criticisms forged in the structuralist paradigm.

Structuralism: Reading the Signs

Structuralism's inception can be traced to the early twentieth-century work of the Swiss linguist mentioned above, Ferdinand de Saussure. When Russian formalists like Roman Jakobson and Boris Tomashevsky were just beginning to meet in Moscow, Saussure was already at work writing his *Cours de linguistique générale* (1916). The volume was groundbreaking. Translated into English as *Course in General Linguistics* (1959), it has been called "the single most influential book in 20th-cent. literary theory."[12] Saussurean concepts were later appropriated and popularized by, among others, French anthropologist Claude Lévi-Strauss, American philosopher Charles Sanders Peirce, and French semioticians Algirdas Greimas and Roland Barthes, all of whom developed their own detailed versions of structuralist study. Saussure's influence can hardly be overstated.

To situate where we're going in relation to where we've been, let me briefly compare the formalist and structuralist paradigms of literary inquiry before turning to the main tenets of structuralism proper. You'll recall from the last chapter that formalists like the New Critics locate meaning in an individual text, which they define as an autotelic, autonomous formal totality. In this sense, literary formalism might be compared to stargazers who find meaning in individual constellations, like Manilius, who believed that someone born under the centaur Sagittarius will enjoy riding horses (*Astronomica* 4.230–34; 1.66–67).

In contrast to the formalists, *structuralists* look for literary meaning in the invisible design of language itself. Structuralists, that is, are less concerned with the form of an individual work than with the universal codes and conventions that make such a work possible. This is why, as we saw above, Longman predicted that structuralism would never catch on in NT scholarship. In the end, he wrote, "understanding the text . . . for many structuralists is not even a concern."[13] The critique that structuralism doesn't advance our interpretation of actual texts has been leveled in the literary field, as well. Eagleton, for example, censures structuralism in his characteristically colorful way:

> Having characterized the underlying rule-systems of a literary text, all the structuralists could do was sit back and wonder what to do next. There was no question of relating the work to the realities of which it treated. . . . The referent, or real object which the sign denoted, was put in suspension so that the structure of the sign itself could be better examined. . . . [But this is] bound to be self-defeating. It is rather like killing a person in order to examine more conveniently the circulation of the blood.[14]

For structuralists, though, the real point is that you have to understand how an entire communicative system operates if you want to understand any one text communicating within that system. In other words, structuralists don't care as much about the constellation Sagittarius because they're focused on understanding the cosmological system in which Sagittarius appears.

Structuralism represents a seamless extension of formalist ideas in certain respects, despite their different critical foci. For one thing, structuralists and formalists share the *hermeneutical* conviction that language and meaning are like static bodies, fixed in the literary firmament. This is not to say that formalists or structuralists necessarily believe that a text can have only *one* meaning. Roland Barthes, in his structuralist phase, referred explicitly to a plurality of potential "structural meanings."[15] The point, rather, is that for formalists and structuralists, literary meaning(s) can be identified and studied systematically (again, not necessarily in a singular way), as long as *disciplinarily*, the critic follows the right principles and practices of discernment. Additionally, although they find meaning in different places (for New Critics, the text; for structuralists, its entire linguistic system), both eschew *extra*textual factors like an author's original intent. Humans can discern constellations in the sky, and identify stars' locations in relation to others, *without* asking whether a divine ("authorial") being "put" them there or intended that they be found.

As we saw in the epigraph at the start of the chapter, Saussure himself uses celestial imagery: "Without language, thought is a vague, uncharted nebula. There are no pre-existing ideas, and nothing is distinct before the appearance of language."[16] For structuralists, language gives ideas form. All reality is textual, insofar as everything we (think we) know is based on and indeed shaped by language. This emphasis on the importance of language in constructing reality so permeated the humanities in the early twentieth century that now it's often called *the linguistic turn*.

Here, let me correct a common misconception: the linguistic turn was not about claiming that there is no reality external to language at all. Historian Frank Ankersmit is right to insist that the linguistic turn should "never be construed as an attack on truth."[17] The structuralists' point is that humans necessarily and inescapably perceive that reality from within human-made, limited linguistic systems. When humans see a picture in a specific configuration of stars—the figure of Aquarius, for instance—it becomes very difficult to see anything else in or around that constellation. Saussure describes this (largely unconscious) phenomenon as *linguistic determinism*.

In terms of literary criticism, the structuralist's goal is to shift critical attention to the active role that interpreters play in drawing connections and conclusions regarding textual elements—elements that are, importantly, *there* to be interpreted. Hindy Najman's explanation is especially clear:

> Constellations depend for their legibility on our interests as readers. Still, they are objectively there. Galaxies exist independently of our interests, whereas constellations such as Orion and the Big Dipper are figures that *we* trace because of their similarity to familiar, earthly images. The stars know nothing of them. Yet the constellations are not merely subjective projections. . . . Similarly, I make no suggestion that the authors of the texts to be discussed were consciously aware of the textual features with which I am concerned. Nevertheless, the constellation is objectively available and is not a subjective projection.[18]

Structuralists do not deny the existence of an objective reality—just humans' ability to apprehend and make sense of that reality outside of language.

Saussure also argued that language is a self-sufficient, interconnected system of symbols, or signs. He distinguished between *signifiers* (the form of representation; here, words) and *signifieds* (the concepts to which those words refer); *signifiers* and *signifieds* together constitute the *sign*, or a concept that exists in the mind, not in physical reality. For example, when I write the letters s-t-a-r, the English word "star" is the *signifier*. What that word evokes in your mind—whether a luminous ball of gas in the sky, the main performer in a show, or a five-pointed star shape—is the *signified*. Together, s-t-a-r and the mental concept it evokes make up the *sign*. Saussure was careful to insist that none of these is the star itself. The actual, material thing to which the sign refers is the *referent*, and only the referent exists in the actual, material world.

This is how, according to Saussure, the structures of language organize and make the world comprehensible in particular ways (as opposed to others), thereby shaping our perceptions of reality. From this *hermeneutical* conviction comes the famous Saussurean distinction between *langue*, the general system of language, and *parole*, a performed utterance within that system. Only within the *langue* can an individual *parole* be meaningful: "Language is a system of interdependent terms in which the value of each term results solely from the simultaneous presence of the others."[19] In other words, the relations between signs, not the signs themselves, impute signifying value. Consequently, on a *disciplinary* level, structuralists are uninterested in analyzing the surface phenomena of a specific *parole;* they seek to explicate the *langue*, the deep structures by which that *parole* becomes comprehensible. Lévi-Strauss, who famously appropriated Saussure's views for anthropological study, described structuralism as "the quest for the invariant, or for the invariant elements among superficial differences."[20]

This structuralist quest gave rise to two contiguous but distinct disciplines: *semiology* and *semiotics* (neither of which should be confused with *semantics*, which has to do with changes in meaning over time). *Semiology* derives from Saussure's imagining of a new "independent science": "A science that studies the life of signs within society . . . I shall call it *semiology* (from the Greek *sēmeion*, 'sign'). Semiology would show what constitutes signs, what laws govern them."[21] *Semiology* is but one branch of the broader science of signs called *semiotics. Semiotics* expands the application of structuralist principles beyond language to include all kinds of *sign systems*, including images, behaviors, and other nonverbal systems of signification.[22]

Saussure also taught that the relationship between *signifiers* and *signifieds* is arbitrary; nothing intrinsic to a given word—say, "star"—makes it the natural or proper sign for the luminous mass of burning gas to which "star" refers. By way of illustration, consider again the metaphor of the constellation, this time as articulated by German philosopher Walter Benjamin:

> Ideas are related to objects as constellations are to stars. This means, in the
> first place, that ideas are neither the concepts of objects nor their laws. They
> do not contribute to the knowledge of phenomena, and in no way can the
> latter be the criteria with which to judge the existence of ideas. . . . Ideas
> are timeless constellations, and *by virtue of the elements' being seen as* points
> in such constellations, phenomena are subdivided and at the same time
> redeemed.[23]

Benjamin's point, much like Saussure's, is that ideas are not *actually* the objects to which they refer, just as constellations are not *actually* lions or scorpions. Phenomena are understood the way they are simply "by virtue of . . . *being seen* as" such.

Decoupling ideas from their referents leads to this conclusion: reality does not determine which signifier should be used for which referent; communities do, and typically not intentionally.[24] That is, convention determines meaning, and communities then pass on those conventions to later generations, like a parent teaching a child to identify the five stars of the Big Dipper's handle. These inherited ways of seeing become largely unconscious and habitual. Jonathan Culler, looking back on his own involvement with literary theory in the 1960s, reflects: "In the structuralist moment there was a growing body of theory—essentially the generalization of the model of structural linguistics—which, it was claimed, would apply everywhere, to all domains of culture [and would] be the key to understanding language, social behavior, literature, popular culture, societies with and without writing, and the structures of the human psyche."[25] In the structuralist paradigm, deep underlying mechanisms of meaning-making animate not only literature, but human consciousness itself.

The system works in two ways. On the one hand, the significance of a given sign depends on its difference from other signs; the North Star, for instance, means something only if it is distinct from all the other "non–North Star" heavenly bodies. Saussure contends that all human thought is organized in terms of binaries: white *is opposed to* black; presence, to absence; speech, to silence; life, to death; male, to female; and so on. On the other hand, even as signs gain meaning from *difference*, they also evoke associations with *similar* signs. "A particular word," Saussure writes, "is like the center of a constellation; it is the point of convergence of an indefinite number of co-ordinated terms."[26] It's worth reiterating: nothing intrinsic to the nature of a given star makes it the center of a constellation; it is the center because humans have agreed to see it as such.

The arbitrary and communal nature of associative significations becomes especially important when we consider the *evaluative* resonances of the hierarchical binaries mentioned above. The two terms are never equal; one side of the opposition is always *privileged*, valued more highly than the other (white is perceived and presented as *better than* black; male, *better than* female, and so on). The privileged concept becomes the center of the social constellation, while its "other" is forced to the margins.

This centering is nicely illustrated by an excerpt from the work of first-century BCE Roman architect Vitruvius:

> Within the area of the entire earthly globe and all the regions at the center of the cosmos, the Roman People has its territories. . . . Just as the planet Jupiter is tempered by running its course between seething Mars and chilly Saturn, so, for the same reason, Italy, in between north and south, partaking of each in her composition, has balanced and invincible qualities. . . . Thus the divine intelligence established the state of the Roman People as an outstanding and balanced region—so that it could take command over the earthly orb. (*De arch.* 6.1.10–11; trans. Rowland)

Vitruvius's rhetorical project is clear. Divinely situated at the center of the earthly orb, which is itself situated at the center of the cosmos, the Roman people, Vitruvius declares, are *innately* better than other populations.

Today, most would consider such judgments arbitrary. They are arbitrary, but not innocent. Valuing one side of dualistic dichotomies over the other serves an (often nefarious) ideological purpose for those who benefit from such valuation. Eventually, this was to become one of the main poststructuralist objections to structuralism.

Let us save that discussion for the next chapter. Now, we turn to a version of structuralist thought that has proven quite influential in NT (especially Gospel) scholarship—narratology.

Narratology

In 1969, Bulgarian narratologist Tzvetan Todorov coined the term "narratology" for the formal critical analysis of narrative (that is, poetics of narrative). Structuralist narratologists (often now called classical narratologists) sought to establish "narrative syntax," that is, transtemporal, transcultural properties and rules that (they believed) govern all stories. Again, the approach presumes an underlying universality: "Narratology is based on the assumption that certain characteristics (universals) are found in *all* narrative texts—from antiquity until modern times."[27]

Narrative theorists argue that certain formative aspects of story are indispensable to an adequate definition of narrative; most typically, these elements include plot, point of view (or focalization), setting, and characterization. Of course, analysis of narrative features is hardly a new phenomenon. As early as Aristotle, we find discussions that isolate the following as constitutive of narrative: spectacle, character, fable (which he equates with plot), diction, melody, and thought (*Poet.* 1450a). Aristotle's privileging of plot is still commonly affirmed today. Narratologist Seymour Chatman, for example, insists, "A narrative without a plot is a logical impossibility."[28]

Let's return again to our celestial imagery to illustrate. A structuralist narratologist would remind us that a constellation is a snapshot. It is, apparently, a moment without momentum. The stars that constitute the constellation of Leo depict a lion hanging in space. There's no action, and therefore, no plot. The myth *behind* Leo, on the other hand, has characters who act in causally connected events. The story is that Leo represents the Nemean Lion with an impenetrable hide who is killed by Hercules in the first of twelve trials. The myth has temporal succession and a teleological end. The story behind the stars, not the constellation itself, is the narrative.

Like Saussurean linguists, structuralist narratologists' aspirations to scientific rigor led them to draw on what they saw as universally applicable linguistic principles to explain narratives. Classical narratologists held that, unlike other forms of discourse and/or knowledge (such as laboratory sciences, lyric poetry, or legal jurisdiction), narrative is based on a universal archetypal subject/predicate plot structure. Just as a sentence requires a subject and a predicate ("The girl [subject, character] throws the ball [predicate, action]"), every story requires certain subjects (often stock characters like heroes, villains, helpers, and so forth) who act in specific ways (the hero receives a task; the villain is punished; the hero is married, and so on). Vladimir Propp called these character acts *functions,* and outlined a set of thirty-one standard functions in Russian fairy tales. Building on Propp's work, A. J. Greimas developed his "actantial" plot model in his *Sémantique structurale* (1966). Greimas's model was made up of distinct elements, or "actants": (1) manipulation (an imbalance is created); (2) competence (trials and temptations test the hero's competence); (3) performance (the hero achieves or fails to achieve the desired goal); and (4) sanction (the hero is acknowledged and balance restored).[29]

Narratology, in its traditional or classical sense, presumes three standard axioms. First, as we saw with the Leo example above, narratives are dynamic and sequential, moving toward some teleological end. Order, sequence, and resolution matter. Second, one should distinguish between the content of a narrative and the way that the narrative is told. Chatman picked up and popularized Russian formalist Viktor Shklovsky's terms for this distinction, *fabula* and *syuzhet,* translating them as *story* and *discourse:* "Story is the *content* of the narrative expression, while discourse is the *form* of that expression."[30] Third, even as we might distinguish critically between story and discourse, a narrative's form and content cannot be separated *hermeneutically;* narrative is constitutive of meaning in and of itself. In other words, narrative is not simply an inconsequential, disposable "container" of ideational or propositional content. The narrative form is crucial to its communication. This brings us to the issue of genre.

Genre Theory

Generic conventions play a crucial role in the composition and comprehension of literature, even as genres are stubbornly ambiguous, "changing, and inherently fuzzy."[31] For most of its two-thousand-year history, genre theory has focused on typological identifications of distinct literary forms. The structuralist literary paradigm fit this classificatory mode quite well, focused as it was on identifying parallels across literary texts and situating literary conventions within larger structural models. Looking back on twentieth-century developments in genre theory, Thomas Beebee identifies the following four stages: (1) production-oriented assessments, or "genre as rules"; (2) evolutionary growth, or "genre as species"; (3) formal analyses of "genre as patterns of textual features"; and (4) socially constructed expectations, or "genre as reader conventions."[32]

Nowhere is modernist genre theory better exemplified than in Northrop Frye's highly influential *Anatomy of Criticism,* published in 1957. Frye takes "the whole of literature" as his focus, insisting that literary criticism exists "to build up a systematic structure of knowledge."[33] Using the quintessential structuralist critique of formalism, Frye's self-proclaimed "polemical introduction" to *Anatomy* rejects the New Critics' "close reading" as "primitive" because it lacks a broader "conceptual framework" that might enable "a systematic comprehension" of literature.[34] Frye's own conceptual framework exemplifies systematic deductive generic analysis. He posits four main literary genres (romance, tragedy, irony/satire, and comedy), the structures of which correspond to a limited number of narrative patterns and cyclical symbols such as the four seasons. Frye also argues that literature is organized around recurring story forms, which he refers to as archetypal myths (*mythoi*).

Scholars like Frye who rigidly employ Beebee's "genre as rules" and/or "genre as patterns of textual features" approaches appear to have inherited ancient theorists' views of genre as determinable based on stable, universally consistent literary conventions. Consider the clear distinctions set forth in the classic work on genre, Aristotle's *Poetics:* "Epic poetry, then, and the poetry of tragic drama, and moreover, comedy and dithyrambic poetry . . . differ one from another in three respects: the media, the objects, and the mode of *mimesis*" (1447a). Or take Horace, who asks, "How can I be called a poet if I ignore, or fail to observe, the established functions and styles in my work? Why, out of diffidence, would I prefer not to know, than to learn?" (*Ars Poetica* 86–91). Joseph Farrell helpfully traces how ancient theorists and poets alike did *not* "regard genre itself as a slippery or even a problematic concept. Instead genre was felt to be . . . immanent and unambiguous." Najman puts it succinctly: "No play could be both a tragedy and a comedy in fifth century BCE Greece."[35] For some scholars of early Christian literature today, these ancient claims about genre provide reason enough to avoid the so-called "imposition of contemporary literary theory" on primary sources.

In recent years, schematic approaches to genre have come under attack for being too rigidly committed to the idea that universal laws govern language across time and tradition. As influential as the classical view has been, genre is considerably more complicated than ancient discussions make them appear. It always has been. For instance, despite clear-cut perceptions like those Najman describes above, ancient theorists themselves often elide description and prescription. We'll consider contemporary genre theory's approach to these complexities in the next chapter's discussion of reader-response criticism.

Marxism

Inspired by nineteenth-century socialist Karl Marx, the grand narrative of Marxism (sometimes referred to as the "Theory of Everything") held that all reality ("the real") is inexorably shaped by the economic system on which a given society is based. The deep underlying universal structure driving Marxism has to do with material economic realities—the conditions constrained and enabled by wealth and poverty. Western capitalism, according to Marx, is built on consumerist ideas and practices, which together fuel an oppressive system of class struggle; those who are oppressed in such a system fail to resist it because they accept their society's reigning ideologies, which appear normal or natural, but always benefit those in power and undermine inclinations toward change. Marx called this "false consciousness."

As a young man at university in Berlin, Marx joined the Young Hegelians, and though he ostensibly resisted Hegel's views, his theories show deep indebtedness to the Hegelian dialectic. Marx and Frederick Engels, in their famous 1848 *Communist Manifesto*, adopted Hegel's dialectic, moving it from the realm of abstract thought to the arena of economic, material reality. They saw history through the lens of a *dialectical materialism*—that is, as a series of conflicts and resolutions that work this way: one view (what Hegel called the *thesis*) gives rise to, and is challenged by, its opposite (*antithesis*), and change finally results through compromise (*synthesis*). Power struggles between owners and workers, rich and poor, exploiters and exploited are pervasive in the modern industrial world; thus, Marx and Engels insisted, the only viable solution is socialism, which rejects the latent contradictions on which those class struggles are built.

In this context, Marx's view of literature acquires a distinctively political focus. Art, after all, is a commodity, or human production. His *evaluation* of literature therefore lies in the extent to which it promotes the rise of the proletariat, or the urban poor who are exploited by wealthy capitalists. Unlike Saussure, the Marxist doesn't view language as a self-contained, abstract signifying system, but rather as a social practice rooted in the materialist conditions in which it's constituted. From a *hermeneutical* standpoint, language instantiates material class divisions and advances an author's cause; as such, a Marxian approach to literature calls for close attention to the author's cultural and political contexts, rather than (as for formalists like the New Critics) prioritizing close attention to "just the words on the page."

It's important to recognize how elusive the concept of ideology can be, even in Marx's own writings. Raymond Williams (an important figure in the rise of cultural studies) rightly insists that "there can be no question of establishing, except in polemics, a single 'correct' Marxist definition of ideology." Williams identifies three conceptions of ideology in Marxist writings: (1) "a system of beliefs characteristic of a particular class or group"; (2) "a system of illusory beliefs—false ideas or false consciousness—which can be contrasted with true or scientific knowledge"; and (3) "the general process of the production of meanings and ideas."[36] Marxist literary critics employ ideology mainly in the second sense, seeking to uncover the false consciousness, or tacit partisanship, that they believe fuels every literary work. A Marxian literary criticism asks whether a text supports and/or undermines classist or imperialist ideologies; how class structure might animate what's happening in a text; or how a text reflects (on) the socioeconomic conditions of its producer(s) and/or recipient(s). Marxist literary criticism, in sum, attends to a text's participation in ideological conflicts over socioeconomic conditions in the time period of its composition.

Whatever the historical successes and failures of Marxism have been, the Marxian literary critics' *disciplinary* goals are idealistic: they seek to unveil the conditions of the writer's material reality; to expose mechanisms of consumerism and consumption underlying (sometimes undermining) a text; to connect the ideological normativities of literature with the materiality of the real world; and, ultimately, to do the foregoing in order to eradicate oppression of all sorts and change the world for the better.

The Frankfurt School

A major movement that drew on and refined Marxian ideas is the so-called Frankfurt School of philosophical thought (whence we get the phrase "Critical Theory"). Most closely associated with Max Horkheimer, Theodor Adorno, Herbert Marcuse, and later Jürgen Habermas, the Frankfurt School sought to develop an all-encompassing Critical Theory that would facilitate "emancipation from slavery" (in all its forms), in order to "create a world which satisfies the needs and powers" of humanity.[37] Joel Weinsheimer's summary of Critical Theory sounds almost Freudian: "Interest has shifted from what a work portrays to what it betrays—typically, the concealed power differentials operative between genders, races, and classes.... The cultural criticism that works to penetrate dark secrets and reveal the hidden truth ... understands its task as exposing the dogshit upon which the palace of culture is erected (in Horkheimer's delicate phrase)."[38] The Frankfurt School rejected Marx's notion that literature is pure economic commodity as too simplistic; to them, language has the potential to "effect significant nonlinguistic, material emancipation."[39] Frankfurt-inspired approaches to literary interpretation (often referred to as *critical hermeneutics*) seek critical objectivity in service of universal liberation.

Walter Benjamin was a fringe member of the Frankfurt School (and constant sparring partner with Adorno). Benjamin assessed the situation differently. On the one hand, like Horkheimer and Adorno, Benjamin held that true art has a singular, authentic "aura," which simply cannot be replicated or reproduced.[40] On the other hand—and in notable contrast to Adorno, Horkheimer, and Georg Lukács—Benjamin held out hope that even mechanically produced art holds countercultural potential, because it provides the masses access to art in a way they had previously been denied.

The Frankfurt School's warnings about Marxism proved accurate. As the twentieth century wore on, technological and industrial developments, along with disenchantments engendered by World War II, destabilized early Marxists' teleological notions of history and human progress. As it turned out, revolution was not inevitable, and dialecticism itself could become totalitarian. Some literary critics (especially certain feminists) rejected Marxism entirely on this basis. Others—usually called "later" or "neo-" Marxists—worked to nuance and adapt Marxian ideas for literary study, rather than dismissing them.

Neo-Marxism

When it comes to literature, neo-Marxists propelled an important shift away from individualistic conceptions of textual interpretation and toward a new kind of critical self-consciousness. Recently, scholars from a number of different arenas have been calling for a return to critical considerations of class systems, laboring bodies, and consumerism in literature. American studies scholars, for example, appeal to the recent financial collapse and the Occupy Wall Street movement in the United States as reason enough to (re)focus on class in/and literature.[41] At its core, though, the neo-Marxist shift considers the products of all cultural systems, including literature, to be ineluctably shaped by particular ideologies. James Kavanagh's summary is apt: "There is no such thing as a social discourse that is nonideological."[42]

Two of today's most prominent proponents of literary Marxism are Terry Eagleton in Britain and Fredric Jameson in the United States. Both agree with Marx that language generally—and literature more narrowly—instantiates material class struggle, but they add that postindustrial societies *also* exploit the middle class (not just proletarian urban workers, as Marx had argued). Eagleton's and Jameson's respective revisions and expansions of Marxism differ from one another in certain respects.

Eagleton, for his part, insists that Marxism is not outdated, despite the fact that forms of capital and labor have changed. In his 2011 volume *Why Marx Was Right*, Eagleton argues that such shifts actually corroborate Marxian views: "Marx himself predicted a decline of the working class and a steep increase in white-collar work [and] foresaw so-called globalisation."[43] With respect to literature, Eagleton argues that exploitation and domination continue to structure society via the market forces of capitalism (including sales and marketing), but also by the inescapable forces of socialization: different classes of readers are taught (by educational systems, by family, and so forth) to make particular aesthetic choices, which then both perpetuate and legitimate class divides. In this, Eagleton resembles Pierre Bourdieu, who (though not a Marxist himself) advances the related notion of *cultural capital*. According to Bourdieu, normative aesthetic preferences (including taste in literature) are perceived as natural, but are actually constructed and circumscribed by the ruling class; as such, literary views function as a symbolic social system of differentiation.[44]

Jameson, for his part, is less concerned with class dynamics and more influenced by Marx's emphasis on the pervasive universality of politically charged ideologies. Jameson's famous dictum—"Always historicize!"—derives from the conviction that literary forms encode their historical contexts' sociopolitical imperatives.[45] Eve Kosofsky Sedgwick critiques the now "sacred status" of this phrase, asking, "*Always* historicize? What could have less to do with historicizing than the commanding, atemporal adverb 'always'?"[46] Still, for neo-Marxists like Jameson, the point is that literature, far from being free or disinterested, functions politically and socially to legitimate hegemonic power structures.

Williams defines *hegemony* as "a lived system of meanings and values—constitutive and constituting . . . the sense of reality for most people in the society . . . beyond which it is very difficult for most members of the society to move . . . [and] which has also to be seen as the lived dominance and subordination of particular classes."[47] The hegemonic culture actively—if at times unconsciously—masks its sanctioning of the status quo by advancing ideologies that appear neutral and natural, but work in their own favor (what French Marxist Louis Althusser describes as *ideological state apparatuses*).[48] Jameson's notion of the *political unconscious* draws on Freudian repression as a resource for exploring the functions of repressed and repressive ideologies in (especially modernist) narratives.

Psychoanalysis

There can be no doubt that modern psychoanalysis began with the Viennese psychiatrist Sigmund Freud. Though others following Freud (most notably, Carl Jung and Jacques Lacan) fundamentally shaped the field of psychoanalysis—and consequently, literary studies—in new and different ways, Freud will be the focus here.[49] Freud was something of a bridge figure; his life spanned the nineteenth and twentieth centuries, and his work and ideas extended far beyond his main discipline of psychoanalysis. As W. H. Auden wrote following Freud's death, "To us he is no more a person / Now but a whole climate of opinion / . . . / He quietly surrounds all our habits of growth."[50]

At base, the conviction underlying Freud's theories is that humans are constantly, unconsciously influenced by repressed desires, defenses, and fears, most of which stem from unprocessed childhood experiences. According to Freud, humans' repressed desires give rise to *complexes* or (in the case of women) hysterical neuroses. Among Freud's most lasting contributions is the idea of the Oedipus complex (the urge to possess one's own mother sexually, and the concomitant, consequent rivalry with the father who already possesses her). Freud also overturned the Cartesian view of the self; prior to Freud (and Marx and Nietzsche), Descartes's *cogito ergo sum* was the standard view of the self, but Freud posited a tripartite human psyche, with reason no longer standing atop the psychic hierarchy. For Freud, the *id* (the seat of desires and passions) is the dominant (and ever disobedient) inner faculty, constantly engaged in a power struggle with the *ego* (which tries to control the id according to the *reality principle*, seeking realistic ways to satisfy its urges) and the *superego* (which adopts society's moral principles to create a picture of the ideal self, punishing and rewarding the self accordingly).

Despite the common perception that Freudian literary analysis is solely concerned with sublimated sexual desires in a text (typically identified as phallic symbols), Freud's own relationship with literature was more complex. The direction of influence flowed both ways: Freud both drew on and was affected by literature (most famously, he derived his idea of the Oedipus complex from the Sophoclean tragedy *Oedipus Rex*), even as Freudian ideas continued to spawn new psychoanalytic approaches to other literary corpora. In a sense, Freud's interpretations of his (often fictional) patients' dreams and memories prefigured the close reading of the New Critics discussed in chapter 2: both assumed that there is always more going on than a surface reading reveals; both held that (textual) meaning always exceeds conscious (authorial) intention, and that careful, detailed analysis will disclose the hidden "textual unconscious."[51] In other words, both assumed that individual words and phrases have a "subtext."

Self-proclaimed psychoanalytic literary critics differ from the New Critics in terms of their respective goals. Whereas New Critics aim to interpret "the text itself," psychoanalytic literary critics seek to uncover the unconscious psychic processes of an author, a character, or a reader, with less concern for what the text actually says.[52] Freud's famous analysis of Hamlet epitomizes the latter: reading between the (characters') lines, Freud claimed to have "translated into consciousness what had to remain unconscious in the mind of the hero [Hamlet]."[53]

The Freudian search to discern a "textual unconscious" coheres with Marxian literary analysis insofar as both aim to reveal a subtext hidden below the surface, and both hold that such subtexts function universally to structure and then perpetuate or challenge normative ideologies. Where psychoanalytical and Marxian literary criticisms differ is in their views of those ideologies' origins. Marxism tends to be concerned with human behavior as determined by systemic social dynamics, whereas psychoanalysis focuses more on the behavior of individuals as determined in and by families of origin. According to the Marxist, then, psychoanalytic approaches to literature are overly concerned with the (author's, character's, reader's) individual psyche, to the exclusion of the social systems that structure human interaction and thereby shape those psyches.

Paul Ricoeur drew on Marx, Freud, and Nietzsche to develop what he famously dubbed the "hermeneutics of suspicion"—a mode of interpretation that assumes that "consciousness is not what it thinks it is."[54] Interpreters assume that, whether due to "the will to power, to social being, to the unconscious psychism," falsehood and guile typify normativity. Therefore, the critical task is to decipher the "ciphering": "The distinguishing characteristic of Marx, Freud, and Nietzsche is the general hypothesis concerning both the process of false consciousness and the method of deciphering. The two go together, since the man of suspicion carries out in reverse the work of falsification of the man of guile."[55] From this perspective, the aim of being a "resistant reader," or reading "against the grain" of a text, is to expose its underlying (but largely invisible) biases, which are (the critic assumes) always in some way inimical to freedom and equality.

Marxism, the Frankfurt School of German philosophy, and psychoanalysis all contributed to Critical Theory. None of them articulates a unified, coherent theory of literature, but the shifts in thinking that they precipitated still carry significant implications for how scholars approach and understand literary texts today.[56]

Feminism (First and Second Waves)

The most familiar account of feminist literary theory is the "three-wave" narrative, which recounts the development of feminist thought in terms of three discrete time periods, or "waves." Each wave has had its own distinctive aims and claims, especially in terms of political and legal issues, but all have shared the goal of eliminating the oppression and marginalization of women in order to establish universal gender equality. In light of this, it will surely strike some as strange that feminism appears in the same chapter as Freud, since the latter, along with his followers like Lacan, are so closely associated with misogynistic and phallocentric aggressions. Feminism's social and political goals obviously stand in direct tension with the problematic gendered assumptions underlying Freudian psychoanalysis. Many literary feminists vehemently reject Freud's concepts; Hélène Cixous's famous notion of *écriture féminine*, or "feminine writing," for example, explicitly resists dominant "phallic" modes of communication. Still, when we consider the outworkings of the first and second waves of feminism in the literary field, we can see modernist hermeneutical assumptions at work that reflect the structuralist paradigm.

Literary critics inspired by feminism's first two waves focus on normative gender binaries as the universal deep structures underlying literature. Recognizing that binaries such as man/woman and masculine/feminine have long shaped literature and literary criticism, feminist literary theory objects specifically to the manifold ways that woman/female has been constructed as man/male's inferior Other. Notice that this is an *evaluative* concern. Like the other approaches we've considered in this chapter, the *hermeneutical* assumption is that the critics' operative categories are fixed; their stars, too, are stable. Elaine Showalter, for example, coined the term *gynocriticism* to refer to "a female framework for the analysis of women's literature" that is "based on the study of female experience."[57] Gynocriticism is built on the premise that there is a distinctly "female framework" of analysis, and that a certain subset of literary texts can be considered "women's literature." In this paradigm, in other words, the assumption is that the male/female binary accurately and consistently reflects reality. The binary itself is not challenged, only the *devaluing* of its female/feminine side.

Feminist literary theorists have critiqued the discipline of literary criticism, and the canon of so-called great books it venerates, as fundamentally patriarchal institutions. Three areas stand out as particularly problematic. First, feminist critics take issue with the general exclusion of women's writings (Showalter's "women's literature") from that revered Western canon; rarely have works authored by women been valued as "classics." Second, they highlight the gender dynamics underlying language itself, objecting, for instance, to the sexism inherent in male-inflected linguistic expressions. Third, feminist literary scholars object to the erasure of women's perspectives from both literature and literary criticism. More often than not, male authors have attempted to portray female characters' experiences, rather than recognizing women's right to voice their own experiences in their own ways; similarly, male literary critics of all persuasions—from Isocrates to Iser—have tended to assume that all readers will adopt the male perspective of a male author and respond in a universally male way.

In a classic feminist reader-response work, *The Resisting Reader*, Judith Fetterley argues that when women read male-authored texts, they undergo a kind of "emasculation": "The consequence of the invocation to identify as male while being reminded that to be male—to be universal—. . . is to be *not female*" is to "experience a peculiar form of powerlessness."[58]

. In response to these androcentric tendencies, feminist literary critics have proposed alternative methods of reading and writing. Patrocinio Schweickart, in a well-known essay titled "Reading Ourselves: Toward a Feminist Theory of Reading," advocates two types of feminist reading strategies aimed at recovering and intentionally valuing the feminine experience: (1) when reading texts written by males, feminist readers ought to employ a hermeneutic of suspicion to uncover the patriarchal ideologies inherent in the text; and (2) when reading texts written by females, they ought to connect in "intimate conversation" with the writer—a conversation that in fact reflects an entire community of women writers and readers who have been ignored but not erased from the world of literature.[59] These arguments were progressive at the time of their publication. Eventually, however, many critics came to see them as essentialist and reductive, and literary theorists moved on to approaches we'll discuss in future chapters, such as third-wave feminism and queer theory.

New Testament Studies: Searching the Stars with Marx

The literary approaches I've just outlined have all entered NT studies with mixed results. Indeed, there are ample examples of NT scholars' varying appropriations and assessments of any of the above discourses; I mentioned some of the mixed reactions to structuralism at the start of this chapter. In this section, I want to focus for illustrative purposes on Marxist interpretation—a literary approach that has conspicuous overlaps with NT (especially Pauline) studies, but that has nevertheless elicited a particularly wide range of responses from NT critics.

In 2007, Roland Boer published a twenty-five-year retrospective on Marxist interpretation in which he celebrated "the vibrancy of Marxist criticism in biblical studies."[60] Yet, just five years later, Neil Elliott lamented that "Marxist interpretation of any part of the Bible has been scarce."[61] More recently, Lawrence Welborn has argued that even when Pauline scholars *have* drawn on Marxist thought, the "poignant irony" is that they've "produced ideological interpretations of Paul that transformed Marx's basic intention into its opposite."[62] So, then, which is it? Is Marxist NT criticism vibrant, scarce, or poignantly ironic?

The answer is, in a sense, all of the above—an assertion that requires some elaboration. Marxist NT criticism is "vibrant" insofar as NT scholars often work with what could be considered Marxian *themes* (class struggle, subversive resistance, slave labor, social stratification, historical development of societies, resource distribution, and so on). It's hardly revelatory to note that topics associated with Marxism stand at the core of several interrelated areas of investigation in NT scholarship, including the complex dynamics of socioeconomic class, status, and material possessions in the early *ekklesiai;* how Roman imperial discourse relates ideologically to early Christian discourse; and the implications of all of the above for feminist treatments of NT texts.[63] In the past decade or so, we've also seen a resurgence of work on issues like urban poverty in the Roman economy, patronage and charity, and the financial practices of first-century communities.[64]

Yet, for all this consanguinity between classical Marxist and Pauline themes, *literary* appropriations of Marxism remain, as Elliott put it, "scarce" in NT scholarship. Rarely does one find NT scholars employing the kinds of Marxist criticism that appear in the field of literary studies. It's telling, for instance, that in Boer's 2007 retrospective, most of the exempla of the Marxist biblical criticism that he describes as so "vibrant" appear in a section on the social sciences, not in the separate section on Marxist literary criticism.[65] When NT scholars employ Marxian concepts, they typically do so in order to discern objective social, material, and historical realia behind the text.

NT scholars'"allergic reaction" to Marx is due, in part, to recognition of historical discrepancies between pre-modern and modern eras.[66] Some argue that Marxist concepts like "class," "economy," or "social status" are simply irrelevant for a preindustrialist world because they developed around uniquely *modern* economic systems. In fact, literary critics like Carolyn Lesjak advocate Marxist interpretation of *contemporary* literature precisely because the discourses of the humanities are so "irreducibly bound to the economy . . . *today.*"[67] For some NT scholars, Marxism is useless when it comes to ancient literature because—as virtually all NT scholars agree—contemporary notions of class and socioeconomic systems do *not* map easily onto the social, political, and economic structures and practices that organized the ancient world.

Still, Marxist literary criticism can reveal how normative modern concepts inform our analysis even when we attempt to avoid them. Dale Martin's influential volume *The Corinthian Body* provides an instructive example of Marxist interpretation at work. Drawing on Marx's emphases on ideology, material conditions, and oppressive class systems, Martin frames his study as an inquiry into "the relation between language and social structures of power" in 1 and 2 Corinthians.[68] He proposes that the Corinthian church was "comprise[d] of a range of socioeconomic positions," and that the theological conflicts to which the letters point "stemmed from conflicts over ideology, differences in world view that correlate with different class positions [and were] . . . rooted in different ideological constructions of the body."[69] Insisting that "religious language must be analyzed ideologically," Martin argues that modern dualistic Western constructions of body, gender, and class are distortive: the "categories and dichotomies that have shaped modern conceptions of the body for the past few centuries . . . *did not exist in the ancient world* as dichotomies."[70] Note that Martin's concerns are literary *and* historical. He uses Marxist theory to expose a number of ways that NT scholars import anachronisms into their interpretations.[71]

And yet, Martin also remains content to keep his analysis almost entirely in the realm of the ancient world (limiting present-day reflections to a two-page postscript). This brings us to Welborn's "poignant irony." Often, Welborn contends, NT scholars who focus on Marxian themes ironically end up working against the Marxist injunction to "contest the assumption that the exploitative relation between classes is inevitable."[72] This is Welborn's critique of Martin's *Corinthian Body*. Careful to underscore that he appreciates Martin's recuperations of Marxian concepts like "class" and "ideology," Welborn marvels at Martin's insistence that he's *not* proposing "to replace some false statement with an objectively true alternative."[73] Welborn asserts that—*unlike* Marx—Martin remains "above the fray, as a cultural anthropologist, rather than a contestant for a different collective organization of power and resources."[74] In other words, even when NT scholars ask how social categories like class and status function in texts like 1 and 2 Corinthians, even when they ask whether Paul critiques or encourages repressive ideologies, they typically stop short of pursuing emancipatory goals in the present.

Turning a critical reflexive eye on these trends, some have argued that NT scholars' "allergic reaction" to Marx is fundamentally self-serving, especially for scholars in the West.[75] Steven Friesen calls this "capitalist criticism"—a way of legitimating and maintaining the status quo of Western capitalism.[76] Put more pointedly, avoiding Marxism (whether intentionally or inadvertently) allows critics to sidestep NT texts' difficult ethical implications regarding the poor, as well as the practicalities of our own power. It's intriguing in this regard that when NT scholars *do* discuss themes that could be considered Marxist, they often don't acknowledge them as such. Instead, scholars like Richard Horsley seem much more comfortable with the labels of "Empire" criticism and even "postcolonial" criticism.[77] But then again, this tendency makes good sense in light of NT "Empire" and "postcolonial" critics' similar tendency to "*relinquish* the central (frequently Marxist-driven) focus on economics and the universal plight of the poor."[78] Picking up Friesen's critique, Welborn suggests that a Marxist literary approach can help to "reclaim" NT texts "from the clutches of Capitalist interpreters."[79]

Welborn is keen to stress that Marxist literary criticism has a lot to offer NT interpreters. This is especially so if we expand our understanding of Marxist concepts. As we've seen, NT scholars commonly equate "ideology" with biased subjectivity. Bockmuehl condemns "self-consciously postmodern forms of ideological criticism" as offering nothing but "a bland discourse of power—in all its tediously bulimic, self-destructive corrosiveness."[80] What if we adopt Eagleton's definition of ideology instead? To Eagleton, ideology is "a particular organization of signifying practices which goes to constitute human beings as social subjects, and which produces the lived relations by which such subjects are connected to the dominant relations of production in society."[81] This definition expands our understanding of ideology beyond narrow—and negative—notions of partiality or one-sidedness. It also refocuses our attention on general Marxist principles, rather than specific instantiations of them. Consequently, one (pre-modern) society's "dominant relations of production" as opposed to another (modern) society's dominant relations of production no longer stand as unbridgeable chasms that render Marxist literary criticism of the NT historically suspect. Instead, as a form of literary theory, Marxism asks us to consider how texts themselves function in a broad ideological sense—that is, how they work to occlude or undermine certain perspectives (like those of slaves, women, and the poor) and valorize others (like those of males, masters, and the elite). This is why Welborn suggests, for example, that a Marxist literary approach can illuminate Paul's "capacity . . . to subvert and overthrow the categories and formulae appropriated from the dominant culture."[82]

Giovanni Bazzana makes a similar appeal in an article titled "Neo-Marxism, Language Ideology, and the New Testament." Drawing on broad

Marxist conceptions of ideology and language, Bazzana objects to the common social-scientific "goal of reconstructing the history and ideological profile of the communities that are presupposed to have stood 'behind' the texts at our disposal." Such projects, Bazzana contends, are "seriously flawed" because they wrongly "construe all the literary and linguistic characters of a given document as necessary products of distinct and identifiable socio-political phenomena."[83] The benefit of a Marxist literary approach is that it facilitates a more nuanced and complex "analysis of language as a social practice that both reinscribes socio-political structures and shapes them through its creative impulses."[84] Marxist ideas can prompt us to ask important questions not only about the sociohistorical realities that NT literature may or may not reflect, but about how NT texts themselves participate in ideological conflicts over class structure or distribution of resources—conflicts that can be operative in any time or place, as texts like Paul's Corinthian correspondences clearly attest.

Structuralism, New Testament Scholarship, and Negative Normativity

In this final section of the chapter, I want to return to the "oddity" mentioned at the start: namely, NT scholars' apparently contradictory assessments of literary criticisms that search for meaning in deep universal structures. As I said, literary approaches like narratology are criticized for being *too* universal (they're "ahistorical"), whereas approaches like feminist literary criticism are faulted for not being concerned *enough* with universally applicable claims (they're "ideological"). To put it another way, the former set of approaches (such as narratology and genre criticism) are seen as inattentive to ancient context(s), and the latter (such as feminism and Marxism) are seen as too focused on present context(s). This chapter's descriptions of these approaches, while necessarily brief, should help us to see that stereotyping certain literary discourses as "ahistorical" or "ideological" is not only far too simplistic; it also, in true structuralist fashion, trades on stable binaries and thereby masks the real disciplinary issues at stake. Importantly, these disciplinary issues do not manifest in the same ways in the field of literary studies, which is one reason that I find literary theory to be such a productive interlocutor for NT interpretation.

Modern NT scholarship is predicated on its own set of deep underlying structural relationships. In a post-Enlightenment era governed by the belief that "science and science alone" is "the measure of reality, knowledge, and truth,"[85] it's not difficult to see how certain constellations of associative schemata could become conflated with each other and opposed to others. Indeed, as modern biblical scholarship developed, a number of interpretive, temporal, and disciplinary dichotomies became elided in a growing mountain of cumulative associations. Many before me have critiqued how definitions of NT scholarship problematically employ dualisms like anachronistic *versus* historical, value-driven *versus* fact-driven, and subjective *versus* neutral. My concern, more narrowly, is with how these disciplinary tendencies negatively impact NT scholars' engagements with contemporary literary theory and literary criticisms.

I contend that simplistic stereotypes of literary approaches persist in the guild because they stand as a constitutive Other to biblical scholarship's binary-based disciplinary self-image. Dominant narratives about NT scholarship conflate multiple binaries in such a way as to create a homogenized picture of literary criticism.[86] A structuralist might ask how the significance of NT studies' self-perception hinges on its differentiation from other disciplines. "Like the center of a constellation," Saussure might say, NT scholarship "is the point of convergence of an indefinite number of [other] co-ordinated" concepts.[87]

We've made note of one such "co-ordinated" concept already: the perception that structuralism, as a synchronic literary approach, is "hair-raisingly *un*historical."[88] Eagleton connects this distancing of structuralism from history with the search for stable human universals: "The laws of the mind [that structuralism] claimed to isolate—parallelisms, oppositions, inversions and the rest—moved at a level of generality quite remote from the concrete differences of human history. From this Olympian height, all minds looked pretty much alike."[89] Structuralism's uneven reception by biblical scholars is due in part to this perception, which admittedly was articulated by early advocates of structuralist biblical study. Patte, for example, explains that "structural methods are in *sharp contrast* to the traditional historical methods [because] rather than being diachronic they are synchronic."[90] Nevertheless, as I've repeatedly emphasized throughout this book, positing *too* sharp a contrast between literary and historical concerns is misleading and unhelpful.

As I've intimated before, the literary/historical dichotomy is not the only specious binary around which we coordinate our definitions of NT scholarship. We're about to wind our way through some of these dichotomizing disciplinary developments; as we do, keep in mind the structuralist principle that nothing inherent to a star's nature makes it the center of a constellation. We saw this previously with Saussure, but it bears repeating: NT scholarship is what it is today because, over time, communities of NT scholars have agreed to see it as such. Here, I can only trace this trajectory in a cursory way, but even brief references should be sufficient to make the point.

First, in the *Eclipse of Biblical Narrative*, Hans Frei meticulously demonstrates a fundamental hermeneutical shift that occurred in biblical studies over the late eighteenth and early nineteenth centuries. By the start of the nineteenth century, Frei writes, "principles of exegesis were pivoted between historical criticism and religious apologetics." In other words, biblical texts had come to be seen *either* as historically accurate "explicative" references to actual persons and events, *or* as theologically motivated "applicative" claims about "universal spiritual truth."[91] Frei also establishes that this historical/theological *interpretive* binary lingered on in biblical scholarship through much of the twentieth century.

A common corollary to this historical/theological distinction was an equally rigid *temporal* divide: history is that which concerns the past, whereas theology concerns the "here and now." Krister Stendahl's well-known distinction between "what the text meant" and "what the text means" was the basic consensus in the twentieth century. Hardly an eyebrow was raised when Yale theologian George Lindbeck tied Stendahl's temporal distinction to a *disciplinary* one, writing that "*history* interprets what the text meant, and *theology* what it means."[92] Scholars continue to employ these associations today. James Crossley, for one, laments the extent to which "the *history* of Christian origins is dominated by *theological* agendas."[93] Roland Boer's efforts to "delink" the Bible from *theology* lead him to criticize Richard Horsley and Gerd Theissen for "succumb[ing] to the temptation to write new gospels, to present a Jesus who can be followed in the *present* world."[94] Note that Crossley and Boer trade on *both* the history/theology and present/past binaries in their ideal constructions of NT scholarship.

The disciplinary distinction between history and theology is often characterized as a difference between *descriptive* and *normative* work.[95] According to this traditional dichotomy, description aims to explicate the "what is" (or "what was") of a given text or event. In contrast, normative work (often described as "political," "ideological," or "advocacy" work) concerns "what ought to be." Purportedly, normative approaches offer judgments about the proper way to understand and/or use a text, offering explicit value judgments about the ends to which interpretation aspires, whereas descriptive approaches self-consciously avoid value judgments about what they're describing.

The normativity/description binary is implicated in another much-disputed disciplinary divide, as well—namely, that between *theology* and *religious studies*. Thomas Lewis explains that "a crucial background assumption—sometimes stated but often not—is that whereas theologians make normative claims, religious studies scholars should *refrain from doing so*. Rather, scholars in religious studies should distinguish themselves from theologians precisely by striving for some type of distance, neutrality, or objectivity in relation to their subject matter, where this is understood to entail analysis regarding what is rather than claims about what ought to be."[96] Lewis also notes that normativity/description and theology/religious studies dichotomies are frequently conflated with a divide between *faith* and *reason*, where faith refers to community-specific beliefs based on un-questioned and unquestion*able* authorities (God, Scripture, Church tradition), and reason refers to universal truths based on tested or empirically verifiable propositions. Christian scholars like Richard Hays marshal these dichotomies when they remind NT interpreters, "When we speak of theological exegesis, particularly when we acknowledge the Spirit's role, we must always remember that we are speaking not chiefly of our own clever readings and constructions of the text but, rather, of the way that God, working through the text, is reshaping us."[97] Lewis summarizes: "Normative claims related to religion are fundamentally a matter of faith, where faith is juxtaposed with reason."[98]

Such dualistic associations (past/present, normative/descriptive, theology/religious studies, faith/reason) form powerful scholarly narratives. Though many of the dynamics inhere differently in distinct institutional and regional locations, one view appears consistently across many different contexts: that is, a negative view of normativity. Most often, normativity is equated with perspectival, subjective, unscholarly work; in contrast, description is seen as disinterested scholarly neutrality. NT scholarship's long-standing lean toward the latter is one reason that NT scholars can so easily label literary approaches like Marxism or feminism "normative," "perspectival," or "ideological," and then actively dismiss or simply ignore them.

But this is exactly why scholars must think critically and reflexively—indeed, we must think *literarily*—about how our normative commitments inflect not only the ancient literary texts we analyze, but the scholarly texts we compose about them. Gary Phillips is right:

> For exegetes: it is no longer possible as responsible professionals to ignore the presence of theory and its impact upon what biblical critics say and do. . . . The fantasy has been dispelled that traditional historical exegesis is neither theoretical nor ideological. Non-theoretical, non-ideological exegesis has never existed except as a romantic construct, itself an ideological imposition on the way exegetes were taught to represent to themselves what it is they said and did.[99]

Taking my point one step further, I would argue that the structuralist literary paradigm is well positioned to help us do this self-critical work. Reading NT scholarship with a heightened awareness of the constructedness of our own arguments can expose the often unacknowledged ways that scholars charge one another with negative normativity, thereby authorizing their own normative claims.

Furthermore, contemporary literary theorists' emphasis on critical reflexivity (in conversation with Critical Theory more broadly, as we saw in chapter 1) can help us see how the "normative is negative" narrative is marshaled rhetorically on opposing sides of scholarly territorial disputes. The very concept of "normativity" becomes a discursive construction used by scholars of otherwise incompatible views toward the same disciplinary end—namely, establishing and maintaining their own interpretive authority. For many, eschewing normative and/or so-called ideological literary criticisms functions implicitly to legitimate the view that *their* interpretive strategies come from an unbiased nonplace (and are, therefore, the *right* ways of reading NT texts), whereas *others'* ways of reading are normative and biased (and are, therefore, *mis*readings). And yet, an inescapable tension stands at the core of the claim that "normativity is negative": decrying others' views as normative (read: biased) is the very means by which scholars (often unintentionally) mask their own biases and claim legitimacy for their own *normative* views.

What I mean is this. The very act of denigrating another perspective as negatively "normative" sets up bordered binaries. It's a dichotomizing act. Yet, quite often, the very same assumptive elisions are found on *both* sides of that divide. It turns out, for example, that *theology* and *religious studies* are actually two sides of the same normativity-averse coin. We've already considered how some scholars conceive of *theology* as biased/faith-based/irrational and *religious studies* as neutral/fact-based/reason-driven. But consider the fact that other scholars hold the exact opposite view: they believe that *theology* is neutral/fact-driven/reason-based and *religious studies* is biased/position-driven.

Consider these examples. As we've seen before, Hays chides contemporary critics for missing "the real work of interpretation," which, he says, "is to *hear* the text, . . . to read and teach Scripture in a way that opens up its message, a way that both models and fosters trust in God." Hays goes on to oppose his view of biblical interpretation to "so much of the *ideological* critique that currently dominates the academy," which, he says, "fails to achieve these ends. Scripture is critiqued but never *interpreted*. The critic exposes but never *exposits*. Thus the word itself recedes into the background, and we are left talking only about the *politics of interpretation*, having lost the capacity to *perform* interpretations. Many of us in the academy are weary of these tactics of critical evasion."[100] Bockmuehl, for his part, isn't just weary; he sees contemporary theory as an outright "attack on biblical theology" that is "distinctly imperial in its ambitions."[101] And Daniel Treier, discussing the relatively new movement of "theological interpretation," suggests similarly that "Christian beliefs can be productive for biblical interpretation, helping us to see what the biblical texts *are really about*."[102]

Notice how, *on both sides* of the theology/religious studies divide, we find scholars claiming (or aiming) to reflect reality by describing "what is" (for historians, "what was"), *and on both sides* of the theology/religious studies divide, we find scholars condemning *others* for advancing normative claims about "what ought to be."[103] What strikes me is the extent to which both sides of the disciplinary divides disown bias and condemn their opponents' "inability to be self-critical."[104] Scholars on both sides often seem not to recognize that there may be additional evidence that might call them to rethink their own reigning paradigms. Even when critics acknowledge ostensibly that absolute neutrality is impossible, they commonly claim (at least relative) neutrality for themselves, and charge others with "*credulity toward their own* favored (but often exegetically disemboweled) revisionist political project."[105]

The story that normativity is negative (while neutral objectivity is positive) is powerful. But the powerful dualisms that fuel this common story are neither innate to nor necessary for scholarly work on the NT. What's more, they keep us from engaging fully with the literary scholarship that can help dislodge them. Discussing the rift between historical and postmodern criticisms, Margaret Mitchell rightly observes that it is "hard to see how reconciliation can be achieved from within the agonistic paradigm, i.e., a starting point that involves a reification of the opposition into a single position, one continually defined not on its own terms, but in contrast to their own."[106]

In my view, the iterations of the structuralist literary paradigm we've discussed in this chapter offer a number of ways to break free from the standard scholarly agonistic paradigm. They do so, in part, by exposing common disciplinary dichotomies as not only constructed, but counterproductive. To echo Hilary Putnam, binaries "have corrupted our thinking . . . not least of all by preventing us from seeing how . . . interwoven and interdependent" artificially polarized categories can be.[107]

Searching for Signs in the Stars: Concluding Thoughts

Throughout this chapter, the hermeneutical conviction that texts function according to universal deep structures has unified otherwise disparate kinds of literary criticism. After presenting structuralism as the quintessential form of this literary paradigm, I introduced the literary approaches of narratology, genre theory, Marxism, psychoanalysis, and early feminism. We considered, for example, how archetypal genre criticism drew literary meaning from a set system of transcultural "timeless" myths, and how early feminist literary critics held that fixed notions of gender animate both literature and readers' responses to it.

As we'll see in the next chapter, postmodernism's challenges to "totalizing" theories have led to significant refinements and revisions of all of the literary approaches discussed above; these advancements have been both welcome and necessary. As I said at the start, what really matters to me is that NT critics engage with the *updated* versions of these literary approaches in a serious and sustained manner. In this chapter, I've sought to remove a major obstacle to such engagement—that is, the outdated and untenable oversimplifications of various literary criticisms that continue to circulate in NT scholarship. I'll close, then, with a hypothetical but likely scenario.

Imagine that in the future, you're reading along in some bit of NT scholarship, and you encounter some blanket statement about literary criticism. Perhaps you run across a specific claim, like "Structuralism is the form of literary criticism that is the most radical in its denigration of history," or perhaps something more general, like a description of psychoanalysis as "subjective," or of feminism as "ideological," or of Marxism as "normative" (implying, of course, that the writer's approach is none of these).[108] My hope is that, after reading this chapter, you won't take such binary-based assertions at face value. I hope that you'll interrogate the criteria by which scholars make such judgments, and that you'll evaluate the merits and pitfalls of specific literary approaches for yourself. Identifying literary approaches in terms of binary formulations has, to adapt Putnam's words, "corrupted our thinking . . . by preventing us from seeing" the benefits of more "interwoven and interdependent" models of interpretation.

As our exploration of the structuralist literary paradigm comes to a close, we do well to remember that the literature of the NT can be like the night sky—at times breathtakingly beautiful, at times dark and mysterious. And just as astronomers study the heavens to understand the stars, so also can we employ literary criticism to interpret the "vague, uncharted nebula" of NT literature—remembering always that literary study offers an aid, not a substitute, for eyes that see.

4 Literary Theory's Copernican Revolution: Poststructuralist Approaches and Beyond

The Copernican Revolution was a revolution in ideas, . . . an epochal turning point in the intellectual development of Western man.
Thomas Kuhn

Truth, Goodness, Beauty—those celestial thrins,
Continually are born; e'en now the Universe,
With thousand throats, and eke with greener smiles,
Its joy confesses at their recent birth.
Henry David Thoreau

In the last chapter, we looked at the structuralist literary paradigm, which searches for meaning in deep universal linguistic structures. In this chapter, we turn to a different literary paradigm—*poststructuralism*—which arose through the 1970s and 1980s largely in response to structuralist views. On a very basic level, the poststructuralist literary paradigm challenges the structuralist hermeneutical conviction that literary meaning comes from stable underlying structures of language. Judith Butler defines poststructuralism as a rejection of "the claims of totality and universality and the presumption of binary structural oppositions." Furthermore, she adds, such structuralist claims "implicitly operate to quell the insistent ambiguity and openness of linguistic and cultural signification."[1] In brief, the difference between these literary paradigms is this: where structuralism embraces universalism, poststructuralism embraces particularism; where structuralism builds up binaries, poststructuralism breaks them down.

I've intimated throughout the book that in NT studies, poststructuralism has been more polarizing than any other literary paradigm. Some NT

scholars, such as Stephen Moore, wholeheartedly embrace poststructuralism's "shape-shifting ability to make the familiar seem startlingly strange
[through] powers of redescription"—powers that Moore says "exceed even
those of historical criticism."[2] Others worry that poststructuralism leads to
relativism, political activism, and/or anachronism. Some adamantly reject
poststructuralism as subjectivity run amok, a form of self-indulgent scholarly navel-gazing that distracts from the real intellectual work of biblical
interpretation. A number of scholars propose that the poststructuralist paradigm might help NT scholars do "the same sorts of things . . . with a new
sharpness and clarity," while others argue that poststructuralist approaches
propagate "extreme textual violence."[3] Does poststructuralism help NT
scholars do what we've always done but better, or is it "a form of autobiography more than anything else"?[4] Is Stanley Porter correct to say that poststructuralism "has ended up exalting itself above the position of the text"?
Or is Moore right that poststructuralism is the most *anti*-authoritarian
mode of interpretation? And if poststructuralism responds to structuralism's perceived weaknesses, why do some NT critics conclude that, *just like*
structuralism, poststructuralism fails to "offer much insight into the text"?[5]

The last chapter drew an analogy between structuralists searching for
meaning in linguistic systems and humans searching for constellations in
the starry night sky. It will help to understand NT scholars' varying responses to poststructuralism if we expand the metaphor of reading constellations to that of humans' changing cosmological views more broadly. The
basic three-act story of human theories about the cosmos is well known.
First was *flat earth theory*. Most people in the ancient world imagined an
anthropocentric, three-storied universe, in which the earth floated about
like a flat disk in an ocean; the sun, moon, and stars were fixed above; and,
in the words of Homer, a dark abyss "dwel[t] beneath earth and the un-
resting sea" (*Iliad* 14.198). Flat earth theory was replaced most famously by
the second-century astronomer Ptolemy, who reasoned that "if [the earth]
were flat, the stars would rise and set for all people together and at the same
time." Since this was demonstrably *not* the case, the earth must be a sphere,
"right in the middle of the heavens, like a geometrical center" (*Almagest*,
Book I). The *Ptolemaic system* (or geocentrism)—the second act—thus saw
the earth as a spinning sphere in the center of the universe. And finally,
in the sixteenth century, Copernicus insisted against Ptolemy that "all the
spheres revolve about the sun as their midpoint, and therefore the sun is the

center of the universe" (*Commentariolus* 3). With the *Copernican system* (or heliocentrism), we came to the current consensus that the earth orbits the sun. Thomas Kuhn describes the Copernican revolution as a "revolution in ideas" with such astonishingly wide-reaching implications that it represents an "epochal turning point" for humankind. In the paradigms of flat earth theory and geocentricism, humans stood at the center of a finite, divinely ordered universe. The Copernican shift to heliocentrism rendered the earth and all of its inhabitants but a small part of something far more complex and mysterious.

Poststructuralism was the Copernican revolution of literary studies. Theorists like Roland Barthes, Michel Foucault, and Jacques Derrida initiated just such a "revolution in ideas," just such an "epochal turning point" in the literary field, by insisting that language, too, is far more complex and mysterious than previously assumed. Just as Copernicus had challenged prevailing notions about the center of the cosmos, poststructuralism challenged the assumptions at the center of earlier literary paradigms.[6] The fact that poststructuralism has generated major debate amongst NT scholars is unsurprising; Copernicus's ideas were vigorously disputed in his day, too. Every new paradigm faces criticism. The *Sturm und Drang* of controversy is simply the predictable price of progress. My concern is with the terms of these debates.

Poststructuralism is so controversial in NT studies because, like Copernicus's theory, it actively challenges the hermeneutical, evaluative, and metadisciplinary convictions that undergird earlier interpretive paradigms. NT scholars need to grapple with these challenges. Unfortunately, widely held and oft-repeated misconceptions about poststructuralism have led many to dismiss the poststructuralist literary paradigm preemptively, without due consideration. But to ignore poststructuralist discourses or deny their importance is to be like those who spurned Copernicus for claiming that the earth revolves around the sun. Most importantly, NT scholars' failure to engage the poststructuralist literary paradigm leads to critical missed opportunities.

My aim with this chapter, therefore, is not so much to explain specific forms of poststructuralist criticism—a number of helpful resources already do that.[7] Rather, my goal is to encourage NT scholars who would otherwise be wary of the poststructuralist literary paradigm to explore its interpretive benefits. I begin by comparing the structuralist and poststructuralist literary paradigms broadly, in order to frame the discussion that follows. I then turn to poststructuralism's impact on the *hermeneutical, evaluative,* and *meta-disciplinary* concerns that constitute the study of literature. The rest of the chapter is organized around these three sets of literary concerns. Under each subcategory, my agenda is threefold: I introduce poststructuralist responses to previous paradigms; interrogate NT scholars' common claims about those responses; and propose ways to reframe the relevant issues. Overall, I want to highlight poststructuralism's potential contributions to literary study of the NT.

Two caveats before we start. Decades ago, one could have drawn fairly clear delineations between the literary approaches we'll discuss in this chapter. Some concerned sex and gender (feminism, womanism, gender studies, queer theory), others asked about societies and cultures (ethnic, minority, and postcolonial criticisms), and so on. It's important to know that now, these forms of literary criticism are so thoroughly intermingled that dividing them into discrete approaches in practice is actually neither possible nor profitable. New strands of literary criticism purposely combine multiple foci. Ecofeminism, for example, draws explicit parallels between the violence perpetrated against the environment and the violence to which women are subjected in patriarchal social systems. Affect theory, which highlights the complex, embodied, affective responses that texts evoke in readers, can be even more expansive and intersectional, drawing, as Ann Cvetkovich does, on "four theoretical allegiances—feminism, critical race theory, Marxism, and queer theory."[8] The point is that today's literary theorists are conversant with and draw on a range of poststructuralist discourses to explore how any number of variables—sexual, social, racial, ethnic, socioeconomic, national, physical, and others—*intersect* and *together* constitute diverse ways of being and forms of meaning-making.[9]

Second, given poststructuralism's nearly ubiquitous influence in the literary field today, I can't even hope to offer a comprehensive account. As one would expect, literary critics have responded to poststructuralism's revolutionary shifts in different ways. Some seek to bring poststructuralism's hermeneutical commitments to bear on specific foci within literature (such as class, status, bodies, gender, and race), an approach exemplified by contemporary literary approaches like ethnic, queer, womanist, or postcolonial criticisms. Critics also have addressed the strengths and weaknesses of the poststructuralist literary paradigm itself—a response evident in the so-called After Theory movement. In this chapter, I introduce the above forms of criticism, but I draw principally on reader-response criticism and deconstruction as two of the most influential and representative strands of the poststructuralist literary paradigm.[10]

Literary Theory's Copernican Revolution: An Overview of Poststructuralism

"Poststructuralism" is something of a misnomer. Despite its "post" prefix, poststructuralism was not chronologically subsequent to structuralism. Nor did poststructuralists reject or abandon all structuralist principles. The poststructuralist literary paradigm simply didn't develop in a straightforward way. But this is the case for all human developments. The cosmological paradigm shifts from flat earth to heliocentric to geocentric theories weren't linear, either, despite the appearance of discrete stages in retrospective recountings (including mine above). Ptolemy was not the first to propose the geocentric model, nor was Copernicus the first to propose heliocentrism; both built on predecessors who were ignored or rejected by their communities, and both faced obstacles when trying to convince others of their views. The same is true of structuralism and poststructuralism, which continue to function in dynamic dialogue, building on, interacting with, and reshaping one another.

The main overlaps between structuralist and (early) poststructuralist literary paradigms are *hermeneutical:* both consider language to be nonreferential, both hold that language shapes our perceptions of reality, and both see linguistic associations as arbitrary insofar as they're not drawn from an internal essence of the thing itself. As Paul Ricoeur puts it, "There is no self-understanding that is not *mediated* by signs, symbols, and texts; in the final analysis self-understanding coincides with the interpretation given to these mediating terms."[11] In other words, structuralists and poststructuralists largely agree that reality is always perceived and constructed discursively; human understanding is never *unmediated.*

Despite these hermeneutical overlaps, however, poststructuralists differ from structuralists insofar as they question the stable underpinnings of the structuralists' finite, orderly universe. Poststructuralists stress that because humans perceive the world from our own partial and particular points of view, our perceptions of reality necessarily change according to shifts in time, location, and culture. People make sense and draw connections— that is to say, people *mean*—differently. According to poststructuralists, perspectivalism undermines structuralism's own claims to universality. But, as we'll see, poststructuralists' hermeneutical views carry significant implications for their evaluative and metadisciplinary positions, as well.

To depict the main difference between structuralists and poststructuralists, let's change our illustrative imagery from heaven back to earth for just a moment. Structuralists think of language as a tree, growing out of and structured around a stable tree trunk of universal dualistic binaries (for example, sane/sick, nature/nurture, body/mind). Poststructuralists, on the other hand, reject universalist claims *a priori* because they see language as too complex and dynamic to have a finalizable common core. Philosophers Gilles Deleuze and Félix Guattari compare language not to a tree, but to a rhizome (from the Greek *rhízōma*, "mass of roots"). A rhizome is a plant stem made up of mutually interlocking roots, ceaselessly spreading across many planes, and constantly connecting with and creating new species.[12] Thus it is that with poststructuralism came "new species" of literary criticism, such as the following identity-based approaches.[13]

Focusing on Women and Gender in Literature: "Third-Wave" Feminism, Womanism, Gender Studies, and Queer Theory

In the previous chapter, we considered how the first two "waves" of feminism challenged the discursive power dynamics that uphold misogyny—in primary sources, in their reception histories, and in contemporary critical theory. Poststructuralism, however, disrupts the universal male/female gender binary on which those early feminist views depended. Near the end of the twentieth century, a new generation of feminists (the so-called third wave) arose that rejected notions of universal womanhood. In opposition to earlier feminists, this generation argued that feminism doesn't depend upon an essential "female" identity; instead, they sought to overcome the limits of the transcultural category "female." Third-wave feminists argued that by insisting on a normative male/female distinction, early feminists unwittingly reinscribed the stereotypes and hierarchies they so actively opposed.

Today, feminist literary theory has unmistakable resonances with other poststructuralist literary approaches like lesbian, gay, and queer criticisms, masculinity studies, and those informed by gender theory, *inter alia*. These approaches all see the formation of sexual and gendered identities as sites of ideological contestation that change over time. Butler's work in particular (most famously, *Gender Trouble* and *Bodies That Matter*) has defined gender as a social construction, rather than an innate fixed aspect of human identity. Butler parses the concept of "gender" as a performative category; she sees gendered identity as the result of repeated sociocultural messages and actions.[14] Deeply informed by projects like Foucault's *History of Sexuality*, which traces the development of sexual identity as a historically contingent cultural construction, literary critics like Butler ask about how texts from different eras construct sex and gender differently.

Focusing on Race, Ethnicity, and Nations in Literature: Minority Discourses and Postcolonialism

Especially following the "quantum leap in the general theory of nationalism and ethnicity in the human sciences" that occurred in the 1970s–1990s (often called the "imperial turn"), literary critics began to focus on the complexities of race, ethnicity, cultures, territories, and nations in literature.[15] The best-known of these approaches, postcolonial criticism, explores how Western rhetoric constructs non-Western cultures as mysterious and dangerous "Others" in order to legitimize colonization, exploitation, and the consolidation of Western power. It's vital to understand that postcolonialism, like feminism, "has never been strictly literary theory, as it has always included anthropology, sociology, and political science, grounded in the experience of real people in particular geographic locations."[16]

Most scholars point to Edward Said's *Orientalism* as postcolonialism's founding text. There, Said analyzes the "otherizing" discourses by which the imperial powers of Britain, Europe, and America constructed negative stereotypes of Eastern nations ("the Orient") and thereby colonialized those territories.[17] Building on and revising Said's pioneering work, postcolonialists like Gayatri Spivak read literature with an eye toward exposing and challenging the West's subjugation of colonized, "subaltern" peoples.[18] In more recent years, *Orientalism* specifically and postcolonialism generally have also been criticized for their own homogenizing tendencies.[19] Ashis Nandy argues that postcolonialism reifies colonialism by making it the dominant defining factor in the colonial/postcolonial binary.[20]

A better approach is to recognize with Homi Bhabha that stereotypes serve the powerful rhetorical purpose of perpetuating "discursive and political practices of . . . hierarchization," but they can never *actually* offer a "secure point of identification."[21] Like Butler's work on gender, Bhabha's

The Location of Culture highlights language's performative power. Bhabha argues that language's fluid indeterminacies allow it to cross boundaries between colonizer and colonized and thereby transform both. Colonization is marked by mutuality and interdependence, an ever-ephemeral, unstable "in-between" space (Bhabha calls it the "Third Space of enunciation"), where oppressed and oppressor influence and co-produce one another.[22] Bhabha's concepts of *hybridity* and *ambivalence* underscore the mixtures and uncertainties of identity construction, and thus provide better alternatives to essentializing binaries like East/West, colonizer/colonized, First World/Third World, center/margins.[23] Furthermore, as Dipesh Chakrabarty observes, literature can simultaneously reflect "contradictory, plural, and heterogenous struggles" *and* legitimate the "schemas that naturalize and domesticate this heterogeneity."[24]

So-called minority criticisms like African American, Native American, Asian, and Latino/a criticisms are similar to postcolonial approaches insofar as they explore the strategies of minoritization (and resistance to it) that operate in and through literature, but they focus more narrowly on specific ethnic groups, cultures, and perspectives. The hermeneutical view that normative concepts like "race" are culturally constructed is crucial to these projects. Henry Louis Gates Jr., author of the landmark work of African American literary criticism, *The Signifying Monkey* (1988), advocates using the word "race" only with quotation marks in order to mark it visibly as "a dangerous trope."[25] Despite appearances, the term "race," insists Gates, is *not* "an objective term of classification."[26] Still, appearances are powerful. Toni Morrison, best known as a novelist but also an astute literary critic, argues that strict, value-laden binaries separating "blackness" from "whiteness" are ubiquitous, always present in literature, and always threatening to undermine efforts toward equality.[27]

Although I've described a focus on women and gender in a separate section from a focus on race, ethnicity, and nations, I want to underscore how in reality, these are neither discrete nor separable categories. Rather, they are inextricably intertwined and mutually reinforcing. Race, gender, nationality, sexuality, class, status, skills—these identity markers and more come together and imbricate each other, and the complex convergences themselves are no less constitutive of identity. All of this is to say that separating certain strands of identity into distinct foci can be a useful analytical step, but should never be seen as reflecting what Kimberlé Crenshaw calls the "structural intersectionality" at work in the world.

Revolutions in Literary Theory and Study of the NT

Now, think back to the so-called literary paradigm shift in NT studies discussed in chapter 2. As we observed in that chapter, accounts that pit traditional historical-critical approaches *over and against* literary-critical approaches reify problematic binaries and don't adequately portray the complexities of the scholarly landscape. I illustrated this by showing how historical-critical form critics, first-wave literary critics, and literary formalists had significant overlapping concerns and assumptions, including these shared assumptions: (1) literary forms evolve out of and develop in response to (typically, an author's) life circumstances (a *hermeneutical* conviction); (2) a work of art stands autonomously as an object of knowledge and its aesthetic sophistication is defined by textual unity (*evaluative* views); and (3) critics must make objective, scientific value judgments about the literariness of texts (a *metadisciplinary* goal).

We can think of the first wave of NT scholars to draw on literary theory—those who turned to literary formalisms—as enacting a kind of Ptolemaic revolution in NT studies. Remember, the Ptolemaic system was not *so* drastically different from its predecessor; the earth remained at the center of the universe in both. And while early generations of literary NT scholars were more open to perspectival differences between readers than earlier biblical critics, they upheld the hermeneutical view that a singular meaning can be determined and (ideally) agreed upon, no matter where one stands. Like Ptolemy, these literary-leaning NT scholars didn't differ *so* drastically from the traditions they ostensibly rejected; modern positivist convictions remained at the center of both. NT scholars' appropriations of formalist and structuralist literary paradigms prompted advantageous changes in NT studies, but they never challenged the core convictions of positivist historical-critical NT scholarship.

This is why poststructuralism represents literary theory's Copernican revolution: the poststructuralist literary paradigm challenges *all* of the above convictions. Poststructuralists refuse to take any of the views shared by prior literary paradigms for granted. They don't hold evolutionary conceptions of literary development or define meaning as authorial intent (*hermeneutical* views); they don't consider literary works to be autonomous objects of knowledge, but they do question whether aesthetic sophistication must be characterized by textual unity (*evaluative* views); and they argue that objective neutral judgments are impossible (a *metadisciplinary* view).

The next part of the chapter is organized around these three sets of topics—hermeneutical, evaluative, and metadisciplinary. Using reader-response criticism and deconstruction as the two main examples of the poststructuralist literary paradigm, we'll move back and forth from poststructuralist ideas to their mixed reception in NT scholarship.

The Copernican Revolution: Poststructuralism in Literary Studies and Biblical Studies

Poststructuralism and Hermeneutical Concerns

As we saw in the previous chapter, structuralists hold the hermeneutical view that humans associate certain signifiers with certain signifieds (and not others), and that we typically do so subconsciously, simply because that's how we're socialized. According to poststructuralists, though, structuralists' universalizing hermeneutical views cannot be maintained when pushed to their logical conclusions. Poststructuralists privilege those who receive a text (whatever one wishes to call them—readers, hearers, audiences, and so forth) because they're the ones who connect signifiers with signifieds and create new ways of understanding.[28]

In many ways, reader-response criticism straddles structuralism and poststructuralism. Wolfgang Iser, one of the founders of the so-called Constance School of reader-response criticism, explains: "The impressions that arise as a result of [the reading] process will vary from individual to individual, but only within the limits imposed by the written as opposed to the unwritten text. In the same way, two people gazing at the night sky may both be looking at the same collection of stars, but one will see the image of a plough, and the other will make out a dipper. The 'stars' in a literary text are fixed; the lines that join them are variable."[29] In order to mean, a text must be read, and in order to comprehend, a reader must draw on preconceived intertextual and extratextual repertoires, habituated reading habits, and socially constructed interpretive frameworks. Thus it is that, with virtually no references to the author at all, Iser presents literary interpretation as the readerly process of anticipation and revision of expectations.[30]

Menakhem Perry similarly emphasizes how the mental processes involved in reading influence interpretive conclusions, especially underscoring the importance of sequence. Perry describes "the effects of the entire reading process" as constitutive of meaning: "[The text's] surprises; the changes along the way; the process of a gradual, zig-zag-like build-up of meanings, their reinforcement, development, revision and replacement; the relations between expectations aroused at one stage of the text and discoveries actually made in subsequent stages; the process of retrospective re-patterning and even the peculiar survival of meanings which were first constructed and then rejected."[31]

Stanley Fish's reader-response criticism considers the text itself to be less important than does Iser's or Perry's. Drawing on Jacques Derrida (to whom we'll soon turn), Fish contends that when a text is read, "it is no longer an object, a thing-in-itself, but an event, something that happens to, and with the participation of, the reader. And it is this event . . . that is, I would argue, the meaning of the sentence."[32] Fish's major (and most controversial) contribution to reader-response theory is his insistence that even when sitting alone in a room, a reader never functions as an isolated individual. Fish's seminal work, *Is There a Text in This Class?* (1980), argues that communities fundamentally shape individuals' perspectives, and thus, "it is *interpretive communities,* rather than either the text or reader, that produce meanings."[33]

Picking up a trend we could already see in the New Critical "intentional fallacy," reader-response critics also insist that the author cannot be the final authoritative arbiter of meaning because the author simply can never be accessed or recovered apart from the text. The author therefore becomes an effect of the text—or, in Roland Barthes's famous formulation, an author can "come back into the Text," but s/he "can only do so as a 'guest.'"[34] The author moves from guest to corpse in Barthes's well-known later essay "The Death of the Author," which concludes by depicting a stark exchange: "It is necessary to overthrow the myth: the birth of the reader must be at the cost of the death of the Author."[35]

The birth of the reader has had a major impact on genre theory. In the last chapter, I gestured toward the fact that genre formation *and* identification are more complex and variable than ancient discussions and many modern theories suggest. Classicists especially have shown how ancient writers oscillate between descriptions of genres as they *are,* and prescriptions of what genres *ought to be.*[36] Even Aristotle, discussing the six elements of tragedy, recognizes that "not a few tragedians *do in fact use these* as qualitative elements; indeed virtually every play has spectacle, the *mimēsis* of character, plot, verbal expression, song, and the *mimēsis* of intellect," but then he turns to "what the arrangement of the particular actions *should be like*" (*Poet.* 1450a-b). Michelle Borg and Graeme Miles are right: "No less than their modern counterparts, ancient genres were contested, hybrid and ambiguous."[37]

Alastair Fowler's famous quip—"Genre is much less of a pigeon hole than a pigeon"—is especially apropos for biblical literature.[38] Leland Ryken and Tremper Longman declare that "nearly every book in the Bible exhibits a mixed-genre format in a degree unparalleled in other literature."[39] The final phrase goes too far in claiming the Bible's uniqueness in this regard, but it is true that NT literature is marked by a mixing and mingling of sub-genres. Harold Attridge memorably describes this generic heterogeneity as "genre bending."[40] This point raises an important question: What is the best way to approach such generic complexities?

Some scholars identify genres using diachronic criteria (time period, author, and geography), while others employ synchronic criteria (thematic elements and literary characterization). It's important, though, to consider both: Identifying genre only by diachronic criteria can homogenize texts by obscuring divergences in both form and content that occur even in texts from the same time period and region. Using only synchronic criteria, on the other hand, can mask the fact that genres shift over time; conventions change, engendering different sets of expectations for readers. Todorov was right: genres are "born from other genres. A new genre is always the trans-formation of one or several old genres: by inversion, by displacement, by combination. . . . [Genre] is a system in constant transformation."[41]

Two strands of contemporary genre theory handle genre more flex-ibly than the classificatory approaches described above: family resemblance theory and prototype theory. The former derives from the Wittgensteinian concept of "family resemblance" as a logical semantic category; examples of a certain genre can have "family resemblances," without necessarily all sharing the same characteristics.[42] The idea of family resemblances is at-tractive for many scholars because it avoids essentialism. Genres are iden-tifiable precisely because they exhibit similarities, but those similarities are not absolute. Still, the theory's flexibility can also be its weakness; the major criticism of this approach is that, taken to its logical extreme, "family re-semblance theory can make anything resemble anything."[43]

Prototype theory offers a corrective to the capaciousness of the fam-ily resemblance model. Built on the insights of the cognitive sciences, the main premise of prototype theory is that humans identify and process all mental categories—including genres—using a "logic of typicality."[44] We assume that certain members of a category are prototypical, while others are peripheral. In doing so, we identify some features as more typical of a certain genre, while other features are less central.[45] Prototypical exemplars then form a schema or template against which we judge each new instance, revising and amending as we confront new data.[46] To give a simple illustration from the literature on cognition, the category "bachelor" is defined as "an unmarried adult male." Yet, few consider the pope to be a "bachelor," because he is *atypical* with respect to the *Gestalt* structure, or schema, in which a typical male progresses through childhood into sexual maturity and marriage.[47] The prototypical view of genre provides an alternative "course between trying to produce unassailable definitions of a particular genre and relaxing into the irresponsibility of family resemblances."[48]

In Heta Pyrhönen's words, "generic competence fluctuates between general fixed interpretive guidelines, functioning as rules of thumb, and the situational judgments of writers and readers about particular texts."[49] Even when we (rightly) reject reductive, reified generic categories, we must still grapple with the messy implications of the well-known Bakhtinian dictum that all discourse is generic.[50] As the (in)famous French intellectual Jacques Derrida put it, there simply "is no genreless text."[51]

Literary theorists tend either to love Derrida and deconstruction, the literary discourse most associated with him, or to hate them. Still, his influence is undeniable; for better or worse, his ideas have permeated multiple academic disciplines. Derrida's impact on literary criticism gained true momentum with his 1970 essay "Structure, Sign, and Play in the Discourse of the Human Sciences" (based on a 1966 lecture that introduced him to the English-speaking world). Derrida's neologisms can make it easy to forget that his ideas developed *within* the context of structuralism, and he actually maintains many structuralist principles.[52] Like Saussure and other structuralists, Derrida believes that language is nonreferential because a linguistic utterance and its referent are inherently different. Where Saussure and Derrida diverge is in the latter's insistence that, despite our *logocentric* desires, an absolute universal meaning is never present in either speech or writing.[53]

Think about it this way: in order to define a word, you must rely on the use of other words, which themselves need to be defined using more words—on and on in what Derrida dubs a never-ending *play of signifiers.* According to Derrida, there is no conclusion to this game, no ultimate *transcendental signifier* that would explain all others. Rather, the play of signifiers is marked by *différance* (another Derridean neologism, combining *differ* and *defer*). *Différance* evokes the way that language, based as it is on binaries, simultaneously depends on difference and defers any absolute, decidable meaning.[54] Consequently, the play of signifiers fundamentally undermines the systematic dichotomies at the core of the structuralists' hermeneutical views—binaries like reader/critic, absence/presence, writing/speech. These concepts, Derrida avers, are not fixed or given, but fluid and constructed; any real distinctions between them will fall apart in the end.

To return to our celestial imagery, the Derridean view is that language functions much like nebulous star clusters, transforming and shifting throughout the galaxy. Astronomers now believe that all celestial bodies are in constant motion. Scientists who measure the heavens in terms of light years know that by the time light touches their telescopes, the stars have already moved on to another place in space. Continually dealing with this lag time, astronomers create maps of the heavens that can only really represent the way things were billions of years ago. Notice that they don't conclude that stars don't really exist and that pursuit of answers is futile. They know they must settle for working approximations. Derrida's view of language is not so different. Just as stars can never be caught, meaning morphs and mutates and eludes our grasp. Like the meandering pathways of what ancient stargazers called the "wandering planets," language develops unpredictably.[55] Nevertheless, like the astronomers, we needn't conclude that meaning doesn't exist and that pursuit of answers is futile. Here, too, we must settle for working approximations.

Rather than trying to reconcile or erase multiple potential interpretations, Derrida proposes, critics can maintain ambiguities and hold mutually viable options in tensive simultaneity. He suggests that we conceive of meanings as undecidable *traces* of the play of signifiers—that is, fleeting mirages of meaning that simultaneously depend on and unsettle contradictions. Derrida argues that any given interpretation of a text's meaning can be countered with a contradictory construal, which can be based on the *very same* text. Barbara Johnson summarizes: "Derrida sees signifying force in the gaps, margins, figures, echoes, digressions, discontinuities, contradictions, and ambiguities of a text. When one writes, one writes more than (or less than, or other than) one thinks. The reader's task is to read what is written rather than simply attempt to intuit what might have been meant."[56] Like Barthes and the reader-response critics discussed above, Derrida disconnects the text from its author or producer, creating space for readers in different contexts, who can always construe a text as something other than what its author intended. For Derrida, meanings are elusive—perhaps best compared not to stars, but to meteors blazing briefly through the night sky.

The hermeneutical views I've just described have led some NT scholars to see poststructuralism as a dangerous usurper to the author's rightful rule as interpretive authority. Hatina, we have seen, warns that poststructuralists hope "authors perish so that *readers may reign.*"[57] Kevin Vanhoozer, in his book *Is There a Meaning in This Text?* (clearly an allusion to Fish), typifies "the text in the age of the reader" as "a ventriloquist's dummy: it serves as an opportunity for *projecting one's own voice.*"[58] Indeed, many conclude that poststructuralism "is an anarchistic, hyper-relativistic form of criticism," and that this "nihilistic" relativism has "chillingly cynical implications" for biblical interpreters.[59]

Some NT scholars would also have us believe that *deconstruction* is paramount to *destruction* of meaning. Deconstruction, they'll declare, is *"designed* to demonstrate how all texts, indeed all human communication, ultimately 'deconstructs' or undermines itself."[60] After all, even Fish describes deconstruction as "a universe of absolute free play in which everything is indeterminate and undecidable."[61] What's more, they'll exclaim, Derrida himself believed that "il n'ya pas de hors-texte" (There is no outside-text)![62] We'll return to this commonly misunderstood Derridean dictum momentarily.

The poststructuralist literary paradigm is seen as especially problematic in certain Christian confessional circles. As Walter Sundberg puts it, the poststructuralist denial "that a unified perspective on the meaning of scripture may be obtained may pose little threat to those ensconced in academia and beholden only to the canons of secular scholarly research. But it is a serious problem for any community of faith that reveres the Bible as the authoritative source of divine revelation and assumes that its fundamental meaning is clear to the average believer and enduring across the ages."[63] Along similar lines, Markus Bockmuehl warns that deconstruction "dismembers" the "quest for truth, beauty, and goodness."[64] Francis Watson cautions that "a Christian faith concerned to retain its own coherence cannot for a moment accept that the biblical texts (individually and as a whole) lack a single, determinate meaning, that their meanings are created by their readers, or that theological interpretations must see themselves as non-privileged participants in an open-ended, pluralistic conversation."[65]

Stay away, these NT scholars warn, because poststructuralism advances "a relativism that borders on the nihilistic."[66] One can imagine poststructuralists aggressively pushing interpreters down the slippery slope of relativism, where the gravitational pull is so strong that meaning disappears into a black hole of oblivion. The problem, though, is that none of the above claims *necessarily* follows from poststructuralist literary principles. This is why NT scholars need to consider more carefully the convergences and divergences of different literary paradigms.

Take the basic example of authorial intent. It's true that formalists, structuralists, and poststructuralists all challenge the idea that authorial intention determines meaning. However, as Stephen Matterson explains, "For structuralists and post-structuralists, the removal of the author from critical consideration was an act of liberation which meant that the text could be scrutinized in the contexts supplied by historical and social discourses, languages outside the text. For the New Critics, removing authorial intentionality was part of a strategy of sealing off the boundaries of the text and ensuring that only the words on the page were the true focus of critical judgement."[67] The New Critical bracketing of the author directs attention to the text itself and *away* from extratextual contexts, while the structuralist and poststructuralist literary paradigms do just the opposite: they direct attention *toward* contextual concerns (in different ways). It's not helpful to generalize about "the text in the age of the reader" when literary critics challenge authorial intentionality in different ways, for different purposes, and with different results.

Furthermore, poststructuralists aren't saying that there *are* no metaphysical or existential truths at all. Foucault introduces his project in *The History of Sexuality* by making this very point: "The object, in short, is to define the regime of power-knowledge-pleasure that sustains the discourse on human sexuality. . . . The essential aim *will not be to determine whether these discursive productions and these effects of power lead one to formulate the truth about sex,* or on the contrary falsehoods designed to conceal that truth, but rather to bring out the 'will to knowledge' that serves as both their support and their instrument."[68] Derrida doesn't allege that all epistemology is futile, either. He doesn't claim that there is no reality, nor does he say that people can't adjudicate between different interpretations. When Derrida says, "Il n'ya pas de hors-texte," he's underscoring that, as humans, "we are *in* a determinate language."[69] Herein lies a subtle but significant distinction: being "*in* a determinate language" does not mean that "there *is* nothing beyond language."[70] On the contrary, Derrida's position (unfortunately obscured by his obfuscatory way of articulating it) is similar to

Saussure's: human understanding will always be mediated and constructed by language. For poststructuralists like Foucault and Derrida, the question of a stable metaphorical Truth outside of linguistic discourse is not at issue; it's altogether beside the point.

Poststructuralists' ultimate goal is not to wrest control from the author or the text, nor to destroy meaning altogether, but to explore the meaning-making activities that reading *always* requires, and to draw attention to their interpretive implications. Reader-response critics in particular wish to account for textual features and the great variety of readerly activities that concretize those features. There's a crucial nuance here that would be easy to miss. Consider this publisher's description of one of the first works of reader-response criticism in NT studies: "First published in hardcover in 1991, Robert Fowler's *Let the Reader Understand* was ahead of its time. Using reader-response criticism, a pioneering method for reading the Gospel of Mark, he *invited contemporary readers to participate* actively in making the meaning of the Gospel."[71]

The blurb presents reader-response critics like Fowler as offering an invitation, as though we could accept or decline an opportunity to be involved in meaning-making. But this is misleading. The reality to which reader-response criticism points is that interpreters of *all* kinds *always* participate in meaning-making. It's simply what happens when we receive and interpret a text. There is no reading without interpretation; there is no "meaning of the Gospel" without readers' active participation.

Derrida reminds us that critics, too, are inescapably entangled and implicated in the very systems we analyze. Deconstruction's disclosing and dismantling of linguistic discrepancies thus extends to the dualisms upon which the field of literary studies is based (literature/criticism, expert/novice, and so forth). As Simon Goldhill puts it, "Derrida has repeatedly interrogated the boundaries between the language of criticism and the language of the objects criticized, between philosophy and literature, between theory and illustration, as he pursues his analysis (and performance) of writing as a practice."[72] Following Derrida, Paul de Man and his colleagues in the "Yale School" of literary theory argued that all "assumedly monadic [that is, unified] totalities" contain "hidden fragmentations" that threaten to unravel textual claims to authoritative stability—and that means *any* text's claim to authoritative stability, including that of the literary critic.[73] The literature/criticism binary itself, insists de Man, is "delusive."[74] This explains, at least in part, why Derrida and deconstructionists provoked such intense antagonism, even from other poststructuralists like Foucault and Pierre Bourdieu.

The poststructuralist literary paradigm doesn't have to undermine our critical enterprise; it can improve it, in part by helping us to refine and revise our conceptual categories. For example, when NT narrative critics began employing reader-response criticism in the 1980s, they recognized that, as John Darr puts it, "to some degree, *the* reader is always *my* reader, a projection of my own experience of reading the text."[75] Through the late 1980s and early 1990s, Darr, along with others like Mary Ann Tolbert, Robert Fowler, and Mark Allan Powell, worked to articulate theoretically nuanced concepts that could address poststructuralists' hermeneutical challenges.[76] This kind of work continues; more recently, the Sixth International Colloquium of the RRENAB (Réseau de la Narratologie et Bible) focused on developing more precise differentiations between historical, implied, and contemporary readers.[77] Examples along these lines could be multiplied.

NT interpreters can learn valuable hermeneutical lessons from poststructuralists about how readers rely on varying presuppositions to make meaning, how these particularities influence interpretive conclusions, and how we as critics are entangled in multiple discursive contexts, as well.

Poststructuralism and Evaluative Concerns

Formalist and structuralist literary paradigms view a literary text as an autonomous object of knowledge, and they judge aesthetic sophistication in terms of textual unity. The poststructuralist literary paradigm asks a more fundamental question—to wit, whether there are universal aesthetic or formal criteria by which we can render evaluative judgments in the first place. This doesn't have to result in nihilism or relativism. Here again, our celestial analogy can clarify. As Iser intimated in the quote above, in China, people have long seen a plough where the West sees the Big Dipper. Poststructuralists are not saying that there *are* no pictures in the stars. They're suggesting that reading a certain configuration of stars as the Big Dipper might be just as valid and valuable as reading that same configuration as the plough. Each constellation may or may not be a legitimate meaning for a particular moment, from a particular place, depending on the evaluative criteria by which we judge legitimacy. To insist that the Big Dipper is the only right way to read that configuration of stars is like refusing to acknowledge that a great many people live in China; it's like insisting that everyone on earth lives or should live in the West.

Reader-response criticism presupposes that people make meaning differently. In this sense, reader-response critics are heir to the German hermeneutical tradition championed by Hans-Georg Gadamer. R. J. Bernstein explains that "hermeneutics, as that discipline that took shape in the nineteenth century, has been a defensive reaction against the universalistic and reductivistic claims made in the name of the sciences. Every defender of hermeneutics, and more generally the humanistic tradition, has had to confront the persistent claim that it is science and science alone that is the measure of reality, knowledge, and truth."[78] Gadamer popularized the notion that every work responds to its particular era's "horizon of expectations." Aesthetic tastes and expectations also change; accordingly, a literary text's reception changes demonstrably through different time periods. In the 1960s and 1970s, Hans Robert Jauss, who was Gadamer's student and Iser's colleague in the "Constance School," pioneered "reception history" or the "aesthetics of reception," which traces those changes in reception over time.[79]

As reader-response critics insist, flesh-and-blood humans are idiosyncratic, possibly connecting stars in ways that can never be entirely dictated, captured, or predicted by anyone, including the critic who observes them drawing the lines. For many poststructuralists, indeterminacies like these shift evaluative criteria away from formal matters like textual unity or the presence of sophisticated conventions, and toward ethical and political concerns. Poststructuralists push us to take responsibility for what we do when we interpret NT literature, and for the criteria by which we adjudicate between alternative readings. Derrida himself was fundamentally ethically and politically motivated (despite the fact that some of his detractors say deconstruction is inherently apolitical). True literature, for Derrida, is defined by its *iterability*—its capacity to be repeated and yet always transformed with each act of repetition. Literature's power—and thus, its value—comes from the fact that it follows established rules even as it remains impossible to translate or replicate in an exact way. Literature always carries the potential to defy convention and subvert unjust power dynamics.

This is poststructuralists' ethical critique of structuralism: because binaries carry implicit value judgments, and because they're implicated in human power relations (as is all communication), they will inevitably serve oppressive ends. Derridean literary critics discern disjunctures and aporias, mark where binaries break down, and preserve the polyvalent potentialities of language, all for an ethical evaluative purpose. They wish to expose and disrupt—that is, they wish to deconstruct—the (apparently neutral, but actually dangerous) dichotomies animating and authorizing literary discourses. There will always be exceptions, of course, but for the most part, poststructuralist literary critics are *not* out to *destroy* literary meaning. More often than not, they're out to expose the implicit but specious ideologies that legitimate certain kinds of literary meaning.

Identifying authors and producers of texts becomes an ethical imperative, since without a locus of responsibility for the discursive practices that shape societies, "there would be no one to be held accountable" for problematic discourses.[80] Let me underscore that poststructuralists' renewed attention to authorial world(s) doesn't depend on a *hermeneutical* view that authorial intent determines meaning, as in earlier literary paradigms. It depends, rather, on an *evaluative* conviction—that is, evaluating a text's underlying ideologies requires identifying an author's and/or culture's ideological presuppositions. When those presuppositions are oppressive to women, marginalized groups, or other non-normative identities, they ought to be exposed and overturned.

Foucault's seminal essay, "What Is an Author?" offers one way to do so without holding to the hermeneutical premise that authorial intention determines meaning. "It is not enough," Foucault contends, "to repeat the empty affirmation that the author has disappeared. For the same reason, it is not enough to keep repeating (after Nietzsche) that God and man have died a common death. Instead, we must locate the space left empty by the author's disappearance, follow the distribution of gaps and breaches, and watch for the openings that this disappearance uncovers."[81] This disappearance, Foucault goes on to argue, uncovers several features in a text that do particular kinds of authorizing work vis-à-vis readers. Foucault labels this the "author function," thereby creating a cultural category for the conditions that gave rise to, and are ultimately responsible for, a literary text.

Donald Pease suggests that Foucault's essay "reactivate[d] the controversy between poststructuralists (who believed only in the environment of textuality) and historicists (who believed in a sociopolitical context for the literary work) over the cultural function of the author."[82] But that's not quite right. Many critics fit neither description. Feminists, womanists, and queer theorists are not historicists who privilege sociopolitical contexts "*over* the cultural function of the author," and although they reject rigid binaries (such as male/female) as poststructuralists do, they don't believe "*only* in the environment of textuality." On the contrary, it's *because* they believe that texts have real-world, extratextual effects that they commit to exposing the unspoken premises that undergird literature.

Many biblical scholars consider poststructuralists' contemporary ethical and political commitments to be a form of "identity politics" that *distorts NT literature.*[83] Hatina, for one, explains that poststructuralists aim "to *gain control over texts,* like science attempts to gain control of the world" and that "stemming *from this political agenda,* the poststructural critics . . . attempt to subvert the traditional approaches."[84] John Barton warns that "attempts to collapse the reading of texts into a single process, as in . . . certain 'committed' or 'advocacy' approaches, are misconceived."[85] Bockmuehl, too, condemns "'synchronic' approaches, with their sociolinguistic, poststructuralist, or broadly literary pursuits, their miscellaneous queer or cultural studies, liberationist or post colonialist ideological criticism, and the sometimes *unabashedly partisan relativism* of their hermeneutics."[86]

To be sure, some contemporary biblical critics do have political agendas. Gay Byron and Vanessa Lovelace introduce their edited volume, *Womanist Interpretations of the Bible,* with the bold declaration, "All interpreters of sacred texts are responsible for exposing and analyzing the power dynamics in both the ancient texts and the interpretations of the texts that have been used to further injustices and global systemic challenges."[87] Byron, Lovelace, and their contributors frequently refer to recent contemporary issues (such as the Black Lives Matter movement), and they unapologetically assert that they want their readers to "be emboldened to read the texts from their own social location and be empowered to take action and work toward . . . transform[ing] the injustices in our society and across the globe."[88]

Still, complaints like Barton's and Bockmuehl's insinuate that "advocacy" leads poststructuralists to *skew* ancient evidence for modern political purposes. Labeling an approach "poststructuralist" thereby becomes a pejorative way of (more or less implicitly) discounting such interpretations as predetermined by biases and therefore intellectually suspect. Even apparently innocuous statements can do this kind of dismissive work. Longman, for instance, explains that identity-focused critics "approach the text with an agenda"; the fact that he uses this descriptor only for poststructuralist approaches implies that poststructuralists are the *only* ones "with an agenda."[89] But as we've seen already, every interpreter approaches the text "with an agenda" in one way or another. Even purportedly neutral and objective processes of "exegesis" ("leading out" the meaning of a text)—so often lauded as preferable to subjective or biased "eisegesis" ("leading in" the meaning)—still function to naturalize certain questions and procedures and not others.

A better way to conceive of approaches like (later) feminist, womanist, queer, ethnic, minority, and postcolonial criticisms is to see them in terms of their shared views and questions. They all (1) accept specific premises about how language works, and then (2) pose research questions about a specific focus or foci based on those premises. For instance, they hold that phenomena like class, bodies, gender, and race are *not* construed in the same ways universally across time and culture. Based on that conviction, these literary critics ask, How do or should our interpretations of literature change if the problematics on which we choose to focus (whether class, race, status, or otherwise) are *not* universally stable, natural "givens"? What does it mean for our understanding of literary texts if these concepts are shaped differently in and by particular cultures and communities? What can a text tell us about the normative perceptions of the time period and culture in which it was written? How do literature and our interpretations of it function to reinforce or resist constructed binaries? The poststructuralist literary paradigm usefully challenges us to pursue answers to these and related questions.

Defining poststructuralist literary approaches as ethically or politically motivated *and therefore distortive* is a major setback for biblical scholars. For one thing, it keeps us from asking crucial questions about antiquity. NT scholars like Denise Buell, Jin Young Choi, Tat-siong Benny Liew, and Eric Barreto pose valuable questions such as these: How can we account for the complexities of ancient portrayals of ethnic, racial, socioeconomic, or sexual differences? How do biblical texts occlude or undermine certain voices (of slaves, women, those with disabilities, and so forth) and valorize the voices of others (certain males, masters, and so forth)? Is it possible to recover and revalue those identities, voices, and experiences that have been devalued, marked as perverse, or otherwise elided in ancient literature?

To reiterate, pursuing answers to such questions (to the extent that it's possible to do so) can be both literary *and* historical in nature. As cultural historian Roger Chartier insists, historical scholarship should focus on literary modes of representation precisely in order "to analyze how a text creates its apparent unity and what historical tensions, rifts and aporias are elided in the process of this particular construction."[90] In the field of early Christian studies, we find such analyses in Bernadette Brooten's famous critique of earlier feminists who "largely failed to include female homoeroticism as part of the history of women or as a subject for gender analysis." We might look to someone like Katherine Shaner, who seeks to uncover the agency of enslaved people, since "ancient materials about enslaved persons primarily reflect masters' perspectives," or to Sheila Briggs, who analyzes NT texts in which, she says, a patriarchal church "has not completely erased" the voice of the oppressed.[91]

Poststructuralism can illuminate a text's own ideological underpinnings; it can also illuminate the ideological underpinnings of scholarly claims about the text. Even as poststructuralists emphasize alterity between past and present, they assume continuity insofar as they consider *all* texts—including scholarly interpretations of literature—to be perspectivally shaped. The poststructuralist literary paradigm therefore stands as a crucial corrective to modern biblical scholarship's entrenched penchant for replicating the ethnocentrism, xenophobia, imperialism, androcentrism, and kyriarchy that we often find in the ancient literature we read. Literary critic Vincent Leitch pulls no punches: "Compulsory objectivity and obligatory critical disinterest, sacred cows of many a theory opponent, often mask blind spots, racial and gender privileges, nationalistic mindsets, and prejudices."[92]

Again, we confront the need for rigorous, unflinching self-assessment—critical reflexivity—regarding our own scholarly assumptions. NT scholars need to ask how our scholarly modes subtly validate themselves and legitimate our conclusions. This means, for instance, asking how our assumptions about alterity or continuity between past and present might be serving *our own* ideological purposes. It's worth repeating: the purpose of critical self-assessment is *not* to skew the historical evidence of ancient literature for modern political purposes. It can actually serve the opposite purpose: it can reveal our blind spots and prejudices so that we might improve our appreciation for and engagements with ancient literature itself.

One of the most egregious examples of the need for reflexive metacritical analysis comes from nineteenth-century biblical scholarship. Near the end of that century, the then-eminent French biblical scholar Ernest Renan advanced what Maurice Olender describes as the "old idea that there is a necessary link between the structure of a language and the spirit it represents—or, to put it another way, the idea that language mirrors the soul of a people."[93] Based on this presupposition, Renan concluded that the "Semitic race" is defective because Semitic languages are, in his estimation, simplistic and narrow. In contrast, Renan declared, "The Aryan language was immensely superior, especially in regard to the conjugation of verbs."[94] Renan's horrifying rhetoric obviously betrays his flawed logic and anti-Semitic presuppositions. Notice, too, how his own essentializing rhetoric was directly linked to his devaluations of biblical rhetoric.

Shawn Kelley has traced how racialized (especially anti-Semitic) discourses like Renan's thoroughly permeated modern biblical scholarship.[95] Kelley's analysis demonstrates why it's *ethically* important to identify first-generation NT literary criticism as a Ptolemaic—not a Copernican—revolution: distinguishing *too* starkly between early literary criticism and historical criticism can mask how both were "objectivist" insofar as they offered "analyses that do not acknowledge their own biases."[96] The point is to recognize how scholarly assessments of biblical literature can be implicated in and give impetus to deleterious discourses. Oppressive and racialized dynamics continue to shape biblical scholarship today, though they might seem subtler than Renan's rhetoric, or at the very least, they might not seem so obvious. But this is often the case. It can be most difficult to identify and evaluate problematic perspectives when we're immersed in them.

In addition to highlighting the devaluation of certain voices in both NT texts and scholarship, poststructuralist perspectivalism can also help shift our posture toward the values expressed in NT literature. For example, we often assume that all cultures conceive of virtues like the transcendental triad of truth, beauty, and goodness in the same ways. Certainly, this assumption undergirds some NT scholars' claims that poststructuralism leads to nihilistic relativism. As you'll recall from earlier, Bockmuehl warns that deconstruction "dismembers" the "quest for truth, beauty, and goodness." But there's a more positive way to reframe the poststructuralist paradigm. We could see it as a refusal to reduce such universal notions to *one* definition. Poststructuralists don't *dis*member, then, they *re*member—like putting pieces back together, they re-member concepts like truth, beauty, and goodness by opening our eyes to ancient perceptions of them. In brief, poststructuralists don't deny that truth, beauty, and goodness exist; they call us to recognize and value the *different* ways that particular cultures and communities perceive and portray truth, beauty, and goodness through literature. This, in turn, *expands* our conceptions of truth, beauty, and goodness.

Another benefit of poststructuralism's challenge to our evaluative norms is that it can help us appreciate and value the differences between our assessments of literature and those of ancient readers. For instance, defining literary sophistication in terms of textual unity ignores the fact that other (especially non-Western, non-contemporary) cultures value(d) different aspects of literature and assess(ed) literary merit according to different evaluative measures. Scholars like Whitney Shiner have highlighted how, in contrast to contemporary expectations for a unified, cohesive narrative plot, many ancient texts show a "greater tolerance for and appreciation of an episodic narrative style."[97] We shouldn't assume that everyone evaluates literature in the same ways.

This is why some NT critics see reception history as offering "hope" for our "troubled discipline."[98] These scholars seek, just as Jauss did, to provide more robust reception histories of specific NT passages and themes (an approach often described in NT studies as *Rezeptionsgeschichte* or *Wirkungsgeschichte*).[99] A. K. M. Adam, for instance, manifests an appreciation of interpretive plurality in his well-known Fish-inspired *Semeia* article "The Sign of Jonah: A Fish-Eye View" by tracing readings of the sign of Jonah logion; with his diachronic account, Adam illustrates how "'correct interpretation' is always relative to particular contexts and interests."[100] In a similar manner, Powell's *Chasing the Eastern Star: Adventures in Biblical Reader-Response Criticism* sets forth patristic, medieval, and contemporary interpretations of the Matthean magi. Víctor Manuel Morales Vásquez's *Contours of a Biblical Reception Theory* considers interpretations of Romans 13 from the first through the thirteenth centuries CE.[101] Again, illustrations could be multiplied.

Poststructuralism prompts us to interrogate our normative evaluative assumptions, so that, for example, we can understand why modern NT interpreters often value a text's literary unity over its ethical implications.[102] Contrary to common caricatures, contemporary literary theory is not about "murdering our past."[103] By destabilizing the normative assumptions on which our evaluative judgments depend, the poststructuralist literary paradigm can help us do better justice to what is left to us from the past, even as it challenges us to define the criteria by which we determine what "better justice" to ancient literature might mean.[104]

Poststructuralism and Metadisciplinary Concerns

In the modern era prior to poststructuralism, most literary critics agreed that the purpose of their discipline was to make objective, scientific value judgments about literature that would stand up to universal scrutiny. As we've just seen, poststructuralism insists on hermeneutical grounds that such objectivity is impossible, and on ethical grounds that everyone is accountable for their interpretive values. This means, moreover, that many poststructuralist literary critics have overtly political metadisciplinary aims: they want their interactions with literature to improve society, usually by advancing equality in some respect. NT scholars like Fernando Segovia, Brian Blount, Randall Bailey, Kwok Pui-lan, and others push us to consider questions like these: What does it mean to read, write, or receive biblical literature "from the margins," and why are these "margins" in the first place? How can critics today identify and critique the legacies of violence and oppressive discourses that linger on in biblical scholarship itself?[105] These NT critics ask such questions *not* because they're "anti-historical" or because they wish to "control" biblical literature, but because they believe that (1) this literature is powerful; (2) this literature represents certain perspectives and occludes others; and (3) scholarly claims about this literature matter.

To be fair, most biblical scholars today would agree that everyone approaches the text from some *position*, or *place*. Most recognize—albeit differently from one another, and to differing degrees—that, as Paul Anderson puts it, "even 'scientific' approaches to objectivity may themselves be distortive, as subjective engagement is required for making any sort of aesthetic, historical, or hermeneutical judgment."[106] Most would also admit that there is no single, definitive interpretation of a text. Today's historical-critical scholars make more nuanced claims than prior generations, yet many continue to hold tightly to the critical goal of objective interpretation even as they recognize its practical impossibility. John Collins, for instance, who situates himself firmly "on the modern side of the modern/postmodern debate," recognizes that authorial intention can "only be reconstructed tentatively" and texts can "take on new meanings in changing circumstances," but still holds that textual meaning "can be established in an objective manner."[107]

Douglas Campbell provides an example of a scholar who denounces others' "naïve presuppositionless objectivity," while basing his own aims and claims on modernist presuppositions about history. Campbell's massive work, *Framing Paul: An Epistolary Biography,* situates the Pauline letters within a chronological "frame" that is based solely on the epistolary data in the NT canon. This frame, Campbell avers, should control interpretation of the letters; consequently, he declares, much current Pauline scholarship is "mistaken because the historical story of the letters it presupposes is corrupt."[108]

Campbell's totalizing positivism is evident not only in his content, but also in his tone: "*Any valid* Pauline interpretation in any historical respect *must* begin with a workable account of the letters' circumstances in relation to one another. We *must* tell the story of their interrelated composition. This is the sine qua non of *all valid* historical interpretation of Paul."[109] Such assertions function to privilege Campbell's version of events and his interpretive priorities; the validity of Pauline scholarship depends on his historical frame. But why "must" historical Pauline interpretation "begin with a workable account of the letters' circumstances in relation to one another"? If we had only one extant Pauline letter in our possession (as is the case with most NT literature), and we therefore could not compare the Pauline text to others, surely our interpretation wouldn't be inherently invalid. More broadly still, we might ask, Is a claim that can't be definitively verified really void of value?

Despite remarking (in a footnote) that "Pauline data is linguistic and thus unstable," Campbell effectively takes for granted that Paul's language is reliably referential.[110] Throughout *Framing Paul,* Campbell's arguments are predicated on the presupposition that the "epistolary data" in Paul's letters reflect historical events *wie es eigentlich gewesen* ("whether or how things actually were").[111] But why should we assume that Paul's letters unambiguously portray historical data? Campbell doesn't explain his assumption. Though he cites Derrida as the inspiration for his title, he misses the opportunity to address the challenges that a nonreferential Derridean theory of language poses to traditional historicist approaches.

Poststructuralists in general, and deconstructionists specifically, push us to take language's irreducible complexities into account—aporias that are notably evident in NT texts themselves. Margaret Mitchell makes this point forcefully with respect to Paul's epistles to the Corinthians: "Modern scholars have been slow to accept what the Corinthian letters demonstrate," which is "that Paul's letters do not and never did have a single, unambiguous meaning. Even in his own lifetime, Paul's letters—that most dynamic of genres—were disputed, his meaning contested and negotiated. . . . In the process of negotiating his own meaning, . . . Paul made recourse to rhetorical *topoi.*"[112] Campbell recognizes that Paul is "imparting his own rhetorical bias to many of his biographical claims," but he characterizes Paul's attempts at persuasion as evidence of "obvious imperfections."[113] But again, we might ask, Why should we equate Pauline rhetoric with imperfections and bias? Why not consider Pauline rhetoric to be its own form of *valid* historical evidence, as Mitchell does?

Historical evidence brings us to another reason that NT scholars are often reticent to engage with the poststructuralist literary paradigm. Many are still under the impression that poststructuralism inevitably leads to anachronism. D. A. Carson expresses one of NT scholars' most frequent complaints about poststructuralist interpretations: They're "so anachronistic as to make a historian wince."[114]

Certainly, *some* poststructuralist writers embrace—indeed, revel in—interpretive anarchy and anachronism. For these critics, deconstruction's decoupling of texts from ancient authors and audiences renders the historians' concerns about anachronism irrelevant; they read literary corpora from different places and times together without misgivings. In NT studies, George Aichele, for instance, reads the Gospel of Mark alongside postmodern fantasy literature, Sharon Jacob reads the Jesus infancy narratives alongside the "texts" of Indian surrogate mothers' life experiences, while Joan Taylor and others read the NT alongside Monty Python's 1979 movie *Life of Brian*.[115] Some purposely "reverse the flow of influence within the hermeneutical process."[116] So we find Patrick Counet discussing John as "a postmodern gospel," Theodore Jennings reading Paul's notion of justice in tandem with Derrida's concept of "the gift," and Pablo Polischuk proposing that the Lukan Prodigal Son's newfound self-awareness reflects Lacan's mirror stage of psychological development.[117]

Perhaps no NT scholar is more identified with poststructuralism than Stephen Moore. For decades (along with numerous co-writers), Moore has been advancing the poststructuralist literary paradigm in all of its manifold manifestations.[118] Moore reinforces the impression that poststructuralism leads to anachronism because his work is saturated with provocative punning and intentionally anachronistic comparisons. He describes Revelation's Bridegroom as a "she-male" looking for "spiritual cunnilingus," and typifies Yahweh's divine anger as "'roid rage" (just one of many descriptions of a God on steroids; others include "bitch-tits" and shrunken testicles).[119]

In a glowing review of Moore's book *God's Gym*, Dale Martin observes that "biblical scholars who bother to read Moore's book at all will find it controversial; the fastidious may find it offensive."[120] Valentine Cunningham appears to be one such fastidious reader: Cunningham derides Moore's interpretations as "monstrous critique," "aweingly awful," and "silly, silly stuff."[121] In "Bible Reading and/after Theory," Cunningham excoriates

Moore as exemplifying his claim that "biblicists have become regular buyers of sexy ideas at the Theory-mongers' brothel."[122] John Collins doesn't seem so offended by Moore's work, though he does declare that it's not "likely *or desirable* that God's gym and God's beauty parlor [alluding to two of Moore's titles] will become the twin towers of biblical interpretation."[123]

It's not surprising that Moore's work has provoked such negative and dismissive responses. Moore's interpretations may strike some as unsavory, or even, in Cunningham's words, as a form of "extreme textual violence," but I would argue that Moore's anachronisms are best understood as the practical, stylistic enactment of his goals for the field of biblical scholarship.[124] Moore flouts scholarly conventions because he hopes, in good Freudian fashion, to needle NT scholars into facing the discipline's ever-present (if variously repressed) normative neuroses; he wants us to ask whether and in what ways biblical studies may be more delusional than revelatory.[125] Moore's playful writing style—iconoclastic as it is—carries serious freight. Perhaps this is why, as Amy-Jill Levine observes, "to some New Testament scholars," Moore's work "represents the THREAT OF _____ [fill in the term: literary studies, poststructuralism, postmodernism, deconstruction]."[126]

But wherein lies the danger, and to whom? None of these discourses should be seen as a "threat" to NT scholars. For one thing, poststructuralist advancements in literary theory don't *require* or *necessarily result* in anachronistic readings. I've been arguing, on the contrary, that even those scholars who choose to pursue *less* anachronistic and *more* historically contextualized readings neglect poststructuralism to their own detriment.[127] The poststructuralist literary paradigm can contribute to a less anachronistic form of NT scholarship in a number of ways, including (but not limited to) the following: it allows for a more capacious view of who and what were operative in any given historical moment; it clarifies how a text's own normative representations can constitute historical evidence; and it exposes our normative presuppositions as historically and culturally contingent through metacritical reflection. Elizabeth Clark's description of a theoretically informed "premodern, textually oriented history" is apropos: "With Hans-Georg Gadamer, it recognizes that since historians' 'horizons' fuse with that of the text, they themselves comprise part of the phenomena to be studied. ... Scholars should seek to understand the differing cultural and moral views of past and present societies—and to recognize the limited and often provincial quality of their own."[128]

While twentieth-century historical criticism succeeded in defamiliar-
izing the Bible "by locating it in a cultural context alien to our own," David
Clines notes, it nevertheless failed to "defamiliarize most of its theological
ideas [such as] ideas of retribution, covenant, sin, the maleness of God,
metaphors of the king and warrior for the divine."[129] Perhaps this can be
explained, again, by the power of language. The vocabularies that we associate with categories like theology, history, religion, and tradition often
do appear in ancient texts (especially in translation), and so, as with truth,
beauty, and goodness, we assume conceptual coherence between "there and
then" and "here and now." Poststructuralist critics insist, though, that the
default construals of *all* the conceptual categories with which we work are
contemporary constructions, shaped by centuries of accrued tradition and
by our particular circumstances. They can hardly be otherwise.

Any poststructuralist form of literary theory could proffer illuminating
illustrations of the above claims. To name but a few: The rapidly growing
literary subfield of ecocriticism (which explores literature and the environment) can helpfully destabilize contemporary Western assumptions about
the earth. Animal studies, a substratum of ecocriticism, challenges modern assumptions about humans and other living beings.[130] Literary scholars
who draw on the discourses of affect theory prompt us to look beyond
Cartesian mind/body dualisms and normative dichotomies between emotions (such as joy *versus* grief), none of which accurately reflects ancient
views about the mind or the body.[131] And concepts from postcolonialism
like hybridity and mimicry suggest more nuanced ways to understand Roman imperialism's impact on and representations in NT literature. Tat-
siong Benny Liew's experiences as a Chinese American, for example, alert
him to the complex realities of the NT as "a collection of texts that was first
written by the colonized but then has become instrumental for colonization [and thus] raise[s] questions concerning multiple and interlocking dif-
ferential relations of power."[132] Because poststructuralist literary discourses
like ecocriticism and affect theory play larger roles in later chapters, I shall
close this section with a subset of literary critics who, in the late twentieth
century, turned poststructuralism's metadisciplinary concerns back on itself.

Resistance, Paranoia, and the "After Theory" Movement

Poststructuralist literary theory "has always also enacted a resistance
to theory."[133] By the late twentieth century, poststructuralism's resistance
to universalizing and emphasis on particularities was leading some crit-

ics to question Critical Theory's (by then) well-established norms. At that time, pronouncements of Theory's demise became something of a cottage industry, later dubbed the "After Theory" movement.[134] Funeral dirges notwithstanding, Theory—and the poststructuralist literary paradigm as part of it—survived and thrived, as scholars like Fredric Jameson increased its nuance and interpretive sophistication.[135]

Eve Kosofsky Sedgwick's influential essay "Paranoid Reading and Reparative Reading, or, You're So Paranoid, You Probably Think This Essay Is about You" epitomizes reflexive critique of the poststructuralist literary paradigm. Pointedly describing the "hermeneutic of suspicion" as "paranoid reading" (also known as reparative reading, recuperative reading, and weak theory), Sedgwick challenges the poststructuralist normativities that were driving Critical Theory at the start of the twenty-first century. Paranoia, she observes, can be self-defeating: "Paranoia seems to require being imitated to be understood, and it, in turn, seems to understand only by imitation. Paranoia proposes both *Anything you can do (to me) I can do worse*, and *Anything you can do (to me) I can do first*—to myself."[136]

Those who cite this essay often miss the fact that Sedgwick doesn't jettison the paranoid reading process; on the contrary, she affirms it as one valid "possibility among other possibilities." Her real challenge is to Critical Theory's status in literary studies as "a mandatory injunction":

> The real force of [Theory's] discoveries has been blunted through *the habitual practices of the same forms of critical theory* that have given such broad currency to the formulae themselves. In particular, it is possible that *the very productive critical habits* embodied in what Paul Ricoeur memorably called the "hermeneutics of suspicion" . . . may have had *an unintentionally stultifying side effect:* they may have made it less rather than more possible to unpack the local, contingent relations between any given piece of knowledge and its narrative/epistemological entailments for the seeker, knower, or teller.[137]

In other words, Sedgwick argues that Theory "stultifies" by *replicating instead of rejecting* the reductive intellectual moves that poststructuralism critiques in structuralism. Her proposed corrective is not an uncritical naïveté but a "reparative" reading that allows for personal responses to literature like surprise, pleasure, wonder, and joy.

More recently, Critical Theory has faced a similar critique wrapped in a different kind of discourse. Amy Allen, following Said's lead, denounces Critical Theory's universalizing impulses as a new form of intellectual imperialism.[138] From this perspective, the German philosopher Jürgen Habermas's influential "Universal Pragmatics" undermines its own purported goal of liberation from monopolizing power discourses; in this sense, according to Allen, later Marxists fall prey to their own critique of earlier Frankfurt School generations.[139] Thinkers like Habermas, Allen avers, recognize that literary inquiry is imbricated with social and political concerns, but their universalist discourse of human progress is actually nothing other than an "unfinished Enlightenment" project, legitimating Western European notions of reality. Bill Ashcroft, Gareth Griffiths, and Helen Tiffin label the very concept of universality "a hegemonic European critical tool."[140] Implicit within this critique is a call for more globalized interdisciplinary (re)engagements with notions of social and political progress that are *not* built on Eurocentric or American imperialistic foundations.[141]

Self-reflexive critique reveals similar dynamics at work in the discipline of biblical studies. As Davina Lopez and Todd Penner observe, "identity-based criticisms—feminist, queer, postcolonial, African American, 'cultural,' and so on" are often seen as an "antidote to the traditionalism that historical criticism is thought to represent." However, as Sedgwick says of Theory, this narrative can have "an unintentionally stultifying side effect."[142] Lopez and Penner explain that when "biblical scholarship is narrated as proceeding in stages, with each stage across time dismissing and/or improving on the previous one," this can simply *replicate* "the same structural narrative about the history of the field as is present within historical-critical narratives about Christian origins." Lopez and Penner caution that "this 'from the one to the many' narrative functions as a myth of origins of sorts that serves more to justify current social relations and hierarchies than it does to say anything substantive about the actual history of the field."[143]

Poststructuralists can help us see that the "actual history of the field" is one of constant negotiation and contestation over (among other things) all three sets of inseparable literary concerns—the hermeneutical, the evaluative, and the metadisciplinary. Goldhill's observation about the field of classics applies to New Testament studies, as well: the discipline "*always has been* a constantly developing, historically contingent, ideologically laden study. What 'modern critical theory' has placed on the agenda is the question of how explicit, how sophisticated and how self-aware a discussion of each and every critic's inevitable commitment to a methodology is to be."[144] Today, scholars in the literary field generally agree that, as Patricia Waugh writes, Theory "is threatening to literary studies only when it adopts a positivistic guise."[145] My view is similar: the poststructuralist literary paradigm is threatening to NT studies only when it adopts a positivistic guise.

Literary Theory's Copernican Revolution: Concluding Thoughts

In 1995, Porter predicted that "deconstruction and related so-called postmodern critical methods, now that they have had their say, and we know what they involve, will fade after an initial burst of energy.... [They have] not offered much insight into the text."[146] Porter's augury has proven false. Deconstruction and other postmodern criticisms have not faded in NT scholarship. On the other hand, John Collins's pronouncement a decade after Porter still rings true: "It is not the case that postmodernists have captured the field. Far from it."[147] In other words, *unlike* Copernicus's geocentrism, the poststructuralist literary paradigm has not replaced its predecessors to enjoy the status of majority opinion.

To be clear, I'm not saying that poststructuralist literary approaches *should* capture the field or replace other paradigms.[148] Other perspectives are vital and shouldn't be neglected. What I am saying is that the poststructuralist literary paradigm shouldn't be so widely and summarily dismissed in NT studies. It can, in fact, *improve* the field. Some biblical scholars have already begun to demonstrate this. Nevertheless, many continue to harbor unfounded suspicions that poststructuralism *must* lead to relativism, political activism, and/or anachronism. In this chapter, I've argued that, despite common caricatures, the poststructuralist literary paradigm can enrich our interpretations of NT texts in their ancient historical contexts *and* sharpen our perspectives on hermeneutical, evaluative, and metadisciplinary literary concerns.[149]

Knowledge about the universe did not stop developing after the Copernican revolution, of course. It famously took Johannes Kepler to figure out that the planets don't move in circles, but in ellipses. It took Henrietta Leavitt to figure out how to measure the universe. And it took Edwin Hubble building on Leavitt's work to discover that the universe is expanding. In the time since Copernicus, we've come to see the cosmos as even more infinite than we had thought. In my view, whatever else we do as NT scholars, we ought to pursue our study with the creativity of a Kepler, the tenacity of a Leavitt, the ingenuity of a Hubble. I've been arguing that the ever-evolving field of literary studies can help us do so.

Like our theories about the universe, literary theory didn't stop developing after its Copernican revolution. In the time since the rise of poststructuralism, literary critics have come to see the study of literature as even more infinite than they had thought. As I mentioned in the introduction, literary theory has multiplied and morphed beyond poststructuralism to include (what some call) "post-poststructuralist" discourses and approaches, most prominently those of cultural studies. In the next two chapters, I present some of the more recent literary developments with reference to two case studies from the NT—first, the Synoptic Gospels (chapter 5), and then, Paul's Corinthian correspondence (chapter 6).

5 The Quest for the Literary Jesus: Reading the Character of Jesus at the Intersection of New Formalism and New Historicism

"Who do *you* say that I am?"
Luke 9.20

Who is Jesus? The answers are legion, and the stakes are high. For centuries, the figure of Jesus has provoked fierce debates. Typically, the four canonical Gospels provide the primary evidence in such debates. Yet even this engenders controversy, since there is no consensus about the *kind* of evidence presented by the Gospel narratives. Do the Gospels provide evidence of the "earthly Jesus," the "historical Jesus," the "Christ of faith," or some combination of these? The disputes rage on, fueled by conflicting convictions about history and literary form, text and context, truth and falsehood.

Scholarly treatments of Jesus provide a conspicuous example of the purported antithesis between historical and literary approaches that I've been challenging throughout this book. In historical Jesus research, scholars continue the now well-established cycle of denouncing previous historical Jesus "quests" only to embark on a new and improved search for the man from Nazareth.[1] Ben Meyer's sweeping claim that historical Jesus research "by common consent has *proved a failure*" is simply untenable.[2] Quests for the Jesus "behind" the Gospels are as popular as ever. Meanwhile, narrative critics have asked how each Gospel depicts Jesus as a particular kind of protagonist. Obvious overlaps notwithstanding, the stereotypes are well known: Matthew's Jesus is the Jewish Rabbi, Mark's Jesus is the Suffering

Servant, Luke's Jesus is the Savior, and John's Jesus is divine.[3] The stories themselves are far more intricate and complex, of course. The point is that NT narrative critics caution against conflating all ancient evidence into one coherent Christ, as though there is one plain answer to the question, *Who is Jesus?* Treating all four Gospels' depictions of Jesus as one portrait is like saying that a Byzantine-era image of the triumphant "Christ Pantocrator" is interchangeable with Salvador Dalí's iconic 1951 depiction, *Christ of Saint John on the Cross.*[4]

Searching for the actual historical person behind a story does differ in important respects from studying the character based on that person in a story. Different questers ask different questions. Those questions, and the presuppositions underlying them, explain why, as Elizabeth Struthers Malbon puts it, "suspicion remains between those questing for the historical Jesus and those questioning the literary-ness of the Gospels."[5] Still, the suspicion is unnecessary; the quests can enrich each other.

This chapter draws together two contemporary literary-theoretical discourses that focus especially on the fraught relationship between history and literary form—New Historicism and New Formalism—in order to propose a new kind of quest: a quest for the literary Jesus.[6] The first part of the chapter introduces the key concepts in these two strands of literary theory and demonstrates the need for them in current Gospel scholarship, with the Gospel of Luke providing an illustrative focal point. The latter part of the chapter brings the broader theoretical reflections to bear on an intercalated set of stories that appears across the Synoptic tradition—the healing stories of Jairus's daughter and the hemorrhaging woman in Mark 5.21–43//Luke 8.40–56//Matthew 9.18–26.

The Gospels, History, and Historiography

New Historicism is a literary movement pioneered by Renaissance scholar Stephen Greenblatt in the 1980s. The distinctive features of New Historicism as a literary approach will be clearer by contrast if we consider modern biblical scholars' dominant views regarding history and historiography. Some biblical scholars have applied New Historicism to biblical literature (and will be discussed below), but as previous chapters have noted, the traditional mode of historical criticism still considers "value-free objectivism and scientific methodism" to be the markers of legitimate NT scholarship. Even when traditional historians recognize that objectivity is impossible, most will agree with John Meier's advice: when "one's vigilance inevitably slips," the proper response is to "admit honestly one's own standpoint [and] try to *exclude* its influence."[7] This methodological commitment to objective historical reconstruction means that, as A. K. M. Adam observes, "even as some scholars submit that this is the postmodern era, most intellectuals and academies continue to *function* comfortably along typically modern lines."[8] In Gospel scholarship, one often finds the interrelated concepts of history, historicity, and historiography conflated along such "typically modern lines."

Consider the Gospel of Luke. The strong influence of an interpreter's historical presuppositions is well illustrated if we compare the conclusions of the late nineteenth-century Religionsgeschichtliche Schule (History of Religions school) to those of the twentieth-century Heilsgeschichtliche Schule (Salvation History School). The former, a group of Protestant theologians at the University of Göttingen, divided early Christianity into two major branches: Jewish followers of Jesus in Palestine, and Hellenistic followers of Jesus outside of Palestine. The Religionsgeschichtliche Schule also held that Jesus himself was human, and only later divinized by Christians who were influenced by Hellenism, like the author of the Gospel of Luke (hereafter, called Luke for convenience). In contrast, the Heilsgeschichtliche Schule held that it was not Hellenism *per se,* but early Christian *heilsgeschichtlich* conviction that dictated Luke's understanding of Jesus. Hans Conzelmann famously proposed that Lukan salvation history should be divided into three distinct stages—the Time of Israel, the Time of Jesus, and the Time of the Church—effectively setting Jesus at the center of world history and the divine plan.[9] These scholars' respective views of early Christian history directly influenced their interpretations of Luke's Jesus (and vice versa).

Here is a specific illustration of these exegetical inclinations. The Gospel of Luke, arguably the most Hellenized of the four canonical Gospels, refers in 2.1 to Caesar Augustus, Roman emperor from 27 BCE to 14 CE. Residents of western Asia Minor had voluntarily set up the (now-famous) Priene inscription to honor the emperor. It reads: "The birthday of the god was for the world the beginning [*archē*] of the gospel [*euangelion*] which has been proclaimed on his account" (*Inscr. Priene* 105,40). Scholars of the Religionsgeschichtliche Schule argued that Luke appropriated terms like *euangelion* from the surrounding imperial context in order to make Christianity less threatening to Rome. They also read whole passages as indicative of Luke's Hellenistic values, such that the Lukan preface and infancy narrative became a presentation of Jesus's beginning (*archē*) in the same mold as the Priene inscription's celebration of Caesar's *archē*.

The Heilsgeschichtliche Schule's theologically inflected interpretive framework prompted its proponents to draw different conclusions about Luke's Jesus. Not so concerned with showing how thoroughly Hellenized Luke was, they instead drew attention to the Lukan emphasis on the inevitability of God's plan.[10] For instance, Conzelmann explained the "Messianic secret" (viewed by many as simply vestiges of Luke's Markan source) by saying that it ensures that Jesus will fulfill his divine purpose; if the people knew Jesus's identity, they would save him from the cross and thereby interrupt the divine plan of salvation.[11]

Especially following Conzelmann, but at least since the days of his teacher Martin Dibelius, scholars have approached the third Gospel as a work of ancient historiography, dubbing its author "the first Christian historian."[12] Certainly, the literary style and content of the Lukan prefaces support this view (Lk. 1.1–4; Acts 1.1–2).[13] The Gospel of Luke begins uniquely, with a complex, technical first-person preface in which the author unabashedly claims to be a reliable historian—that is, an informed, authoritative storyteller. And like the historian Thucydides before him, Luke insists that he values accuracy (*akribeia*) for a purpose, assuring Theophilus that he has written "so that (*hina*) [he] might know for certain the things about which [he has] been taught" (Lk. 1.3–4).[14]

Whatever the precise genre of Luke-Acts (and/or the other Gospel narratives), it bears repeating that in the ancient world, history and historiography were more capacious and flexible concepts than our modern categories. Indeed, scholars of antiquity have decisively challenged traditional modern boundaries between historical "fact" and imaginary "fiction" with respect to ancient narratives, and it's fairly commonplace amongst those who study ancient literatures and cultures to recognize that ancient writers conceived of and crafted their literary genres differently than we do.[15] Most NT scholars will readily cede these points. Most will agree that post-Enlightenment ideals of historical (re)construction are foreign to ancient historiographical narratives, and that, as classicist Christina Kraus observes, ancient historians "constructed their works with techniques that were as much at home in oratory or the novel as with what we might call 'historical research.'"[16] And yet, it remains the case that many NT historical critics "continue to *function* comfortably along typically modern lines" by approaching the Gospels as though they were written according to modern academic conventions of history writing.[17]

Craig Blomberg's *The Historical Reliability of the Gospels* provides an unqualified exemplar of this kind of positivist discourse. Blomberg aims "to provide answers to the questions of historicity which will stand up to serious academic scrutiny."[18] As a foil to his approach, Blomberg sets up a straw man, mischaracterizing contemporary literary approaches (which he calls "the new hermeneutic") this way: "If no objective meaning is recoverable, then no reliable history is recoverable, because readers can never be sure whether or not they have misunderstood the gospels by thinking that they were supplying historical information when in fact they were not." Blomberg then outlines the "obvious flaws" in the postmodern perspective, concluding that it "confuses facts with their interpretations" and ends in "complete relativism."[19] Blomberg and others perceive—and erroneously portray—literary approaches as rendering historical inquiry futile. Few advocates of literary theory's New Historicism, however, would agree.

New Historicism

New Historicism aims to situate literary texts within their historical contexts, while resisting "old" historicism's positivist assumptions about objectivity and human progress. Stephen Greenblatt's conceptions of history are deeply informed by concomitant advancements in cultural studies, especially Clifford Geertz's contributions to cultural anthropology. Greenblatt describes his own classic work, *Renaissance Self-Fashioning,* as a "poetics of culture."[20] New Historicism incorporates many of the poststructuralist insights we explored in the last chapter, including Derridean deconstruction of binaries and Foucauldian discursive analyses that show how the sociopolitical power struggles of particular times and cultures shape sociocultural phenomena like sexuality, crime, and mental illness. For New Historicists, literature doesn't recount unmediated bare facts from the past; it presents one of many possible interpretations of events that occurred in the past. Literary analysis requires paying attention to the web of cultural discourses in which that text could first interpret and represent—that is, could first *mean*—something about the past.

New Historicism thereby shifts the critic's posture toward both history and literature. On the one hand, New Historical literary critics approach history itself as a text, to be interpreted in the same ways that we interpret literature; at the same time, they treat literature as cultural artifacts that can teach us about history. Gina Hens-Piazza explains that "New Historicism views literature and history as essentially the same. Traditionally, a constructed history formed the stable backdrop against which unstable literary texts were read and interpreted. New Historicism abandons these distinctions between literature and history. It views both as story and involved in the fashioning of each other."[21] To use Louis Montrose's well-known phrase, New Historicism holds together "the historicity of texts and the textuality of history."[22]

In many ways, then, New Historicism mirrors Hayden White's work in critical historiography. Both emphasize that all accounts *from* the past and all accounts *of* the past will be inherently *partial*, in both senses of that word: they will be fragmentary, or limited, and they will privilege one perspective over others. Our historical accounts will be fragmentary because our extant evidence from every ancient culture is selected and selective. "History," as Daniel Fulda puts it, "must always and as a matter of principle be *selected* (*erlesen*) [and] can in no easy or simple way merely be *read* (*gelesen*)."[23] In this fragmentary partiality inheres a perspectival partiality; every written account of a historical event—ancient or modern—will inevitably (if implicitly) constitute an argument for one particular construal of the world over and against other potential configurations.

Throughout this book, I've been challenging the common perception that literary approaches to NT texts are anti- or ahistorical. Luke Timothy Johnson is correct: "Literary critics . . . think that historical critics pay too little attention to the rhetoric of the compositions and too much attention to the putative reconstruction of their historical situation . . . but they do not thereby abandon historical imagination."[24] Biblical scholars like Lori Rowlett, Gina Hens-Piazza, Stephen Moore, and Claire Clivaz have recognized that New Historicism provides a way of attending to the rhetoric of the compositions while maintaining a robust historical imagination. Despite these important advancements, as Clivaz explains, the work of "thinking history and poetics together" remains a desideratum for biblical scholars because, "*as opposed to New Historicism*, the biblical sciences have kept the dichotomy between 'history' and 'poetics' intact while developing their own 'Narrative Criticism.'"[25] We'll return to New Historicism below. First, we turn to the literary side of the persistent "history" and "poetics" divide to which Clivaz refers.

The Gospels, Characterization, and Narrative Form

Along with NT scholarship's "literary turn" in the latter half of the twentieth century came newfound interest in the construction of Jesus as a literary character in a narrative. This methodological shift took a variety of forms, including the rise of distinct subdisciplines like "narrative christology" and "narrative criticism," and increased interest in literary characterization, identity construction, and the impact of the narrative form on meaning-making. In fact, Robert Tannehill explicitly defines narrative christology as an approach that "tak[es] seriously the narrative form . . . in discussing [a] Gospel's presentation of Jesus Christ."[26]

For early NT literary critics, taking the narrative form seriously meant, in part, reconceiving Jesus's identity based on literary strategies of characterization, rather than drawing conclusions based on theological or historical views of Jesus's ontological essence (saying, for example, that Jesus *is* God's anointed one, and the narrative reflects this; or that Jesus *wasn't* a political threat, and the narrative reflects this).[27] Consider again the "Messianic secret" in Luke. While redaction critics view Jesus's injunctions to silence as traces of his Markan source, and proponents of the Heilsgeschichtliche Schule viewed them as facilitating God's will, narrative critics ask instead what those speech acts reveal about Jesus's identity in relation to other Lukan characters.[28] As in all narratives, literary figures in the Gospels are characterized vis-à-vis one another, both explicitly and implicitly. What do we find when we look at Jesus's interactions with other characters? With whom does he associate? With whom does he agree and disagree? NT scholars like John Darr have helped us see how Jesus's character is "built" within a mutually illuminating dialectic: "Intermediate characters help the reader to construct the many images projected upon Jesus," and concomitantly, those characters "are evaluated in light of their responses to him."[29] Any understanding of Jesus as a literary character should therefore take into account the "web of interrelationships" established by the narrative in which he appears.[30]

Reading Jesus literarily not only prompts us to attend to his interactions with other characters, but also to situate those interactions within their broader narrative context—a context that, as reader-response critics remind us, unfolds sequentially. The beginning of a story is thus especially important. Because a narrative's linear order influences the audience's perceptions of its meanings, "the perspectives established at the beginning, when we are seeking to orient ourselves in this new narrative world, will continue to operate until they are decisively challenged."[31]

Luke's Gospel establishes early on that Jesus is, to use Joseph Fitzmyer's description, the "heaven-sent mouthpiece of God."[32] In Luke 2.41–51, after searching for the young Jesus, his parents find him in the Jerusalem Temple impressing everyone—including the Jewish teachers (*didaskaloi*)—with his "understanding" (*sunēsis*, 2.46–47).[33] Jesus's *sunēsis* includes his understanding of Jewish tradition, as well as his own self-understanding. Mark Coleridge is correct: this scene is when "Jesus is born in the narrative as prime interpreter."[34] Indeed, throughout Luke's Gospel, Jesus interprets not only the Scriptures, but also himself (see, for example, 4.20–21; 9.22; 17.25; 24.27, 45).

Jesus's first public sermon in his hometown of Nazareth is a case in point. It's fairly axiomatic in Lukan studies to read Jesus's dual scriptural- and self-interpretation in this synagogue scene as a kind of charter or blueprint for his mission on earth (4.16–30). Reading from the scroll of Isaiah, Jesus indicates that God's Spirit has anointed him *in order to* "bring good news to the poor, . . . to proclaim release to the captives and recovery of sight to the blind, to let the oppressed go free, to proclaim the year of the Lord's favor" (Lk. 4.18–19). The reading culminates in Jesus's declaration, "Today this Scripture has been fulfilled in your hearing" (4.21).

But the scene isn't only a blueprint for the actions of Luke's Jesus; it also stands as a kind of Gospel in synecdoche—a proleptic preview of the story to come. The Jesus we meet here embodies themes that are characteristic of the third Gospel as a whole. First, Jesus's role as God's *anointed* one, or Messiah (from the Hebrew *mashiach*, "anointed one," in Greek translation, *Christos*, or "Christ"), coheres with Luke's twin prioritizing of the Holy Spirit and the divine will. For Luke, God's Spirit anoints, directs, and empowers God's chosen leaders, and God's Spirit directs unfolding events in the world (salvation history).[35] Second, Jesus refers to himself as an anointed *prophet*, like the Hebrew prophets of old (4.14–24, esp. v. 24). This resonates with Luke's broader focus on welcoming Gentiles (universal salvation) because the Hebrew prophets were unjustly rejected by their own people and well received by "foreigners" (such as the widow at Zarephath and Naaman the Syrian in 4.26–27). And finally, in Luke 4.18–19, Jesus reads from Isaiah 61 in order to highlight his role as champion for the despised and/or marginalized "others" (in his context, the sick and the poor, women, tax collectors and "sinners," slaves, and so forth). Intriguingly, the citation doesn't include Isaiah 61.2b ("to proclaim . . . the day of vengeance of our God"), an omission that reflects Luke's broader concern with God's mercy, forgiveness, peace, and healing (for all, but markedly for the poor and downtrodden).

The description I've just set forth is hardly controversial; these are oft-repeated claims about the third Gospel's depiction of Jesus. Unfortunately, the familiarity of this profile can give the mistaken impression that Luke's characterization of Jesus is straightforward and simple. In reality, debates continue about who Luke's Jesus "is." Is he cast in the Hellenistic mold of a noble Master forming disciples? Is he depicted as a wise philosopher in the Platonic tradition dialoguing at Hellenistic symposia? Or, perhaps, a conquering Jewish Messiah planning a political revolution?[36]

Even if we can draw descriptions together to see Luke's Jesus as *simultaneously* wise teacher, Spirit-anointed prophet, triumphant Savior, and more, some claims aren't merely matters of degree. Some declarations about Luke's Jesus diametrically oppose one another. So, for example, we find Daniel Marguerat asserting that Luke uniquely "intègre l'affectif dans la caractérisation,"[37] while Fitzmyer argues that Luke erases from Mark "anything that smacks of the violent, the passionate, or the emotional."[38] Or we might contrast Stephen Moore's claim that Luke is "mirroring Roman imperial ideology, deftly *switching Jesus for Caesar*," with Paul Walaskay's assertion that "Luke had no intention . . . of challenging the ideal of *pax Augusta*."[39]

Debates continue, too, over the Lukan use of gender stereotypes to portray the character of Jesus. Drawing on Greco-Roman discussions of gender, some scholars argue that Luke's Jesus is the epitome of masculine authoritative power: he is educated, elite, and in full possession of classic Hellenistic virtues like self-control, intelligence, and noble duty. Critics like Colleen Conway have argued that compared to other NT texts, "Luke's work is the *most explicitly* concerned with showing Jesus and the leading figures of the emerging Christian community as models of masculinity."[40] Luke, for example, refers frequently to Jesus as "Lord" (*kyrios*, 7.13, 19; 10.1, 41; 11.39; 13.15; 17.5) and "Savior" (*sōtēr*, 2.11; compare 1.47)—titles and descriptions that customarily were employed for powerful Roman men like the emperor and/or to describe the apotheosis of elite figures like Julius Caesar. Luke also has a Roman centurion defer to Jesus with an explicit comparison to his own authoritative role as a superior officer: "I say to this one, 'Go,' and he goes, and to another, 'Come,' and he comes, and to my slave, 'Do this,' and he does it" (7.8).

Other critics counter, however, that Luke's Jesus is not only or even primarily depicted as an honorable Greco-Roman male. Brittany Wilson argues that "more often than not," Luke's male characters—not least, Jesus himself—"look *unmanly* in comparison to elite masculine norms," and that this Lukan "tension between manliness and unmanliness" actually reflects the paradox at the heart of the gospel message.[41] That is, Wilson argues that Luke's Jesus may be a powerful Savior, but he's also a feminized suffering Messiah. Fitzmyer goes so far as to call the idea of a suffering Messiah an "exclusively Lucan theologoumenon."[42] Fitzmyer overstates his case, but the point is that the Messianic call to suffer and die is a prominent Lukan motif that complicates the view that Luke's Jesus is only or primarily portrayed as a powerful Hellenistic *kyrios.*

Notice that each of the scholars above supports her or his claims about Luke's Jesus with references to the Gospel itself; these conclusions hardly represent a descent into "complete relativism," nor are they simply unfounded fabrications.[43] I stressed in the previous chapter that, contrary to the declamations of some, the poststructuralist literary paradigm doesn't have to result in absolute interpretive relativism. Even Derridean deconstruction doesn't require that all readings be considered equally valid or compelling. Narratives engender multiple interpretive possibilities, but interpretive latitude can be limited in a number of ways, depending on the criteria established.

Here's a quick example. Literary critic Mark Ledbetter critiques Lukan scholars for taking the Gospel narrative's claims that Jesus is authoritative at "face value." Ledbetter himself argues that the Lukan Jesus is indistinguishable from the Evil One (Beelzeboul).[44] Ledbetter's reading is predicated upon a *strictly* episodic approach; that is, he looks *only* at the episode in Luke 11.14–26. But that's a methodological decision he made prior even to looking at Luke's Jesus. One could choose instead—and many have—to read this scene as just one data point in a larger unfolding narrative plot. *If* one makes the latter methodological choice, then attention to the entire narrative militates against Ledbetter's conclusion.

What we need, then, is a way to acknowledge and analyze multiple interpretations of a literary text, even as we recognize various kinds of interpretive limitations. New Formalism provides exactly that.

New Formalism

The formalist literary paradigm we discussed in chapter 2 recently has been revived under the moniker "New Formalism." Heather Dubrow first used the phrase "New Formalism" in 1989 as a corrective to what she saw as an uncritically radical turn toward cultural studies at the expense of form and literary aesthetics.[45] Although New Formalism can't be reduced to one perspective, Verena Thiele offers a concise summation. New Formalists, she writes, ask "how to hone form (back) into a viable theoretical shape and to (re)assign it a critically interventive power."[46]

Dubrow and others kept developing the idea of New Formalism after her 1989 address, but the movement truly gained traction following Marjorie Levinson's programmatic 2007 essay "What Is New Formalism?"[47] Levinson identifies two strains of New Formalism, defining each by its posture toward history: an *activist strain* (which aims to recover a "historically informed formalist criticism")[48] and a *normative strain* (which, maintaining a strict dichotomy between history and art, considers form the purview of the latter alone).[49] Levinson summarizes: "In short, we have a new formalism that makes a continuum with new historicism and a backlash new formalism."[50] Levinson's repeated insistence that New Formalism was, in 2007, a "movement rather than a theory or a method" prompted subsequent attempts to theorize along New Formalist lines.[51]

Whereas *normative* New Formalists see a new need for "the defense of the literary,"[52] Annette Federico typifies *activist* New Formalists as "seek[ing] a compromise between the New Critical bent toward nonhistorical and aesthetic reading and the important work of historicists, Marxists, and feminists from the 1980s and after."[53] Because activist New Formalists view form and content as embedded in particular social and historical contexts, they appreciate references to external background information where a strictly New Critical or "old" formalist approach would not. They ask whether there is "a way to combine a wish to delve into the aesthetic complexity of a literary work with a concern for its life in politics and history."[54] Despite normative and activist New Formalists' distinctive inclinations vis-à-vis history, they share certain aims. Both strands of New Formalism seek (albeit in different ways) to recover earlier formalists' valuing of form and structure, while addressing critiques of formalism's earlier iterations.

One such critique came from New Formalists themselves. They rejected the earlier formalists' disciplinary view that critics must offer objective value judgments about a text. Thiele writes that instead, New Formalism "suggests that a text's formal features, its aesthetics, in close conjunction with cultural context, convey a politically and historically significant literary experience that is both intentional and affective."[55] New Formalists critique "old" formalism's views of proper scholarship because the latter requires the effacement of an embodied, situated interpreting self. Pushing the critique further, New Formalists argue that this apparent sense of disembodied interpretation functions rhetorically to conceal—and more importantly, to legitimate—scholars' ideological positions by capitalizing on "restrictive ideas of form's *givenness* (whether as container, or adornment, or genre, or verse-form, or speech act)."[56]

An additional theoretical development is especially relevant for NT scholars. As I suggested above, New Formalists embrace multiple possible readings where their predecessors would not have done so. Daniel Schwarz lauds New Formalism as a "pluralistic approach, which allows for multiple perspectives."[57] This is a critically significant methodological point. NT scholars' overwhelming tendency—amongst historical and literary critics alike—has been to entertain multiple possible factors in the reading process and then to choose between them using careful, historically informed logic, all with the goal of producing a single, integrated interpretation. New Formalism suggests that this step of isolating a single reading loses something essential to the textual exchange.

In answer to the overarching question of "how to hone form (back) into a viable theoretical shape and to (re)assign it a critically interventive power," New Formalists offer a "myriad of answers and kaleidoscopically fragmented visions." These multiple answers and visions are predicated upon "a common supposition, namely that literary theory is changing, that New Criticism is not nefarious, that Russian formalism has never been disreputable, that post-structuralism, despite its prefix, does not mark the end of structure, and that New Historicism is not the catch-all that it has been frequently made out to be."[58] I share these assumptions. I offer the following case study as just one of the "myriad of answers" regarding how we might "hone form (back) into a viable theoretical shape" in Gospel studies.

Jesus, Jairus's Daughter, and the Hemorrhaging Woman

We'll focus here on two miracle stories that appear across the triple tradition: the twinned accounts of Jairus's daughter and the hemorrhaging woman (Mk. 5.21–43//Lk. 8.40–56//Matt. 9.18–26).[59] These Synoptic parallels clearly reflect use of the same source materials, as the fundamental plot structure is the same in each: the precipitating event is that a leader in the synagogue comes to Jesus in search of help for his daughter, who is dead (Matthean version) or dying (Markan and Lukan versions). Suddenly, the narrative is interrupted by a woman who comes up behind Jesus as he is teaching. The woman has been bleeding for twelve years, and she seeks healing. In all three versions, the woman touches Jesus's garment and is miraculously healed of her infirmity; in all three versions, Jesus commends the woman for her faith. The narrative then returns to the ruler's predicament. When Jesus eventually arrives at the ruler's home, he's mocked by the mourners outside, but ultimately heals the man's daughter, raising her up from her deathbed.

Traditional historical critics situate these stories in their historical first-century *Sitz im Leben* in order to answer the question, What happened? Scholars have long sought to diagnose the woman's medical condition. What was really wrong with her? In 1903, Wilhelm Ebstein concluded that she was hemorrhaging from the womb; nearly one hundred years later, J. Keir Howard inexplicably asserted that her "dysfunctional uterine bleeding" was not real, but "psychologically generated."[60] Sometimes, though, scholars' results belie their claims to have uncovered ancient realities. Ironically, in their efforts to recover the history "behind" the narrative, these scholars have diagnosed the woman in modern medical terms that would have been incomprehensible in ancient cultures. A New Historicist also seeks to understand the first-century context of these stories, but in order to answer different kinds of questions. Instead of asking, What was this woman's disease?, a New Historicist might ask, How does this culture interpret a woman who's been bleeding for twelve years? What does this account tell us about the discourses of power and exclusion at work in the Mediterranean world of the late first century CE?

Scholars like Bruce Malina and Jerome Neyrey draw on the social sciences and cultural anthropology to answer such questions. Most commonly, they appeal to physical, individual, and social boundaries between "clean" and "unclean," or "pure" versus "impure." Malina, for instance, writes that in the NT world, examples of "the unclean" as a category "include persons suffering from skin disorders or unusual, abnormal bodily flows such as menstruation, seminal emission, suppuration. In these instances the personal boundaries of the individual prove to be porous; the individual is not whole."[61] A sociological perspective foregrounds the social boundaries instantiated by such purity/impurity concepts, as well as the ritual guidelines for inclusion or exclusion that accompany and sustain them. As

Mary Douglas famously argued, "The only way in which pollution ideas make sense is in reference to a total structure of thought whose keystone, boundaries, margins and internal lines are held in relation by rituals of separation."[62]

Others draw similar conclusions based on ancient physiognomic discourse, the interpretation of character based on physical appearance.[63] If "the physical body and the corporate social body were thought to mirror each other," then an imperfect physical body "had the potential of defiling the social body."[64] If physical imperfections or ailments were viewed as visible manifestations of invisible impurity, then, "as undesirables, the physically and mentally imperfect functioned materially and symbolically as metaphors or paradigms for religious and social transgressions."[65] In antiquity, personal porosity could pollute the polis. Drawing on this sociocultural context, critics argue that the hemorrhaging woman's individual body threatens to contaminate the corporate body; her bodily boundary transgressions are dangerous because they can cause concomitant social boundary transgressions.

Many NT critics have assumed that the clean/unclean binary behind these pericopes is religiously inflected. For many, Jewish ritual purity laws represent the pivotal link between these stories (and even, for some, extending beyond into wider literary contexts). William Lane expresses the traditional view in his 1974 commentary on Mark: "A detail which may have contributed to the association of Ch. 5:21–42 with Ch. 5:1–20 is Jesus' contact with the unclean, since the man of the tombs (who is probably a Gentile), the flow of blood and the presence of death all involve Jesus in ceremonial uncleanness."[66] Interpreters like Lane often point out that the two other times that the Greek terms for "flow" (*rhusis*) and "blood" (*haima*) appear together in the Bible are in Leviticus: "If a woman has a flow of blood (the LXX has *rhusei haimatos*) for many days, not at the time of her impurity, or if she has a discharge beyond the time of her impurity, all the days of the discharge she shall continue in uncleanness; as in the days of her impurity, she shall be unclean" (15.25), and "If a man lies with a woman having her sickness and uncovers her nakedness, he has laid bare her flow and she has laid bare her flow of blood (the LXX has *tēn rhusin tou haimatos autēs*); both of them shall be cut off from their people" (20.18).

According to this line of interpretation, the hemorrhaging woman breaks the Levitical laws regarding menstruation by appearing in public; she should have been in a state of social and religious quarantine.[67] Joel

Marcus, for example, takes the "surreptitiousness of the woman's approach to Jesus" as "an indirect indication that she is ritually unclean and is violating a taboo by being out in public."[68] If the Levitical stipulations situate the hemorrhaging woman in a state of perpetual impurity, then she personifies boundary transgression and deserves to be rebuked, or at least shunned, for appearing in public and touching Jesus.[69]

Yet, Jesus doesn't condemn the woman. Marla Selvidge and others conclude that through his restraint, Jesus "subtly shatters the legal purity system and its restrictive social conditioning."[70] This interpretative stance construes Jesus as a countercultural rebel who departs from exclusionary misogynistic Jewish thinking to advance a more inclusive egalitarian (some say feminist) agenda. Moreover, Jesus honors the woman by drawing her out of the crowd, inviting public attention (especially in the Lukan version) in a world where, according to Malina, "to honor a person is to acknowledge publicly that his or her actions conform with social oughts."[71] Jesus becomes an inclusive rebel, erasing the dominant value distinctions of his day and restructuring normative Jewish schemas dividing insiders from outsiders.

But what if Shaye Cohen is correct that Levitical purity laws are historically irrelevant to this story? Cohen, pointing up the distinction in Jewish law between a normal menstruant (*nidda*) and a woman bleeding outside her menstrual cycle (*zaba*), concludes that "the Gospel story about the woman with a twelve-year discharge, clearly a case of *zaba*, does not give any indication that the woman was impure or suffered any degree of isolation as a result of her affliction."[72] Cohen also counters the story's allegedly "feminist" or "egalitarian" trajectory on historical grounds: "There is no evidence that the intent or immediate effect of these laws was to discriminate against women," since Jewish laws also instructed men about bodily discharge.[73] Other critics aver that menstruation isn't in view in this Synoptic story at all, since (1) the Gospels avoid the most common ancient terms for menstruation, and (2) menstrual purity laws applied in the first century CE only to those who lived close to the Jerusalem Temple.[74]

Interpretations like those I've just outlined might seem New Historicist in nature, since they aim to contextualize the story within the cultural and historical conditions that produced it. The difference between traditional historical criticism and New Historicism is subtle, and really concerns a perceptual realignment regarding both text and extratext. Traditional historical critics prioritize the specific historical backgrounds, or extratexts, "behind" a text, and conceive of textual meaning as dependent on those extratexts. On both sides of the interpretive debate regarding the hemorrhaging woman, traditional historical critics *presuppose* a given historical reality (Levitical purity laws *are* or *are not* operative), and use *that* to explain Jesus's actions (thus, Jesus *is* or *is not* challenging societal and/or religious norms).[75] New Historicists, in contrast, consider the literary text as a cultural artefact in its own right, one that not only is shaped by but actively shapes specific sociohistorical contexts.

As "a sensibility rather than a method," New Historicism prompts us to ask different kinds of questions about biblical texts.[76] How, for example, does this Synoptic pericope interpret the predicament of a woman who has bled for twelve years? How does it understand a man like Jesus, whose garment miraculously heals? What kinds of cultural work does this account accomplish, and how does that work differ across Synoptic versions and in their varied receptions? What kinds of claims does the story make, and where can we discern struggle and contestation in the midst of those claims? In other words, a New Historicist wants to know how the story functions as a participant in the complex cultural discourses of its day, and how these interconnected realms shape one another.

Traditional historical critics have inquired about the woman's miraculous healing with questions like these: How did the healing actually work? Did the woman drain Jesus's power? If so, would that power have been visible—comparable, for example, to the Greek physician Eudemus's list of observable bodily leakage ("vomiting, gastric evacuations, urination, sweats, hemorrhage and normal bleeding piles")? If Jesus's power is a finite commodity, then is the woman committing an illicit act by taking it without his knowledge? And more broadly still: How were healing, touch, and gender related in the ancient imagination?[77]

Certainly, such questions yield intriguing possibilities. A traditional historian might note, for example, that this is one of several examples in the NT wherein the transfer of power doesn't require human contact; touching a holy person's garment can engender miraculous healing, as well (see Mk. 6.56; compare Matt. 9.20; 14.36; Lk. 8.44; Acts 19.11–12). This may, in turn, reflect the view, held by some in antiquity, that one's garments are connected to the self (compare Plutarch's *Life of Sulla*, 35.4).[78] It may also, or instead, reflect specific economic configurations. On the ramifications of the woman's action, Neyrey argues, "If someone secretly obtained healing or some other benefit without the healer's knowledge and remuneration, this might be considered a form of theft."[79]

While these possibilities are fascinating, New Historicists would note that none of the Synoptic parallels of this story seems particularly interested in the mechanics of the miracle or its economic implications. The stories themselves are cultural artefacts participating in ongoing ancient discourses, and not one stipulates whether or how the woman's action accesses Jesus's power, nor does it seem to matter whether that power is visible. In Mark and Luke, Jesus perceives the power leaving him, which could imply that there's a finite amount from which he senses depletion, but even so, there's no mention of remuneration; as Mary Rose D'Angelo writes, "Jesus' parting commendation of her faith simply concedes to her what she has already taken from him: the power with which to supply her weakness."[80] As a historically attuned form of literary criticism, New Historicism focuses primarily on what the narratives *do* tell us, and how those features function rhetorically to advance particular worldviews.

We can add to this New Historicist perspective the New Formalists' point that stories participate in the discourses of their day through the "critically interventive power" of literary form.[81] The historical and social-scientific interpretations described above pay little attention to the Synoptic stories' literary form. When modern NT scholars *do* attend to form, they tend not to see form as "critically interventive," as New Formalists do. Instead, NT form critics and narrative critics alike take a classificatory approach, prioritizing recurrent structural features as a means of source identification and/or generic classification.

Rudolf Bultmann and Martin Dibelius, for example, identified similarities between the hemorrhaging woman/Jairus's daughter pericopes and other ancient accounts of miraculous healings (or, to use Dibelius's term, *Novellen*).[82] David Rhoads, an early NT narrative critic, adopted Robert Alter's concept of the type-scene—a story recounted multiple times, with varied details but stable plot elements—in order to categorize the accounts of Jairus and the hemorrhaging woman as "Suppliant with Faith" type-scenes, wherein faithful people come to Jesus for healing, either for themselves or on behalf of a dependent.[83] Along similar lines, Antoinette Clark Wire identifies these pericopes as "demand stories," in which "the demanding party from the first takes an active part in the struggle and overcomes."[84]

NT form critics and narrative critics alike also recognize the literary technique of intercalation as significant.[85] The hemorrhaging woman's story is couched within a narrative frame, or what James Edwards calls a "host pericope."[86] Mark's version is paradigmatic:[87]

(A1) 5.21–24—Jairus asks Jesus to help his daughter
(B) 5.25–34—Jesus heals the hemorrhaging woman
(A2) 5.35–43—Jesus raises Jairus's daughter

The narrative sandwiching organizes the episodes into a larger chiasmus—that is, "an extended pattern of paralleled and inverted elements, often with a deliberate focus on the central segment"—which many consider an invitation to treat the outer and inner stories as mutually illuminating aspects of one interpretive puzzle.[88] I am indebted to many of these previous treatments of the Gospels' literary form. Still, classificatory approaches like those just described represent what the New Formalists consider "restrictive ideas of form's *givenness*"; they often mistakenly assume that form works according to static, stable, timeless convention.[89]

Narrative and reader-response critics have helpfully shifted attention to the intercalated structure's narratological effects. In Mark and Luke, for example, the delay caused by Jesus's interactions with the woman along the road creates the narrative time necessary for the girl to die before Jesus reaches her. In all three versions, bracketing the story of Jairus's daughter increases the dramatic suspense for readers who must wait to discover what will happen; the delay then heightens the miraculous nature of Jesus's healing when he does arrive.[90] Not only that, but the woman's arrival on the scene disrupts the readers' expectations of the plot flow. While the Jairus story begins with clear generic signals that suggest that a miracle is coming, nothing tells readers to expect a disruption. The introduction of the woman creates surprise, increases narrative dissonance, and compels readers to stay engaged in the story.

The sandwich structure also invites comparison between characters through the use of a literary foil—that is, a character who "through contrast underscores the distinctive characteristics of another."[91] NT scholars generally cannot agree about whether the hemorrhaging woman ought to be compared to the dying girl, Jairus, or Jesus. Advocates of the dying girl as literary foil point to semantic parallels between the two stories, such as the repetition of the number twelve (*dōdeka*) in descriptions of the girl and the woman, and Jesus's use of the vocative "Daughter" (*thugatēr*) to address them both. Additionally, in both accounts, the healing itself happens immediately (Luke twice uses *parachrēma*, Mark uses his favorite word, *euthus*, and Matthew says *apo tēs hōras*).

Other scholars argue that "the true foil for the woman is not the little girl, but her father Jairus."[92] Indeed, Jairus and the woman both come to

Jesus with faith in his ability to heal. Both believe in the efficacy of Jesus's physical presence; the woman wants to touch him, while Jairus asks him to come to his home to heal his daughter. In the Markan and Lukan versions, both Jairus and the woman express their desperation by falling down (*piptō*) at Jesus's feet. Both characters are contrasted with the unbelieving surrounding crowds, and both experience a miracle in reward for their faith.[93]

Still other interpreters hold that "the obvious comparison" is between the woman and Jesus.[94] Consider their respective uses of power: in the outer narrative, Jesus is the active agent of healing power, intentionally touching the girl to heal her. The girl herself remains a passive figure, acted upon by the change agent of the story. In the inner story, the woman is the active agent, intentionally reaching out to Jesus to receive healing; in this case, Jesus himself remains passive—Mark and Luke even underscore that the woman receives healing without his permission or knowledge. The woman, then, is the change agent of the inner story.[95]

Intercalation invites comparison not just in terms of identifying parallels between characters, but in terms of contrasts, as well. Indeed, many interpreters have observed social reversals at work in these stories. Take the contrasts between Jairus and the woman. In a first-century Hellenistic Jewish world, Jairus, as a synagogue leader, a father, and a (presumably) healthy male, likely would have occupied a venerated social position; standing at the center of his community/ies, he represents the values of those in power. It's appropriate to his station, then, that he approaches Jesus face to face. The hemorrhaging woman, on the other hand, is marginal in this first-century *Sitz im Leben:* she's unnamed, chronically ill, and probably poor; in Mark, at least, she's already spent everything she had on physicians.[96] The difference between Jairus and the woman is even more pronounced in the Markan and Lukan versions than in the Matthean version, since Jairus is named in Mark and Luke, but remains unnamed in Matthew. Mark and Luke also highlight the gravity of the woman's condition by mentioning that she's incurable (Mk. 5.26; Lk. 8.43).[97] It's therefore unsurprising that unlike Jairus, the woman approaches Jesus from behind. Yet, as the plot unfolds, these respective positions change. As Marcus and others have observed, "their fortunes seem to be suddenly reversed." The woman begins "at the opposite end of the social, economic, and religious spectrum from Jairus," but in the end, "his loss of time becomes her gain."[98] By the end of the inner story, the woman has taken center stage, whereas in the second installment of the outer story, Jairus fades from view.

Our earlier literary question, though, remains: Who are the appropriate foils in these intercalated tales? What's the most productive comparison between characters? New Formalism offers a useful way beyond the impasse by posing a new question altogether: Why choose at all? As we saw above, New Formalism embraces interpretive multiplicity. All three characters—the dying girl, Jairus, and Jesus—can function as foils to the hemorrhaging woman, and vice versa. For the New Formalist, determining that *one* character is a definitively "better" foil for another is fairly pointless. It's far more important to recognize the rhetorical effects of juxtaposing various characters to one another within the Gospel's "web of interrelationships."[99]

Who or what are these characters being connected in the Gospel's "web of interrelationships"? Above, I made note of early NT literary critics' attention to literary characterization as an aspect of narrative form. Considerations of "who Jesus is" often turn on how one conceives of the active agents in literature. There are two major approaches to characterization—the *referential* and the *nonmimetic*—and they've given rise to a "seemingly implacable conflict" (in both literary and biblical studies).[100] Historical critics, on the one hand, tend to rely on a *referential* approach—they take the figure of Jesus in the Gospels as referring to someone who exists/existed (in some sense) outside of the text. Poststructuralists, on the other hand, read the Jesus in the Gospels through a *nonmimeticist* lens—they take him to be a semiotic representation, circumscribed by and accessible only in the narrative form through which he's encountered.[101] Drawing on Mieke Bal's oft-quoted formulation, poststructuralists see literary characters as "fabricated creatures . . . paper people, without flesh and blood."[102] Importantly, for strict antimimeticists, the latter is true even when a narrative refers to actual, flesh-and-blood historical persons. Extratextual historicity aside, literary characters exist within a constructed, *constricted* narrative story world; they are nonactual individuals insofar as they have been crafted by an author (or authors) in particular ways (which, importantly, could have been narrated otherwise).

The mimetic/antimimetic dichotomy presents interpreters with what literary critic Alex Woloch describes as an "unpalatable choice: language *or* reference, structure *or* individuality."[103] I've argued elsewhere that in order to move beyond this unpalatable choice, NT interpreters should follow literary critics in distinguishing between different modes or "layers" of inquiry.[104] As we saw in chapter 3, the standard example of such layers is the narratological distinction between *story* (what is told) and *discourse* (how it is told). Techniques of characterization operate in the realm of the discourse, while characters' behaviors, qualities, virtues, and vices belong to the domain of the story world.[105] John Frow is correct: "One way of moving beyond the tied dichotomy of structuralist reduction and humanist plenitude (of the actant and the fully human character)" is "to recast them as distinct *levels* of analysis."[106]

Woloch's helpful reconfiguration of characterizational dynamics "recasts theoretical conflict back into literary process" in order to "make the tension between structure and reference generative of, and integral to, narrative signification." Characters, in other words, are "always emerging at the juncture between structure and reference."[107] To describe how this works, Woloch develops the concepts of the *character-space* and the *character-system:*

> The *character-space* marks the intersection of an implied human personality . . . with the definitively circumscribed form of a narrative. . . . The implied person behind any character is never directly reflected in the literary text but only partially inflected: each individual portrait has a radically contingent position within the story as a whole; our sense of the human figure (*as* implied person) is inseparable from the space that he or she occupies within the narrative totality.

Character-spaces then give rise to a *character-system,* or a "distributional matrix," by which "the discrete representation of any specific individual is intertwined with the narrative's continual apportioning of attention to different characters who jostle for limited space within the same fictive universe."[108]

To put these concepts into terms more familiar to NT scholars, critics involved in the social-scientific Context Group have long recognized the pervasive influence of agonism in the ancient world; this observation has advanced our understanding of how, on the level of the story, Jesus is characterized through conflict (*agōn*) with his adversaries. Yet NT scholars rarely consider how characters compete for space and attention on the level of the discourse, as well—a point suggested by the etymology of the word *protagonist* itself (proto-agonist). Because Jesus is the protagonist, his character-space only arises relative to—and in asymmetric relationship with—the character-spaces of others (the deuteragonist, tritagonist, and so on), all of whom interact within the character-system created by the narrative structure. Although Woloch doesn't claim the "New Formalist" label, he offers one way to bring form "(back) into a viable theoretical shape and to (re)assign it a critically interventive power."[109]

We've already seen how contextualizing these stories historically can illuminate the social and cultural dynamics at play between characters. New Formalism invites us to ask how these dynamics function *in conjunction with* the narrative's formal features. Fredric Bogel issues a New Formalist call to "pay closer attention to the cultural significance or valence of literary forms and conventions. Onto the pre-formalist and formalist interest in genres and conventions has been grafted an attention to their cultural, social, and political weight."[110] For example, as noted above, a historian might ask, How did this healing happen? and What were its consequences? Candida Moss, discussing the flow of power between Jesus and the woman, remarks that "the mechanics of the healing" entail a "reversal of fortunes for the physician and patient."[111] Taking a New Formalist perspective, I would add that the mechanics of form organize, enact—and even in some ways threaten to undo—such reversals. The following paragraphs unpack this claim.

Consider again the chiasmus created by the two stories. Drawing on cognitive stylistics to bridge the gap between the "activist" and "normative" strands of New Formalism, Karin Kukkonen insists that "form organizes content and provides a pattern of thinking." Consequently, a chiasmus functions not only as a "repetition that reverses grammatical structures," but also as "an inversion of the power relationship between participants. . . . The chiasmus inverts relationships between content."[112] Patrick O'Neill makes a similar observation when he writes, "The relationship between nested narratives is always one of mutual relativization, while the embedding narrative is ultimately always in a position to colour fundamentally our reception of an embedded narrative, it may itself always in turn be challenged or even displaced altogether by the narrative it embeds."[113]

While Jairus pleads with Jesus to heal his daughter, the woman—with her excessive blood flow—interrupts the narrative flow. The reader's perception of the interruption is filtered through the woman's perspective, who is described not only as having bled for twelve years, but as incurable (Lk. 8.43).[114] The narration, that is, foregrounds the woman's experience (narratologists discuss this aspect of narration in terms of focalization).

The narrator's control of knowledge and perspective guides readers in their interpretive judgments of this scene. Readers—unlike the other characters in the story—see the woman in the crowd, readers are told the reason for her presence, and readers watch her come up behind Jesus and touch his garment. Readers' privileged information can make it difficult for them to remain neutral "outside" observers. The narrative development turns on the discrepancies in knowledge between characters and readers. The way the story is told aligns readers' perspectives with the woman's, *in contrast to* the disciples' and Jesus's perspectives. For example, Jesus's question in Luke 8.45 ("Who touched me?") and the readers' knowledge of the answer heighten the tension and create dramatic irony. With these reader-elevating strategies of focalization, the narrator effectively creates a cohort of informed insiders; as Paul Duke puts it, "Irony rewards its followers with a sense of community."[115] Irony situates readers over and against the disciples, who "are shown to have little faith in Jesus and little understanding of why Jesus would ask who touched Him in such a mob."[116]

From a New Formalist perspective, what's remarkable about these intercalated tales is that "the chiasmus inverts relationships between content"—that is, Jesus and Jairus are decentered as the central active agents, while the woman takes center stage as the protagonist at the inner core of a framed narrative.[117] In a world that has marginalized this woman in more ways than one, she is suddenly right in the center of the action—both literally and figuratively—while Jairus, the respectable Jewish leader who embodies the social center, is relegated to the margins of the narrative.

Moreover, if we accept the formalist premise that form itself communicates, then we can see the interruption of the story as a literary instantiation of an important theological message, one with ramifications for our understanding of the Synoptic narratives' depictions of Jesus: those in the center don't deserve Jesus's attention more than those on the margins. Jesus doesn't prioritize those with power, nor even those whose need seems more urgent. This is especially striking when one considers that in Mark and Luke, Jairus's daughter has not yet died when the woman stops Jesus. The woman has been bleeding for twelve years—the entirety of the young girl's life. Presumably, a few more hours while Jesus attends to a dying girl wouldn't make much of a difference in this woman's condition. Nevertheless, Jesus stops and Jairus's plotline is put on hold. Indeed, it's only *because* Jairus's story stops on the level of the discourse that the woman's blood flow stops on the level of the story. In this regard, what happens on the level of the story occurs simultaneously on the level of the discourse such that form and content mirror and reinforce one another.

And yet. New Formalism also points up intricate and contradictory connections between the body *of* the text (its form) and the bodies *in* the text. Heeding Sasha Roberts's call for "reconciliation between new

formalism and feminist criticism," we might turn again to ancient constructions of gendered bodies.[118] We saw above how a social-scientific approach like Malina's emphasizes the porosity of female bodies in terms of a
strict dichotomy between pure (solid) and impure (leaky) bodies, and how
many interpreters have linked these discourses with ancient Jewish purity
laws. But ancient ideas of gendered bodies weren't always tied to discourses
of purity and impurity. Ancient Greek physiological formulations also distinguish between female bodies as porous and male bodies as contained:
"In women the nature of glands . . . is loose textured . . . but in males both
the compactness and the solidity of their bodies contribute greatly to the
glands not becoming big. . . . The female, on the other hand, is loose textured and spongy" (*Gland*. 16, L. VIII. 572).[119]

Further, as Cohen rightly points out, "underlying the Hippocratic characterization of male and female flesh is a value judgment: firm and com-
pact is good/loose and spongy is bad."[120] This view continued to hold sway
long beyond the time of Hippocrates. Ann Ellis Hanson demonstrates that
"post-Hippokratic female physiology continue[d] to view woman as a crea-
ture of excess."[121] Reading this Synoptic pericope in that historical context,
then, some argue that the story overturns normative gender expectations.
If *both* the woman and Jesus are "porous, leaky creatures," then in terms of
ancient construals of gender, Jesus's masculinity is threatened.[122] In contrast, the woman's healed body becomes more "bounded," more male, and
as such, more valuable.[123]

A New Formalist interpretive lens allows us to see hierarchical gender
disparities operating not only on the level of sentience, but on the level
of the sentence—not only on the level of bodily form, but on the level of
narrative form. Woloch's concepts of character-space and character-system
remind us that characters are created through asymmetry of attention on
the discourse level. Consider again the fact that Jairus's story "forms a pa-
renthesis" around the woman's story. In terms of character-space, this could
be read in two contrasting ways: on the one hand, it could be read in feminist terms as an unusual centering of a female character, on the levels of
both form and content. As the woman's story is recounted, Jairus and his
concerns fade into the background. On this reading, the woman is liberated
not only from her physical ailment, but also from the larger societal structures that oppress and constrict her.[124]

On the other hand, the intercalated form could also effectively render
the woman little more than a parenthetical remark—an aside, a departure

from the more important (male-dominated) storyline.[125] Jairus does re-appear once the woman has been healed, whereas we never see or hear from the woman again. From this perspective, the form moves the woman from the margins to the center, but her story—like her healed body—remains bounded within the structure of the outer (male-dominated) frame narra-tive and contained within strictures of dominant (male-elevating) norms. In this case, Jesus sends the woman back into the world of her oppressors, "healed," but hardly liberated.

My reticence to argue definitively for one or another of the above pos-sibilities as the "right" reading shouldn't be construed as an endorsement of interpretive relativism or anarchy. To reiterate, narrative form limits our interpretive options even as it gives rise to multiple potential meanings. In my view, one benefit of New Historicism and New Formalism is that together, they can help us reshape our own perceived disciplinary bound-aries, which often unnecessarily limit our conceptions of how the Gospel narratives work as literary structures. Allowing for capacious—sometimes contradictory—considerations of the Gospel narratives' formal features can open up pathways toward a more richly textured *and* widely contextualized literary Jesus.

The Quest for the Literary Jesus: Concluding Thoughts

All of this brings us back to the question with which we began: *Who is Jesus?* As we saw at the start of the chapter, the regrettable rift between historical and literary approaches in NT studies has resulted in essentially two different quests: a quest for an extratextual Jesus and a quest for the (Matthean, Markan, Lukan, or Johannine) protagonist Jesus. Yet, neither approach adequately explains how and why readers of the very same narra-tive, all searching for Jesus, keep arriving at *different destinations*.

New Historicism and New Formalism together provide one way to unite these estranged forms of inquiry into a quest that is attuned to liter-ary form, but *not* ahistorical. They help us see Luke's characterization as presenting neither a purely *paper Jesus* nor an extratextual *historical Jesus*, but rather, a paradoxical protagonist Jesus who is constructed and circum-scribed by the Gospel's dynamic narrative form and by the concrete, real-world readers who instantiate it.

The literary-theoretical discourses we've discussed in this chapter also suggest that answers to the question of who Jesus is will always call for clarification, and always give rise to more questions: Who is Jesus *in which story?* Who is Jesus *according to whom?* Who is Jesus *compared to whom?* Who is Jesus, and *why does that matter?* The Gospel stories should be read as participants in debates that were already ongoing at the time of their earliest circulation. Kenneth Burke's image of rhetoric as "unending conversation" paints the right picture:

> Imagine that you enter a parlor. You come late. When you arrive, others have long preceded you, and they are engaged in a heated discussion, a discussion too heated for them to pause and tell you exactly what it is about. In fact, the discussion had already begun long before any of them got there, so that no one present is qualified to retrace for you all the steps that had gone before. You listen for a while, until you decide that you have caught the tenor of the argument; then you put in your oar. Someone answers; you answer him; another comes to your defense; another aligns himself against you, to either the embarrassment or gratification of your opponent, depending upon the quality of your ally's assistance. However, the discussion is interminable. The hour grows late, you must depart. And you do depart, with the discussion still vigorously in progress.[126]

Each Gospel story of Jesus is its own powerful voice amongst many—one form of literary argumentation in the "unending conversations" that are always at work rhetorically constituting, deconstructing, and reconfiguring human social systems and relations.

None of this should surprise us; it's been true since the beginning. According to the Gospels, even during Jesus's own lifetime, people gave different answers when Jesus himself posed the question, "Who do *you* say that I am?" (Lk. 9.20).[127] And so, we might ask, and even attempt to answer—Who is the literary Jesus?

But the quest should never end there.

6 The Corinthian Corpus and Epistolary Embodiment: Reading Paul's Epistles with Affect Theorists and Ecocritics

> For now, we see through a glass in obscurity;
> but then face to face: now I know in part;
> but then shall I know fully.
> *1 Corinthians 13.12*

Whereas the last chapter focused on narrative, this chapter turns to the epistolary literature of the New Testament. Specifically, we'll consider the two extant epistles sent by the apostle Paul to the *ekklesia* in Corinth, which are so concerned with matters of literary interpretation that Margaret Mitchell has called them "a correspondence course in practical, indeed, tactical hermeneutics." In this chapter, I seek to challenge traditional scholarly modes of approaching Paul's epistles to the Corinthians by engaging two recent trends in poststructuralist literary criticism: the move to draw on affect theory, and the increased interest in ecocriticism.

As Mitchell rightly says, Paul's correspondence course in hermeneutics is practical. At the same time, we shouldn't let modern associations with practicality cloud the fact that it is also intensely personal and deeply emotional. Paul takes a particularly heated tone in chapters 10–13 of the second letter, where he famously defends himself against some opponents who are typically associated with the "super apostles" of 2 Corinthians 11.5 and 12.11. In "the first recorded moment of Pauline interpretation by someone other than Paul himself," we learn their complaint: "His letters are weighty and powerful, but the bodily presence weak, and the spoken word (*logos*) contemptible" (2 Cor. 10.10). Instead of denying that his physical self-presentation drastically differs from his epistolary self-presentation, Paul appears to corroborate it, admitting that he is "humble when face to face with" the Corinthians yet "bold" in his writing (2 Cor. 10.1).

Pauline scholars tend to accept that Paul's "authorial *parousia* is at such odds with the epistolary *parrêsia*."[1] Historical critics especially have proffered numerous hypotheses about Paul's purported bodily defects (his "weak" body) and lauded his rhetorical prowess (his "bold" writing).[2] The consequence of accepting this claim at face value, however, is that Pauline interpreters unintentionally reinscribe the argument of Paul's opponents. Like the super apostles, scholars pit Paul's powerful epistolary voice *over and against* his "weak" body, thereby maintaining a strict binary between Bold Epistolary Paul and Weak Corporeal Paul.

That binary becomes even more problematic when juxtaposed with another commonplace in Pauline scholarship: the assumption that epistles indicate absence and lack, while physical bodies represent presence and power. This view reverses the prior dichotomy, creating a *Weak* Epistolary Paul and a *Bold* Corporeal Paul. Paul also seems implicitly to support this assumption, assuring the Corinthians that, although "absent in body," he is "present in spirit" (1 Cor. 5.3), and referring repeatedly to his desire to visit them in person (see, for example, 2 Cor. 12.14; 13.1). A letter, from this perspective, constitutes a less appealing, less powerful stand-in for an absent Paul (Weak Epistolary Paul), in contrast to his (obviously preferable) physical presence (Bold Corporeal Paul).

The quintessential example of this perspective in modern scholarship is Robert Funk's widely accepted thesis regarding "apostolic *parousia*." According to Funk, Paul considered his apostolic presence "under three different but related aspects at once: the aspect of the letter, the apostolic emissary, and his own personal presence." Moreover, Funk insists that all three communication strategies—written letters, sent emissaries, and physical presence—instantiate Paul's apostolic *parousia*. This latter point provides a useful corrective to those who consider presence *only* in terms of the physical body. Less helpful, however, is Funk's concomitant claim that letters "may be *less* effective," since they do not "bear the apostolic power to the same degree as Paul's personal presence."[3] In other words, Funk privileges corporeal presence *over and against* epistolary presence, thereby maintaining value-laden distinctions between a letter writer's physical, material body and the immaterial thoughts expressed in a letter. But as Mitchell rightly argues contra Funk, that evaluative hierarchy (Paul-envoy-letter) is unnecessary and improbable; it's more likely that Paul evaluated each circumstance individually and, at times, decided that an emissary or a letter might, in fact, be *more* effective than his physical presence (as suggested in 2 Cor. 10.10).[4]

Which is it? Is the Epistolary Paul a powerful *rhētor*, or is he *less* effective by virtue of his absence? Alternatively, is the Corporeal Paul weak and contemptible, or physically present and thus *more* powerful? In my view, the problem lies with the questions themselves. Either way—whether we ascribe to a Weak/Bold Epistolary Paul or a Weak/Bold Corporeal Paul—another problematic dichotomy remains intact: that between the Corporeal Author Paul and the Disembodied Epistolary Paul. In other words, both construals maintain a dichotomy between the *content* of Paul's letters—his abstract, *immaterial* recorded thoughts—and the Paul who conceived and composed them—the bodily *material* author. Either way, the interpreter's goal is the same: to exegete, or "lead out," the immaterial contents of a corporeally absent Paul's mind and heart (theological truth and/or his thoughts and desires).

However, a strict separation between a (Corporeal) Author Paul and a (Disembodied) Epistolary Paul raises several other unresolved issues. For one thing, it presupposes a stable text and a singular authorial voice. And yet, both are difficult to establish. NT scholars are intimately familiar with our fragmentary manuscript evidence and the long, intricate history of textual changes by scribes and copyists; these material realities considerably complicate the notion of one solid, determinable text. Not only that, but twentieth-century redaction critics convinced most NT scholars that 1–2 Corinthians actually represent compilations of many fragments from multiple embedded letters.[5] In addition, identifying one singular authorial voice is elusive, partly because Paul's letter writing was a collective enterprise (see 1 Cor. 1.18–31; 2.6–16; 16.21), but also because the very idea of a solitary, identifiable writing subject "behind" a text is a modern construct (see the discussion of Foucault's famous "What Is an Author?" essay in chapter 4).[6] Modern scholarly discussions of ancient epistles have traditionally been dominated by debates over authorship, authenticity, pseudepigraphy, forgery, and fakes. But as Laura Nasrallah and others have noted, our anxieties about these matters don't reflect ancient priorities. Even when ancient writers express concern about textual authenticity in language that sounds similar to our own, they do so from within a "different ethical system."[7]

Problems like those above attest to the need for an alternative approach to 1–2 Corinthians—one that's less focused on identifying a unified authoritative voice and/or an original textual autograph, one that doesn't presuppose modern dichotomies (such as presence/absence, mind/body, written/spoken, authentic/inauthentic) or modern values (like presence is power, absence is weakness). The traditional scholarly discussions don't necessarily reflect *ancient* views about bodies, texts, authors, or agency. Too often, they simply replicate instead of interrogating the dichotomizing epistolary rhetoric in the letters themselves.

The following discussion looks first at the epistolary rhetoric in 1–2 Corinthians and in traditional Pauline scholarship. The next section highlights advancements by Pauline scholars who have drawn on Critical Theory and thereby paved the way for a fresh literary approach to Paul's letters. I then demonstrate how literary critics' recent engagements with affect theory and ecocriticism can open up conceptual space for considering the Corinthian correspondence differently, and the final section advances a new proposal regarding the Epistolary/Corporeal Paul and the corpus of his Corinthian correspondence.

Epistolary Binaries, Ancient and Modern

As noted at the start of the chapter, letters—*qua* letters—are not peripheral to the content of 1–2 Corinthians.[8] Throughout 1 and 2 Corinthians, Paul attempts to correct what he considers to be the Corinthians' misinterpretations of what he has written. The very fact that these letters were written and exchanged demonstrates that, as Mitchell insists, they "do not and never did have a single, unambiguous meaning. Even in his own lifetime, Paul's letters—that most dynamic of genres—were disputed, his meaning contested and negotiated."[9]

Paul repeatedly foregrounds the writing and interpreting of letters: he refers to his own previous and current epistles (1 Cor. 5.9, 11; 14.37; 16.21; 2 Cor. 1.13; 2.3–4; 3.1; 7.8, 12; 10.10–11), letters written by the Corinthians (1 Cor. 7.1; 16.3), and his own motivation(s) for writing (1 Cor. 4.14; 9.15; 2 Cor. 2.4, 9; 7.8; 9.1; 10.9; 13.10). We might consider such references a form of self-theorizing—moments of epistolary reflexivity. What kind of epistolary theory does the Corinthian correspondence reflect?

For one thing, Paul assures the Corinthians that as long as his physical presence with them is delayed, his letters constitute authentic substitutes, true expressions of his spirit and desires when he is physically absent. "Though absent in body," he tells them, he's "present in spirit,"

> and as if present I have already pronounced judgment in the name of the Lord Jesus on the man who has done such a thing. When you are assembled, and my spirit is present with the power of our Lord Jesus, you are to hand this man over to Satan for the destruction of the flesh, so that his spirit may be saved in the day of the Lord. (1 Cor. 5.3–5)

Repeatedly, Paul juxtaposes his physical presence with them to his absence from them:

> Perhaps I will stay with you or even spend the winter. . . . I do not want to see you now just in passing, for I hope to spend some time with you, if the Lord permits. (1 Cor. 16.6)

> I wanted to come to you first. . . . I wanted to visit you on my way to Macedonia, and to come back to you from Macedonia and have you send me on to Judea. (2 Cor. 1.15)

> Let such people understand that what we say by letter when absent, we will also do when present. (2 Cor. 10.11)

> I warn them now while absent, as I did when present on my second visit, that if I come again . . . (2 Cor. 13.2)

Epistles, then, appear to be Paul's go-betweens—literal lettered *pages,* metaphorically carrying communication of the heart from one absent party to another.

This epistolary logic appears across ancient epistolary theorizing, and in ancient letters themselves. Ps.-Demetrius, for example, describes epistles as "conversations halved" (*De elocutione* 223) that "reveal the author's soul" (227). "A letter," he explains, "is designed to be the heart's good wishes" (231). Pliny the Younger famously writes to his wife, Calpurnia (referring to letters she's already written him), "You write that my being absent from you causes you no little sadness, and that your one consolation is to grasp my writings as a substitute for my person" (*Ep.* 6.7).[10] In his *Moral Letters to Lucilius,* Seneca writes, "I thank you for writing to me so often; for you are revealing your real self to me in the only way you can. *I never receive a letter from you without being in your company forthwith.* If the pictures of our absent friends are pleasing to us, though they only refresh the memory and lighten our longing by a solace that is unreal and insubstantial, how much more pleasant is a letter, which brings us real traces, real evidences of an absent friend" (*Ep.* 40.1). Seneca later writes that this is just as epistolary correspondence should be: "I prefer that my letters should be just what my conversation would be if you and I were sitting in one another's company or taking walks together" (*Ep.* 75.1). It was a stock motif—cliché, even—in antiquity that letters provide privileged access to the private inner thoughts and feelings of a physically absent other.

The conviction that a letter does what an absent person cannot do also undergirds the common ancient practice of sending letters of introduction or recommendation—Cicero called them *litterae commendaticiae*—with someone to vouch for the letter bearer's trustworthiness and procure the hospitality of those who would receive him (*Ad Fam.* 5.5 § 1). Ps.-Demetrius's letter-writing manual explains:

> The commendatory type, which we write on behalf of one person to another, mixing in praise, at the same time also speaking of those who had previously been unacquainted as though they were (now) acquainted. In the following manner:
>
> So-and-so, who is conveying this letter to you, has been tested by us and is loved on account of his trustworthiness. You will do well if you deem him worthy of hospitality both for my sake and for his, and indeed for your own. For you will not be sorry if you entrust to him words or deeds of a confidential nature. Indeed, you, too, will praise him to others when you see how useful he can be in everything.[11]

The practice appears in the NT, as well (see Acts 18.27). Paul wrote letters of recommendation for others (Rom. 16.1–2; 1 Cor. 16.10–11; 2 Cor. 8.22–23; Eph. 6.21–22; Col. 4.7–8, 10; Philemon), but insisted he didn't need one himself (2 Cor. 3.2–3).[12]

Ancient conceptions of epistles seem clearly to cohere with ours today. Routinely, Pauline scholars note that letters create "an alternative form of social relationship, one which functions to establish or maintain a relationship when the parties to it cannot meet face-to-face."[13] Antitheses like body/mind and presence/absence also inform the standard conceptual separation between a letter's *content* (disembodied recorded thoughts) and the (embodied) person who conceived and composed them. One need only think of NT scholars' extensive efforts to posit an actual travel itinerary—the real-world movements of Paul's physical body through the Mediterranean—based on his references to visiting the Corinthian church (1 Cor. 16.6; 2 Cor. 1.15; 12.14, 20–21).[14] It seems fairly self-evident that 1–2 Corinthians are the material bearers of the immaterial contents of an absent Paul's mind and heart (theological truth and/or his thoughts and desires).

I contend, however, that the epistolary theories just set forth above actually obscure significant differences between ancient and modern conceptions, and thus skew our understandings of Paul's rhetoric. In every chapter of this book, I've challenged the notion that literary interpretation is ahistorical, or unconcerned with extratextual issues. Here, I argue that (1) the poststructuralist literary paradigm exposes how contemporary ideas about ancient letters can be too reductionistic and, in some respects, anachronistic; and (2) recent developments in poststructuralist literary theory can help us to do better justice to ancient views vis-à-vis the Corinthian correspondence. Before I make my case, let's look at some other ways that assumptions of continuity between antiquity and today have led to anachronistic interpretations of Pauline literature.

One famous example is Krister Stendahl's argument about Paul's supposedly individualistic introspection. In the mid-twentieth century, Stendahl pointed out that throughout Western history, "the Apostle Paul has been hailed as a hero of the introspective conscience." This perception informed interpretations of passages like Romans 7.15 ("I do not do what I want, but I do the very thing I hate"), which were seen as clear evidence of Paul's divided psyche. Yet, Stendahl argued that the very notion that Paul *had* an "introspective conscience" is a product of Western (especially Protestant) Christianity: "[Bultmann states that] continuity in the human self-consciousness is the common denominator between the New Testament and any age of human history. This presupposition is stated with the force of an a priori truth."[15]

As Stendahl warned, such "tacit" universalizing presuppositions play a "subtle and distorting role in historians who do not give account of their presuppositions but work within an unquestioned Western framework."[16] Scholars have helpfully interrogated other presumed "common denominators," as well. Proponents of the "New Perspective" on Paul, for example, object to "unquestioned Western frameworks" like the theological dichotomy between faith and good works, or the supposedly clear rift between Jews and Christians in the first century.[17]

More recent Pauline scholarship has pushed these trajectories even further through engagements with Critical Theory. In the introduction, I adopted Jonathan Culler's definition of Critical Theory (often just called Theory): "discourses that come to exercise influence outside their apparent disciplinary realm because they offer new and persuasive characterizations of problems or phenomena of general interest: *language, consciousness, meaning, nature and culture, the functioning of the psyche, the relations of individual experience to larger structures, and so on.*"[18] Interestingly, the Corinthian correspondence has drawn more attention from Theory-inspired Pauline scholars than other books of the NT.[19] Recently, these scholars have been overturning long-standing assumptions of continuity, especially regarding issues of embodiment and materiality. Because these shifts provide a productive preamble to the literary reading of 1–2 Corinthians that I'll propose, I want to walk through a few of them together.

The Corinthian Corpus and Critical Theory

I mentioned Dale Martin's now classic work *The Corinthian Body* in chapter 3. It was Martin's engagements with Critical Theory that led him to question Western constructions of the body, gender, and class in previous scholarship on 1–2 Corinthians. Against previous scholars who conceived of class (in a modern sociological sense) as static economic status (defined in terms of income), Martin argues that ancient conceptions of class are less "a matter of rich or poor or something in between," and more about relations of exploitation. Instead, "it is economic *relationship,* rather than wealth per se, that is important for analysis of early Christianity."[20] Drawing Theory into his readings of Paul's rhetoric (and ancient comparanda), Martin demonstrates how "categories and dichotomies that have shaped modern conceptions of the body for the past few centuries ... *did not exist in the ancient world* as dichotomies."[21] For example, "it is not at all clear that what we moderns mean by 'matter' ... has much relation to what ancient philosophers meant by *hyle.*" This is why Martin concludes, against so many prior Pauline scholars, that we ought to interrogate "the often unrecognized implications of our own constructions of the bodies of ourselves and others," and "avoid introducing into the Corinthian debate a concern regarding matter and nonmatter."[22]

We find another example of a Theory-informed historical approach to Paul in Nasrallah's contribution to the 2014 edited volume *Corinth in Con-*

trast. Nasrallah's chapter, titled, "'You Were Bought with a Price': Freedpersons and Things in 1 Corinthians," is attentive to both historical and ideological concerns, asking what historical realities the texts might obscure, and what we can know about the material lives of Paul's embodied recipients. Adducing extratextual evidence of slavery and manumission practices that were operative in and around ancient Corinth (including inscriptions and other material realia), Nasrallah rejects several misperceptions regarding slavery and status in the ancient world. For instance, she points out that Aristotle's reference to the slave as a "tool" (*Pol.* 1253b30–32) troubles the modern distinction between "humans" and "things." If enslaved humans can be things, Nasrallah asks, "how would those who first received this letter have understood its use of terminology associated with slavery theologically and materially?" More generally, she writes, "We may also ask what would it mean to write history in light of a sliding scale of being in which distinctions not only between humans as persons and humans as commodities, but also between things, humans, animals, and other creatures, might not be clear."[23] Drawing on ancient sources, Nasrallah concludes that Paul's reminder to the Corinthians that they were "bought with a price" (1 Cor. 6.20; 7.23) effectively "asks the hearers or readers to think of themselves as things on the market."[24]

With respect to the ideological power dynamics of Paul's Corinthian correspondence, scholars like Elisabeth Schüssler Fiorenza, Elizabeth Castelli, and Margaret Mitchell (among others) have drawn special attention to Paul's rhetoric as evidence of his efforts to exert apostolic control.[25] Traditionally, NT scholars have sought to identify and classify Paul's rhetorical strategies according to the classical rules set forth in ancient rhetorical handbooks.[26] In contrast, scholars like Schüssler Fiorenza, Castelli, and Mitchell read Paul's rhetoric as a form of ideological argumentation and seek to illuminate asymmetrical power dynamics therein.

Unfortunately, many interpreters fail to do justice to the fact that these letters are Paul's *written attempts to persuade.* The tendency throughout the long history of Pauline interpretation has been to read Paul's epistles as though his apostolic authority was already unquestioned at the time of their composition or earliest reception. However, Joseph Marchal makes the perceptive point that this assumption "fail[s] to measure Paul's letters the way he likely expected them to be received: as attempts at persuasion." In fact, Marchal continues, "to presume that Paul was already authoritative and his arguments always already accepted seems to misunderstand how these letters function." Reading 1–2 Corinthians as anything *other* than attempts at persuasion, in other words, does "a disservice to Paul and the manifest effort he expended to persuade through these letters."[27] Assuming that the letters have always been authoritative documents domesticates them and divests them of the power to persuade. Antoinette Clark Wire underscores the irony of this tendency: "Because an argument Paul makes cannot be rejected as unconvincing, it also cannot convince. In this way the authority we attribute to Paul prevents him from persuading us."[28]

Notably, rhetorical contestations over power are evident in Paul's letters *even when* his recipients are imagined to have renounced hierarchy in favor of a "discipleship of equals" (to use Schüssler Fiorenza's now-famous formulation).[29] Anna Miller, for instance, argues that the Corinthians considered themselves a democratic *ekklesia* marked by equality. Yet, Miller still contends that speech is "a site of struggle between Paul and his Corinthian audience," and therefore represents "a key to understanding the contestation over power that marks [1 Corinthians] as a whole."[30] Giovanni Bazzana draws on neo-Marxist linguistic theories to demonstrate how such contestations can work even on a granular grammatical level. Bazzana argues that attention to a text's "speech structures, its genre, the ideological weight embedded in its very syntax and grammar" allows critics to "emphasize, as an appropriate and productive subject of analysis, what a text can 'do,' at the socio-political level."[31]

Critical Theory can help us to expose anachronistic assumptions in Pauline scholarship and illuminate the ideological dimensions of Paul's writing. It can also clarify what's at stake in critical readings of Paul's letters. As we saw in chapter 1, Critical Theory sees *all* literature—including scholarly interpretations—as ideologically determined. Further, because normative assumptions are inescapable, critical reflexivity is always necessary. Turning a critical eye on scholarly processes means that as readers, we ought to ask how our assumptions about alterity or continuity between past and present might be serving our own ideological purposes.

Slavery provides a clear example: for most of the nineteenth century, readers of the NT assumed that ancient enslavement, which was ubiquitous in the Roman Empire, was fairly synonymous with slavery in the modern world—an assumption that clearly served the interests of modern slaveholders who found in NT texts warrant for their practices. Today, it's well known that ancient slavery differed significantly from modern slavery in scope, ideology, and actual practice, and yet, such differences only recently began to change NT scholars' interpretations of slavery-related passages.[32] For instance, in 1 Cor. 7.20–21, Paul instructs the Corinthians to "remain in the condition in which you were called," launching major interpretive debates about whether Paul intends for this to be read literally or figuratively. Nasrallah, in her chapter about freedpersons and things in 1 Corinthians, critiques interpreters on both sides who "neutralize the passage's revolutionary idea of seeking freedom, on the one hand, or its horrifying quietism of staying enslaved, on the other."[33] Critical Theory prompts us to ask not only what's at stake in Paul's ideological claims *but also* what's at stake in scholarly treatments of them.

To date, this growing body of Theory-inspired Pauline scholarship has focused mainly on *author*- and *recipient*-related issues (such as attempts to recover Paul's ideological intentions, or attempts to imagine how the letters' embodied recipients would have responded). Rarely have critics focused on the third component of the communication triad: *the letters themselves.* Scholars of antiquity who *do* foreground letters *qua* letters tend to treat material objects like illuminated manuscripts, scribal marginalia, textual variants, or palimpsestic pages as windows onto lost historical processes.[34] Consequently, epistles remain inanimate, lifeless objects, and binaries like mind/matter, presence/absence, and material/immaterial remain mutually exclusive categories.

Let's go back to the question of how to understand the purported distinction between a Weak Corporeal Paul "behind" the letter and a Bold Epistolary Paul "in" the letter. Jennifer Glancy's *Corporal Knowledge* productively challenges the binaries implicit in the Bold Epistolary Paul/Weak Corporeal Paul debate. Glancy contends that modern conceptions of mind *versus* matter lead us to miss how Paul's own body constitutes a form of knowing: "Because NT scholars have not acknowledged that relationships of power were embodied, they *have not appreciated the centrality of Paul's body* to the superapostles' campaign against him."[35]

Glancy appeals to ancient somatic reasoning, according to which the body constitutes a form of knowing, to argue that passages like Paul's "boasting of beatings" (2 Cor. 11.22–25) do not present a Bold Epistolary Paul at all. Quite the opposite: "The debility of Paul's somatic presentation" in the letters actually would have "*undermined* his claim to authority." Paul, then, makes a surprising rhetorical move when, instead of refuting the perception that his body is weak, he equates his physical infirmities with Jesus's.

Glancy concludes, "By pointing to his own storytelling body, Paul claims his dubious corporal knowledge as a source of improbable power."[36] Indeed, by pointing to Paul's "storytelling body" herself, Glancy reminds us that "rhetoric was a corporal practice," and that Paul's corporality ought to enter into scholarly considerations of his rhetorical strategies in the letters.[37] *Corporal Knowledge* admirably destabilizes normative assumptions regarding strength and weakness, bodies and words. And yet, even in Glancy's nuanced discussion, the epistles themselves remain inert, passive objects.

The letters are rendered *immaterial*, in both senses of that word: their significance rests in their *immaterial* (abstract) content (Paul's thoughts and wishes), while their epistolarity (the fact that they are material written texts) remains *immaterial* (insignificant). Conceiving of epistolarity in this way might *seem* natural in a capitalist system that treats objects as commodities that are created and circulated for human consumption. Texts generally, and letters more narrowly, seem to us to be inert matter (ink on a page or even pixels on a screen), the purpose of which is to transfer abstract non-matter (words, ideas) to and from active human agents (senders and receivers). To us, a letter is what Scott Elliott describes as "a mechanism of conveyance for the transfer of meaning."[38] We think, in other words, that humans "do things" with letters, but letters do not "do things" with humans.

But scholars in the literary field, especially those who focus on eighteenth-century epistolary novels, insist that the work of composing, producing, sending, and interpreting letters always requires more than abstract, disembodied cognitive activity, and always gives rise to more than abstract, immaterial consequences.[39] Furthermore, as Marx and his followers insist, ideology and human production are never "just" about ideas: "As individuals express their life, so they are. What they are, therefore, coincides with their production, both with *what* they produce and with *how* they produce."[40] More significantly still for NT scholars, modern notions of epistolarity don't necessarily reflect ancient conceptions of objects, agency, or texts.

Remember Martin's admonition: The "categories and dichotomies that have shaped modern conceptions of the body for the past few centuries . . . *did not exist in the ancient world* as dichotomies."[41] Of course, Martin is referring to human corporeal bodies, but I suggest that we can approach the letters themselves this way—they, too, are material bodies, though of a different kind. I contend that the letters themselves *do* matter, *as matter*. We need an approach that will help us intentionally set aside modern dichotomies so we can think about letters as *more* than merely *immaterial.* In my view, recent developments in literary theory pave the way for a literary approach that does just that.

The Corinthian Corpus: A Proposal

In short, my proposal is this: Instead of treating a Pauline epistle as a passive stand-in for a (weak or bold) absent apostle, it makes more sense to understand it as a powerful *alternative* form of presence. In the literary realm, recent years have seen a rise in two different forms of criticism: those inspired by affect theory, and those influenced by ecological concerns. These contemporary developments can help us rethink our epistolary presuppositions with respect to the Pauline corpus.

In previous chapters, we've seen how every successive paradigm in literary studies incorporates critiques of previous paradigms, and these shifts are often later dubbed "turns." Recently, partly in response to the twentieth-century "linguistic turn," literary scholarship has taken what some call a "corporeal turn," a "nonhuman turn," and/or a "material turn." Brian Massumi, discussing the linguistic turn, writes, "A common thread running through the varieties of social constructivism currently dominant in cultural theory holds that everything, including nature, is constructed in discourse. The classical definition of the human as the rational animal returns in new permutation: the human as the chattering animal. Only the animal is bracketed: the human as the chattering of culture."[42]

The "material turn" rejects the view of the human as merely "the chattering of culture" to ask instead how corporeality, embodiment, and matter (living or nonliving) shape and reflect the literary. Materialism is complicated, of course, referring to more than tangible objects and artifacts. With respect to literature, materiality concerns (1) the texts themselves—manuscripts, papyri, printed documents, and so forth; (2) the material culture and socioeconomic conditions reflected in a given literary text, or in which that text is produced and/or read; and (3) the embodied, visceral effects that texts engender vis-à-vis humans and the world.[43] Literary scholars take various stances with respect to these interconnected issues, but overall, the "material turn" recognizes that texts are significant not merely on an immaterial level, but materially, as well. In order to do justice to this dimension of literature, literary critics have begun to draw on discourses like affect theory and ecocriticism.

Affect Theory

As Marta Figlerowicz has stated, there simply is "no single definition of affect theory."[44] Most affect theorists ask how bodies, emotions, feelings, perceptions, and cognition are related, but there are so many iterations of this cluster of concerns that the singular phrase "affect theory" can itself be misleading. Definitions appear to be up for grabs, depending upon the frameworks, intentions, and critical proclivities of the interpreter in question. For example, many affect theorists follow Massumi, who differentiates between *emotions* (which are perceived and understood cognitively) and *affects* (which are, to use Massumi's oft-cited description, "irreducibly bodily and autonomic").[45] Still others, however, agree with Ruth Leys, who finds the emotion/affect distinction meaningless and insists that it "cannot be sustained."[46]

Given such basic definitional disagreements, it might be surprising to learn that with respect to literary studies, affect theory does have an acknowledged point of origin: retrospectives consistently cite 1995 as inaugurating the "affective turn" in literary criticism. It was in that year that two key publications appeared: Eve Kosofsky Sedgwick and Adam Frank's "Shame in the Cybernetic Fold: Reading Silvan Tomkins," and Brian Massumi's essay "The Autonomy of Affect."[47] In "Shame in the Cybernetic Fold," Sedgwick and Frank introduced a new generation of literary and cultural theorists to the psychobiological work of Silvan Tomkins. Decades earlier, Tomkins had investigated what he termed "affect theory," by which he meant hardwired neurobiological responses such as joy, anguish, and shame. Massumi's 1995 article "The Autonomy of Affect" drew on the work of contemporary French philosopher Gilles Deleuze, who conceived of affect in poststructuralist terms—that is, in terms of nonlinguistic, perceptual "intensity."[48]

The "Tomkins" and "Deleuze-Spinoza" modes of affect theory are distinct, but the two groundbreaking publications of 1995 set a new shared agenda: "The turn to affect . . . returned critical theory and cultural criticism to bodily matter, which had been treated in terms of various constructionisms under the influence of poststructuralism and deconstruction. The turn to affect points instead to a dynamism immanent to bodily matter and matter generally."[49] Affect theorists insisted that the linguistic turn had rendered reality *merely* the result of socially constructed language, and completely occluded matter. Literary critics who agreed with that position therefore sought to (re)incorporate bodily responses into literary-theoretical discussions.

Affect theory has gained considerable traction since 1995, particularly in the past decade or so; still, individual theorists continue to run in different directions.[50] Affect theorists interested in literature differ from one another in terms of their critical goals and consequent posture toward texts. The lineage of some can be traced back through the halls of the Frankfurt School to Freudian psychoanalysis; they practice a type of psychoanalytic criticism, by which the critic becomes the *analyst* and assesses a text or character as *analysand*.[51] Others are heirs to one of the main correctives Marxism offered with respect to capitalism: they emphasize human sociality over hyper-individualism.[52] This has led to a special focus on the social effects of "trauma as part of the affective language that describes life under capitalism."[53] Moreover, affect theorists like Sara Ahmed and Lauren Berlant advocate a personal, *affected* form of engagement, rejecting traditional scholarly approaches in favor of reading affects as a mode of social and cultural critique.

An intriguing paradox lies at the heart of literary critics' engagements with affect theory. Affect theory generally stresses the inexpressibility of the affects and the limits of reason—but the affectivity with which literary theorists are concerned is expressed in words. This paradox can be productive, however. Affect theory's unique contribution to the literary field (and, by extension, to the field of biblical studies) can be the very insight that emotion *and* affectivity—(re)cognition *and* (ir)rationality alike—play interconnected, often indistinguishable roles in textual interpretation. Fruitful critical inquiry arises precisely at the junction where affective reactions exceed cognitive capacities *and* catalyze interpreters' rational responses to literary texts.[54]

In the relatively short time span of affect theory's influence on literary studies, a tension has arisen regarding the proper object of study. On the one hand, early affect theorists, recognizing the complicated interstices between affect, emotion, embodiment, and cognition, reconfigured the operative critical questions. Ahmed, for example, wrote, "Rather than asking 'What *are* emotions?'" we should be asking, "What do emotions *do?*"[55] Sedgwick advocated a similar move "from the rather fixated question Is a particular piece of knowledge true, and how can we know? to the further questions": "What does knowledge *do*—the pursuit of it, the having and exposing of it, the receiving again of knowledge of what one already knows? *How*, in short, is knowledge performative, and how best does one move among its causes and effects?"[56] In light of these shifts, some literary scholars began asking how affect contributes to literature's rhetorical potency. In direct contrast to the formalist New Critics' affective fallacy (discussed in chapter 2), these scholars place the many ways that texts *affect* human beings at the center of their study.

Other affect theorists want to *de*center human subjects. As one of many "theoretical threads that intertwine" in a larger movement that Stephen Moore has recently dubbed "nonhuman theory," this line of thinking interrogates the implicit "us" left unspoken in formulations like Ahmed's ("What do emotions do [to/for/in us]?") and Sedgwick's (the "ones" who pursue, receive, and perform knowledge). These scholars interact with affect theory, but they prefer *not* to treat affect "as always being, in the end, *for us*."[57] Advocates of the so-called post-human turn object to human-centeredness, pushing back against scholarly obsessions with "naming where subjectivity begins and ends."[58]

Affect theorists' divergent moves toward and away from the human are in tension with one another, but that tension is not intractable; it is entirely possible to bring these impulses into productive dialogue with one another to illuminate literature. For example, we might consider the human body as the center of immaterial intellectual existence *and* material sensuous experience, even as we consider whether, or to what extent, our interests in human subjectivity can be intimately "bound up with fantasies of a human uniqueness in the eyes of God, of escape from materiality, or of mastery of nature."[59] Additionally, as Moore argues, "nonhuman theory" provides a corrective to anachronistic assumptions by "effect[ing] an unprecedented erosion of the Western conception of 'the human' that has coalesced since the Enlightenment." The erosion of modern assumptions about the human, consequently, "pair[s] well with early Christian texts that long precede that epochal amalgamation and that testify to other notions of the human in its relations with the nonhuman."

This brings us to another theoretical discourse that similarly confronts "human exceptionalism, classically expressed as a conceptual dualism of the human and the nonhuman (animals, plants, inorganic entities)"—namely, ecocriticism.[60]

Ecocriticism

The term "ecocriticism," coined by William Rueckert in 1978, now takes several forms in literary theory.[61] For some, it means reading so-called nature writers like Thoreau, while for others, it means highlighting environ-ment-related themes in any literary corpus (biology- or landscape-related metaphors, allusions, and so forth); for still others, ecocriticism entails rec-ognizing and honoring the generative role literature can play in enlivening the imagination and inspiring creative solutions to environmental prob-lems. For the latter group, literature itself can function, in Rueckert's words, as "the verbal equivalent of fossil fuel."[62]

In NT scholarship, ecological themes appear most often in discus-sions of Christian theology and praxis. David Horrell, for example, argues that in addition to "the obvious eco-texts" in Romans (8.19–23) and Colos-sians (1.15–20), "a broader ecological engagement with Paul" can "resource a Christian response to our contemporary ecological crisis."[63] Some, like the international team of scholars involved in the "Earth Bible" project, seek "ecojustice" through their rereadings of biblical texts. Still, relatively few NT scholars address ecology or the environment, and even fewer engage the ecocriticism that has arisen in the field of literary studies.[64]

As Horrell indicates, current environmental crises like global warm-ing, pollution, and human consumption propel much of this work. Conse-quently—and unsurprisingly—ecologically inflected literary studies tend to be explicitly ethical and praxis-focused; ecocritics rarely attempt to be "objective" or value-neutral in the post-Enlightenment sense. Some early practitioners of ecocriticism were stridently anti-Theory, impatient with what they perceived as critical theorists' obscurity, practical impotence, and problematic dissociations with the material world. The main disciplin-ary goal for ecocritics is to advance environmental justice. Many oppose anthropocentrism as a violent and destructive way of being in the world, emphasizing instead the dire need for human shifts toward sustainability and away from indiscriminate consumption of natural resources (even the phrase "natural resources" can problematically imply that nature is there for humans to *use*). They also point out that the trajectory of influence goes both ways: environmental spaces (and the biodiversities within them) shape human beings, not just the other way around.

Resisting literary theory's long-standing anthropomorphism, ecocriti-cism expands the literary critic's conceptual resources on two levels. First, it broadens the horizons of study by investigating certain normative as-sumptions about the world. For example, many readers (ancient and mod-ern) hold the Aristotelian view that "man alone of the animals has *logos*" (*Pol.* 1253a8). Ecocritics point out that this isn't the only way of construing the world; there were exceptions even in antiquity (the Greek biographer Plutarch, for one, considered animals to be rational beings).[65] Second, attending to our own fragile contingencies in relation to nonhuman matter expands the literary critic's methodological and stylistic repertoires. For some critics, at least, decentering human subjectivity has opened space for personal, subjective perspectives in literary scholarship.[66] Pure, positivist objectivity is impossible; the critic is, after all, only human.

Jane Bennett proposes that we think in terms of an "ecology of things"—that is, a conception of the world as an interconnected whole in which humans act, but are not, ultimately, the *only* actors. Humans also are acted *upon*. Inspired by the Spinozan notion of affect's capacity to act, Bennett argues that inanimate things reciprocally and actively shape the environment as "vibrant matter." That is, *many* kinds of bodies (human, textual, cultural, biological) are constantly converging and constituting one another.[67]

Bennett's vibrant matter is closely related to another critical discourse called "thing theory."[68] Thing theorists also argue that inanimate things can have their own transformative capacities. Bill Brown, drawing on Heidegger, distinguishes between *objects* and *things:* "We look *through* objects because there are codes by which our interpretive attention makes them meaningful, because there is a discourse of objectivity that allows us to use them as facts. A thing, in contrast, can hardly function as a window."[69] In other words, it's not the innate essence of things but our "discourse of objectivity"—our normative practices, our conditioned *habitus*—that leads us to think of objects as inert and passive. As counterintuitive as it may seem to us, tangible physical things can have the capacity to make a difference and create change. Sociologists refer to this as "material agency."[70]

Material Agency, Epistolary Embodiment

With these concepts in mind, we return to the topic of epistolarity. Could it be that we tend to look *through* letters as windows, rather than *at* them as active *things*, because a modern "discourse of objectivity" conditions us to do so? How might it shift our discussions of Paul's Corinthian correspondence if, instead of assuming that letters are passive objects passed between people, we considered them to be *things*, with a kind of material agency? What if we thought of epistles as *vibrant* matter, located somewhere on the ancient "sliding scale of being," where, as Nasrallah puts it, distinctions between humans and things, agents and objects simply "might not be clear"?[71]

Let me forestall potential misunderstanding. When I speak of epistolary agency, I do not mean to advance what Dale Martin describes as the "myth of textual agency"—the "common assumption" that "the Bible 'speaks' and our job is just to 'listen.'"[72] Martin has in mind Christians who, like Clark Pinnock, consider the Bible to be "the Word that issues forth when the Spirit takes the Word and renders it the living voice of the Lord. Therefore, it is not a text we can master through techniques but a text that wants to master us."[73] Pinnock declares that as a divine agent, the biblical text "masters" the reader. This is not what I mean when I refer to Paul's epistles as having "material agency." I agree completely with Martin that texts "must be interpreted by human beings," and that readers are ethically accountable for their active role in interpretive meaning-making—even when (especially when!) those readers consider the Bible to be divinely inspired.[74] My concern here, though, is with ancient views, according to which written words *could* engender actual, material effects—effects that neither authors nor readers could entirely control—and thus *could* have material agency.

For those who worry that my references to material agency and thing theory anachronistically impose modern concepts onto ancient texts, my argument is the exact opposite: these concepts provide useful vocabulary for grasping ancient views about the powers and abilities of language. Indeed, concepts had a tangible dimension to them long before Paul's day. Ekaterina Haskins describes archaic Greece, for example, as "a world in which concepts do not possess an existence apart from their material instantiations."[75] I contend that considering Paul's letters as "vibrant matter" with material agency is not only entirely *plausible* in light of ancient ideologies and conceptions of language, but does better justice to them.[76]

Material agency was a familiar concept in the ancient world. It was common to believe that humans were not the only active agents in the world, and that things could "do things." Moreover, for much of antiquity, writing was construed as a magical practice imbued with numinous power.[77] Written words could easily be active agents, with a kind of supernatural ability to engender real, material effects in the world. Examples from antiquity abound. Curse tablets, for example (commonly called *defixiones* or *katadesmoi*), enacted a spell that brought one person under the power of another.[78] Inscriptions also could exert influence over passersby. As Joshua Englehardt and Dimitri Nakassis put it, inscriptions could "impose their will upon readers . . . neatly reversing our 'commonsense' expectation of an active human subject and a passive material object."[79]

The power of letters is also evident in ancient anxieties over what David Fredrickson calls "epistolary duplicity"—that is, the ever-present possibility that a letter will fail to do what it purports to do.[80] Writing about epistles in ancient Mesopotamia, Piotr Michalowski observes, "The idea that a letter could kill its bearer is indicative of the ideological danger of written communication: letters can be falsified, altered, or simply lost."[81] William Harris, in his well-known study of ancient literacy, underscores the "surprisingly sinister import" of ancient letters: "They are authoritative and deceptive at the same time. . . . It is remarkable how much the letters of Thucydides—political of course—are instruments of death, betrayal, and deceit."[82] These are distinct discourses, with different textual and generic corpora in view, but the point is that modern epistolary presuppositions can miss or obscure how, in the ancient *Weltanschauung*, the power of words far exceeded the ability to induce cognitive intellectual assent.

Contemporary affect theory helpfully highlights how the composition of and responses to literary texts are not only (or always) cognitive or conscious. The editors of a 2014 thematic issue of *Biblical Interpretation* devoted to affect theory, Stephen Moore and Jennifer Koosed, recognize that the task its contributors "are faced with—at least those interested in close reading/exegesis, and most are—is a challenge of creative adaptation. What might affect theory look like transmuted into affect criticism?" In addition to Moore and Koosed, scholars like Maia Kotrosits, Erin Runions, and Jennifer Knust have also been drawing on affect theory in order to pose a provocative question: How might scholarly work on the Bible change if we were to recognize the inevitable influence of affectivity and emotion on our scholarly endeavors?[83]

As I mentioned above, affect theory expands literary critics' repertoires by drawing attention to aspects of literature that are routinely ignored, and by allowing for personal subjective responses in modern critical scholarship. In NT studies, Kotrosits, for instance, explores the "non-conscious, affective aspects" of early Christians' traumatic experiences in an imperial world. What's more, her work is unapologetically personal: "I won't attempt to separate my professional, institutional, and relational histories from this account of affect theory within biblical studies, not only because to do so would deprive this essay of any kind of meaningful 'perspective,' but because we are more or less starved for models of intellectual history that do justice to the fully relational ways in which thoughts unfold, the way disciplines and institutions enable and constrain, and the incidental and sometimes circular fashion in which insights pop up."[84]

Kotrosits's description of the Acts of the Apostles fits the Corinthian correspondence, as well; Paul's letters to the Corinthian community are also a "chronicle of the desperate brokering of fragile agency and inclusion." Given the early Jesus-followers' precarious relationship to "fraught and ambivalent" questions of social belonging, agency, and inclusion, the language of 1 and 2 Corinthians certainly would have had material embodied effects for Paul and for his recipients.[85] Consequently, the common scholarly practice of envisaging epistles as immaterial occludes how the acts of composing, receiving, and interpreting them would have been marked *not* primarily by modern constructions of a conscious, disembodied rationality, but by material, visceral, "non-conscious" affectivity.

Ancient writers educated in the classical rhetorical tradition would have learned about specific ways by which words actively conjure up presence. Aristotle, for instance, describes rhetoric as language that can "bring before the eyes" (*Rhet.* 3.11), while Quintilian commends speech by which "images of things absent are represented to the mind, so that we seem to see them with our eyes and have them in our presence" (*Inst. Or.* 6.2.29). Dionysius of Halicarnassus defines *enargeia*, often translated "vividness" or "actuality," as "the power of bringing what is said before the senses," such that the audience can "consort with the characters . . . as if they were present" (*On Lysias* 7).[86] While contemporary socio-rhetorical critics use the term *rhetography* to refer to written and visual imageries intersecting in the minds of readers, it is worth emphasizing that for ancient rhetoricians, the effects of *enargeia* are not just visual.[87] Note that in the quotation above, Dionysius mentions "the senses" more generally.

Enargeia is language that persuades *not* just by rational argument, but by engaging the audience's embodied senses and emotions. Rutger Allan, Irene de Jong, and Casper de Jonge underscore this feature of *enargeia:* "Apart from visual effects, the rhetoricians and commentators also point to acoustic effects, which are for instance created by onomatopoetic words that mimetically suggest the sounds of the action described. By 'seeing' and 'hearing' the events, the listener becomes deeply involved. . . . Such effects will often result not only in cognitive but also in emotional involvement of the audience."[88] Quintilian especially emphasizes that *enargeia*'s graphic quality is persuasive because it involves the audience immersively by rendering present that which is absent.

Like *enargeia*, *ekphrasis* is based on the notion that words create images in the mind's eye; whereas *ekphrasis* is typically associated today with descriptions of visual art, in antiquity it was not specific to topic or literary genre.[89] The first-century *rhētor* Theon defines *ekphrasis* as "a descriptive (*periēgēmatikos*) speech (*logos*), which leads (*agōn*) the thing shown vividly before the eyes" (*Prog.* 11). It's not insignificant that Theon casts the *logos*—*not* the author or audience—as the active subject who does the "leading" (*agōn*). What's more, the adjective *periēgēmatikos* (typically translated "descriptive") is related to *periagō* ("to lead around"). This suggests that much like Pausanias's travel guide of Greece, *Hellados Periegesis*, the *logos* is leading readers around on a kind of visual tour. Robyn Whitaker summarizes: "*Ekphrasis* seeks to do the impossible: to use what is unseen to produce something seen, thus creating a visual representation through the medium of language."[90]

Also like *enargeia*, *ekphrasis* functions persuasively by evoking emotion. Both techniques stand in contrast to a bald statement of facts; the latter, as Quintilian stresses, "does not touch the emotions" (*Inst. Or.* 8.3.69). This is relevant when we consider the famously emotional language of 1 and 2 Corinthians. Especially 2 Corinthians has been described as "a tumult of conflicting emotions."[91] Indeed, Paul passionately appeals to the emotions of his recipients and expresses his own emotions (2 Cor. 1.1–2.13; 5.2, 4, 14; 6.6, 10; 7.4–16; 11.2–3, 11, 29; 12.9, 15, 20–21; 13.9).[92] And yet, most scholarly treatments fail to acknowledge the bodily, unconscious, irrational responses such references encode and invoke. Kotrosits is correct: most readers

> view these affective changes and [Paul's] relationships as functions of his ideological principles. In other words, if Paul is angry with the Corinthians, it is because they are behaving in a way that is not compatible with his ideals. Or if Paul is frustrated, it is because the Corinthians are thick headed. But this conceptualization of Paul in relationship is still indebted to the thinking that casts Paul as primarily a distant ideologue, a moral superior, or a knowing and transcendent apostle.[93]

In my view, the picture of a logical, rational Paul is an unfortunate residual corollary to the anachronistic image of "Paul, hero of the introspective conscience" that Stendahl exposed in the last century.

Note that my argument is *not* that Paul drew on rhetorical handbooks and treatises, nor that he *intentionally* used these specific strategies. My point, rather, is that in light of ancient hermeneutical conceptions about humans, matter, and language, we shouldn't consider 1 and 2 Corinthians as passive objects with only immaterial (abstract, cognitive) import. From an ancient perspective, words wield power. Not insignificantly, this appears to be how fourth-century preacher John Chrysostom conceives of epistolarity in his homily on Paul's Corinthian correspondence (*Hom. On 1 Cor.* 7.2). Chrysostom refers to words, or letters (*grammata*), as having power (*dynamis*); he says that anyone who thinks that an epistle is merely inanimate "parchment and ink" (*chartē kai melan*) is "inexperienced" (*apeiros*), whereas the "experienced" (*empeiros*) reader will "hear a living voice, and . . . converse with the absent friend." Chrysostom assumes that Paul's written epistles could evoke a "living voice."[94]

Such critical realignment has a number of interpretive benefits when it comes to 1 and 2 Corinthians. As discussed previously, many scholars reinscribe the argument of Paul's opponents by pitting Paul's authoritative, incorporeal epistolary voice *over and against* his "weak" body (2 Cor. 10.10). I suggest that instead, we imagine the letters effectively engendering a different manifestation of Pauline presence. To pick up Whitaker's description of *ekphrasis* (cited above), we might say that 1 and 2 Corinthians "do the impossible": they produce a *re*-presentation of Paul that is made of words but is also, in a sense, more than words. Paul's letters function as more than merely indicators of his corporeal absence; they make him legible, "leading" him "vividly before the eyes" of the Corinthians. English translations of 1 Corinthians 5.3 render the phrase *hōs parōn* "as if present" (ASV, CEB, ESB, NCV, NIRV, NRS, RSV), or "as though present" (KJV, NKJV, JUB, NLT, NAS, TYN), which implies that the subject is not present, but we could also translate the phrase, "as one who is present." When we read Paul's apparently dichotomous descriptions of himself, we can avoid an absolute distinction between presence/absence by imagining him as both simultaneously: he somehow *is* present in his absence. The letters, in other words, engender an equally powerful form of presence—one I suggest we describe as *epistolary embodiment*.

This concept appears in the Corinthian correspondence itself. Recall the ancient practice of sending letters of recommendation mentioned above. Apparently, the fact that Paul carried no such letter himself was problematic for some Corinthians and may have given them reason to oppose him. Instead of affirming their perception (as he does regarding his "humble" presence versus his "bold" writing), Paul turns his lack of a literal letter to his advantage, playing with literal and metaphorical senses of *epistolē* to assert that, in fact, he doesn't need one. The reason, he writes, is that his Corinthian recipients already embody an epistle:

> Are we beginning to commend ourselves again? Surely, we do not need, as some do, letters of recommendation to you or from you, do we? You your-selves are our letter, written on our hearts, to be known and read by all; and you show that you are a letter of Christ, prepared by us, written not with ink but with the Spirit of the living God, not on tablets of stone but on tablets of human hearts. (2 Cor. 3.1–3)

Paul's depiction of the Corinthians as letters of Christ has caused no small amount of consternation for NT scholars. As Timothy Marquis puts it, "Paul's letter metaphor in verses 1–3 *almost defies neat and orderly interpre-tation,* as the Corinthians are figured as letter, letter recipient, and letter sender. . . . Insofar as the Corinthians are depicted as receivers and sources of Paul's recommendation and introduction, they are likewise depicted as parties in a social transaction with God over the services of the apostle."[95]

The notion of epistolary embodiment I'm advocating has the advantage of maintaining complexity vis-à-vis materiality, textuality, agency, and so-cial relations. Ancient concepts like *ekphrasis* and *enargeia,* and associations of writing with embodment also add a level of tangibility to Mitchell's helpful reframing of Paul's dispute with his opponents in 2 Corinthians. Mitchell describes the issue in terms of competing verbal *portraits* of Paul: "Paul ensures his testimonial against [the Corinthians'] apparently miscon-strued authorial intent by painting a retrospective self-portrait—of himself as letter writer, composing the controversial missive with tears streaming down his face."[96] Reading Paul's epistolary embodiment, or "verbal self-portrait," in light of ancient theories of language like *ekphrasis* suggests that the Corinthian letters constitute "a correspondence course" not just in "tac-tical hermeneutics"—as Mitchell puts it—but also in what we might call *tactile* hermeneutics.[97]

Conceiving of 1 and 2 Corinthians as material agents makes sense of another curiosity, as well: Paul refers repeatedly to his own letters (1 Cor. 5.9, 11; 14.37; 16.21; 2 Cor. 1.13; 2.3–4; 3.1; 7.8, 12; 10.10–11), but his assessments of them appear to conflict. On the one hand, Paul insists that his written words have power and efficacy. He implies that his letters will create the changes he wishes to see in the Corinthian community: "*I write these things while I am away from you, so that* when I come, I may not have to be severe" (2 Cor. 13.10). Elsewhere, he unabashedly marshals divine authority in an ideologically loaded description of his writing: "*What I am writing* to you is a command of the Lord" (1 Cor. 14.37). Similar to the way that, as Glancy argued, Paul conflates his scarred body with the body of Christ and expects "that in the stripes of his own flesh the story of Jesus' passion could be read," Paul conflates his instructions with the Lord's commands and hopes that they, too, will be read as one and the same corpus.[98]

On the other hand, Paul is aware that his letters might not create the change he desires. Immediately after depicting himself as the Lord's legal stenographer in the statement just cited (1 Cor. 14.37), Paul acknowledges that his writing might not be received as such: "Anyone who does not recognize this is not to be recognized" (1 Cor. 14.38). Several times, he indicates that earlier letters didn't work in the ways that he had hoped (see, for example, 1 Cor. 5.9–13; 2 Cor. 2.1–4); his worry that his return to Corinth will be marked by disappointment implies that the current letter might not engender change, either: "For I fear that when I come, I may find you not as I wish" (2 Cor. 12.20). Certainly, these statements attest to Paul's recognition that the Corinthian *recipients* of his letters are unpredictable. But they also suggest that letters themselves elude human control.

Indeed, epistolary realities are rarely as straightforward as rhetoric *about* epistles makes them seem—no less in antiquity than today. Fredrickson, reflecting on ancient discussions about letters, observes, "While joyous letter recipients touted the miraculous appearance of the absent writer, their jubilation often turned to grief as they realized, as they themselves often said, that the fictive presence they held in their hands actually turned them more deeply to the absence of their loved one. . . . Ancient epistolary theory was naïve, or perhaps very cunning, to claim that letters delivered presence and voice without countervailing effects."[99] Letters render Paul present to the Corinthians, but traces of "countervailing effects" (see 2 Cor. 7.7–8) simultaneously trouble the notion that letters can do so in a straightforward, clear way.

The epistolary form instantiates the precariousness of dialogic exchange and invites us "to read the envelope of contingency that surrounds any letter."[100] Importantly, this differs from the common scholarly move of appealing to the "envelope" of contingencies to explain away textual enigmas. By way of illustration, consider scholars' treatments of Paul's assertion, "To all I have become all things" (1 Cor. 9.22). The most common explanation of this claim is that Paul's flexible self-presentation reflects his missionary strategy—in other words, he responds to contextual contingencies and adapts his message according to his audiences' needs. Such formidable Pauline scholars as Hans Conzelmann, Günther Bornkamm, and Gordon Fee all agree that Paul's "apparently chameleonlike stance" represents the justified means by which he spreads the gospel.[101] Yet, this again merely replicates the binaries in the text, instead of interrogating them. Elliott rightly points out that attempts to disambiguate Paul's claim subject him "again to a system dependent upon dichotomy."[102]

How might modern conceptions of letters as passive things serve an ideological purpose for us as critics (even unintentionally)? One possible answer is that conceiving of the letters' contents as Paul's disembodied, immaterial thoughts maintains Pauline apostolic authority. The poststructuralist literary paradigm can help us see how, ideologically, such a methodological move assumes—indeed, amplifies—Pauline apostolic authority, and with it, the NT critic's claims about Paul's message. Here's how it works. As Melanie Johnson-DeBaufre points out, it's difficult to question the authority of Paul the Letter Writer if he's considered to be "someone who claims the authority to write one's life and whose 'mind' is constructed beyond the texts in which his or her 'I' is inscribed."[103] Along the same lines, Fredrickson observes that the tendency to consider Paul's "writing as the [disembodied] expression of his ideas or the contents of his commands" easily lends itself to constructions of Paul as All-Powerful Apostle: "The letter itself necessarily shapes an authoritative Paul, benevolent or otherwise, whose expertise concerning his own mind cannot be surpassed," and whose voice becomes "a faint copy of divine sovereignty."[104]

Notice how this Letter Writer Paul's unsurpassed authority *depends* on his bodily absence. Paul's incorporeal words presuppose his corporal lack. In other words, the presence/absence dichotomy is doing rhetorical work for Paul. When scholars accept such binaries at face value, we're reinscribing the dichotomies at play in ancient rhetorical arguments. Schüssler Fiorenza is right: "As diverse as are [contemporary] interpretations and their implications for the understanding of the community in Corinth, they all follow Paul's dualistic rhetorical strategy without questioning or evaluating it."[105] This is why Fredrickson expands his charge (cited above, that ancient epistolary theorists are misleading) to argue that modern Pauline interpreters are "equally naïve, or again maybe very shrewd, when they claim to have discovered Paul's intentions in a letter and then use the letter to prove their claim."[106] The Disembodied Epistolary Paul's unsurpassed authority, conflated with divine command, serves a legitimating function for those who claim explanatory power.

Instead of pinning Paul down for our own purposes, we can (try to) retain the ambiguities in the text. Elliott, inspired by French theorist Roland Barthes, discerns in Paul's writing "a degree of resistance to deciding between any two options, or among many, with an implicit invitation to his readers to think differently about him and thus also about themselves."[107] In this chapter, I've suggested one way we can think differently about Paul—namely, reading his rhetoric as engendering a complex and different manifestation of Pauline presence. Recasting our conceptions of the (Bold or Weak) Epistolary Paul in this way suggests that when Paul says he is "absent in body" but "present in spirit," he's not emphasizing his physical absence but affirming a different—still *real*—kind of presence (1 Cor. 5.3–5).

In sum, actively resisting modern binaries offers us "an implicit invitation" to think differently about Paul's letters. It's more historically appropriate to consider ancient epistles *not* in either/or terms, but paradoxically as both/and: both mind and matter, both signified absence and embodied presence, both inanimate objects and autonomous things. The poststructuralist literary paradigm also offers us "an implicit invitation" to think differently about scholarly fixations on fixing Paul by turning a critical eye on our own ideological complexities and complicities.

The Corinthian Corpus and Epistolary Embodiment: Concluding Thoughts

Scholarship on 1–2 Corinthians is still in many ways mired in modern dichotomies that operated differently in antiquity (if at all). With respect to epistolarity, scholars remain largely preoccupied with questions about Paul's intentions in writing, the redactional processes "behind" the letters, and the constitution and practices of the Corinthian community receiving them. In this chapter, I've suggested that the poststructuralist literary paradigm exposes anachronisms in the common assumptions about epistolarity that continue to guide NT scholars, and also offers an alternative way forward.

Affect theorists, for example, emphasize the embodied dimensions of producing and responding to literature, reminding us that humans are not rational minds alone, but visceral, sentient beings. Ecocritics, for their part, caution against (mis)reading texts through anthropocentric lenses, inviting an expanded focus that includes nonhuman matter. And thing theorists suggest that inert objects can engender real (as opposed to merely immaterial, cognitive) effects in the world. Drawing these conceptual shifts together, I've suggested that we consider Paul's letters in terms of *epistolary embodiment*. That is, instead of treating a Pauline epistle as a passive stand-in for a (weak or bold) absent apostle, we can think of it as a powerful *alternative* form of presence.

The poststructuralist literary paradigm makes visible aspects of NT texts that might have been occluded by the largely unquestioned presumptions of twentieth-century NT scholars, especially regarding the functions of Paul's epistolary rhetoric in 1–2 Corinthians. When NT scholars treat Paul's letters themselves as *immaterial,* they maintain a problematic stable divide between Paul the Embodied Letter Writer and Paul the Disembodied Epistolary Voice. I've argued instead that ancient views about the powers and abilities of language commend material agency as a useful concept for approaching Paul's letters. Epistles are better understood as *things* that (perhaps inexplicably to us) impact the world and in some way, render Paul both absent from and present with the believers in Corinth. This shift helps us take seriously the extent to which letters remain out of human control.

As Paul puts it, we see only "in obscurity" (1 Cor. 13.12). Counterintuitively for some, the poststructuralist literary paradigm can facilitate more fine-grained descriptions of the places where ancient and contemporary cultures converge and diverge. It can illuminate the role that texts play in advancing or dismantling ideological conceptions and valuing or eliding historical agents. At the same time, poststructuralist literary theory holds scholars ethically responsible for thinking through the complications and implications inherent to our critical claims. One of the ways it does so is by cautioning us against artificially imposing interpretive clarity on texts— acting, that is, as though we "know fully"—when in fact, texts express themselves only "in part."

7 Literary Theory and the New Testament: Concluding Travel

The political thrust of this book, then, is first, to persuade colleagues and students that there is a way out of these predicaments, and second, to offer ideas to those trying to find their way in the labyrinthine land of a humanities without boundaries. Such a land can only unify through travel, through learning foreign languages, through encounters with others.
Mieke Bal

This book began in a bay—specifically, George Guthrie's Bay of Biblical Studies—a chaotic place, filled with boats of scholars who fish for meaning differently and deride one another's "catches" as useless or self-serving. "The bay has gotten crowded," Guthrie declares, "and we must ask what we are to do about it."[1] In a sense, this whole book represents an acceptance of Guthrie's invitation: my claim throughout has been that one thing "we can do about it" is travel upstream to explore the rich intellectual resources available to us in the Lake of Literary Studies.

I trust that by now, it's clear that I believe NT scholars have yet to take full advantage of all that literary scholarship has to offer, and that this is not just unfortunate, but dire for our discipline. Literary matters are at the heart of NT interpretation. It's a "labyrinthine land," as Mieke Bal puts it, but "such a land can only unify through travel." I hope to have convinced you that travelling with literary theory can be a magnificent, enlivening, and illuminating adventure.

Let's look back for a moment at the journey that this book has taken. In chapter 1, we sought common ground—some shared intellectual space in which to stage a meeting between literary and biblical studies. To get our bearings, we used Meyer Abrams's four aesthetic orientations (universe-oriented mimetic approaches, author-oriented expressive approaches, audience-oriented pragmatic approaches, and text-oriented objective approaches) to categorize different forms of literary criticism, and we identified three major sets of concerns (hermeneutical, evaluative, and metadisciplinary) that have always animated literary theory. In that chapter, our peregrinations took us from literary studies to biblical studies, from biblical studies to literary studies ... there and back again. That back-and-forth rhythm typifies the interdisciplinary travel I've been commending all along.

With chapter 2, we ventured with literary formalists into the *terra firma* of literary form. Chapter 3 took us stargazing for signs and symbols with the structuralists. In chapter 4, poststructuralists pushed us to take a step back and contemplate shifting human perceptions of language, and of the universe itself. Then, in chapters 5 and 6, we wound our way through NT literature, with special stops in the Synoptic Gospels and Paul's Corinthian corpus. A number of different companions accompanied us along the way: New Historicists and New Formalists joined us in chapter 5, and affect theorists and ecocritics came along in chapter 6. All in all, we've covered a lot of ground.

Now, finally, we come to the end of our journey. These chapters have offered glimpses of the many ways that literary theory and literary criticism can deepen and enrich our understandings of NT literature and the worlds from which that literature emerged. My hope is that these glimpses have piqued your interest in pursuing your own journey with contemporary literary studies. If this book has made you want to travel on with literary theory, it will have served its purpose.

At the risk of being overly didactic, permit me to offer some parting advice.

Guideposts for the Journey

First, pursue a journey of true interdisciplinarity. Don't simply stop by a particular kind of literary criticism, learn a few terms, and move on—like a tourist who visits the Eiffel Tower and learns a little French to use at a dinner party, but never learns the culture. As I once heard a colleague comment after a candidate job talk, "Well, that was just traditional scholarship with a little postcolonialism sprinkled on top." Make your engagements with literary theory and literary criticism substantive and rigorous so that they can also be transformative.

The boundaries of literary studies are constantly shifting. In my view, this is not a weakness, but a strength. The fact that literary studies resides flexibly at the interstices of many disciplines means that it has richer potential to advance NT scholarship. Of course, NT interpretation has always involved multiple disciplines (history, philology, and theology, among others), but the relationships between those disciplines are often unclear. Sometimes, this means that NT scholars engage multiple discourses in an additive rather than integrative way. Real interdisciplinary engagement with literary studies allows us to expand our interpretive horizons without sacrificing critical precision. In other words, literary theory and literary criticism offer NT interpreters a way to "move from a muddled multidisciplinarity to a productive interdisciplinarity."[2]

Second, if I may offer a warning: remember that scholarly rhetoric about literary studies is rhetorical. It seeks to persuade. Be prepared for these attempts at persuasion, just as a traveler who happens upon a lively open-air market can anticipate vendors loudly pushing their wares. NT scholars' contradictory evaluations of literary approaches that I've highlighted throughout the book illustrate how rhetoric *about* literary theory is itself rhetorical. NT critics' associations with, assumptions about, and assessments of literary approaches are rarely, if ever, neutral.

All scholarly rhetoric seeks to persuade, even in discourses that are purportedly objective. Thus it is that Kenneth Burke can refer to the "necessarily suasive nature of even the most unemotional scientific nomenclatures."[3] The point to notice here is that evaluations of literary studies—my own included—are designed to persuade their audiences of their positions. I hope to have persuaded you not to take scholarly rhetoric *about* literary theory or literary criticism—my own included—at face value, but to think carefully about the assumptions on which they're built and the functions they fulfill.

Finally, don't be afraid to go to new places, but don't forget where you've been. NT scholars have a fair amount of ambivalence about "new" versus "old" interpretations. On the one hand, I often hear biblical scholars sigh, with the author of Ecclesiastes: "Of making many books there is no end, and much study is a weariness of the flesh" (12.12). Nevertheless, the expectation is ubiquitous—from publishers to dissertation advisors to tenure and promotion committees—that NT scholars will advance "new" interpretations. Contributions to NT scholarship are judged in part by the degree to which they convince others to consider fresh perspectives and as-yet unarticulated arguments. Newness pushes the field forward. On the other hand, the "new" can be fetishized to such a degree that previous contributions are denigrated, dismissed, or forgotten altogether. Sensing danger, some defend the "old" views, at times vehemently in person or in print, at times quietly in staunch rejections of so-called bad scholarship. Newness threatens consensus.

Of course, we need both tradition and innovation. The conviction that "there is nothing new under the sun" didn't stop the author of Ecclesiastes from writing something new, from offering his perspective on and to the world (1.6). Biblical literature embodies the cultural moment in which it arises. In this, it's like all literature—looking ahead to new possibility and looking back to lessons from the past. Literature can challenge the presumptions of our predecessors, pushing us to imagine new possibilities and inspiring us to pursue new ways of being. And literature can uphold the status quo, authorizing us to cling to our biases and look away from injustice. It's a "labyrinthine land ... [that] can only unify through travel." Travelling with contemporary literary theory can offer fresh insights, but as I've also sought to show throughout this book, every recent development in literary studies is shaped by previous literary paradigms.

Concluding Thoughts on Concluding Travel

Explorations of literary theory and literary criticism can seem circuitous, disorienting, even arduous at times. Still, I like Culler's reflection on the literary-theoretical journey: "This point of arrival," he writes, "is very different from the point of departure." This is true even when arriving means returning home to the very same place whence we departed. Herein lies the paradox inherent to both text and travel: we need to leave home in order to return. When we do, we often find that home has—and we ourselves have—changed. The familiar has become new. Culler is right: "As the genre of the picaresque has long shown us, you have to leave home and, often, to travel a long way." This is the way "to make your fortune."[4]

I hope this book has alleviated potential concerns about leaving home. I hope you're convinced that the journey is worth the effort—that there is, in fact, fortune to be found. I hope that the book motivates and facilitates future scholarly innovation and collaboration in literary interpretation of the NT. I also hope that more NT scholars will look to literary studies as we seek to understand the ineluctable power of NT literature and come to terms with the implications of our own interpretive endeavors.

What's at stake when we read the literature of the NT is no less than what makes human beings who we are—where we have been, where we are headed, and how we should relate to one another and the rest of the world along the way. Literary analysis is both pressing and necessary because the literature we interpret represents, for so many, the word and the will of God. There's an urgency to this journey.

Above all, therefore, I hope that after reading this book, you want to embark on your own explorations through the New Testament's literary landscapes. The itinerary is inexhaustible.

"In my end is my beginning," wrote T. S. Eliot in "Four Quartets."

May this end be your beginning.

Abbreviations

AB	Anchor Bible
ANRW	*Aufstieg und Niedergang der römischen Welt*
AsTJ	*Asbury Theological Journal*
B&CT	*The Bible & Critical Theory*
BibInt	*Biblical Interpretation*
BSac	*Bibliotheca Sacra*
CBQ	*Catholic Biblical Quarterly*
CI	*Critical Inquiry*
ETL	*Ephemerides Theologicae Lovanienses*
HNT	*Handbuch zum Neuen Testament*
Int	*Interpretation*
JAAR	*Journal of the American Academy of Religion*
JBL	*Journal of Biblical Literature*
JECS	*Journal of Early Christian Studies*
JR	*Journal of Religion*
JSNT	*Journal for the Study of the New Testament*
JSOT	*Journal for the Study of the Old Testament*
LQ	*Lutheran Quarterly*
MLQ	*Modern Language Quarterly*
Neot	*Neotestamentica*
NICNT	New International Commentary on the New Testament
NovT	*Novum Testamentum*
NTS	*New Testament Studies*
PMLA	*Publications of the Modern Language Association*
RevExp	*Review and Expositor*

TAPA	*Transactions of the American Philological Association*
TynBul	*Tyndale Bulletin*
TZ	*Theologische Zeitschrift*
USQR	*Union Seminary Quarterly Review*
ZNW	*Zeitschrift für die neutestamentliche Wissenschaft und die Kunde der Älteren Kirche*

Notes

Introduction

1. Guthrie, "Boats in the Bay," 24.
2. Guthrie, "Boats in the Bay," 25.
3. Guthrie, "Boats in the Bay," 24.
4. Moore and Sherwood, *Invention of the Biblical Scholar*, 11.
5. Adam, *Postmodern Biblical Criticism*, vii.
6. Culler, *Literary in Theory*, 3.
7. Emphasis added. Culler, *Literary in Theory*, 4.
8. Emphasis added. Franklin and Sparks, *Life of Benjamin Franklin*, 156.
9. Eagleton, *Literary Theory*, viii.
10. Culler, *Literary in Theory*, 4.
11. Dickens, *Old Curiosity Shop*, 181.
12. Moore and Sherwood, *Invention of the Biblical Scholar*, 8.
13. Moore and Sherwood, *Invention of the Biblical Scholar*, 41.
14. Greenblatt and Gunn, "Introduction," 5.
15. The scholarly literature on this question is immense.
16. Wellek and Warren, *Theory of Literature*, 22.
17. Ellis, *Theory of Literary Criticism*, 44.
18. This is why, in my view, the idea that we can read "the Bible as literature" simply needs no defense; cf. Ryken, *How to Read*; Ryken, *Words of Life*.
19. All written poetry and prose communicates, even if its message is that it is meant to communicate nothing. See, e.g., Shillingsburg, "Text as Communication."
20. Emphasis added. Culler, *Literary in Theory*, 15, 4.
21. Goulimari, *Literary Criticism and Theory*; also see, similarly, Selden, *Theory of Criticism*; and Moore, *Gospel Jesuses*, 3.
22. Emphasis added. Greenblatt and Gunn, "Introduction," 5.
23. Too, *Idea of Ancient Criticism*, 2.
24. Bockmuehl, *Seeing the Word*, 48–49.
25. Eagleton, *Literary Theory*, viii.
26. Spencer, "Acts and Modern Literary Approaches," 412.
27. De Jong, *Narratology and Classics*, v.

28. I consider the four canonical Gospels and Acts to be narrative, the Apocalypse of John to be a narrative embedded in an epistle, and the rest of the books of the NT to be epistles. For more on genre, see especially chapters 1 and 3.

29. Poland, "The New Criticism," 459–460.

30. During, "The Postcolonial Aesthetic," 498.

31. Ryan, "Introduction to the Encyclopedia of Literary and Cultural Theory," xiii.

32. Thiele, "New Formalism(s)," 16.

33. Bal, *Travelling Concepts*, 14.

34. Pollock, "Golden Gate," 194.

35. Ashton, "Narrative Criticism," 145.

36. Guthrie, "Boats in the Bay," 24.

Chapter 1. Biblical Studies and Literary Studies

1. Guthrie, "Boats in the Bay," 24.

2. Soulen and Soulen, *Handbook of Biblical Criticism*, 105.

3. Moore, *Bible in Theory*, 375.

4. Moore, *God's Beauty Parlor*, 9.

5. Anderson and Moore, "Introduction," 4.

6. Hawkins, "Bible as Literature," 197. See Norton, *English Bible as Literature*; also, Royalty, *Origin of Heresy*. Medieval interpreters like Augustine, Aquinas, and Dante adapted the work of Neoplatonists like Plotinus in their explorations of figurative and literal scriptural signification. The third-century philosopher Plotinus revived Plato's view that literature mimetically reflects—and thus for Plato, is inherently inferior to—an ideal Form, but Plotinus validated literary art as a reflection of both eternal essence and the artist's creativity and wisdom.

7. See Darwin, *Origin of Species;* and Schleiermacher, *Hermeneutics*, esp. 216. Scholarly approaches inevitably shape the object of study: conceptions of the Bible itself shifted during the Enlightenment, as well. Jonathan Sheehan has traced four distinct interpretive modes (philology, morality, historiography, and aesthetics) by which, he argues, Enlightenment thinkers essentially created separate Bibles—the *textual/philological* Bible, the *pedagogical* Bible, the *historical* Bible, and the *poetic* Bible. According to Sheehan, these diverse Bibles were united "beneath a single enormous banner," creating an "Enlightenment Bible." Sheehan, *Enlightenment Bible*, 220.

8. Frei, *Eclipse of Biblical Narrative*, 282.

9. Moore and Sherwood, *Invention of the Biblical Scholar*, x. On this shift, see, e.g., Legaspi, *Death of Scripture*.

10. Emphasis original. Petersen, *Literary Criticism*, 10.

11. Koch, *Growth of the Biblical Tradition*.

12. Among many examples, Daniel Patte distinguishes between structural analysis and literary criticism (*Structural Exegesis*, 1–2). Decades later, William Baird's

monumental three-volume account of NT scholarship continues to employ "literary criticism" in this way. See, e.g., Baird, *New Testament Research,* 279.

13. Muilenburg's address was published as "Form Criticism and Beyond," 8.

14. Standard accounts notwithstanding, Muilenburg wasn't the first to draw attention to the literary or rhetorical dimensions of biblical texts. Even in medieval times (often falsely perceived as rhetoric's Dark Ages), writers produced treatises on biblical rhetoric (see, e.g., several examples in Miller, Prosser, and Benson, *Readings in Medieval Rhetoric*). In the modern period, as well, biblical scholars were already analyzing biblical texts from a literary perspective. In an earlier article, Muilenburg himself named NT scholars who had been doing so. "Literary Forms," 40. See, e.g., Amos Wilder's 1955 SBL presidential address, published as "Ancient Rhetoric."

15. Beardslee, *Literary Criticism;* Petersen, *Literary Criticism;* see also Maier and Tollers, "Introduction"; and Frye, "Gospel Criticism."

16. On the Gospels as Hellenistic historiography, see, e.g., van Unnik, "Luke's Second Book." On Luke-Acts as apologetic historiography à la Josephus's *Jewish Antiquities,* see Sterling, *Historiography and Self-Definition.* On Greco-Roman *Bioi,* see Burridge, *What Are the Gospels?* Other proposals include institutional history (e.g., Cancik, "Culture, Religion, and Institutions," and "Hairesis, Diatribe, Ekklesia"); rhetorical history (e.g., Yamada, "Rhetorical History"); and oral history (Byrskog, *Story as History*); Harrington, *Hebrews,* 5. Most discussions of Revelation cite John Collins's definition of the apocalyptic genre in "Morphology of a Genre," 9, and the two key additional points in Adela Yarbro Collins, "Apocalypticism," 7.

17. On the challenges involved in identifying poetry in the NT, see, e.g., Peppard, "How to Do Things with Indentations."

18. François Bovon, "La structure canonique," argues that this two-part structure is grounded in and arose out of the nature of the Christian faith itself (i.e., event = narration and declaration = epistle).

19. See, e.g., Betz, "Literary Composition"; Betz, *Galatians;* Betz, *Second Corinthians 8 and 9;* and Betz, *Sermon on the Mount.* See also Kennedy, *New Testament Interpretation;* Stowers, *Diatribe;* and Stowers, *Rereading of Romans.* Betz's thesis is disputed by, e.g., Classen, "Paulus," 15–27.

20. Blomberg, *Parables,* 171; Perrin, *Symbol and Metaphor,* 145–146; D'Entrevernes, *Signes et paraboles;* Via, *Parables;* Crossan, *In Parables;* Crossan, "Servant Parables"; Crossan, "Parable and Example."

21. Alter, *Art of Biblical Narrative;* Sternberg, *Poetics of Biblical Narrative;* Rhoads and Michie, *Mark as Story;* Culpepper, *Anatomy of the Fourth Gospel;* Kingsbury, *Matthew as Story;* Tannehill, *Narrative Unity of Luke-Acts.* Daniel Patte was a particularly strong proponent of structuralist exegesis. See, e.g., Patte, *Structural Exegesis;* Patte, *Structural Commentary;* and Patte, *Structural Introduction.*

22. Pearson, "New Testament Literary Criticism," 243.

23. Tannehill, *Sword of His Mouth*, 7.

24. Petersen, "Literary Criticism in Biblical Studies," 35; Haynes and McKenzie, *To Each Its Own Meaning* (interestingly, the 2013 self-proclaimed "sequel" to the latter volume abandons these divisions; see Kaltner and McKenzie, *New Meanings*); Möller, "Renewing Historical Criticism," 149.

25. Muilenburg, "Literary Forms," 42. See also Pearson, "New Testament Literary Criticism," 249; Frye, *Anatomy of Criticism*, 315; Wilder, *Early Christian Rhetoric*, xxv (emphasis added); and Longman, *Literary Approaches*, 5.

26. Aune, "Literary Criticism," 126, 133.

27. See, e.g., Long, *Ancient Rhetoric and Paul's Apology*.

28. Emphasis added. Gamble, *Textual History*, 12.

29. Emphasis added. Mitchell opposes her methodology to those who argue for unity based on *theological* coherence. Mitchell, *Paul and the Rhetoric of Reconciliation*, 5.

30. Koch, *Growth of the Biblical Tradition*, 69.

31. Rhoads, "Narrative Criticism and the Gospel of Mark," 413.

32. Witherington, *New Testament Rhetoric*, 131–132; cf. several contributions in Porter and Dyer, *Paul and Ancient Rhetoric*.

33. Emphasis added. Porter, "Literary Approaches," 78.

34. Alter, *Art of Biblical Narrative*, 13.

35. Moore, "Modest Manifesto," 5.

36. Elliott, *Reconfiguring Mark's Jesus*, 4, 24.

37. Emphasis added. Petersen, *Literary Criticism*, 18.

38. Emphasis added. Wilder, *Early Christian Rhetoric*, xxvii.

39. Emphases added. Nadella, *Dialogue Not Dogma*, 5.

40. Emphasis added. Leitch, *Literary Criticism*, 33.

41. Leitch, *Literary Criticism*, 33.

42. Emphasis added. Abrams, *Mirror and the Lamp*, 5.

43. Richards, *Principles of Literary Criticism*, 2.

44. Richards, *Principles of Literary Criticism*, chapter 2. Also see, e.g., Elliott and Attridge, *Theory after "Theory"*; Williams, "The Posttheory Generation"; McQuillan et al., *Post-Theory*; and Bové, *In the Wake of Theory*.

45. Abrams, *Mirror and the Lamp*, 3, 3–5.

46. Abrams, *Mirror and the Lamp*, 14.

47. Abrams, *Mirror and the Lamp*, 22.

48. Wordsworth, "Preface to the Second Edition of *Lyrical Ballads*," 435.

49. Hirsch, *Validity in Interpretation*, 5.

50. Abrams, *Mirror and the Lamp*, 26.

51. Ricoeur, *From Text to Action*, 17.

52. Abrams, *Mirror and the Lamp*, 15.

53. Emphasis added. Sidney, "Apology for Poetry," 158. Sidney was drawing on Horace's *Ars Poetica*.

54. This line has long been the subject of scholarly debate.
55. Leitch, "Primer of Recent Critical Theories," 140.
56. Abrams, *Mirror and the Lamp*, 7, 6.
57. Abrams, *Mirror and the Lamp*, 6.
58. Emphasis added. Abrams, *Mirror and the Lamp*, 4.
59. Auerbach, *Mimesis*, 14.
60. Wilder, *Early Christian Rhetoric*, 125.
61. *International Standard Bible Encyclopedia*, s.v., "Rhetorical Criticism"; Hays, *Reading Backwards*, 56–57.
62. Merenlahti, *Poetics*, 21.
63. Rhoads, "Narrative Criticism and the Gospel of Mark," 412. See also, e.g., Tannehill, *Narrative Unity;* Darr, *On Character Building*; Talbert, *Reading Luke;* Malbon and Berlin, *Characterization in Biblical Literature;* Tolbert, "How the Gospel of Mark Builds Character"; Aletti, *L'art de raconter Jésus-Christ;* Marguerat and Bourquin, *Pour lire les récits bibliques;* and Meynet, *L'Évangile selon saint Luc.*
64. Fowler, *Let the Reader Understand*, 48; Gowler, "Hospitality and Characterization," 214; Camery-Hoggatt, *Irony in Mark's Gospel*, x; Powell, *What Is Narrative Criticism?*, 97.
65. Fowler, *Let the Reader Understand*, 23; Maxwell, *Hearing between the Lines*, 1.
66. Powell, *What Is Narrative Criticism?*, 91–96; emphasis added to Elliott, *Reconfiguring*, 5; Moore and Sherwood, *Invention of the Biblical Scholar*, x.
67. Emphasis added. Resseguie, "Reader-Response Criticism," 309.
68. Along these lines, it is telling that the critic Moore commends for being theoretically and practically consistent is Temma Berg, a literary critic who is "unacquainted with New Testament scholarship." Moore, *Literary Criticism*, 104.
69. Moore, *Literary Criticism*, 104.
70. Emphasis added. Resseguie, "Reader-Response Criticism," 309.
71. Moore, *Literary Criticism*, 66–67.
72. Similarly, Moore later notes with disappointment that although the contemporary reader and the "textually prescribed reader" jockey for position in Gary Phillips's "History and Text," the "contest swiftly goes to the latter." Moore, *Literary Criticism*, 104.
73. Powell, *What Is Narrative Criticism?*, 12.
74. Tannehill, "Disciples in Mark," 394.
75. Shively, *Apocalyptic Imagination*, 57. For a more recent (re)consideration of authorial intent, see Shively, "Intentionality and Narrative Worldmaking."
76. Kennedy, *New Testament Interpretation*, 11.
77. Kennedy, *New Testament Interpretation*, 3, 5.
78. Culler, *Literary in Theory*, 4.
79. Moore, *Bible in Theory*, 375.
80. Emphasis added. Culler, *Literary in Theory*, 3.
81. Emphasis added. Culler, *Literary in Theory*, 3.

82. Emphasis added. Lin, *Erotic Life of Manuscripts*, 146.
83. Barton, *Reading the Old Testament*, 235.
84. Stevenson, *Dr. Jekyll and Mr. Hyde*, 50.
85. Goldhill, "Failure of Exemplarity," 51.
86. Fox, *Beyond Health*, 180.
87. Moore and Sherwood, *Invention of the Biblical Scholar*, 15.
88. See, e.g., Johnson-DeBaufre, *Jesus among Her Children*, 11–17; and Schüssler Fiorenza, *Rhetoric and Ethic*, 196–197.
89. Schüssler Fiorenza, "Ethics of Biblical Interpretation," 4.
90. Bultmann, "Ist voraussetzungslose Exegese möglich?"; Guthrie, "Boats in the Bay," 27; Barton, *Reading the Old Testament*, 235. In his postscript to *Derrida's Bible*, Barton recants his earlier assessment to an extent. Barton, "Beliebigkeit."
91. Moore and Sherwood, *Invention of the Biblical Scholar*, 130.
92. Schleiermacher, *Hermeneutics*, 96.
93. Gadamer, *Truth and Method*, 295.
94. Ricoeur, *Freud and Philosophy*, 8.
95. Geertz, *After the Fact*, 114.
96. Eagleton, *Literary Theory*, viii.
97. Frye, "Age of Sensibility," 130–131.
98. Frye, *Anatomy of Criticism*, 23.
99. Crossan, *In Parables*, 13.
100. Emphasis original. Stein, *Parables of Jesus*, 69.
101. Emphasis original. Hays, *Conversion of the Imagination*, 198.
102. Emphasis added. Wilder, *Early Christian Rhetoric*, xxvii.
103. Stein, *Parables of Jesus*, 69.
104. Spencer, "Acts and Modern Literary Approaches," 412.
105. Lentricchia, "Last Will and Testament," 59.
106. Leitch, *Literary Criticism*, 26–27.
107. Emphasis added. Carey, *Jesus' Cry from the Cross*, 34; van Seters, "Response," 6; emphasis added to Hatina, "Intertextuality and Historical Criticism," 29–31.
108. Powell, *What Is Narrative Criticism?*, 201.
109. Emphasis added. Ashton, "Narrative Criticism," 141, 159, 165.
110. Ashton, "Narrative Criticism," 144, 145.

Chapter 2. What Makes the Stone Stony

1. On the related Swiss-German tradition (*Werkinterpretation*), see Enders, *Die Werkinterpretation;* on the French iteration of what we will discuss as "close reading," see, e.g., Blechmann, "Probleme der Explication Française." Vincent Leitch describes over six different formalisms in *American Literary Criticism*, esp. in chapters 2, 3, and 9.
2. Strier, "How Formalism Became a Dirty Word," 208.
3. Poland, *Literary Criticism*, 4–5.

4. Strier, "How Formalism Became a Dirty Word," 208.

5. De Man, *Allegories of Reading*, 4.

6. Emphasis added. Poland, *Literary Criticism*, 4–5.

7. Some parts of this discussion reflect portions of Dinkler, "New Formalist Approach."

8. Baldick, *Criticism and Literary Theory*, 10–11.

9. Steiner, *Russian Formalism*, 9. Roman Jakobson is perhaps most responsible for bringing Russian formalism—and, ultimately, structuralism—to the West. After starting the Moscow Linguistic Circle in 1915, Jakobson emigrated from Moscow to Prague, where he helped to found the Prague Linguistic Circle with other formalist scholars like René Wellek, then went on to Paris, where he influenced seminal structuralists Claude Lévi-Strauss and Roland Barthes, and finally settled in the United States, teaching literature in New York and Boston.

10. Erlich, *Russian Formalism*, 171–172.

11. Eichenbaum, "Theory of the 'Formal Method,'" 103.

12. Emphasis added. Žirmunskij, "K voprosu o 'formal'nom metode,'" 154. English is cited in Steiner, "Russian Formalism," 12.

13. Quoted in Steiner, *Russian Formalism*, 23.

14. Emphasis added. Shklovsky, "Art as Technique" (also translated elsewhere as "Art as Device"), 12.

15. Quoted in Bakhtin and Medvedev, *Formal Method*, 117. This thoroughgoing critique of formalism was originally published in 1929.

16. Jakobson, "Dominant," 751.

17. Tynyanov, "Literary Fact," 33.

18. Dodd, *Parables*, 5. Dodd specifically critiques form criticism in "Framework of the Gospel Narratives."

19. Blomberg, *Parables*, 171.

20. Jülicher, *Die Gleichnisreden Jesu*. Against Jülicher, see his contemporaries Bugge, *Die Haupt-Parabeln Jesu*; Fiebig, *Altjüdische Gleichnisse*; and Fiebig, *Die Gleichnisreden Jesu*.

21. Dodd, *Parables*; Jeremias, *Parables*; Cadoux, *Parables*; Funk, *Language*; Via, *Parables*; Via, *Kerygma and Comedy*.

22. Via, *Parables*, ix. See also, e.g., Hedrick, *Parables as Poetic Fictions*; Jones, *Art and Truth*; Crossan, *In Parables*, esp. 10–22; and Resseguie, "Defamiliarization," esp. 151.

23. Emphasis added. Zimmermann, *Puzzling the Parables*, 31.

24. Funk, *Language*, 4; Funk, *Parables and Presence*, esp. 26–107.

25. See, e.g., Reed, *Dialogues of the Word*; Nadella, *Dialogue Not Dogma*; Boer, *Bakhtin and Genre Theory*.

26. Bakhtin, *Rabelais*, 8–10.

27. Nadella, *Dialogue Not Dogma*, 109, 110.

28. Leon Trotsky's major critique of Russian formalism was first published in 1926. Trotsky, *Literature and Revolution.*

29. Eichenbaum, English cited in Steiner, *Russian Formalism*, 2.

30. Emphasis added. Tynyanov, "On Literary Evolution," 162.

31. Stalin reportedly said this in a speech at Maxim Gorky's home on October 26, 1932. Quoted in Elliott, "Engineers of the Human Soul," 6.

32. Dubrow, "Foreword," xi. Standard accounts of the movement are now being updated to reflect these distinctions. See, e.g., Donald J. Childs's recent updating of his earlier entry to *The Encyclopedia of Contemporary Literary Theory*, s.v., "New Criticism"; and Childs, *Birth of New Criticism.*

33. Spingarn, "New Criticism," 29.

34. Interestingly, though, Ransom discusses critics who are not the ones typically associated with New Criticism today. Ransom, *New Criticism.*

35. Matterson, "New Criticism," 166.

36. Wellek himself later wrote that *Understanding Poetry* did more "than any other single book to make the techniques of the New Criticism available in the classrooms of American colleges and universities and to present the techniques of analysis as something to be learned and imitated." *Encyclopedia of World Literature in the 20th Century*, s.v., "Literary Criticism."

37. Lentricchia, *After the New Criticism.*

38. Eliot, introduction to *The Wheel of Fire*, xxii.

39. But cf. E. D. Hirsch's staunch defense of authorial intention in *Validity of Interpretation*, and the discussion of Hirsch in Lentricchia, *After the New Criticism.*

40. Emphasis original. Wimsatt and Beardsley, "Affective Fallacy," 21.

41. MacLeish, "Ars Poetica," 107.

42. Matterson, "New Criticism," 172.

43. Culler, *Literary in Theory*, 9.

44. See, e.g., Eliot, "Tradition and the Individual Talent"; Wellek and Warren, *Theory of Literature*, 39–40.

45. Wimsatt and Beardsley, "Intentional Fallacy," 4; Wimsatt and Beardsley, "Affective Fallacy," 21.

46. Wellek, "Literary Theory," 6.

47. Wimsatt and Beardsley, "Intentional Fallacy," 4, 5.

48. Though we want to avoid overly facile equations of formalism with Kantian aesthetics or some generic concept of beauty, this New Critical view of literary art overlaps with Kant's argument that the "purposiveness" of nature gives rise to aesthetic judgment. On Kant, see, e.g., Crawford, *Kant's Aesthetic Theory;* Kaufman, "Red Kant," and Kaufman, "Negatively Capable Dialectics."

49. Via, *Parables*, 70.

50. Scott, *Jesus, Symbol-Maker*, 11.

51. Malbon, "Narrative Criticism," 25.

52. Wimsatt and Beardsley, "Intentional Fallacy," 5.

53. New Critics did expand previous notions of literary canon to include modernist literature.

54. Moore and Sherwood, *Invention of the Biblical Scholar*, x.

55. Ransom, "Criticism, Inc.," 328.

56. Eichenbaum, "Theory of the 'Formal Method,'" 103.

57. In contrast to American New Critics who turned away from scientific discourse, Richards was *also* committed to science. His two most influential works were *Principles of Literary Criticism* and *Practical Criticism*.

58. Ransom, "Poetry," 139. See also Brooks, "Metaphor and the Tradition," 1–17.

59. Emphasis original. Richards, *Practical Criticism*, 174.

60. Petersen, *Literary Criticism*, 12. Classic studies in form criticism include Jolles, *Einfache Formen;* Seeberg, *Die Didache;* Dibelius, *From Tradition to Gospel;* Bultmann, *Synoptic Tradition;* and Schmidt, *Der Rahmen der Geschichte Jesu.* Introductions to form criticism abound. See, e.g., Buss, *Biblical Form Criticism; Anchor Bible Dictionary*, s.v. "Form Criticism: New Testament"; and Berger, "Hellenistische Gattungen."

61. Dibelius, *From Tradition to Gospel*, 3.

62. Of course, this can easily collapse into circular reasoning, since any discrete formal categories are created by the form critic based on the texts. Bultmann admitted this. *Synoptic Tradition*, 5.

63. Joseph Fitzmyer, an ardent defender of historical criticism, lists source and redaction criticisms as refinements of historical criticism, not strictly examples of it. Fitzmyer, *Interpretation of Scripture*, 64–66.

64. Brooks and Warren, *Understanding Poetry*, 18.

65. Muilenburg, "Form Criticism and Beyond," 9.

66. Rhoads, "Narrative Criticism," 413; Malbon, *Mark's Jesus*, 251.

67. Pearson, "New Testament Literary Criticism," 249; emphasis added to Aune, "Literary Criticism," 126, 133.

68. Wellek and Warren, *Theory of Literature*, 157.

69. Cited in Jakobson, *Language in Literature*, 47, 49.

70. Russian formalists were not the first to consider literary developments in evolutionary terms. French thinkers at the turn of the twentieth century discussed literary forms in terms of what Thomas Beebee later called a "genre as species" approach. *Ideology of Genre*, 2–3. See Brunetière, *L'évolution de la poésie lyrique;* and Brunetière, *L'évolution des genres;* also see Manly, "Literary Form"; and, more recently, Neumann and Nünning, "Einleitung."

71. NT form critics followed the lead of Hebrew Bible scholar Gunkel, *Einleitung in die Psalmen.*

72. Overbeck, "Über die Anfänge der patristischen Literatur," 429.

73. Petersen, *Literary Criticism*, 12. Still, form criticism arose out of Romanticism's interest in folklore, which itself corrected many Enlightenment assumptions.

74. Emphasis original. Bultmann, *Synoptic Tradition*, 347–348.

75. See, e.g., Dibelius's discussion of intermediate forms (*Mischformen*), which have formal features from more than one generic category. Dibelius, *From Tradition to Gospel*, 43.

76. Bousset, *Kyrios Christos*, 98–106; Bultmann, "Zur Frage des Wunders," 215. See also Bultmann, *Synoptic Tradition*, 370.

77. Twelftree, *Jesus the Miracle Worker*, 35.

78. Klauck, "Adolf Jülicher," 111; cf. Scott, *Hear Then the Parable*, 72. To Jülicher's similitudes (*Gleichnisse*), parables (*Parabeln*), and exemplary stories (*Beispieler-zählungen*), Bultmann added the category of figures (*Bildworte*). *Synoptic Tradition*, 174–179.

79. See, e.g., Cadoux, *Parables of Jesus*; Jeremias, *Parables of Jesus*, esp. 20–21; and Cadoux, "Zum Gleichnis vom verlorenen Sohn."

80. Jeremias, *Parables of Jesus*, 25. Kingsbury, "Parable Interpretation," 589. A more recent self-proclaimed revival of Jeremias is Blomberg, *Interpreting the Parables*, 10.

81. See, e.g., Derrida, "The Law of Genre"; and Wellek, "Evolution in Literary History."

82. Kingsbury, "Parable Interpretation," 587–588. See also Kingsbury, "Ernst Fuchs' Existentialist Interpretation."

83. Funk, *Language*. Funk's conception of "authentic" (unadulterated, unconventional) language also shows Heideggerian influence, though Funk ignores Heidegger's specific grounding of authentic language in the German people (*Volk*) and the Greco-Germanic linguistic tradition. Crossan, *In Parables*. Similarly, Kingsbury describes his own approach as a form of redaction criticism. "Parable Interpretation," 596.

84. Kelley, *Racializing Jesus*, 180. See, e.g., Via, *Kerygma and Comedy*.

85. Funk, *Language*, 4; Funk, *Parables and Presence*, esp. 26–107.

86. Dodd, *Parables*, 5.

87. A.-J. Levine advocates defamiliarization of common (Christian) readings of the parables. *Short Stories by Jesus*, esp. 25. See also Resseguie, "Defamiliarization," esp. 151; and Cronjé, "Defamiliarization."

88. See, e.g., Bultmann, *Synoptic Tradition*, esp. 371–374; and Bultmann, "Gospels," 89.

89. Emphasis original. Bultmann, *Theology of the New Testament*, 1:86; Bultmann, *Synoptic Tradition*, 373–374.

90. Burridge, *What Are the Gospels?*, 11.

91. See, e.g., Bornkamm, *Jesus of Nazareth*, 218; and Wellek and Warren, *Theory of Literature*, 157.

92. Malbon, "Narrative Criticism," 25.

93. Poland, *Literary Criticism*, 4. In the literary field, critiques of New Criticism grew especially strong in the 1970s. See, e.g., Graff, *Poetic Statement*; and Graff, *Literature against Itself*, esp. 129–149.

94. Kjärgaard, *Metaphor and Parable*, 173.

95. Frye, "Literary Perspective," 194.

96. Culpepper, *Anatomy of the Fourth Gospel*, 6.

97. Reinhartz, "Building Skyscrapers on Toothpicks," 59–60.

98. See, e.g., Tannehill, *Narrative Unity*. Cadbury (*Making of Luke-Acts*) appears to have been the first to hyphenate the two books. Other major contributions to this discussion include Verheyden, *Unity of Luke-Acts*; O'Toole, *Unity of Luke's Theology;* Parsons and Pervo, *Rethinking the Unity;* and Walters, *Assumed Authorial Unity.*

99. Tannehill, *Narrative Unity*, 1.

100. Holladay, *Acts*, 34–36.

101. Holladay, *Acts*, 67.

102. O'Brien, *Use of Scripture*, 2.

103. Farrer, *St. Matthew and St. Mark*, 18.

104. Schmidt first popularized the distinction between *Hochliteratur* and *Kleinliteratur* in "Die Stellung der Evangelien."

105. Wilder, *Early Christian Rhetoric*, 36.

106. Emphasis added. Porter, "Literary Approaches," 84.

107. See, e.g., Dibelius, *From Tradition to Gospel*, 1; Bultmann, *Synoptic Tradition*, 371–372. Form critics were not the first to evaluate the biblical texts as literarily wanting. Matthew Arnold, for example, in the nineteenth century, judged the Gospels to be "but a matter of infinitely little care and attention . . . a mere slight framework, in which to set the doctrine and discourses of Jesus." *Literature and Dogma*, 171.

108. Dibelius, *From Tradition to Gospel*, 1.

109. Emphasis added. Overbeck, "Über die Anfänge der patristischen Literatur," 432–433.

110. This is also, famously, the view of James Kugel (whose work focuses on the Hebrew Bible). For arguments applicable to the NT, as well, see Kugel, "Bible and Literary Criticism."

111. Strier, "How Formalism Became a Dirty Word," 209.

112. Bockmuehl, *Seeing the Word*, 48–49.

113. Gamble, *Books and Readers*, 19; Aune, "Form Criticism," 143.

114. Deissmann, *Light from the Ancient East*, 10.

115. Dibelius, *From Tradition to Gospel*, 3.

116. This was also the aim of the history of religions school (*Religionsgeschichte*) introduced by Friedrich Max Müller (1823–1900). On the integration of a history of religions approach and NT form criticism, see Kümmel, *New Testament*, esp. 206–324, 342–362.

117. Kant, *Critique of Judgment*, 341.

118. Emphasis added. Von Harnack, "Fifteen Questions," 165–166, along with Karl Barth's response, "Fifteen Answers," 167–170.

119. English quoted in Steiner, *Russian Formalism*, 1.

120. Poland, *Literary Criticism*, 74.
121. Wellek and Warren, *Theory of Literature*, 157.
122. Composition criticism similarly conceives of a text's meaning in terms of its theological content, separable from its literary form. See Perrin's discussion in *Redaction Criticism*, 65–67.
123. Beardslee, *Literary Criticism*, 2.
124. Wilder, *Early Christian Rhetoric*, 125, 36, 37.
125. Wilder draws especially on the observations of Eduard Norden in, e.g., Norden, *Die antike Kunstprosa*, 493; Norden, *Agnostos Theos*.
126. See also Erich Auerbach's praise for Hebrew Bible narration as "fraught with background." *Mimesis*, 12. The phrase "fraught with background" has taken on a life of its own, eliciting both positive and negative responses from some of the most prominent Hebrew Bible scholars of the twentieth century, e.g., Barr, "Reading the Bible as Literature," 10–11; Alter, *Art of Biblical Narrative*, 17, 114–115; Berlin, *Poetics and Interpretation*, 138–139; and Yee, "'Fraught with Background.'" More generally, but with reference to Auerbach, see Hawkins, "Bible as Literature and Sacred Text," esp. 208.
127. Wilder, *Early Christian Rhetoric*, 37, 25.
128. This ought to be distinguished from the late twentieth-century poetry movement called "New Formalism." On the latter, see McPhillips, *New Formalism*; Walzer, "Dana Gioia"; and Walzer, *Ghost of Tradition*.
129. Thiele, "New Formalism(s)," 16.

Chapter 3. Searching for Signs in the Stars

1. Manilius's *Astronomica* is an impressive five-volume account of the study of the heavens. Rich and wide-ranging, the *Astronomica* provides detailed accounts of the constellations, signs of the zodiac, Stoic beliefs, divination, and the many mythical stories that had been preserved about the eternal beings of the celestial realm.
2. De Saussure, *Course in General Linguistics*, 112.
3. Eagleton, *Literary Theory*, 198.
4. Rogerson, "Recent Literary Structuralist Approaches," 166.
5. Patte, *What Is Structural Exegesis?*, 2. Other key works from that time include Barthes et al., *Analyse structurale et exégèse biblique;* and Léon-Dufour, *Exégèse et herméneutique*.
6. Longman, *Literary Approaches*, 37.
7. Emphasis added. Porter, "Literary Approaches," 83 n. 21. Porter faults R. R. Melick Jr. for "confusing" structuralism and rhetorical criticism with literary criticism, referring to Melick, "Literary Criticism."
8. Bailey, "Guidelines for Interpreting," 29.
9. Castelli et al., *Postmodern Bible*, 117.
10. Longman, *Literary Approaches*, 37.

11. Elliott, "Marxism," 35.

12. Fowler and Fowler, "Literary Theory and Classical Studies," 872.

13. Longman, *Literary Approaches*, 37.

14. Eagleton, *Literary Theory*, 95.

15. Barthes, "L'analyse structurale," 188.

16. De Saussure, *Course in General Linguistics*, 112.

17. Ankersmit, *Historical Representation*, 36.

18. Najman, "Idea of Biblical Genre," 316; Najman is building on Benjamin, *German Tragic Drama*.

19. De Saussure, *Course in General Linguistics*, 114.

20. Lévi-Strauss, *Myth and Meaning*, 8. See also Lévi-Strauss, *Structural Anthropology*.

21. De Saussure, *Course in General Linguistics*, 16.

22. In 1975 the center for the analysis of religious texts (CADIR) opened in Lyon, which focused especially on biblical texts and semiology.

23. Emphasis added. This oft-cited passage appears in the "Epistemo-Critical Prologue" (*Erkenntniskritische Vorrede*) to Benjamin's 1928 study of German tragedy, *German Tragic Drama*, 34–35.

24. Lévi-Strauss distinguishes between history and anthropology based on the view that the former concerns *conscious* human acts, while the latter concerns the *unconscious*. *Structural Anthropology*, 1–27.

25. Culler, *Literary in Theory*, 23.

26. De Saussure, *Course in General Linguistics*, 126.

27. Tolmie, *Narratology and Biblical Narratives*, 1.

28. Chatman, *Story and Discourse*, 47.

29. Greimas, *Maupassant*. For a useful introduction to the semiotic approach to plot for NT scholars, see Patte, *Structural Exegesis*.

30. Shklovsky, "*Syuzhet* Construction and General Stylistic Devices"; Chatman, *Story and Discourse*, 23.

31. Frow, *Genre*, 52. See, similarly, Duff, "Key Concepts," xiii.

32. Beebee, *Ideology of Genre*, 2–3. More recently, see Neumann and Nünning, "Einleitung," 3; and Christine Mitchell's addition to Beebee's taxonomy in "Power, *Eros*, and Biblical Genres," 31.

33. Frye, *Anatomy of Criticism*, 9, 18.

34. Frye, *Anatomy of Criticism*, 15, 12.

35. Farrell, "Classical Genre," 386; Najman, "Idea of Biblical Genre," 311.

36. Williams, *Marxism and Literature*, 56.

37. Horkheimer, *Critical Theory*, 246.

38. Weinsheimer, Foreword, xiii. Contra Weinsheimer, Adorno, not Horkheimer, said that culture stinks because "its mansion is built of dogshit" (gebaut aus Hundsscheisse). Adorno, *Negative Dialektik*, 359.

39. Gallagher, *Hermeneutics and Education*, 11.

40. Walter Benjamin, "Work of Art."
41. See, e.g., Lawson, *Class.*
42. Kavanagh, "Ideology," 311.
43. Eagleton, *Why Marx Was Right,* 3; cf. Rosen, "Terry Eagleton's Republic of Letters," who argues that Eagleton is now (ironically) a New Critic.
44. Bourdieu, *Distinction.*
45. Jameson, *Political Unconscious,* 9.
46. Sedgwick, "Paranoid Reading," 125.
47. Williams was heavily influenced by the Italian Marxist Antonio Gramsci, who coined the term. Williams, *Marxism and Literature,* 110.
48. Althusser, "Idéologie et appareils idéologiques d'État."
49. See, e.g., Lacan, *Ego in Freud's Theory;* Lacan, "Agency of the Letter"; and Sugg, *Jungian Literary Criticism.*
50. Auden, "In Memory of Sigmund Freud," 271.
51. See, e.g., Bloom, *Poetry and Repression;* Freud's writings have been submitted to such analyses, as well, in, e.g., Derrida, "Freud and the Scene of Writing."
52. Typically, critics of this view refer to Marie Bonaparte's biographical interpretation of Edgar Allan Poe as the paramount negative example of "applied psychoanalysis." *Life and Works of Edgar Allan Poe.*
53. Freud, *Interpretation of Dreams,* 310.
54. Ricoeur, *Freud and Philosophy,* 34.
55. Ricoeur, *Freud and Philosophy,* 34.
56. Specific aspects of Marxism, psychoanalysis, and Frankfurt School philosophy have been variously appropriated in literary studies, and specialized concepts have been adopted and adapted toward new literary-critical ends. To give just one example, Peter Brooks suggests that narrative plot is structured by an interplay between what Freud called *condensation* (which works to unite the disparate images of a dream) and *displacement* (which transposes the dreamer's most shameful desires onto apparently irrelevant details). "Freud's Masterplot."
57. Showalter helpfully traces three phases of feminist approaches to literature up to and through the 1970s. Showalter, "Toward a Feminist Poetics," 131.
58. Fetterley, *Resisting Reader,* xiii.
59. Schweickart, "Reading Ourselves," 52.
60. Boer, "Marxist Biblical Criticism," 316.
61. Emphasis added. Elliott, "Diagnosing an Allergic Reaction," 3. The journal is open access and can be found at http://novaojs.newcastle.edu.au/ojsbct/index.php/bct.
62. Welborn, "Marxism and Capitalism in Pauline Studies," 362.
63. See, e.g., Boer, "Marx, Postcolonialism and the Bible"; and Boer and Økland, *Marxist Feminist Criticism.*
64. See, e.g., the recent Fortress handbook: Blanton and Pickett, *Paul and Economics.*
65. Boer, "Marxist Biblical Criticism," 299. The literary section lists only four names as examples (I. J. Mosala, Tina Pippin, Jorunn Økland, and Alan Cadwallader).

66. Elliott, "Diagnosing an Allergic Reaction," esp. 3–12.
67. Emphasis added. Lesjak, "Reading Dialectically," 237.
68. Martin, *Corinthian Body*, xv.
69. Martin, *Corinthian Body*, xvi–xvii, xv. Martin draws especially on the conceptions of ideology expressed in Thompson, *Ideology and Modern Culture* and Giddens, "Four Theses on Ideology."
70. Martin, *Corinthian Body*, 251, 3.
71. Including his own teacher. Meeks, *First Urban Christians*, 53–55.
72. Welborn, "Marxism and Capitalism in Pauline Studies," 365.
73. Martin, *Corinthian Body*, xv.
74. Welborn, "Marxism and Capitalism in Pauline Studies."
75. Elliott, "Diagnosing an Allergic Reaction," 3.
76. Friesen, "Poverty in Pauline Studies," 336. One of the first to make this point with reference to Marxism was Miguez-Bonino, "Marxist Critical Tools."
77. Horsley is the most prominent example. See, among others, Horsley, *Paul and Empire;* Horsley, "Submerged Biblical Histories"; Horsley, *Paul and Politics;* and Horsley, *In the Shadow of Empire.*
78. It's also unsurprising that, in contrast to NT studies, Marxism has had a far more direct influence on classical liberation theology, a discipline in which concern for the poor in the present remains paramount. Emphasis added to Moore and Segovia, "Postcolonial Biblical Criticism," 6.
79. Welborn, "Marxism and Capitalism in Pauline Studies," 395.
80. Bockmuehl, *Seeing the Word*, 106.
81. Eagleton, *Ideology*, 18.
82. Welborn, "Marxism and Capitalism in Pauline Studies," 395.
83. Bazzana, "Neo-Marxism," 20.
84. Bazzana, "Neo-Marxism," 16.
85. Bernstein, *Beyond Objectivism and Relativism*, 46.
86. In this section, I draw readily on Dinkler, "Beyond the Normative/Descriptive Divide."
87. De Saussure, *Course in General Linguistics*, 126.
88. Emphasis added. Eagleton, *Literary Theory*, 95.
89. Eagleton, *Literary Theory*, 95.
90. Importantly, Patte *also* advocated the use of historical-critical methods. Patte, *What Is Structural Exegesis?*, 14.
91. Frei, *Eclipse of Biblical Narrative*, 124.
92. Stendahl, "Biblical Theology, Contemporary." Emphasis added to Lindbeck, "Story-Shaped Church," 162.
93. Emphasis original. Crossley, *Why Christianity Happened*, 2.
94. Boer, "Marxist Biblical Criticism," 301, 315.
95. Note that the use of "normative" here differs from the "normative" strand of New Formalism discussed in chapter 5.
96. Lewis, *Why Philosophy Matters*, 45.

97. Hays, "Reading the Bible with the Eyes of Faith," 94.
98. Lewis, *Why Philosophy Matters*, 45.
99. Phillips, "Exegesis as Critical Praxis," 9, 12.
100. Emphases original. Hays, *Conversion of the Imagination*, 198.
101. Bockmuehl, *Seeing the Word*, 106.
102. Emphasis added. Treier, *Introducing Theological Interpretation*, 34.
103. The recent rise of self-proclaimed *secularist studies* over and against the normativity that secular theorists consider endemic to *both* theology and religious studies demonstrates further the rhetorical power of negative normativity as a discursive construction. In biblical studies, see, e.g., Avalos, *End of Biblical Studies;* and Boer, *Secularism and Biblical Studies;* in religious studies, see, e.g., McCutcheon, *Manufacturing Religion.*
104. Bockmuehl, *Seeing the Word*, 106.
105. Emphasis added. Bockmuehl, *Seeing the Word*, 51.
106. Mitchell, *Birth of Christian Hermeneutics*, 156 fn. 55, responding to Aichele, Miscall, and Walsh, "An Elephant in the Room."
107. Putnam, *Collapse of the Fact/Value Dichotomy*, 3.
108. Mercer, *Norman Perrin's Interpretation*, 69.

Chapter 4. Literary Theory's Copernican Revolution

1. Butler, *Gender Trouble*, 40.
2. Moore, *Poststructuralism and the New Testament*, 117.
3. Cunningham, "Aw(e)ful Necessity of Bible Re-Reading," 50.
4. Bockmuehl, *Seeing the Word*, 49; and, similarly, Porter, "Literary Approaches to the New Testament," 121. Some biblical scholars self-consciously embrace this label, creating what's now referred to as autobiographical criticism. See, e.g., Moore, "True Confessions and Weird Obsessions"; Staley, *Reading with a Passion;* and Kitzberger, *Autobiographical Biblical Criticism.*
5. Porter, "Literary Approaches to the New Testament," 121; Moore, *Poststructuralism and the New Testament*, 117; Seeley, *Deconstructing the New Testament*, 1. Recall Longman on structuralism: *Literary Approaches*, 37.
6. Cultural studies represents a confluence of a number of disciplines, including literary structuralism and poststructuralism, anthropology, history, postcolonialism, and (especially Lacanian) psychoanalysis. One of its main contributions to literary studies has been denying value-laden distinctions between "high" (elite) and "low" (popular) literature. Kuhn, *Copernican*, 1.
7. A recent introduction to poststructuralism and biblical studies is Aichele, *Play of Signifiers.*
8. Don't confuse affect theory with affective stylistics, a more specific form of reader-response theory developed by Stanley Fish. Cvetkovich, *Archive of Feelings*, 19.
9. Kimberlé Williams Crenshaw coined the popular term "intersectionality" to refer to these interconnected, cumulative dynamics. Crenshaw, "Mapping the

Margins"; see also McCall, "Complexity of Intersectionality." Liew specifically invokes Crenshaw in "Queering Closets and Perverting Desires," 252. Among many examples of such work in biblical studies, see Kwok, *Postcolonial Imagination;* Dube, Mbuvi, and Mbuwayesango, *Postcolonial Perspectives;* Wimbush, *African Americans and the Bible.*

10. Unfortunately, restricting the focus in this way means we'll ignore other significant considerations and conversations in the field. But then again, this illustrates one of poststructuralism's primary principles: for every narrative that's told, a counternarrative goes unspoken. In order to articulate one vantage point, a speaker must mute another.

11. Ricoeur, *From Text to Action,* 15. Closely related, but from a sociological perspective, is the classic volume by Berger and Luckmann, *Social Construction of Reality.*

12. Deleuze and Guattari, *A Thousand Plateaus.*

13. Note that my discussion of identity here differs from the "sudden popularity of Christian identity as an optic" that Maia Kotrosits identifies (and challenges) in *Rethinking Early Christian Identity,* 3. On the latter, see, e.g., Boyarin, *A Radical Jew;* Lieu, *Christian Identity;* and Lieu, *Neither Jew nor Greek?*

14. Butler, *Gender Trouble;* Butler, *Bodies That Matter.*

15. David-Fox, Holquist, and Martin, "The Imperial Turn," 705.

16. Hasseler and Krebs, "Academic Uses of the Postcolonial," 96.

17. Said, *Orientalism.*

18. Notably, Spivak was the first to translate Derrida's *De la grammatologie.* Spivak, *In Other Worlds;* Spivak, "Can the Subaltern Speak?"

19. See, e.g., Elmarsafy, Bernard, and Attwell, *Debating Orientalism;* Harris, "An Awkward Silence"; and Lazarus, *Postcolonial Unconscious.*

20. Nandy, *Intimate Enemy.*

21. Bhabha, *Location of Culture,* 96.

22. Bhabha, *Location of Culture,* 34.

23. On the problematic legacy of the term "hybrid," see Young, *Colonial Desire;* Acheraïou, *Questioning Hybridity;* and Werbner, "Essentialising Essentialism, Essentialising Silence," 228–230.

24. Chakrabarty, *Provincializing Europe,* 42.

25. Gates, "Race," 4; Gates, *Signifying Monkey.*

26. Gates, "Introduction," 5.

27. Morrison, *Playing in the Dark.*

28. On the applicability and relevance of references to "readers" who more likely were *hearers,* see chapter 1.

29. Iser, "Reading Process," 287.

30. Iser, *Act of Reading,* 38; Iser, *Implied Reader.* On Iser in biblical studies, see Schwáb, "Mind the Gap."

31. Perry, "Literary Dynamics," 41.

32. Fish, *Is There a Text in This Class?,* 25.

33. Emphasis added. Fish, *Is There a Text in This Class?*, 2.
34. Barthes, "From Work to Text," 418. See also Barthes, *S/Z*.
35. This essay shifts Barthes from structuralism into poststructuralism. Barthes, "Death of the Author," 142. See also Burke, *Death and Return of the Author.*
36. See, e.g., Dinkler, "What Is a Genre?"; Alexander, "Typology of Intertextual Relations," esp. 69; Harrison, *Generic Enrichment;* Tissol and Batstone, *Defining Genre;* and Depew and Obbink, *Matrices of Genre.*
37. Borg and Miles, "Introduction," 1.
38. Fowler, *Kinds of Literature*, 37.
39. Ryken and Longman, "Introduction," 29.
40. Attridge, "Genre-Bending."
41. Todorov, *Genres in Discourse*, 15.
42. Wittgenstein was writing about games, not literary genres (*Philosophical Investigations*, 31–32), but Alastair Fowler popularized and adapted Wittgenstein's insights for literary genres in *Kinds of Literature*, 41; cf. Fishelov, "Genre Theory." Richard Burridge uses the concept in *What Are the Gospels?*, 42; see the review by Collins, "Genre and the Gospels."
43. Swales, *Genre Analysis*, 51. See also David Fishelov's critique in *Metaphors of Genre*, 54.
44. Frow, *Genre*, 54. Prototype theory developed out of empirical research in linguistics, psychology, and anthropology, and was later brought into conversations about genre. For useful summaries of key concepts and figures related to prototype theory and human categorization generally, see Lakoff, *Women, Fire, and Dangerous Things*, 12–44. Vernon Robbins and the Rhetoric of Religious Antiquity group have been exploring similar concepts in biblical studies; Robbins, citing Lakoff, writes, "It gradually has become evident that the sociorhetorical concept of 'rhetorolect' is, from the perspective of cognitive science, some kind of Idealized Cognitive Model (ICM)." *Invention of Christian Discourse*, 104.
45. Rosch, "Cognitive Representations." The most cited illustration from Rosch's studies is the category "bird": participants did not identify each bird using a mental list of features (such as wings, beaks, and feathers), but rather by comparing new birds to a prototypical example (such as robin or sparrow). Some birds are like the exemplar, while others (like ostriches or flamingos) are less typical and peripheral to the category.
46. Benjamin Wright describes three sets of variables comprising a cognitive template: (1) necessary or "compulsory" properties (a dog is an animal); (2) "default" properties (a dog has four legs); and (3) optional properties (the dog is black). Wright, "Joining the Club," 266. See also Mandler, *Stories;* and Rumelhart, "Schemata."
47. Sinding, "After Definitions," 193–194.
48. Swales, *Genre Analysis*, 52.

49. Pyrhönen, "Genre," 118.
50. Bakhtin, "Speech Genres." Bakhtin's point effectively nullifies the distinction between *Kleinliteratur* and *Hochliteratur* discussed in chapter 2.
51. Derrida, "Law of Genre," 65.
52. Culler, *On Deconstruction*.
53. Derrida critiques Saussurean structuralism for being *logocentric*—that is, privileging the word (*logos*) over all else.
54. Barthes, too, writes that "the book itself is only a tissue of signs, in imitation that is lost, infinitely deferred." "The Death of the Author," 147.
55. See, e.g., Pliny, *Nat. Hist.* 2.32. Cicero says that this is wrong in *De Natura Deorum* 2.51.
56. Johnson, "Writing," 46.
57. Emphasis added. Hatina, "Intertextuality and Historical Criticism," 29–30.
58. Emphasis added. Vanhoozer, *Is There a Meaning in This Text?*, 164.
59. Klein, Blomberg, and Hubbard, *Introduction to Biblical Interpretation*, 75; Bockmuehl, *Seeing the Word*, 49. Bockmuehl cites David Clines, who says that interpreters focus on "producing interpretations they can sell" in Clines, "A World Established on Water," 79.
60. Emphasis added. Klein, Blomberg, and Hubbard, *Introduction to Biblical Interpretation*, 75.
61. Fish, *Is There a Text in This Class?*, 268.
62. Derrida, *De la grammatologie*, 227; cf. Vanhoozer, *Is There a Meaning in This Text?*, 211.
63. Sundberg, "Social Effect," 69.
64. Bockmuehl, *Seeing the Word*, 49.
65. Watson, *Text and Truth*, 97.
66. Bockmuehl, *Seeing the Word*, 49.
67. Matterson, "New Criticism," 171.
68. Emphasis added. Foucault, *History of Sexuality*, 11–12.
69. Derrida, "Dialogue," 111.
70. Derrida, "Dialogue," 123.
71. Emphasis added. Bloomsbury, "Let the Reader Understand," https://www.bloomsbury.com/uk/let-the-reader-understand-9781563383380/.
72. Goldhill, "Failure of Exemplarity," 53.
73. De Man, *Allegories of Reading*, 249.
74. De Man, *Allegories of Reading*, 19.
75. Darr, *On Character Building*, 25; and Darr, *Herod the Fox*, 34–36.
76. See, e.g., Tolbert, *Sowing the Gospel*; Fowler, *Let the Reader Understand*; and Powell, "Expected and Unexpected Readings."
77. Burnet, Luciani, and van Oyen, *Le lecteur*.
78. Bernstein, *Beyond Objectivism and Relativism*, 46.
79. See, e.g., Jauss, "Theorie der Gattungen und Literatur des Mittelalters."

80. Pease, "Author," 113.
81. Foucault, "What Is an Author?," 105.
82. Pease, "Author," 113.
83. A cautionary note: It's vital to identify the context in which one encounters the phrase "identity politics." Some use it positively to refer to their own work, while opponents and skeptics use it to refer to others' work negatively.
84. Hatina, "Intertextuality and Historical Criticism," 29–30.
85. Barton, *Nature of Biblical Criticism*, 6.
86. Bockmuehl, *Seeing the Word*, 32.
87. Byron and Lovelace, "Introduction," 15.
88. Byron and Lovelace, "Introduction," 15. Similarly, see Anderson, *Ancient Laws and Contemporary Controversies*. On ethics and NT scholarship more broadly, see Patte, *Ethics of Biblical Interpretation*.
89. Longman, *Literary Approaches*, 40.
90. Chartier's work in cultural history shares affinities with the French *Annales* school. Chartier, *Cultural History*, 13–14.
91. Brooten, *Love between Women*, 14; Shaner, *Enslaved Leadership*, xv; Briggs, "Can an Enslaved God Liberate?," 138.
92. Leitch, *Living with Theory*, 23.
93. Olender, *The Languages of Paradise*, 55.
94. Renan, *History of the People of Israel*, 7.
95. Kelley, *Racializing Jesus*, esp. 177. See also Kelley, "Race, Aesthetics, and Gospel Scholarship," esp. 200.
96. Levine, "Feminist Criticism," 156.
97. Shiner, "Creating Plot in Episodic Narratives," 155.
98. Lyons, "Hope for a Troubled Discipline?," 210, responding to Aichele, Miscall, and Walsh, "Elephant in the Room."
99. See, e.g., Bond, Schröter, and Keith, *Reception of Jesus*.
100. Adam, "Sign of Jonah," 177.
101. Powell, *Chasing the Eastern Star*. The volume builds on Powell's earlier article, "Magi as Kings"; Vásquez, *Contours of a Biblical Reception Theory*.
102. Reinfandt, "Reading Texts," 49.
103. Stone, "History and Post-Modernism," 218; Windschuttle, *Killing of History*.
104. Moore makes a similar point explaining why he employs "nonhuman theory": "These theoretical threads pair well with early Christian texts that long precede [Western Enlightenment conceptions of "the human"] and that testify to other options of the human in its relations with the nonhuman, notions other than the anthropocentric conceptions that have generated the Anthropocene, which is to say our current Age of Extinction." *Gospel Jesuses*, 2.
105. See, among many others, De La Torre, *Reading the Bible from the Margins*; Blount, *Can I Get a Witness?*; Blount et al., *True to Our Native Land*; Liew, *What Is Asian American Hermeneutics?*; Buell, *Why This New Race?*; Buell and

Johnson Hodge, "The Politics of Interpretation"; Nasrallah and Schüssler Fiorenza, *Prejudice and Christian Beginnings;* Segovia, *Decolonizing Biblical Studies;* Bailey, Liew, and Segovia, *They Were All Together;* Barreto, *Ethnic Negotiations;* Choi, *Postcolonial Embodiment;* and Lin, *The Erotic Life.*

106. Anderson, *From Crisis to Christ,* xii.

107. Collins, *Bible after Babel,* 4.

108. Campbell, *Framing Paul,* 12.

109. Emphases added. Campbell, *Framing Paul,* 12.

110. Campbell, *Framing Paul,* 13 n. 14.

111. The meaning of this famous phrase is debated. Von Ranke, *Geschichten der romanischen und germanischen Völker,* vii.

112. Mitchell, *Birth of Christian Hermeneutics,* 10.

113. Campbell, *Framing Paul,* 21.

114. Carson, "Matthew," 328.

115. Aichele, *Phantom Messiah;* Jacob, *Reading Mary;* Taylor, *Jesus and Brian.* See also, e.g., Colbertson and Wainwright, *Bible in/and Popular Culture.*

116. Kreitzer, *New Testament in Fiction and Film,* 19.

117. Counet, *John, a Postmodern Gospel;* Jennings, "Justice as Gift"; Polischuk, "Metacognitive Perspective."

118. Especially relevant are Moore, *Bible in Theory;* and Moore and Sherwood, *Invention of the Biblical Scholar.*

119. Moore, *God's Beauty Parlor,* 222; Moore, *God's Gym,* 12.

120. Martin, "Review of Stephen D. Moore," 736.

121. Cunningham, "Aw(e)ful Necessity of Bible Re-Reading," 50. Cunningham opposes Theory in the literary field as well in *Reading after Theory.*

122. Cunningham, "Bible Reading and/after Theory," 651.

123. Collins, *The Bible after Babel,* 3, alluding to Moore, *God's Gym,* and Moore, *God's Beauty Parlor.*

124. Cunningham, "Aw(e)ful Necessity of Bible Re-Reading," 50.

125. See Moore's own related comments in Moore, *Poststructuralism and the New Testament,* 117.

126. Levine, "Foreword/Preface/Introduction/Preamble/Exordium," xii.

127. Moore and Sherwood, *Invention of the Biblical Scholar,* 132.

128. Clark, *History, Theory, Text,* 156.

129. Clines, "Possibilities and Priorities," 85.

130. Rueckert, "Literature and Ecology," 109. Of course, critics were concerned with nature-related themes long before this.

131. See, e.g., Tomkins, *Affect, Imagery, Consciousness.* For an example in NT scholarship, see Dinkler, "Reflexivity and Emotion."

132. Liew, *What Is Asian American Biblical Hermeneutics?,* xii. See also, e.g., Liew, "Postcolonial Criticism"; Segovia and Sugirtharajah, *Postcolonial Commentary;* and Dinkler, "Reading Power(s) and Potential(s)."

133. Waugh, "Introduction," 21.
134. See, e.g., Elliott and Attridge, *Theory after "Theory"*; Williams, "The Posttheory Generation"; McQuillan et al., *Post-Theory;* Bové, *In the Wake of Theory;* and Patai and Corral, *Theory's Empire.* Responses to the latter include Holbo, *Framing Theory's Empire;* and Leitch, *Literary Criticism,* 26–27.
135. Jameson mounts a full-fledged defense of Theory as not only valuable but *necessary* in *Valences of the Dialectic.*
136. Sedgwick, "Paranoid Reading," 131.
137. Sedgwick, "Paranoid Reading," 124–125.
138. Allen, *End of Progress.*
139. German philosopher Jürgen Habermas worked to recuperate human reason as the universal means to liberation. See, e.g., Habermas, *Philosophical Discourse.* Recent critiques and developments of this view include Honneth, *Pathologies of Reason;* and Jay, *Reason after Its Eclipse.*
140. Ashcroft, Griffiths, and Tiffin, *Empire Writes Back,* 149.
141. In addition to Allen, *End of Progress,* see Domingues, *Global Modernity.*
142. Penner and Lopez, *De-Introducing the New Testament,* 12–13.
143. Penner and Lopez, *De-Introducing the New Testament,* 15.
144. Emphasis added. Goldhill, "Failure of Exemplarity," 51.
145. Waugh, "Introduction," 21.
146. Porter, "Literary Approaches," 121.
147. Collins, *Bible after Babel,* 3.
148. Penner and Lopez rightly criticize such linear portrayals of the field. *De-Introducing the New Testament,* 12–13.
149. The reverse is true, as well: biblical texts can dislodge the normativities implicit in contemporary concepts. See, e.g., Badiou, *Saint Paul,* 5–7.

Chapter 5. The Quest for the Literary Jesus

1. Developments over the past half century in the field of "historical Jesus research" are well known. See the excellent account in Meier, *A Marginal Jew;* and the discussion and citations in Keith, "Narratives of the Gospels," 428–429.
2. Emphasis added. Meyer, *Aims of Jesus,* 13.
3. Whether these varying accounts of Jesus are commensurable with one another or reflective of the actual historical Jesus is beside the point here.
4. Gaventa says something similar in *Mary,* 2.
5. Malbon, *Mark's Jesus,* 251. On the uneasy relationship between literary and historical approaches to the Gospels, see Reinhartz, "Building Skyscrapers on Toothpicks," and in the same volume, Conway, "There and Back Again"; and Attridge, "Some Methodological Considerations."
6. Portions of this chapter reflect sections of the following: Dinkler, "Narratological Jesus Research"; "New Formalist Approach"; and "Building Character on the Road to Emmaus."

7. Emphasis added. Meier, *Roots of the Problem,* 6.

8. Adam, *Postmodern Biblical Criticism,* 4.

9. Conzelmann, *Theology of St. Luke* (the German original was aptly titled *Die Mitte der Zeit*).

10. On divine causation as a key programmatic theme throughout Luke's two-volume work, see Squires, *Plan of God in Luke-Acts;* and Cosgrove, "Divine Δεῖ in Luke-Acts."

11. Conzelmann, *Theology of St. Luke,* 76–77. Following Wrede, *Das Messiasgeheimnis in den Evangelien,* scholars have discussed Jesus's commands to silence almost exclusively with respect to the Gospel of Mark, where they appear more frequently. See, e.g., Luz, "Secrecy Motif and Marcan Christology"; Räisänen, *"Messianic Secret" in Mark;* and Tuckett, "Messianic Secret."

12. Dibelius, "First Christian Historian." Dibelius inspired Marguerat, *First Christian Historian.* Gregory Sterling has nuanced that view by proposing that Luke-Acts is apologetic historiography like Josephus's *Jewish Antiquities* in Sterling, *Historiography and Self-Definition.* C. Clifton Black, "Mark as Historian," has countered that the appellation of "first Christian historian" actually belongs to the author of the earliest Gospel, Mark.

13. The following compare Luke 1.1–4 with prefaces of Greco-Roman and Jewish historiographies: Earl, "Prologue-form in Ancient Historiography."; van Unnik, "Once More"; Dillon, "Previewing Luke's Project"; Callen, "Preface of Luke-Acts"; Schmidt, "Rhetorical Influences and Genre"; and Robbins, "Prologues and Greco-Roman Rhetoric." Contrast these with the view set forth by Loveday Alexander, *Preface to Luke's Gospel,* who argues that the Lukan preface matches the genre of an ancient scientific treatise.

14. See, e.g., Thucydides, *Hist.* 1.22.2–4. For a recent thorough discussion of the term "investigate" (*parēkoloutheō*) in Luke 1.3, see Moessner, "Luke as Tradent."

15. Bowersock, *Fiction as History;* Gill and Wiseman, *Lies and Fiction;* Luther, Röder, and Schmidt, *Wie Geschichten Geschichte schreiben.*

16. Kraus, "History and Biography," 415. We might add that often, their *purposes* for writing also would have been "as much at home" with those of orators and novelists. See, e.g., Quintilian's definition of historiography in *Institutio Oratoria* X.1.31.

17. Adam, *Postmodern Biblical Criticism,* 4.

18. Originally published in 1987 and reissued in a "thoroughly updated" version in 2007. Blomberg, *Historical Reliability,* 10.

19. Blomberg, *Historical Reliability,* 93.

20. Greenblatt, *Renaissance Self-Fashioning,* 5.

21. Hens-Piazza, "New Historicism," 61.

22. Montrose, "Professing the Renaissance," 20.

23. Emphases original. Fulda, "'Selective' History," 182–183.

24. Johnson, *Contested Issues,* 206.

25. Emphasis added. Clivaz, "'Asleep by Grief,'" 6. See, e.g., Rowlett, *Joshua and the Rhetoric of Violence;* Hens-Piazza, *The New Historicism;* Hens-Piazza, "New Historicism"; and Moore's introduction to the thematic issue of *BibInt* in 1997, "The New Historicism," and the contributions therein.

26. This article is widely considered the founding document of narrative Christology. Tannehill, "Mark as Narrative Christology," 57. Though Tannehill's article concerns the Gospel of Mark, scholars have since read the other Gospels through the lens of narrative christology, as well, e.g., Coleridge, *Birth of the Lukan Narrative;* Hamm, "What the Samaritan Leper Sees"; and Rowe, *Early Narrative Christology.* On "narrative criticism" and the Gospel of Luke, see Tannehill, *Narrative Unity of Luke-Acts;* Kurz, *Reading Luke-Acts;* and Dinkler, *Silent Statements.*

27. Literary characterization is an enormous and ever-expanding area of research in both literary and biblical studies; we simply can't do it justice here. In addition to Dinkler, "Building Character," and the citations therein, see the following recent publications: Dicken and Snyder, *Character and Characterization;* Skinner and Hauge, *Character Studies;* Dicken, *Herod as a Composite Character;* Bennema, *Encountering Jesus;* Bennema, *Theory of Character;* Hunt, Tolmie, and Zimmermann, *Character Studies;* Campbell, *Of Heroes and Villains;* and Skinner, *Characters and Characterization.*

28. See, e.g., Thiselton, "Christology in Luke." Austin, *How to Do Things with Words;* Searle, *Speech Acts;* Searle, *Expression and Meaning.*

29. Darr, *On Character Building,* 41, 42.

30. Darr, *On Character Building,* 41.

31. Tannehill, "Beginning to Study," 188.

32. Fitzmyer, *Luke (X–XXIV),* 1032.

33. Luke 2.46 is the only time in Luke that *didaskalos* describes someone other than Jesus. On this, see Kilgallen, "Foreshadowing of Jesus."

34. Coleridge, *Birth of the Lukan Narrative,* 222–223.

35. Shelton, *Mighty in Word and Deed;* Shepherd, *Narrative Function;* Wenk, *Community-Forming Power;* Hur, *Dynamic Reading.*

36. On Jesus as Master of disciples, see, e.g., Robinson, "Theological Context"; on Jesus at symposia, see de Meeûs, "Composition de Lc, XIV"; Delobel, "L'onction par la pécheresse"; Steele, "Modified Hellenistic Symposium?"; and Smith, "Table Fellowship"; on Jesus as political conqueror, see, e.g., the debates in *JSNT* over Dale Martin's thesis that the disciples carried swords in Gethsemane *in order to instigate* a military battle into which the heavenly host would intervene. Martin, "Jesus in Jerusalem," esp. 4–5; Fredriksen, "Arms and the Man," esp. 314–315; Downing, "Swords for Jesus," esp. 328–331; Martin, "Response to Downing and Fredriksen."

37. Marguerat, "Luc, metteur en scène des personnages," 283.

38. Fitzmyer, *Luke (I–IX),* 94.

39. Emphasis original. Moore, *Empire and Apocalypse*, 37; Walaskay, *And So We Came to Rome*, 28.

40. Conway, *Behold the Man*, 129. See also, e.g., Matthews, "Weeping Jesus."

41. Wilson, *Unmanly Men*, 21.

42. Fitzmyer, *To Advance the Gospel*, 259. On the Jewish suffering Messiah, see Klausner, *Messianic Idea*, 519–531; cf. Boyarin, "Suffering Christ."

43. Blomberg, *Historical Reliability*, 55.

44. Ledbetter, "Telling the Other Story," 292.

45. Douglas Bruster traces Dubrow's first use to a 1989 MLA session titled "Toward the New Formalism: Formalist Approaches to Renaissance New Historicism and Feminism," in Bruster, "Shakespeare and the Composite Text."

46. Thiele, "New Formalism(s)," 16.

47. See, e.g., Strier, "How Formalism Became a Dirty Word"; Kaufman, "Everybody Hates Kant"; and Wolfson, *Formal Charges*. Levinson, "What Is New Formalism?," 559. The special issue of the journal *Representations* 104 (2008) is devoted to form.

48. Breslin, *From Modern to Contemporary*, xiv. See also Hunter, "Formalism and History"; and Rooney, "Form and Contentment."

49. Examples include Bérubé, "Aesthetics and the Literal Imagination"; and Harpham, *Character of Criticism*.

50. Levinson, "What Is New Formalism?," 559. Levinson draws on Wolfson, "Reading for Form," for this distinction.

51. See, e.g., Thiele and Tredennick, *New Formalisms and Literary Theory*.

52. Rooney, "Form and Contentment," 25.

53. Federico, *Close Reading*, 19.

54. Federico, *Close Reading*, 19.

55. Thiele, "New Formalism(s)," 16.

56. Bogel, *New Formalist Criticism*, 85.

57. Schwarz, *In Defense of Reading*, xiii.

58. Thiele, "New Formalism(s)," 16.

59. In this section, I treat the Synoptics together because of the similarities between the stories; I point out differences where relevant.

60. Ebstein, *Die Medizin im Neuen Testament*, 97; Howard, *Disease and Healing*, 94.

61. Malina, *New Testament World*, 179–180.

62. Douglas, *Purity and Danger*, 51.

63. Classicists have considered embodiment through the lens of literary characterization, especially drawing on physiognomy. Elizabeth Evans, for example, who created a catalogue of ancient physiognomic principles, declared that after Aristotle, physiognomy assumed "a vigorous role in the study of personality *and the art of characterization in ancient literature.*" Emphasis added. Evans, *Physiognomics*, 11.

64. Parsons, *Body and Character*, 135.

65. Vlahogiannis, "Disabling Bodies," 28.
66. Lane, *Mark,* 190 n. 35.
67. See, e.g., Theissen, *Miracle Stories,* 134.
68. Marcus, *Mark 1–8,* 357.
69. For a brief survey of the major Greek writers' terms for menstruation, see Selvidge, "A Reaction." See also Lev. 12.2; 15.19; 20.18; Ezek. 36.17.
70. Selvidge, "A Reaction," 622.
71. Luke underscores the public nature of Jesus's response. In contrast to the Markan text ("[The woman] came in fear and trembling and fell down before him, and told him the whole truth" [5.33]), Luke has, "[The woman] came trembling, and falling down before him declared why she had touched him before all the people, and how she had been healed immediately" (8.47). Malina, *New Testament World,* 31.
72. Cohen, "Menstruants and the Sacred," 275. Cohen says that this "important point" is "unappreciated" by Selvidge, "A Reaction," and by Witherington, *Women in the Ministry of Jesus,* 71–75.
73. Cohen, "Menstruants and the Sacred," 276. See, among others, Lev. 15.2–15, 32–33; 22.4; Num. 5.2.
74. See, e.g., Fonrobert, *Menstrual Purity;* Fonrobert, "Menstrual Laws and Jewish Culture"; Levine, "Discharging Responsibility"; Cohen, "Menstruants and the Sacred."
75. Still others rightly point out from a metacritical perspective that interpretations like these can reify and perpetuate misogynistic and anti-Jewish views. See, e.g., Kinukawa, "Story of the Hemorrhaging Woman"; Dube, "Fifty Years of Bleeding"; Kelley, *Racializing Jesus.*
76. Hens-Piazza, "New Historicism," 61.
77. Galen, *On Prognosis,* 3.15; 618K; D'Angelo, "Gender and Power," 98.
78. Resseguie argues that Jesus's "clothing is identical to his selfhood." *Narrative Criticism,* 139.
79. Neyrey, "Miracles," 22.
80. D'Angelo, "Gender and Power," 99.
81. Thiele, "New Formalism(s)," 16.
82. Bultmann, *Synoptic Tradition,* 214; Dibelius, *From Tradition to Gospel,* 43.
83. Rhoads, "Syrophoenician Woman," drawing on Alter, *Art of Biblical Narrative,* 47–52.
84. Wire, "Gospel Miracle Stories," 102. Examples of other "demand stories" in the Synoptic Gospels include the accounts of the leper (Mk. 1.40–45); the father of the boy with the demon (Lk. 9.38–42); the ten lepers (Lk. 17.11–19); the Canaanite woman (Matt. 15.21–28); and the centurion (Matt. 8.5–13).
85. Most assume that intercalations such as this one originated with Mark. See, e.g., von Dobschütz, "Zur Erzählerkunst des Markus"; Schenke, *Wundererzählungen,* 198; Koch, *Bedeutung,* 139; cf. Twelftree, *Jesus the Miracle Worker,* 73.
86. Edwards, "Markan Sandwiches," 201.

87. See, e.g., Fowler, *Let the Reader Understand,* 145–146.

88. Bailey and Vander Broek suggest that on a micro-level, chiasm is a literary *device,* whereas on a macro-level, it's a literary *form.* Bailey and Vander Broek, *Literary Forms,* 181–182.

89. Bogel, *New Formalist Criticism,* 85.

90. See, e.g., Shepherd, "Markan Intercalation"; and Bultmann, *Synoptic Tradition,* 214; cf. Matthew, where the girl is already dead before Jairus approaches Jesus.

91. Harmon and Holman, *Handbook,* 216.

92. Camery-Hoggatt, *Irony in Mark's Gospel,* 138.

93. On the possibility that the woman's faith is in Jesus as a *magician,* see Edwards, "Markan Sandwiches," 204; Witherington, *Women in the Ministry of Jesus,* 73.

94. Moss, "Man with the Flow of Power," 516.

95. See, e.g., Powell, "'Passivity' of Jesus."

96. On the significance of proper names, see Beck, *Discipleship Paradigm;* Reinhartz, *Why Ask My Name?;* and Bauckham, *Gospel Women.*

97. Several early manuscripts reflect a Lukan change here. Whereas Mark tells his readers that the woman spent all her money on doctors, Luke (traditionally, but not likely, the "Beloved Physician") simply says that no one could help her.

98. Marcus, *Mark 1–8,* 366.

99. Darr, *On Character Building,* 41.

100. Woloch, *One vs. the Many,* 15.

101. On the former, see Beardslee, "What Is It About?" On the latter, see, e.g., Moore, *Jesus Begins to Write;* Elliott, *Reconfiguring Mark's Jesus;* and Donaldson, "Cyborgs."

102. Bal, *Narratology,* 115.

103. Woloch, *One vs. the Many,* 17.

104. Dinkler, "Building Character."

105. Other layers have been posited as well (such as Mieke Bal's *fabula, story,* and *text*). Bal, *Narratology,* 18.

106. Frow, *Character and Person,* 15.

107. Woloch, *One vs. the Many,* 17.

108. Woloch, *One vs. the Many,* 13.

109. Thiele, "New Formalism(s)," 16.

110. Bogel, *New Formalist Criticism,* 76.

111. Moss, "Man with the Flow of Power," 516.

112. Kukkonen, "Form as a Pattern of Thinking," 166.

113. O'Neill, *Fictions of Discourse,* 65.

114. Gary Yamasaki discusses this in terms of narratorial control of information flow. *Point of View,* 58. On the functions of knowledge acquisition in biblical narrative, see Sternberg, *Poetics,* esp. 153–185.

115. Duke, *Irony,* 38–39.

116. Witherington, *Women in the Ministry of Jesus,* 73.

117. Kukkonen, "Form as a Pattern of Thinking," 166.

118. Roberts, "Feminist Criticism." One self-proclaimed "attempt to answer that call" is Scott-Baumann, *Forms of Engagement,* 9.
119. See, e.g., Aristotle, *Historia Animalium* 1.220–23; and the discussion in Dean-Jones, "Menstrual Bleeding."
120. Cohen, "Menstruants and the Sacred," 115.
121. Hanson, "Medical Writers' Woman," 333.
122. Moss, "Man with the Flow of Power," 516.
123. See, e.g., Wilson, *Unmanly Men,* 199; and Moss, "Man with the Flow of Power," 515.
124. Douglas, *What's Faith Got to Do with It?*; Grant, *White Women's Christ.*
125. Resseguie, *Narrative Criticism,* 138.
126. Burke, *Philosophy of Literary Form,* 110–111.
127. Compare the explicitly polyvalent responses in GTh. 13.

Chapter 6. The Corinthian Corpus and Epistolary Embodiment

1. All non-biblical quotations in this and the prior paragraph are from Mitchell, *Birth of Christian Hermeneutics,* 81.
2. See, e.g., Martin, *Corinthian Body,* 52–53.
3. Funk, "Apostolic *Parousia*," 249, 259.
4. Mitchell, "New Testament Envoys," 642.
5. Though some scholars do argue for unity. See, e.g., Mitchell, *Paul and the Rhetoric of Reconciliation,* 184–304; Fee, *First Epistle,* 15; Long, *Ancient Rhetoric;* and Engberg-Pedersen, "Unity of 2 Corinthians." The scholarly literature regarding "partition theories" is vast. See, e.g., Nongbri, "Possible Material Evidence"; Stewart-Sykes, "Ancient Editors"; Yeo, *Rhetorical Interaction,* esp. 78–83; Betz, *Second Corinthians 8 and 9;* and Schmithals, "Korintherbriefe als Briefsammlung."
6. On which, see Murphy-O'Connor, "Co-Authorship"; Murphy-O'Connor, *Paul the Letter-Writer,* 33–34; Richards, *Paul and First-Century Letter Writing;* and Foucault, "What Is an Author?"
7. Nasrallah, "'Out of Love for Paul,'" 74.
8. See Becker's well-developed discussion in *Letter Hermeneutics.*
9. Mitchell, *Birth of Christian Hermeneutics,* 10.
10. See also, e.g., Poster and Mitchell, *Letter-Writing Manuals.*
11. Trans. in Malherbe, *Ancient Epistolary Theorists,* 33. See also the many examples in Stowers, *Letter Writing.*
12. Macguire, "Letters and Letter Carriers"; Baird, "Letters of Recommendation"; Kim, *Form and Function.*
13. Petersen, *Rediscovering Paul,* 53. So, similarly, Meeks, *First Urban Christians,* 109; and Aune, *Literary Environment,* 197.
14. See, e.g., Campbell, *Framing Paul,* esp. 74–121.
15. Stendahl, "Introspective Conscience," 199, 208.
16. Stendahl, "Introspective Conscience," 208. Scholars now largely reject the individualistic view of Paul. See, e.g., Barth, "Social Character of Justification";

Dahl, "Doctrine of Justification"; Martin, "Anti-Individualistic Ideology"; cf. Engberg-Pedersen, "Philosophy of the Self," 179–194; Burnett, *Salvation of the Individual;* and Nicolet-Anderson, *Constructing the Self.*

17. See, e.g., Becker and Reed, *Ways That Never Parted;* Dunn, *New Perspective.*

18. Emphasis added. Culler, *Literary in Theory,* 4.

19. See, e.g., Økland, *Women in Their Place,* focuses on 1 Cor. 11–14; Martin, *Corinthian Body,* on the whole Corinthian correspondence; Nasrallah, "'You Were Bought with a Price,'" on 1 Cor. 6–7; Welborn, "Towards Structural Marxism as a Hermeneutic," on 1 Cor. 15.30–32; and Welborn, "'That There May Be Equality,'" on 2 Cor. 8.13–15.

20. Martin, *Corinthian Body,* xvi.

21. Martin, *Corinthian Body,* 3.

22. Martin, *Corinthian Body,* 251, 106–107.

23. Nasrallah, "'You Were Bought with a Price,'" 54.

24. Nasrallah, "'You Were Bought with a Price,'" 72.

25. Schüssler Fiorenza, "Rhetorical Situation"; Castelli, *Imitating Paul;* Mitchell, *Birth of Christian Hermeneutics.*

26. See, e.g., Betz, *Der Apostel Paulus;* Kennedy, *New Testament Interpretation;* Long, *Ancient Rhetoric;* and Wuellner, "Greek Rhetoric."

27. Marchal, "Female Masculinity," 99.

28. Wire, *Corinthian Women Prophets,* 10.

29. Among others, see Schüssler Fiorenza, *Discipleship of Equals.*

30. Miller, "Not with Eloquent Wisdom," 324.

31. Bazzana, "Neo-Marxism," 18, 20.

32. Among others, see, e.g., Bartchy, *First Century Slavery;* Nasrallah, "'You Were Bought with a Price'"; Shaner, *Enslaved Leadership;* Bradley, *Slaves and Masters;* Martin, *Slavery as Salvation;* Glancy, "Obstacles to Slaves' Participation"; Osiek, "Female Slaves"; Harrill, *Slaves in the New Testament;* and Glancy, *Slavery in Early Christianity.*

33. Nasrallah, "'You Were Bought with a Price,'" 66.

34. Such studies look, for example, at scribal practices as linked to and implicated in ancient economies; changes in the tools employed in letter writing and distribution; or reconstructions of the Roman Empire's "postal service" as a mechanism of imperial rule. See, e.g., Luijendijk, *Greetings in the Lord;* Poster, "Economy of Letter-Writing"; Haines-Eitzen, *Guardians of Letters;* Gamble, *Books and Readers;* Lowden, "Word Made Visible"; and Kloppenborg, "Literate Media."

35. Emphasis added. Glancy, *Corporal Knowledge,* 44. As an exception, Glancy points to Harrill, "Invective against Paul," 211. Glancy builds especially on the theoretical work of practice-oriented Pierre Bourdieu and phenomenologist Maurice Merleau-Ponty.

36. Glancy, *Corporal Knowledge,* 26.

37. Glancy, *Corporal Knowledge,* 14.

38. Elliott, "What Is Paul?," 121.
39. In 1982, two prominent literary critics separately suggested (albeit in different ways) that the epistolary form of Samuel Richardson's novel *Clarissa* enabled advocacy of cultural revolution against the bourgeoisie: Eagleton, *Rape of Clarissa;* and Castle, *Clarissa's Ciphers.* See also Elizabeth Cook's *tour de force, Epistolary Bodies.*
40. Marx and Engels, *German Ideology,* 42.
41. Emphasis added. Martin, *Corinthian Body,* 3.
42. Massumi, "Autonomy," 100.
43. Elvey, *The Matter of the Text,* is one of the few works to engage NT texts through an ecological lens of textual materiality.
44. Figlerowicz, "Affect Theory," 3.
45. Massumi, *Parables,* 28.
46. Leys, "Turn to Affect," 434 n. 2.
47. Sedgwick and Frank, "Shame in the Cybernetic Fold"; Massumi, "Autonomy."
48. Deleuze, *Negotiations.* Deleuze is perhaps best known for his collaboration with French psychoanalyst Félix Guattari. Together, they obviously were in dialogue with Freud. See, e.g., Deleuze and Guattari, *Anti-Oedipus;* and Deleuze and Guattari, *A Thousand Plateaus.* Their work, in many ways, continues to set the terms of Continental philosophy today.
49. Clough, "Affective Turn," 206–207.
50. Ahmed, *Cultural Politics;* Ahmed, *Promise of Happiness;* Berlant, *Cruel Optimism;* Sedgwick, *Touching Feeling;* Gilroy, *After Empire;* Ngai, *Ugly Feelings;* Probyn, *Blush;* Massumi, *Parables;* Gregg and Seigworth, *Affect Theory Reader.*
51. Brooks avers that readers interpret texts dialogically, in a *transference* process similar to the way in which a patient (*analysand*) and doctor (*analyst*) work together to reconstruct and understand the past through dream interpretation in "The Idea of a Psychoanalytic Literary Criticism."
52. Clough and Halley, *Affective Turn.*
53. Cvetkovich, *Archive of Feelings,* 19.
54. Hogan discusses this in terms of "perceptual emotion triggering." *Affective Narratology,* esp. 46–47. See also Hogan, *What Literature Teaches Us.*
55. Emphasis added. Ahmed, *Cultural Politics,* 4.
56. Sedgwick, "Paranoid Reading," 124.
57. Brinkema, *Forms of the Affects,* 31.
58. Moore, *Gospel Jesuses,* 2. See also, *inter alia,* Spinks, "Thinking the Post-Human."
59. Bennett, *Vibrant Matter,* ix.
60. Moore, *Gospel Jesuses,* 2, 4.
61. Rueckert, "Literature and Ecology," 109. Of course, critics were concerned with nature-related themes long before 1978.
62. See, e.g., Buell, *Environmental Imagination;* Carroll, "Ecology of Victorian Fiction"; and Rueckert, "Literature and Ecology," 109.
63. Horrell, "A New Perspective," 3, 7.

64. See, e.g., White, "Our Ecological Crisis"; Wainwright, "Reading Matt 21:12–22 Ecologically"; Wainwright, "'Hear Then, the Parable of the Seed'"; Wainwright, "Images, Words, and Stories"; Wainwright, "Place, Power, and Potentiality"; Koosed, *Bible and Posthumanism;* and Moore and Kearns, *Divinanimality.* The Earth Bible team met in South Australia in the early 2000s. See especially Habel, *Readings from the Perspective of Earth;* and Habel and Balabanski, *The Earth Story in the New Testament.* Burbery, "Ecocriticism and Christian Literary Scholarship" does concern literary ecocriticism. In classics, see Schliephake, *Ecocriticism.*

65. On this, see, e.g., Newmyer, *Animals, Rights, and Reason.*

66. Ahmed mentions feminist and queer thought as examples of what she calls "'touchy feely' styles of thought." *Cultural Politics,* 207.

67. Bennett, *Vibrant Matter,* esp. xii.

68. Brown, "Thing Theory"; Nilges and Sauri, *Literary Materialisms;* Boscagli, *Stuff Theory;* Tischleder, *Literary Life of Things;* Morrison, *Literature of Waste.*

69. Brown, "Thing Theory," 4.

70. Giddens, *Constitution of Society,* esp. 14. Giddens's work is based largely on Bruno Latour's actor-network theory.

71. Nasrallah, "'You Were Bought with a Price,'" 54.

72. Martin, "Myth of Textual Agency," 1.

73. Pinnock, *Scripture Principle,* 156.

74. Martin, "Myth of Textual Agency," 1.

75. Haskins, *Logos and Power,* 82.

76. This section of the chapter reflects and develops parts of Dinkler, "Between Intention and Reception."

77. On the "numinous power of writing" in antiquity, see, e.g., Schniedewind, *How the Bible Became a Book,* esp. 24–34. On how spoken narratives could "transmit power in a religious or magical sense," see Frankfurter, "Narratives That Do Things," 105.

78. See, e.g., Gager, *Curse Tablets.*

79. Englehardt and Nakassis, "Introduction," 8. See, similarly, Winter's work on inscribed monuments. See, e.g., Winter, "Agency Marked."

80. Fredrickson has Philippians in view, but his remarks apply to Paul's letters more generally in *Eros and the Christ,* 152–153.

81. Michalowski, *Letters from Early Mesopotamia,* 3.

82. Harris, *Ancient Literacy,* 88.

83. Koosed and Moore, "From Affect to Exegesis," 386. See, e.g., Kotrosits, *How Things Feel;* Kotrosits, *Rethinking Early Christian Identity;* Kotrosits, "The Rhetoric of Intimate Spaces"; Runions, "From Disgust to Humor"; and Knust, "Who's Afraid of Canaan's Curse?"

84. Kotrosits, *Rethinking Early Christian Identity,* 113 n. 61. Some NT scholars interested in affect draw more from the social sciences than from literary theory. See, e.g., Barton, "Eschatology and the Emotions"; and Lawrence, "Emotions in Protest."

85. Kotrosits, *Rethinking Early Christian Identity*, 100; on Acts, see esp. 85–116.

86. Usher, *Dionysius of Halicarnassus*. See, recently, Allan, de Jong, and de Jonge, "From *Enargeia* to Immersion."

87. Jeal, "Visual Interpretation."

88. Allan, de Jong, and de Jonge, "From *Enargeia* to Immersion," 36.

89. See, e.g., Webb, *Ekphrasis*, 62–84 and citations therein.

90. Whitaker, *Ekphrasis*, 15.

91. Strachan, *Second Epistle of Paul to the Corinthians*, xxix.

92. Drawing on classical rhetorical categories, Welborn identifies several of these passages as pathetic proofs in "Paul's Appeal." On pathetic proofs in ancient rhetoric generally, see Martin, *Antike Rhetorik*, 160–166.

93. Kotrosits, "The Rhetoric of Intimate Spaces," 134.

94. So, similarly, Krueger: "By late antiquity, the connection between logos and body always already underlies the craft of composition; the practice of writing is the embodiment of the logos." *Writing and Holiness*, 134.

95. Marquis, *Transient Apostle*, 108.

96. Mitchell, *Birth of Christian Hermeneutics*, 102.

97. Mitchell, *Birth of Christian Hermeneutics*, 81, 16.

98. Glancy, *Corporal Knowledge*, 46. Elsewhere, Paul demotes his writing from the status of divine command ("I do not say this as a command. . . . In this matter I am giving my advice," 2 Cor. 8.8, 10). I take this as a rhetorical ploy in response to the failure(s) of his previous letter(s); he still concludes that section by citing Scripture in support of his instructions (2 Cor. 8.14).

99. Fredrickson, *Eros and the Christ*, 152–153.

100. Fevret, *Romantic Correspondence*, 56.

101. Fee, *First Epistle*, 423; Bornkamm, "Missionary Stance," esp. 194–197; Conzelmann, *1 Corinthians*, esp. 159–161.

102. Elliott, "What Is Paul?," 120.

103. Johnson-DeBaufre, "Narrative," 365.

104. Fredrickson, *Eros and the Christ*, 153.

105. Schüssler Fiorenza, *Rhetoric and Ethic*, 111.

106. Fredrickson, *Eros and the Christ*, 153.

107. Elliott, "What Is Paul?," 136.

Chapter 7. Literary Theory and the New Testament

1. Guthrie, "Boats in the Bay," 24.

2. Bal, *Travelling Concepts*, 25.

3. Burke, *Rhetoric of Motives*, 45.

4. Culler, "Philosophy and Literature," 48.

Bibliography

Abrams, Meyer. *The Mirror and the Lamp: Romantic Theory and the Critical Tradition*. Oxford: Oxford University Press, 1953.

Acheraïou, Amar. *Questioning Hybridity, Postcolonialism and Globalization*. New York: Palgrave Macmillan, 2011.

Adam, A. K. M., ed. *Handbook of Postmodern Biblical Interpretation*. St. Louis: Chalice, 2000.

———. "The Sign of Jonah: A Fish-Eye View." *Semeia* 51 (1990): 177–191.

———. *What Is Postmodern Biblical Criticism?* Minneapolis: Fortress, 1995.

Adorno, Theodor. *Negative Dialektik*. Frankfurt am Main: Suhrkamp, 1966. Reprinted in *Gesammelte Schriften*, vol. 6, edited by Rolf Tiedemann. Frankfurt am Main: Suhrkamp, 1973. Page references are to the 1973 edition.

Ahmed, Sara. *The Cultural Politics of Emotion*. 2nd ed. New York: Routledge, 2013.

———. *The Promise of Happiness*. Durham, NC: Duke University Press, 2010.

Aichele, George. *Phantom Messiah: Postmodern Fantasy and the Gospel of Mark*. New York: T&T Clark International, 2006.

———. *The Play of Signifiers: Poststructuralism and Study of the Bible*. Brill Research Perspectives. Leiden: Brill, 2016.

Aichele, George, Peter Miscall, and Richard Walsh. "An Elephant in the Room: Historical-Critical and Postmodern Interpretations of the Bible." *JBL* 128, no. 2 (2009): 383–404.

Aletti, Jean-Noël. *L'art de raconter Jésus-Christ: L'écriture narrative de l'Évangile de Luc*. Paris: Seuil, 1989.

Alexander, Loveday. *The Preface to Luke's Gospel: Literary Convention and Social Context in Luke 1.1–4 and Acts 1.1*. Cambridge, UK: Cambridge University Press, 1993.

Alexander, Philip. "A Typology of Intertextual Relations Based on the Manchester-Durham Typology of Anonymous and Pseudepigraphic Jewish Literature of Antiquity." In *Between Text and Text: The Hermeneutics of Intertextuality in Ancient Cultures and Their Afterlife in Medieval and*

Modern Times, edited by Michaela Bauks, Wayne Horowitz, and Armin Lange, 66–88. Göttingen: Vandenhoeck & Ruprecht, 2013.

Allan, Rutger J., Irene J. F. de Jong, and Casper C. de Jonge. "From *Enargeia* to Immersion: The Ancient Roots of a Modern Concept." *Style* 51, no. 1 (2017): 34–51.

Allen, Amy. *The End of Progress: Decolonizing the Normative Foundations of Critical Theory.* New York: Columbia University Press, 2016.

Alter, Robert. *The Art of Biblical Narrative.* New York: Basic Books, 1981.

Althusser, Louis. "Idéologie et appareils idéologiques d'État (notes per une recherche)." *La Pensée* 151 (1970): 3–38.

Amador, J. D. Hester. *Academic Constraints in Rhetorical Criticism of the New Testament: An Introduction to a Rhetoric of Power.* Sheffield: Sheffield Academic, 1999.

Anderson, Cheryl. *Ancient Laws and Contemporary Controversies: The Need for Inclusive Biblical Interpretation.* New York: Oxford University Press, 2009.

Anderson, Janice Capel, and Stephen D. Moore. "Introduction: The Lives of Mark." In *Mark and Method: New Approaches in Biblical Studies,* edited by Janice Capel Anderson and Stephen D. Moore, 1–22. Minneapolis: Fortress, 1992.

Anderson, Paul N. *From Crisis to Christ: A Contextual Introduction to the New Testament.* Nashville: Abingdon, 2014.

Ankersmit, Frank. *Historical Representation.* Stanford, CA: Stanford University Press, 2001.

Arnold, Matthew. *Literature and Dogma: An Essay towards a Better Apprehension of the Bible.* New York: Macmillan, 1874.

Ashcroft, Bill, Gareth Griffiths, and Helen Tiffin. *The Empire Writes Back: Theory and Practice in Postcolonial Literatures.* London: Routledge, 1989.

Ashton, John. "Narrative Criticism." In *Studying John: Approaches to the Fourth Gospel,* 141–165. Oxford: Clarendon Press, 1994.

Attridge, Harold W. "Genre-Bending in the Fourth Gospel." *JBL* 121, no. 1 (2002): 3–21.

———. "Some Methodological Considerations Regarding John, Jesus, and History." Paper presented at the Princeton Conference on John, Jesus, and History, March 2016.

Auden, W. H. "In Memory of Sigmund Freud." In *Collected Poems,* edited by Edward Mendelson, 271–274. New York: Modern Library, 2007.

Auerbach, Eric. *Mimesis: The Representation of Reality in Western Literature.* Translated by Willard R. Trask. Princeton: Princeton University Press, 1953.

Aune, David E. "Form Criticism." In *The Blackwell Companion to the New Testament,* edited by David E. Aune, 140–155. Malden, MA: Blackwell, 2010.

———. "Literary Criticism." In *The Blackwell Companion to the New Testament,* edited by David E. Aune, 116–139. Malden, MA: Blackwell, 2010.

Austin, J. L. *How to Do Things with Words.* 2nd ed. Cambridge, MA: Harvard University Press, 1975.

Avalos, Hector. *The End of Biblical Studies.* Amherst, NY: Prometheus, 2007.

Badiou, Alain. *Saint Paul: The Foundation of Universalism*. Translated by Ray Brassier. Stanford, CA: Stanford University Press, 2003.

Bailey, James L., and Lyle D. Vander Broek. *Literary Forms in the New Testament*. Louisville: Westminster John Knox, 1992.

Bailey, Mark L. "Guidelines for Interpreting Jesus' Parables." *BSac* 155 (1998): 29–38.

Bailey, Randall C., Tat-siong Benny Liew, and Fernando F. Segovia, eds. *They Were All Together in One Place? Toward Minority Biblical Criticism*. Atlanta: Society of Biblical Literature, 2009.

Baird, William R. *History of New Testament Research*. Vol. 2, *From Jonathan Edwards to Rudolf Bultmann*. Minneapolis: Augsburg Press, 2003.

———. "Letters of Recommendation: A Study of II Cor 3:1–3." *JBL* 80, no. 2 (1961): 166–172.

Bakhtin, Mikhail. "Discourse in the Novel." In *The Dialogic Imagination: Four Essays*, edited by Michael Holquist, translated by Caryl Emerson and Michael Holquist, 259–422. Austin: University of Texas Press, 1981.

———. "The Problem of Speech Genres." In *Speech Genres and Other Late Essays*, edited by Caryl Emerson and Michael Holquist, translated by Vern W. McGee, 60–102. Austin: University of Texas Press, 1986.

———. *Problems of Dostoevsky's Poetics*. Edited and translated by Caryl Emerson. Minneapolis: University of Minnesota Press, 1984.

———. *Rabelais and His World*. Translated by Helene Iswolsky. Bloomington: Indiana University Press, 1984.

Bakhtin, Mikhail, and Pavel Medvedev. *The Formal Method in Literary Scholarship: A Critical Introduction to Sociological Poetics*. Translated by Albert J. Wehrle. Baltimore: Johns Hopkins University Press, 1991.

Bal, Mieke. *Narratology: Introduction to the Theory of Narrative*. 2nd ed. Toronto: University of Toronto Press, 1997.

———. *Travelling Concepts in the Humanities: A Rough Guide*. Toronto: University of Toronto Press, 2002.

Baldick, Chris. *Criticism and Literary Theory, 1890 to the Present*. London: Longman, 1996.

Barr, James. "Reading the Bible as Literature." *Bulletin of the John Rylands University Library of Manchester* 56 (1973): 10–33.

Barreto, Eric D. *Ethnic Negotiations: The Function of Race and Ethnicity in Acts 16*. Tübingen: Mohr Siebeck, 2010.

Bartchy, S. Scott. *Mallon Chrēsai: First Century Slavery and the Interpretation of 1 Corinthians 7:21*. Missoula, MT: Society of Biblical Literature for the Seminar on Paul, 1973.

Barth, Karl. "Fifteen Answers to Professor von Harnack." In *The Beginnings of Dialectic Theology*, edited by James M. Robinson, translated by Keith R. Crim, 167–170. Richmond: John Knox, 1968.

Barth, Markus. "Jews and Gentiles: The Social Character of Justification." *Journal of Ecumenical Studies* 5, no. 2 (1968): 241–267.

Barthes, Roland. "L'analyse structurale du récit: A propos d'Actes X–XI." In *Exégèse et herméneutique,* edited by Xavier Léon-Dufour, 181–204. Paris: Seuil, 1971.

———. "The Death of the Author." In *Image, Music, Text,* translated by Stephen Heath, 142–48. New York: Hill and Wang, 1977.

———. "From Work to Text." In *Literary Criticism: A Reading,* edited by B. Das and J. M. Mohanty, 413–420. Calcutta: Oxford University Press, 1985.

———. *S/Z: An Essay.* Translated by Richard Miller. New York: Farrar, Straus, & Giroux, 1974.

Barthes, Roland, François Bovon, Franz J. Leenhardt, Robert Martin-Achard, and Jean Starobinski. *Analyse structurale et exégèse biblique.* Neuchâtel: Delachaux et Niestlé, 1971.

Barton, John. "Beliebigkeit." In *Derrida's Bible (Reading a Page of Scripture with a Little Help from Derrida),* edited by Yvonne Sherwood, 301–303. New York: Palgrave Macmillan, 2004.

———. *The Nature of Biblical Criticism.* Louisville: Westminster John Knox, 2007.

———. *Reading the Old Testament: Method in Biblical Study.* Philadelphia: Westminster, 1984.

Barton, Stephen. "Eschatology and the Emotions in Early Christianity." *JBL* 130 (2011): 571–591.

Bauckham, Richard. *Gospel Women: Studies of the Named Women in the Gospels.* Grand Rapids, MI: Eerdmans, 2002.

Bazzana, Giovanni B. "Neo-Marxism, Language Ideology, and the New Testament." *B&CT* 8, no. 2 (2012): 16–26.

Beardslee, William A. *Literary Criticism of the New Testament.* Philadelphia: Fortress, 1970.

———. "What Is It About? Reference in New Testament Literary Criticism." In *The New Literary Criticism and the New Testament,* edited by Elizabeth Struthers Malbon and Edgar V. McKnight, 367–386. Sheffield: Sheffield Academic, 1994.

Beck, David. *The Discipleship Paradigm: Readers and Anonymous Characters in the Fourth Gospel.* Leiden: Brill, 1997.

Becker, Adam H., and Annette Yoshiko Reed, eds. *The Ways That Never Parted: Jews and Christians in Late Antiquity and the Early Middle Ages.* Minneapolis: Fortress, 2007.

Becker, Eve-Marie. *Letter Hermeneutics in Second Corinthians: Studies in Literarkritik and Communication.* Translated by Helen S. Heron. London: T&T Clark, 2004.

Beebee, Thomas O. *The Ideology of Genre: A Comparative Study of Generic Instability.* University Park, PA: Pennsylvania State University Press, 1994.

Bender, John B., and David E. Wellbery. *The Ends of Rhetoric: History, Theory, Practice.* Stanford, CA: Stanford University Press, 1990.

Benjamin, Walter. *The Origin of German Tragic Drama.* Translated by John Osborne. London: Verso, 1977.

———. "The Work of Art in an Age of Mechanical Reproduction." In *Illuminations,* edited by Hannah Arendt, translated by Harry Zohn, 217–252. New York: Harcourt Brace Jovanovich, 1968.

Bennema, Cornelis. *Encountering Jesus: Character Studies in the Gospel of John.* 2nd ed. Minneapolis: Augsburg Press, 2014.

———. *A Theory of Character in New Testament Narrative.* Minneapolis: Fortress, 2014.

Bennett, Jane. *Vibrant Matter: A Political Ecology of Things.* Durham, NC: Duke University Press, 2009.

Berger, Klaus. "Hellenistische Gattungen im neuen Testament." *ANRW* 25, no. 2 (1984): 1031–1432.

Berger, Peter, and Thomas Luckmann. *The Social Construction of Reality.* Garden City, NY: Doubleday, 1966.

Berlant, Lauren. *Cruel Optimism.* Durham, NC: Duke University Press, 2011.

Berlin, Adele. *Poetics and Interpretation of Biblical Narrative.* Sheffield: Almond, 1983.

Bernstein, R. J. *Beyond Objectivism and Relativism: Science, Hermeneutics, and Praxis.* Oxford: Basil Blackwell, 1983.

Bérubé, Michael. "Aesthetics and the Literal Imagination." In *Falling into Theory: Conflicting Views on Reading Literature,* edited by David Richter, 391–398. Boston: Bedford, 2000.

Betz, Hans Dieter. *Der Apostel Paulus und die sokratische Tradition: Eine exegetische Untersuchung zu seiner "Apologie" 2 Korinther 10–13.* Tübingen: Mohr Siebeck, 1972.

———. *Galatians: A Commentary on Paul's Letter to the Churches in Galatia.* Hermeneia. Philadelphia: Fortress, 1979.

———. "Literary Composition and Function of Paul's Letter to the Galatians." *NTS* 21, no. 3 (1975): 353–379.

———. *Second Corinthians 8 and 9: A Commentary on Two Administrative Letters of the Apostle Paul.* Hermeneia. Philadelphia: Fortress, 1985.

———. *The Sermon on the Mount: A Commentary on the Sermon on the Mount, including the Sermon on the Plain (Matthew 5:3–7:27 and Luke 6:20–49).* Hermeneia. Minneapolis: Fortress, 1995.

Bhabha, Homi. *The Location of Culture.* London: Routledge, 1994.

Black, C. Clifton. "Mark as Historian of God's Kingdom." *CBQ* 71, no. 1 (2009): 64–83.

Blechmann, W. "Probleme der Explication Française." *Germanisch-Romanische Monatsschrift* 38 (1957): 383–392.

Blomberg, Craig L. *The Historical Reliability of the Gospels.* 2nd ed. Downers Grove, IL: InterVarsity, 2007.

————. *Interpreting the Parables*. Downers Grove, IL: InterVarsity, 1990.

Bloom, Harold. *Poetry and Repression: Revisionism from Blake to Stevens*. New Haven: Yale University Press, 1976.

Bloomquist, L. Gregory. "The Intertexture of Lukan Apocalyptic Discourse." In *The Intertexture of Apocalyptic Discourse in the New Testament*, edited by Duane F. Watson, 45–68. Leiden: Brill, 2002.

Blount, Brian K. *Can I Get a Witness? Reading Revelation through African American Culture*. Louisville: Westminster John Knox, 2005.

Blount, Brian K., Clarice Martin, Cain Felder, and Emerson Powery, eds. *True to Our Native Land: An African American Commentary on the New Testament*. Minneapolis: Fortress, 2007.

Bockmuehl, Markus. *Seeing the Word: Refocusing New Testament Study*. Grand Rapids, MI: Baker Academic, 2006.

Boer, Roland, ed. *Bakhtin and Genre Theory in Biblical Studies*. Atlanta: Society of Biblical Literature, 2007.

————. "Marx, Postcolonialism and the Bible." In *Postcolonial Biblical Criticism: Interdisciplinary Intersections*, edited by Stephen D. Moore and Fernando F. Segovia, 166–183. London: T&T Clark, 2005.

————, ed. *Secularism and Biblical Studies*. London: Equinox, 2010.

————. "Twenty-Five Years of Marxist Biblical Criticism." *Currents in Biblical Research* 5 (2007): 298–321.

Boer, Roland, and Jorunn Økland, eds. *Marxist Feminist Criticism of the Bible*. Sheffield: Sheffield Phoenix, 2008.

Bogel, Fredric V. *New Formalist Criticism: Theory and Practice*. New York: Palgrave Macmillan, 2013.

Bonaparte, Marie. *The Life and Works of Edgar Allan Poe: A Psychoanalytic Interpretation*. Translated by J. Rodker. London: Imago, 1949.

Bond, Helen, Jens Schröter, and Chris Keith, eds. *The Reception of Jesus in the First Three Centuries*. 2 vols. London: Bloomsbury T&T Clark, forthcoming.

Booth, Wayne C. *Modern Dogma and the Rhetoric of Assent*. Chicago: University of Chicago Press, 1974.

Borchert, Gerald. "The Conduct of Christians in the Face of the 'Fiery Ordeal' (1 Pet 4:12–5:11)." *RevExp* 79, no. 3 (1982): 451–462.

Borg, Michelle, and Graeme Miles. "Introduction." In *Approaches to Genre in the Ancient World*, edited by Michelle Borg and Graeme Miles, 1–5. Newcastle upon Tyne: Cambridge Scholars, 2013.

Bornkamm, Günther. *Jesus of Nazareth*. Translated by Irene and Fraser McLuskey with James M. Robinson. New York: Harper, 1960.

————. "The Missionary Stance of Paul in 1 Corinthians 9 and in Acts." In *Studies in Luke-Acts: Essays Presented in Honor of Paul Schubert*, edited by L. E. Keck and J. L. Martyn, 194–207. Nashville: Abingdon, 1966.

Boscagli, Maurizia. *Stuff Theory: Everyday Objects, Radical Materialism*. New York: Bloomsbury, 2014.

Bourdieu, Pierre. *Distinction: A Social Critique of the Judgment of Taste.* Translated by Richard Nice. Cambridge, MA: Harvard University Press, 1979.

Bousset, Wilhelm. *Kyrios Christos: A History of the Belief in Christ from the Beginnings of Christianity to Irenaeus.* Translated by John E. Steely. Nashville: Abingdon, 1970.

Bové, Paul. *In the Wake of Theory.* Middletown, CT: Wesleyan University Press, 1992.

Bovon, François. "Foi chrétienne et religion populaire dans la première epître de Pierre." *Études Théologiques et Religieuses* 53 (1978): 25–41.

———. "La structure canonique de L'Evangile et de l'Apotre." *Cristianesimo nella Storia* 15 (1994): 559–576.

Bowersock, G. W. *Fiction as History: Nero to Julian.* Berkeley: University of California Press, 1994.

Boyarin, Daniel. *A Radical Jew: Paul and the Politics of Identity.* Berkeley: University of California Press, 1994.

———. "The Suffering Christ as a Jewish Midrash." In *Religion und Politik: Das Messianische in Theologien, Religionswissenschaften und Philosophien des zwanzigsten Jahrhunderts,* edited by Gesine Palmer and Thomas Brose, 209–224. Tübingen: Mohr Siebeck, 2013.

Bradley, Keith. *Slaves and Masters in the Roman Empire: A Study in Social Control.* New York: Oxford University Press, 1987.

Breslin, James. *From Modern to Contemporary: American Poetry, 1945–1965.* Chicago: University of Chicago Press, 1984.

Briggs, Sheila. "Can an Enslaved God Liberate? Hermeneutical Reflections on Philippians 2:6–11." *Semeia* 47 (1989): 137–53.

Brinkema, Eugenie. *The Forms of the Affects.* Durham, NC: Duke University Press, 2014.

Brooks, Cleanth. "Metaphor and the Tradition." In *Modern Poetry and the Tradition,* 1–17. Chapel Hill: University of North Carolina Press, 1939.

———. *The Well Wrought Urn: Studies in the Structure of Poetry.* Orlando: Harcourt, 1947.

Brooks, Cleanth, and Robert Penn Warren. *Understanding Fiction.* 2nd ed. New York: Appleton-Century-Crofts, 1959.

———. *Understanding Poetry.* 3rd ed. New York: Holt, Rinehart and Winston, 1964.

Brooks, Peter. "Freud's Masterplot." In *The Critical Tradition: Classic Texts and Contemporary Trends.* 3rd ed., edited by David H. Richter, 882–892. Boston: Bedford/St Martin's 1989.

———. "The Idea of a Psychoanalytic Literary Criticism." In *Discourse in Psychoanalysis and Literature,* edited by Shlomith Rimmon-Kenan, 1–18. New York: Methuen, 1987.

Brooten, Bernadette. *Love between Women: Early Christian Responses to Female Homoeroticism.* Chicago: University of Chicago Press, 1996.

Brown, Bill. "Thing Theory." *CI* 28, no. 1 (2001): 1–22.

Brunetière, Ferdinand. *L'évolution de la poésie lyrique en France au dix-neuvième siècle*. Paris: Hachette, 1894.

———. *L'évolution des genres dans l'histoire de la littérature*. Paris: Hachette, 1890.

Bruster, Douglas. "Shakespeare and the Composite Text." In *Renaissance Literature and Its Formal Engagements*, edited by Mark David Rasmussen, 43–66. Basingstoke: Palgrave, 2002.

Buell, Denise Kimber. *Why This New Race: Ethnic Reasoning in Early Christianity*. New York: Columbia University Press, 2005.

Buell, Denise Kimber, and Carolyn Johnson Hodge. "The Politics of Interpretation: The Rhetoric of Race and Ethnicity in Paul." *JBL* 123, no. 2 (2004): 235–251.

Buell, Lawrence. *The Environmental Imagination: Thoreau, Nature Writing, and the Formation of American Culture*. Cambridge, MA: Harvard University Press, 1995.

Bugge, Christian A. *Die Haupt-Parabeln Jesu*. Giessen: J. Rickersche Verlagsbuchhandlung, 1903.

Bultmann, Rudolf. *The History of the Synoptic Tradition*. Rev. ed. Translated by John Marsh. New York: Harper & Row, 1963.

———. "Ist voraussetzungslose Exegese möglich?" *TZ* 13 (1957): 409–417.

———. *Theology of the New Testament*. 2 vols. Translated by Kendrick Grobel. Waco, TX: Baylor University Press, 2007.

———. "Zur Frage des Wunders." In *Glauben und Verstehen: Gesammelte Aufsätze von Rudolf Bultmann*. Bd. 1, 214–228. Tübingen: Mohr Siebeck, 1954.

Burbery, Timothy J. "Ecocriticism and Christian Literary Scholarship." *Christianity & Literature* 61 (2012): 189–214.

Burke, Kenneth. *The Philosophy of Literary Form: Studies in Symbolic Action*. Berkeley: University of California Press, 1941.

———. *A Rhetoric of Motives*. Berkeley: University of California Press, 1969.

Burke, Sean. *The Death and Return of the Author: Criticism and Subjectivity in Barthes, Foucault and Derrida*. 2nd ed. Edinburgh: Edinburgh University Press, 1998.

Burnet, Régis, Didier Luciani, and Geert van Oyen, eds. *Le lecteur: Sixième Colloque International du RRENAB, Université Catholique de Louvain, 24–26 mai 2012*. Leuven: Peeters, 2015.

Burnett, Gary W. *Paul and the Salvation of the Individual*. Leiden: Brill, 2001.

Burridge, Richard A. *What Are the Gospels? A Comparison with Greco-Roman Biography*. Cambridge, UK: Cambridge University Press, 1992.

Buss, M. J. *Biblical Form Criticism in Its Context*. Sheffield: Sheffield Academic, 1999.

Butler, Judith. *Bodies That Matter: On the Discursive Limits of "Sex."* New York: Routledge, 1993.

———. *Gender Trouble: Feminism and the Subversion of Identity*. New York: Routledge, 1990.

Byron, Gay, and Vanessa Lovelace. "Introduction: Methods and the Making of Womanist Biblical Hermeneutics." In *Womanist Interpretations of the Bible: Expanding the Discourse,* edited by Gay Byron and Vanessa Lovelace, 1–18. *Semeia* 85. Atlanta: Society of Biblical Literature Press, 2016.

———. *Symbolic Blackness and Ethnic Difference in Early Christian Literature.* New York: Routledge, 2002.

Byrskog, Samuel. *Story as History—History as Story: The Gospel Tradition in the Context of Ancient Oral History.* Tübingen: Mohr Siebeck, 2000.

Cadbury, Henry Joel. *The Making of Luke-Acts.* London: Macmillan, 1927.

Cadoux, A. T. *The Parables of Jesus.* London: James Clarke, 1931.

Callen, Terrance. "The Preface of Luke-Acts and Historiography." *NTS* 31, no. 4 (1985): 576–581.

Camery-Hoggatt, Jerry. *Irony in Mark's Gospel: Text and Subtext.* New York: Cambridge University Press, 1992.

Campbell, Douglas A. *Framing Paul: An Epistolary Biography.* Grand Rapids, MI: Eerdmans, 2014.

Campbell, Keith. *Of Heroes and Villains: The Influence of the Psalmic Lament on Synoptic Characterization.* Eugene, OR: Wipf & Stock, 2013.

Cancik, Hubert. "Hairesis, Diatribe, Ekklesia: Griechische Schulgeschichte und das Lukanische Geschichtswerk." *Early Christianity* 2, no. 3 (2011): 312–334.

———. "The History of Culture, Religion, and Institutions in Ancient Historiography: Philological Observations Concerning Luke's History." *JBL* 116, no. 4 (1997): 673–695.

Carey, Holly J. *Jesus' Cry from the Cross: Towards a First-Century Understanding of the Intertextual Relationship between Psalm 22 and the Narrative of Mark's Gospel.* London: T&T Clark, 2009.

Carroll, Joseph. "The Ecology of Victorian Fiction." *Philosophy and Literature* 25 (2001): 295–313.

Carson, D. A. "Matthew." In *The Expositor's Bible Commentary,* vol. 8, edited by F. E. Gaebelein, 1–599. Grand Rapids, MI: Zondervan, 1984.

Castelli, Elizabeth A. *Imitating Paul: A Discourse of Power.* Louisville: Westminster John Knox, 1991.

Castelli, Elizabeth A., Stephen D. Moore, Gary A. Phillips, and Regina M. Schwartz, eds. *The Postmodern Bible: Bible and Culture Collective.* New Haven: Yale University Press, 1995.

Castle, Terry. *Clarissa's Ciphers: Meaning and Disruption in Richardson's "Clarissa."* Ithaca, NY: Cornell University Press, 1982.

Chakrabarty, Dipesh. *Provincializing Europe: Postcolonial Thought and Historical Difference.* Princeton: Princeton University Press, 2000.

Chartier, Roger. *Cultural History: Between Practices and Representations.* Translated by Lydia G. Cochrane. Ithaca, NY: Cornell University Press, 1988.

Chatman, Seymour. *Story and Discourse: Narrative Structure in Discourse and Film.* Ithaca, NY: Cornell University Press, 1978.

Childs, Donald J. *The Birth of New Criticism: Conflict and Conciliation in the Early Work of William Empson, I. A. Richards, Laura Riding, and Robert Graves.* Montreal: McGill-Queen's University Press, 2013.

Choi, Jin Young. *Postcolonial Embodiment of Discipleship: An Asian and Asian American Feminist Reading of the Gospel of Mark.* New York: Palgrave Macmillan, 2015.

Claassen, Jo-Marie. *Ovid Revisited: The Poet in Exile.* London: Bloomsbury Academic, 2008.

Clark, Elizabeth A. *History, Theory, Text: Historians and the Linguistic Turn.* Cambridge, MA: Harvard University Press, 2004.

Classen, Carl Joachim. "Paulus und die antike Rhetorik." *ZNW* 82, nos. 1–2 (1991): 1–33.

Clines, David J. A. "Possibilities and Priorities of Biblical Interpretation in an International Perspective." *BibInt* 1, no. 1 (1993): 67–87.

———. "A World Established on Water (Psalm 24): Reader-Response, Deconstruction and Bespoke Interpretation." In *The New Literary Criticism and the Hebrew Bible,* edited by J. Cheryl Exum and David J. A. Clines, 79–90. Sheffield: Sheffield Academic, 1993.

Clivaz, Claire. "'Asleep by Grief' (Lk 22:45): Reading from the Body at the Crossroads of Narratology and New Historicism." *B&CT* 3 (2006): 1–29.

Clough, Patricia Ticineto. "The Affective Turn: Political Economy, Biomedia, and Bodies." In *The Affect Theory Reader,* edited by Melissa Gregg and Gregory Seigworth, 206–225. Durham, NC: Duke University Press, 2010.

Clough, Patricia T., with Jean Halley, eds. *The Affective Turn: Theorizing the Social.* Durham, NC: Duke University Press, 2007.

Cohen, Shaye J. D. "Menstruants and the Sacred in Judaism and Christianity." In *Women's History and Ancient History,* edited by Sarah B. Pomeroy, 273–299. Chapel Hill: University of North Carolina Press, 1991.

Coleridge, Mark. *The Birth of the Lukan Narrative: Narrative as Christology in Luke 1–2.* Sheffield: Sheffield Academic, 1993.

Collins, Adela Yarbro. "Genre and the Gospels." *JR* 75 (1995): 239–246.

———. "Introduction: Early Christian Apocalypticism." *Semeia* 36 (1986): 1–11.

Collins, John J. *The Apocalyptic Imagination: An Introduction to Jewish Apocalyptic Literature.* 2nd ed. Grand Rapids, MI: Eerdmans, 1998.

———. *Beyond the Qumran Community: The Sectarian Movement of the Dead Sea Scrolls.* Grand Rapids, MI: Eerdmans, 2009.

———. *The Bible after Babel: Historical Criticism in a Postmodern Age.* Grand Rapids, MI: Eerdmans, 2005.

———. "From Prophecy to Apocalypticism: The Expectation of the End." In *The Encyclopedia of Apocalypticism,* vol. 1, edited by John J. Collins. New York: Continuum, 2000.

———. "Introduction: Towards the Morphology of a Genre." *Semeia* 14 (1979): 1–20.

———. *Scriptures and Sectarianism: Essays on the Dead Sea Scrolls.* Tübingen: Mohr Siebeck, 2014.

———. "Sectarian Consciousness in the Dead Sea Scrolls." In *Heavenly Tablets: Interpretation, Identity, and Tradition in Ancient Judaism,* edited by L. LiDonnici and A. Lieber, 177–192. Leiden: Brill, 2007.

Conway, Colleen. *Behold the Man: Jesus and Greco-Roman Masculinity.* New York: Oxford University Press, 2008.

———. "There and Back Again: Johannine History on the Other Side of Literary Criticism." In *Anatomies of Narrative Criticism: The Past, Present, and Futures of the Fourth Gospel as Literature,* edited by Tom Thatcher and Stephen D. Moore, 77–91. Leiden: Brill, 2008.

Conzelmann, Hans. *1 Corinthians.* Hermeneia. Philadelphia: Fortress, 1975.

———. *The Theology of St. Luke.* Translated by Geoffrey Buswell. New York: Harper & Brothers, 1960.

Cook, Elizabeth. *Epistolary Bodies: Gender and Genre in the Eighteenth-Century Republic of Letters.* Stanford, CA: Stanford University Press, 1996.

Cook, Stephen. *Prophecy and Apocalypticism: The Post-Exilic Social Setting.* Minneapolis: Fortress, 1995.

Cosgrove, Charles H. "The Divine Δεῖ in Luke-Acts." *NovT* 26 (1984): 168–190.

Counet, Patrick Chatelion. *John, a Postmodern Gospel: Introduction to Deconstructive Exegesis Applied to the Fourth Gospel.* Leiden: Brill, 2000.

Crawford, Donald. *Kant's Aesthetic Theory.* Madison: University of Wisconsin Press, 1974.

Crenshaw, Kimberlé. "Mapping the Margins: Intersectionality, Identity Politics, and Violence against Women of Color." *Stanford Law Review* 43 (1991): 1241–1299.

Cronjé, J. Van W. "Defamiliarization in the Letter to the Galatians." In *A South African Perspective on the New Testament,* edited by J. H. Petzer and P. J. Hartin, 214–227. Leiden: Brill, 1986.

Crossan, John Dominic. *In Parables: The Challenge of the Historical Jesus.* New York: Harper & Row, 1973.

———. "Parable and Example in the Teaching of Jesus." *Semeia* 1 (1974): 63–104.

———. "The Servant Parables." *Semeia* 1 (1974): 17–62.

Crossley, James G. *Why Christianity Happened: A Sociohistorical Account of Christian Origins (26–50 CE).* Louisville: Westminster John Knox, 2006.

Culbertson, Philip, and Elaine M. Wainwright, eds. *The Bible in/and Popular Culture: A Creative Encounter.* Atlanta: Society of Biblical Literature, 2010.

Culler, Jonathan. *The Literary in Theory.* Stanford, CA: Stanford University Press, 2007.

———. *On Deconstruction: Theory and Criticism after Structuralism.* Ithaca, NY: Cornell University Press, 1982.

———. "Philosophy and Literature: The Fortunes of the Performative." *Poetics Today* 21, no. 3 (2000): 48–67.

Culpepper, R. Alan. *Anatomy of the Fourth Gospel: A Study in Literary Design.* Philadelphia: Fortress, 1983.

Cunningham, Valentine. "The Aw(e)ful Necessity of Bible Re-Reading." In *Visions and Revisions: The Word and the Text,* edited by Roger Kojecký and Andrew Tate, 43–51. Newcastle upon Tyne: Cambridge Scholars, 2013.

———. "Bible Reading and/after Theory." In *The Oxford Handbook of the Reception History of the Bible,* edited by Michaël Lieb, Emma Mason, Jonathan Roberts, and Christopher Rowland, 649–674. Oxford: Oxford University Press, 2011.

———. *Reading after Theory.* Oxford: Blackwell, 2002.

Cvetkovich, Ann. *An Archive of Feelings: Trauma, Sexuality, and Lesbian Public Cultures.* Durham, NC: Duke University Press, 2003.

Dahl, Nils A. "The Doctrine of Justification: Its Social Function and Implications." In *Studies in Paul: Theology for the Early Christian Mission,* 95–120. Minneapolis: Fortress, 1977.

D'Angelo, Mary Rose. "Gender and Power in the Gospel of Mark: The Daughter of Jairus and the Woman with the Flow of Blood." In *Miracles in Jewish and Christian Antiquity: Imagining Truth,* edited by John C. Cavadini, 83–109. Notre Dame, IN: University of Notre Dame Press, 1999.

Darr, John. *Herod the Fox: Audience Criticism and Lukan Characterization.* Sheffield: Sheffield Academic, 1998.

———. *On Character Building: The Reader and the Rhetoric of Characterization in Luke-Acts.* Louisville: Westminster John Knox, 1992.

Darwin, Charles. *On the Origin of Species by Means of Natural Selection, or The Preservation of Favoured Races in the Struggle for Life.* London: J. Murray, 1859.

David-Fox, Michael, Peter Holquist, and Alexander M. Martin. "The Imperial Turn." *Kritika: Explorations in Russian and Eurasian History* 7 (2006): 705–712.

Dean-Jones, Leslie. "Menstrual Bleeding according to the Hippocratics and Aristotle." *TAPA* 119 (1989): 177–192.

Deissmann, Adolf. *Light from the Ancient East: The NT Illustrated by Recently Discovered Texts of the Graeco-Roman World.* Translated by L. R. M. Strachan. London: Hodder and Stoughton, 1927.

de Jong, Irene. *Narratology and Classics: A Practical Guide.* Oxford: Oxford University Press, 2014.

De La Torre, Miguel. *Reading the Bible from the Margins.* Maryknoll, NY: Orbis, 2002.

Deleuze, Gilles. *Negotiations, 1972–1990.* Translated by Martin Joughin. New York: Columbia University Press, 1995.

Deleuze, Gilles, and Félix Guattari. *Anti-Oedipus: Capitalism and Schizophrenia.* Translated by Robert Hurley, Mark Seem, and Helen R. Lane. Minneapolis: University of Minnesota Press, 1972.

———. *A Thousand Plateaus: Capitalism and Schizophrenia.* Translated by Brian Massumi. Minneapolis: University of Minnesota Press, 1980.

Delobel, J. "L'onction par la pécheresse: La composition littéraire de Lc., VII, 36–50." *ETL* 42 (1966): 414–475.

de Man, Paul. *Allegories of Reading: Figural Language in Rousseau, Nietzsche, Rilke, and Proust.* New Haven: Yale University Press, 1979.

de Meeus, X. "Composition de Lc. XIV et genre symposiaque." *ETL* 37 (1961): 847–870.

D'Entrevernes, Groupe. *Signes et paraboles: Sémiotique et texte évangélique.* Paris: Seuil, 1977.

Depew, Mary, and Dirk Obbink, eds. *Matrices of Genre: Authors, Canons, and Society.* Cambridge, MA: Harvard University Press, 2000.

Derrida, Jacques. *De la grammatologie.* Paris: Minuit, 1967.

———. "Dialogue with Jacques Derrida." In *Dialogues with Contemporary Continental Thinkers: The Phenomenological Heritage: Paul Ricoeur, Emmanuel Levinas, Herbert Marcuse, Stanislas Breton, Jacques Derrida,* edited by Richard Kearney, 105–126. Manchester: Manchester University Press, 1984.

———. "Freud and the Scene of Writing." In *Writing and Difference,* translated by Alan Bass, 196–231. Chicago: University of Chicago Press, 1978.

———. "The Law of Genre." Translated by Avital Ronell. *CI* 7, no. 1 (1980): 55–81.

———. *The Other Heading: Reflections on Today's Europe.* Translated by Pascale Anne-Brault and Michael Naas. Bloomington: Indiana University Press, 1992.

———. "Structure, Sign, and Play in the Discourse of the Human Sciences." In *The Structuralist Controversy: The Languages of Criticism and the Sciences of Man,* edited by Richard Macksey and Eugenio Donato, 247–265. Baltimore: Johns Hopkins University Press, 1970.

de Saussure, Ferdinand. *Course in General Linguistics.* Edited by Perry Meisel and Haun Saussy. Translated by Wade Baskin. New York: Columbia University Press, 1959.

Dibelius, Martin. *An die Kolosser, Epheser, an Philemon.* HNT 12. Tübingen: Mohr, 1953.

———. "The First Christian Historian." In *Studies in the Acts of the Apostles,* edited by Heinrich Greeven, translated by Mary Ling, 123–137. New York: Scribner, 1956.

———. *From Tradition to Gospel.* 2nd ed. Translated by Bertram Lee Woolf. New York: Charles Scribner's Sons, 1935.

Dicken, Frank. *Herod as a Composite Character in Luke-Acts.* Tübingen: Mohr Siebeck, 2014.

Dicken, Frank, and Julia Snyder, eds. *Character and Characterization in Luke-Acts.* London: Bloomsbury T&T Clark, 2016.

Dickens, Charles. *The Old Curiosity Shop.* London: Chapman and Hall, 1841.

Dillon, R. J. "Previewing Luke's Project from His Prologue (Luke 1:1–4)." *CBQ* 43 (1981): 205–227.

Dinkler, Michal Beth. "Beyond the Normative/Descriptive Divide: Hermeneutics and Narrativity." In *Verstehen und Interpretieren,* edited by Andreas Mauz. Paderborn: Ferdinand Schöningh, 2019.

———. "Building Character on the Road to Emmaus: Lukan Characterization in Contemporary Literary Perspective." *JBL* 136, no. 3 (2017): 687–706.

———. *How to Do Things with Stories: Biblical Narrative as Rhetoric.* Cambridge: Cambridge University Press, under contract.

———. "Narratological Jesus Research: An Oxymoron?" In *Jesus, quo vadis? Entwicklungen und Perspektiven der aktuellen Jesusforschung Conference Proceedings*, edited by Eckart Schmidt, 187–230. Biblisch-theologische Studien. Neukirchen-Vluyn: Neukirchener Verlag, 2018.

———. "A New Formalist Approach to Narrative Christology: Returning to the Structure of the Synoptic Gospels." *Hervormde Teologiese Studies* 73, no. 1 (2017): 1–11.

———. "Reading Power(s) and Potential(s) in Jesus' 'Triumphal Entry' (Luke 19:28–40)." *RevExp* 112 (2015): 525–541.

———. "Reflexivity and Emotion in Narratological Perspective: Reading Joy in the Lukan Narrative." In *Mixed Feelings and Vexed Passions in Biblical Literature: Emotions of Divine and Human Figures in Interdisciplinary Perspective*, edited by F. Scott Spencer, 265–286. Atlanta: Society of Biblical Literature Press, 2017.

———. *Silent Statements: Narrative Representations of Speech and Silence in the Gospel of Luke.* Berlin: Walter de Gruyter, 2013.

Docherty, Thomas. *After Theory.* Edinburgh: Edinburgh University Press, 1996.

Dodd, C. H. "The Framework of the Gospel Narrative." In *New Testament Studies*, 1–11. Manchester: Manchester University Press, 1953.

———. *The Parables of the Kingdom.* London: Nisbet, 1935.

Domingues, José Maurício. *Global Modernity, Development, and Contemporary Civilization: Towards a Renewal of Critical Theory.* New York: Routledge, 2012.

Donaldson, Laura E. "Cyborgs, Ciphers, and Sexuality: Re: Theorizing Literary and Biblical Character." *Semeia* 63 (1993): 81–96.

Douglas, Kelly Brown. *What's Faith Got to Do with It? Black Bodies/Christian Souls.* New York: Maryknoll Books, 2005.

Douglas, Mary. *Purity and Danger: An Analysis of Concepts of Pollution and Taboo.* New York: Routledge, 2002.

Downing, F. Gerald. "Dale Martin's Swords for Jesus: Shaky Evidence?" *JSNT* 37, no. 3 (2015): 326–333.

Dube, Musa W. "Fifty Years of Bleeding: A Storytelling Feminist Reading of Mark 5:24–43." In *Other Ways of Reading: African Women and the Bible*, edited by Musa W. Dube, 50–60. Atlanta: Society of Biblical Literature, 2001.

Dube, Musa W., Andrew Mbuvi, and Dora Mbuwayesango, eds. *Postcolonial Perspectives in African Biblical Interpretations.* Atlanta: Society of Biblical Literature, 2012.

Dubrow, Heather. Foreword to *New Formalisms and Literary Theory*, edited by Verena Theile and Linda Tredennick, vii–xviii. New York: Palgrave Macmillan, 2013.

Duff, David. "Key Concepts." In *Modern Genre Theory*, edited by David Duff, x–xvi. London: Routledge, 2014.

Duke, Paul D. *Irony in the Fourth Gospel.* Atlanta: John Knox, 1985.

Dunn, James D. G. *The New Perspective on Paul: Collected Essays.* Tübingen: Mohr Siebeck, 2005.

Dunning, Benjamin H. *Aliens and Sojourners: Self as Other in Early Christianity.* Divinations: Rereading Late Ancient Religion. Philadelphia: University of Pennsylvania Press, 2008.

During, Simon. "The Postcolonial Aesthetic." *PMLA* 129 (2014): 498–503.

Eagleton, Terry. *After Theory.* New York: Basic Books, 2003.

———. *Ideology: An Introduction.* London: Verso, 1991.

———. *Literary Theory: An Introduction.* Minneapolis: University of Minnesota Press, 1983.

———. *The Rape of Clarissa: Writing, Sexuality and Class Struggle in Samuel Richardson.* Minneapolis: University of Minnesota Press, 1982.

———. *Why Marx Was Right.* New Haven: Yale University Press, 2011.

Earl, D. "Prologue-form in Ancient Historiography." *ANRW* 1, no. 2 (1972): 842–856.

Ebstein, Wilhelm. *Die Medizin im Neuen Testament und im Talmud.* Stuttgart: Enke, 1903.

Edwards, James R. "Markan Sandwiches: The Significance of Interpolations in Markan Narratives." *NovT* 31 (1989): 193–216.

Eichenbaum, Boris. "The Theory of the 'Formal Method.'" In *Russian Formalist Criticism: Four Essays,* edited and translated by Lee T. Lemon and Marion J. Reis, 99–140. Lincoln: University of Nebraska Press, 1974.

Eliot, T. S. Introduction to *The Wheel of Fire,* by G. Wilson Knight, xi–xix. London: Methuen, 1930.

———. "Tradition and the Individual Talent." In *Selected Essays,* 13–22. London: Faber and Faber, 1932.

Elliott, David. "Engineers of the Human Soul: Painting of the Stalin Period." In *Soviet Socialist Realist Painting, 1930s–1960s,* edited by Matthew Cullerne Bown and David Elliott, 1–17. Oxford: Museum of Modern Art, 1992.

Elliott, Jane, and Derek Attridge, eds. *Theory after "Theory."* London: Routledge, 2011.

Elliott, Neil. "Diagnosing an Allergic Reaction: The Avoidance of Marx in Pauline Scholarship." *B&CT* 8 (2012): 3–15.

———. "Marxism and the Postcolonial Study of Paul." In *The Colonized Apostle: Paul through Postcolonial Eyes,* edited by Christopher D. Stanley, 34–50. Minneapolis: Fortress, 2011.

Elliott, Scott S. *Reconfiguring Mark's Jesus: Narrative Criticism after Poststructuralism.* Sheffield: Sheffield Phoenix, 2011.

———. "What Is Paul? Mythology and the Neutral in 1 Corinthians 9:19–23." In *Simulating Aichele: Essays in Bible, Film, Culture and Theory,* edited by Melissa C. Stewart, 120–139. Sheffield: Sheffield Phoenix, 2015.

Ellis, John. *The Theory of Literary Criticism: A Logical Analysis.* Berkeley: University of California Press, 1974.

Elmarsafy, Ziad, Anna Bernard, and David Attwell, eds. *Debating Orientalism.* New York: Palgrave Macmillan, 2013.

Elvey, Anne. *The Matter of the Text: Material Engagements between Luke and the Five Senses.* Sheffield: Sheffield Phoenix, 2011.

Enders, Horst, ed. *Die Werkinterpretation.* Darmstadt: Wissenschaftliche Buchgesellschaft, 1967.

Engberg-Pedersen, Troels. "Philosophy of the Self in the Apostle Paul." In *Ancient Philosophy of the Self,* edited by Pauliina Remes and Juha Sihvola, 179–194. Heidelberg: Springer, 2008.

———. "The Unity of 2 Corinthians as Reflected in the Account of Paul's and Titus' Travels between Ephesus, Macedonia and Corinth and the Theology of 2:14–17." Paper presented at the Society of Biblical Literature annual meeting, San Francisco, CA, November 19, 2011.

Englehardt, Joshua, and Dimitri Nakassis. "Introduction: Individual Intentionality, Social Structure, and Material Agency in Early Writing and Emerging Script Technologies." In *Agency in Ancient Writing,* edited by Joshua Englehardt, 1–18. Boulder, CO: University Press of Colorado, 2013.

Erlich, Victor. *Russian Formalism: History-Doctrine.* The Hague: Mouton, 1955.

Evans, Elizabeth. *Physiognomics in the Ancient World.* Philadelphia: American Philosophical Society, 1969.

Farrell, Joseph. "Classical Genre in Theory and Practice." *New Literary History* 34, no. 3 (2003): 383–408.

Farrer, Austin. *St. Matthew and St. Mark.* Westminster: Dacre, 1954.

Federico, Annette. *Engagements with Close Reading.* London: Routledge, 2016.

Fee, Gordon D. *The First Epistle to the Corinthians.* NICNT. Grand Rapids, MI: Eerdmans, 1987.

Fetterley, Judith. *The Resisting Reader: A Feminist Approach to American Fiction.* Bloomington: Indiana University Press, 1978.

Fevret, Mary. *Romantic Correspondence: Women, Politics and the Fiction of Letters.* Cambridge, UK: Cambridge University Press, 1993.

Fiebig, Paul A. *Altjüdische Gleichnisse und die Gleichnisse Jesu.* Tübingen: Mohr Siebeck, 1904.

———. *Die Gleichnisreden Jesu in Lichte der rabbinischen Gleichnisse des neutestamentlichen Zeitalters.* Tübingen: Mohr Siebeck, 1912.

Figlerowicz, Marta. "Affect Theory Dossier: An Introduction." *Qui Parle: Critical Humanities and Social Sciences* 20, no. 2 (2012): 3–18.

Fish, Stanley. *Is There a Text in This Class? The Authority of Interpretive Communities.* Cambridge, MA: Harvard University Press, 1980.

Fishelov, David. "Genre Theory and Family Resemblance—Revisited." *Poetics* 20 (1991): 23–38.

———. *Metaphors of Genre: The Role of Analogies in Genre Theory.* University Park, PA: Pennsylvania State University Press, 1993.

Fitzmyer, Joseph A. *The Gospel according to Luke (I–IX): Introduction, Translation, and Notes.* AB 28. Garden City, NY: Doubleday, 1986.

———. *The Gospel according to Luke (X–XXIV): Introduction, Translation, and Notes.* AB 28A. Garden City, NY: Doubleday, 1986.

———. *The Interpretation of Scripture: In Defense of the Historical-Critical Method.* New York: Paulist, 2008.

———. *To Advance the Gospel: New Testament Studies.* New York: Crossroad, 1981.

Flannery, Frances. "Dreams and Visions in Early Jewish and Early Christian Apocalypses and Apocalypticism." In *The Oxford Handbook of Apocalyptic Literature,* edited by John J. Collins, 104–120. Oxford: Oxford University Press, 2014.

Fonrobert, Charlotte. *Menstrual Purity: Rabbinic and Christian Reconstructions of Biblical Gender.* Stanford, CA: Stanford University Press, 2000.

———. "The Woman with a Blood-Flow (Mark 5:24–34) Revisited: Menstrual Laws and Jewish Culture in Christian Feminist Hermeneutics." In *Early Christian Interpretation of the Scriptures of Israel: Investigations and Proposals,* edited by Craig A. Evans and James A. Sanders, 121–140. Sheffield: Sheffield Academic, 1997.

Foucault, Michel. *The History of Sexuality.* Vol. 1, *An Introduction.* Translated by Robert Hurley. New York: Vintage Books, 1978.

———. "What Is an Author?" In *The Foucault Reader,* edited by Paul Rabinow, 101–120. New York: Pantheon, 1984.

Fowler, Alastair. *Kinds of Literature: An Introduction to the Theory of Genres and Modes.* Cambridge, MA: Harvard University Press, 1982.

Fowler, Don, and Peta Fowler. "Literary Theory and Classical Studies." In *The Oxford Classical Dictionary,* 3rd ed., edited by Simon Hornblower and Antony Spawforth, 871–875. New York: Oxford University Press, 1996.

Fowler, Robert M. *Let the Reader Understand: Reader-Response Criticism and the Gospel of Mark.* Minneapolis: Fortress, 1991.

Fox, Nicholas J. *Beyond Health: Postmodernism and Embodiment.* New York: Free Association, 1999.

Frankfurter, David. "Narratives That Do Things." In *Religion: Narrating Religion,* edited by Sarah Iles Johnston, 95–106. MacMillan Interdisciplinary Handbooks. New York: MacMillan Reference USA, 2016.

Franklin, Benjamin, and Jared Sparks. *The Life of Benjamin Franklin: Containing the Autobiography, with Notes and a Continuation.* Boston: Tappan, Whittemore, and Mason, 1848.

Fredrickson, David E. *Eros and the Christ: Longing and Envy in Paul's Christology.* Minneapolis: Fortress, 2013.

Fredriksen, Paula. "Arms and the Man: A Response to Dale Martin's 'Jesus in Jerusalem: Armed and Not Dangerous.'" *JSNT* 37, no. 3 (2015): 312–325.

Frei, Hans W. *The Eclipse of Biblical Narrative: A Study in Eighteenth and Nineteenth Century Hermeneutics.* New Haven: Yale University Press, 1974.

Freud, Sigmund. *The Interpretation of Dreams.* In *The Basic Writings of Sigmund Freud.* Translated by A. A. Brill. New York: Modern Library, 1938.

Friesen, Steven J. "Poverty in Pauline Studies: Beyond the So-called New Consensus." *JSNT* 26, no. 3 (2004): 323–361.

Frow, John. *Character and Person.* Oxford: Oxford University Press, 2014.

———. *Genre.* New York: Routledge, 2006.

Frye, Northrop. *Anatomy of Criticism.* Princeton: Princeton University Press, 1957.

———. "Towards Defining an Age of Sensibility." In *Fables of Identity: Studies in Poetic Mythology.* New York: Harcourt, Brace & World, 1963.

Frye, Roland Mushat. "Literary Criticism and Gospel Criticism." *Theology Today* 36, no. 2 (1979): 207–219.

———. "A Literary Perspective for the Criticism of the Gospels." In *Jesus and Man's Hope,* vol. 2 (Perspective 2), edited by Donald G. Miller and Dikran Y. Hadidian, 193–221. Pittsburgh: Pittsburgh Theological Seminary, 1971.

Fulda, Daniel. "'Selective' History: Why and How 'History' Depends on Readerly Narrativization, with the Wehrmacht Exhibition as an Example." In *Narratology beyond Literary Criticism: Mediality-Disciplinarity,* edited by Jan Christoph Meister with Tom Kindt and Wilhelm Schernus, 173–194. New York: Walter de Gruyter, 2005.

Funk, Robert W. "The Apostolic *Parousia:* Form and Significance." In *Christian History and Interpretation: Studies Presented to John Knox,* edited by William R. Farmer, C. F. D. Moule, and Richard R. Niebuhr, 249–268. Cambridge, UK: Cambridge University Press, 1967.

———. *Language, Hermeneutic, and the Word of God.* New York: Harper & Row, 1966.

———. *Parables and Presence: Forms of the New Testament Tradition.* Philadelphia: Fortress, 1982.

Gadamer, Hans-Georg. *Truth and Method.* 2nd ed. Translated by Joel Weinsheimer and Donald Marshall. New York: Crossroad, 1989.

Gaertner, Jan Felix, ed. *Writing Exile: The Discourse of Displacement in Greco-Roman Antiquity and Beyond.* Leiden: Brill, 2007.

Gager, John G. *Curse Tablets and Binding Spells from the Ancient World.* New York: Oxford University Press, 1992.

Galen. *On Prognosis.* Edited and translated by Vivian Nutton. *Corpus Medicorum Graecorum* 5.8.1. Berlin: Akademie-Verlag, 1979.

Gallagher, Shaun. *Hermeneutics and Education.* Albany: State University of New York Press, 1992.

Gamble, Harry Y. *Books and Readers in the Early Church: A History of Early Christian Texts.* New Haven: Yale University Press, 1995.

———. *The Textual History of the Letter to the Romans: A Study in Textual and Literary Criticism.* Grand Rapids, MI: Eerdmans, 1977.

Gates, Henry Louis, Jr. "Introduction: Writing 'Race' and the Difference It Makes." In *"Race," Writing and Difference,* edited by Henry Louis Gates Jr., 1–20. Chicago: University of Chicago Press, 1986.

————. *The Signifying Monkey: A Theory of Afro-American Literary Criticism.* New York: Oxford University Press, 1988.

Gaventa, Beverly Roberts. *Mary: Glimpses of the Mother of Jesus.* Columbia, SC: University of South Carolina Press, 1995.

Geertz, Clifford. *After the Fact: Two Countries, Four Decades, One Anthropologist.* Cambridge, MA: Harvard University Press, 1995.

Genette, Gérard. "Rhetoric Restrained." In *Figures of Literary Discourse,* translated by Alan Sheridan, 103–126. Oxford: Blackwell, 1982.

Giddens, Anthony. *The Constitution of Society: Outline of the Theory of Structuration.* Berkeley: University of California Press, 1984.

————. "Four Theses on Ideology." *Canadian Journal of Political and Social Theory* 7 (1983): 8–21.

Gill, Christopher, and Tim Wiseman, eds. *Lies and Fiction in the Ancient World.* Austin: University of Texas Press, 1993.

Gilroy, Paul. *After Empire: Melancholia or Convivial Culture?* London: Routledge, 2004.

Glancy, Jennifer A. *Corporal Knowledge: Early Christian Bodies.* New York: Oxford University Press, 2010.

————. "Obstacles to Slaves' Participation in the Corinthian Church." *JBL* 117, no. 3 (1998): 481–501.

————. *Slavery in Early Christianity.* Minneapolis: Fortress, 2006.

Goldhill, Simon. "The Failure of Exemplarity." In *Modern Critical Theory and Classical Literature,* edited by Irene de Jong and J. P. Sullivan, 51–73. Leiden: Brill, 1994.

————. "The Limits of the Case Study: Exemplarity and the Reception of Classical Literature." *New Literary History* 48, no. 3 (2017): 415–435.

Goulimari, Pelagia. *Literary Criticism and Theory: From Plato to Postcolonialism.* New York: Routledge, 2015.

Gowler, David B. "Hospitality and Characterization in Luke 11:37–54: A Socio-Narratological Approach." *Semeia* 64 (1993): 213–251.

Graff, Gerald. *Literature against Itself.* Chicago: University of Chicago Press, 1979.

————. *Poetic Statement and Critical Dogma.* Evanston, IL: Northwestern University Press, 1970.

Grant, Jacquelyn. *White Women's Christ and Black Women's Jesus: Feminist Christology and Womanist Response.* Atlanta: Scholars Press, 1989.

Greenblatt, Stephen. *Renaissance Self-Fashioning: From More to Shakespeare.* Chicago: University of Chicago Press, 1980.

Greenblatt, Stephen, and Giles B. Gunn. "Introduction." In *Redrawing the Boundaries: The Transformation of English and American Literary Studies,* edited by Stephen Greenblatt and Giles B. Gunn, 1–11. New York: MLA, 1992.

Greimas, A. J. *Maupassant: The Semiotics of Text.* Philadelphia: Benjamins, 1988.

Gunkel, Hermann. *Einleitung in die Psalmen: Die Gattungen der religiösen Lyrik Israels.* Göttingen: Vandenhoeck & Ruprecht, 1933.

Guthrie, George H. "Boats in the Bay: Reflections on the Use of Linguistics and Literary Analysis in Biblical Studies." In *Linguistics and the New Testament: Critical Junctures*, edited by Stanley E. Porter and D. A. Carson, 23–35. Sheffield: Sheffield Academic, 1999.

Habel, Norman C., ed. *Readings from the Perspective of Earth*. The Earth Bible 1. Sheffield: Sheffield Academic, 2000.

Habel, Norman C., and Vicky Balabanski, eds. *The Earth Story in the New Testament*. The Earth Bible 5. Sheffield: Sheffield Academic, 2002.

Habermas, Jürgen. *The Philosophical Discourse of Modernity: Twelve Lectures*. Translated by Frederick Lawrence. Cambridge, MA: MIT Press, 1987.

Haines-Eitzen, Kim. *Guardians of Letters: Literacy, Power, and the Transmitters of Early Christian Literature*. Oxford: Oxford University Press, 2000.

Hamm, Dennis. "What the Samaritan Leper Sees: The Narrative Christology of Luke 17:11–19." *CBQ* 56 (1994): 273–287.

Hampton, Timothy. *Writing from History: The Rhetoric of Exemplarity in Renaissance Literature*. Ithaca, NY: Cornell University Press, 1990.

Hanson, Ann Ellis. "The Medical Writers' Woman." In *Before Sexuality: The Construction of Erotic Experience in the Ancient Greek World*, edited by David M. Halperin, John J. Winkler, and Froma I. Zeitlin, 309–337. Princeton: Princeton University Press, 1990.

Harmon, William, and C. Hugh Holman. *A Handbook to Literature*. 8th ed. Upper Saddle River, NJ: Prentice Hall, 1999.

Harpham, Geoffrey. *The Character of Criticism*. London: Routledge, 2006.

Harrill, J. Albert. "Invective against Paul (2 Cor 10:10), the Physiognomics of the Ancient Slave Body, and the Greco-Roman Rhetoric of Manhood." In *Antiquity and Humanity: Essays on Ancient Religion and Philosophy Presented to Hans Dieter Betz on His 70th Birthday*, edited by Adela Yarbro Collins and Margaret M. Mitchell, 189–213. Tübingen: Mohr Siebeck, 2001.

———. *Slaves in the New Testament: Literary, Social and Moral Dimensions*. Minneapolis: Fortress, 2006.

Harrington, Daniel J. *The Letter to the Hebrews*. Collegeville, MN: Liturgical, 2006.

Harris, Ashleigh. "An Awkward Silence: Reflections on Theory and Africa." *Kunapipi: Journal of Postcolonial Writing* 34, no. 1 (2012): 28–189.

Harris, William V. *Ancient Literacy*. Cambridge, MA: Harvard University Press, 1989.

Harrison, Stephen. *Generic Enrichment in Vergil and Horace*. Oxford: Oxford University Press, 2007.

Haskins, Ekaterina. *Logos and Power in Isocrates and Aristotle*. Columbia, SC: University of South Carolina Press, 2004.

Hasseler, Terri, and Paula Krebs. "Losing Our Way after the Imperial Turn: Charting Academic Uses of the Postcolonial." In *After the Imperial Turn: Thinking with and through the Nation*, edited by Antoinette Burton, 90–101. Durham, NC: Duke University Press, 2003.

Hatina, Thomas R. "Intertextuality and Historical Criticism in New Testament Studies: Is There a Relationship?" *BibInt* 7 (1999): 28–43.

Hau, Lisa Irene. *Moral History from Herodotus to Diodorus Siculus.* Edinburgh: Edinburgh University Press, 2016.

Hawkins, Peter S. "The Bible as Literature and Sacred Text." In *The Oxford Handbook of English Literature and Theology,* edited by Andrew Hass, David Jasper, and Elisabeth Jay, 197–213. Oxford: Oxford University Press, 2007.

Haynes, Stephen R., and Steven L. McKenzie, eds. *To Each Its Own Meaning: An Introduction to Biblical Criticisms and Their Application.* Louisville: Westminster John Knox, 1999.

Hays, Christopher M. *Luke's Wealth Ethics: A Study in Their Coherence and Character.* Tübingen: Mohr Siebeck, 2010.

Hays, Richard B. *The Conversion of the Imagination: Paul as Interpreter of Israel's Scripture.* Grand Rapids, MI: Eerdmans, 2005.

———. *Reading Backwards: Figural Christology and the Fourfold Gospel Witness.* Waco, TX: Baylor University Press, 2014.

———. "Reading the Bible with the Eyes of Faith: Theological Exegesis from the Perspective of Biblical Studies." In *Sharper Than a Two-Edged Sword: Preaching, Teaching and Living the Bible,* edited by Michael Root and James J. Buckley, 82–101. Grand Rapids, MI: Eerdmans, 2008.

———. "'The Righteous One' as Eschatological Deliverer: A Case Study in Paul's Apocalyptic Hermeneutics." In *Apocalyptic and the New Testament: Essays in Honor of J. Louis Martyn,* edited by Joel Marcus and Marion Soards, 191–215. Sheffield: Sheffield Academic, 1989.

Hedrick, Charles. *Parables as Poetic Fictions: The Creative Voice of Jesus.* Peabody, MA: Hendrickson, 1994.

Hellholm, David. "The Problem of the Apocalyptic Genre and the Apocalypse of John." *Semeia* 36 (1986): 13–64.

Hens-Piazza, Gina. "New Historicism." In *New Meanings for Ancient Texts: Recent Approaches to Biblical Criticisms and Their Applications,* edited by Steven L. McKenzie and John Kaltner, 59–76. Louisville: Westminster John Knox, 2013.

———. *The New Historicism.* Minneapolis: Fortress, 2002.

Hirsch, E. D., Jr. *Validity in Interpretation.* New Haven: Yale University Press, 1967.

Hogan, Patrick Colm. *Affective Narratology: The Emotional Structure of Stories.* Lincoln: University of Nebraska Press, 2011.

———. *What Literature Teaches Us about Emotion.* Cambridge, UK: Cambridge University Press, 2011.

Holbo, John, ed. *Framing Theory's Empire.* West Lafayette, IN: Parlor, 2007.

Holladay, Carl R. *Acts: A Commentary.* Louisville: Westminster John Knox, 2016.

Honneth, Axel. *Pathologies of Reason: On the Legacy of Critical Theory.* Translated by James Ingram. New York: Columbia University Press, 2009.

Horkheimer, Max. *Critical Theory: Selected Essays.* Translated by Matthew J. O'Connell et al. New York: Herder and Herder, 1972.

Horrell, David. "A New Perspective on Paul? Rereading Paul in a Time of Ecological Crisis." *JSNT* 33 (2010): 3–30.

Horsley, Richard A. *In the Shadow of Empire: Reclaiming the Bible as a History of Faithful Resistance*. Louisville: Westminster John Knox, 2008.

———, ed. *Paul and Empire: Religion and Power in Roman Imperial Society*. Harrisburg: Trinity, 1997.

———, ed. *Paul and Politics: Ekklesia, Israel, Imperium, Interpretation*. Harrisburg: Trinity, 2000.

———. "Submerged Biblical Histories." In *The Postcolonial Bible*, edited by R. S. Sugirtharajah, 152–173. Sheffield: Sheffield Academic, 1998.

Howard, J. Keir. *Disease and Healing in the New Testament: An Analysis and Interpretation*. New York: University Press of America, 2001.

Hunt, Steven, D. Francois Tolmie, and Ruben Zimmermann, eds. *Character Studies in the Fourth Gospel*. Tübingen: Mohr Siebeck, 2013.

Hunter, J. Paul. "Formalism and History: Binarism and the Anglophone Couplet." *MLQ* 61, no. 1 (2000): 109–129.

Hur, Ju. *A Dynamic Reading of the Holy Spirit in Luke-Acts*. Sheffield: Sheffield Academic, 2001.

Iser, Wolfgang. *The Act of Reading: A Theory of Aesthetic Response*. Baltimore: Johns Hopkins University Press, 1978.

———. *The Implied Reader: Patterns of Communication in Prose Fiction from Bunyan to Beckett*. Baltimore: Johns Hopkins University Press, 1974.

———. "The Reading Process: A Phenomenological Approach." *New Literary History* 3, no 2 (1972): 279–299.

Jacob, Sharon. *Reading Mary, the Mother of God, alongside Indian Surrogate Mothers: Violent Love, Oppressive Liberation, and Infancy Narratives*. New York: Palgrave, 2015.

Jakobson, Roman. "The Dominant." In *Selected Writings: Poetry of Grammar, Grammar of Poetry*, vol. 3, edited by Stephen Ruddy, 751–756. The Hague: Mouton, 1981.

———. *Language in Literature*. Edited by Krystyna Pomorska and Stephen Rudy. Cambridge, MA: Belknap, 1987.

Jameson, Fredric. *The Political Unconscious: Narrative as a Socially Symbolic Act*. Ithaca, NY: Cornell University Press, 1981.

———. *Valences of the Dialectic*. New York: Verso, 2009.

Jauss, Hans Robert. "Theorie der Gattungen und Literatur des Mittelalters." In *Alterität und Modernität der mittelalterlichen Literatur: Gesammelte Aufsätze 1956–1976*, edited by Hans Robert Jauss, 327–358. Munich: Fink, 1977.

Jay, Martin. *Reason after Its Eclipse: On Late Critical Theory*. Madison: University of Wisconsin Press, 2016.

Jeal, Roy. "Visual Interpretation: Blending Rhetorical Arts in Colossians 2.6–3.4." Paper presented at the Society of Biblical Literature annual meeting, November 2013.

Jennings, Theodore W., Jr. "Justice as Gift: Thinking Grace with the Help of Derrida." In *Derrida's Bible: Reading a Page of Scripture with a Little Help from Derrida,* edited by Yvonne Sherwood, 181–198. New York: Palgrave Macmillan, 2004.

Jeremias, Joachim. *The Parables of Jesus.* 2nd ed. Translated by S. H. Hooke. New York: Charles Scribner's Sons, 1972.

———. "Zum Gleichnis vom verlorenen Sohn, Luk. 15,11–32." *TZ* 5 (1949): 228–231.

Johnson, Barbara. "Writing." In *Critical Terms for Literary Study,* edited by Frank Lentricchia and Thomas McLaughlin, 39–49. Chicago: University of Chicago Press, 1995.

Johnson, Luke Timothy. *Contested Issues in Christian Origins and the New Testament.* Leiden: Brill, 2013.

———. *The Literary Function of Possessions in Luke-Acts.* Missoula, MT: Scholars Press, 1977.

Johnson-DeBaufre, Melanie. *Jesus among Her Children: Q, Eschatology, and the Construction of Christian Origins.* Cambridge, MA: Harvard University Press, 2005.

———. "Narrative, Multiplicity, and the Letters of Paul." In *The Oxford Handbook of Biblical Narrative,* edited by Danna Nolan Fewell, 362–375. Oxford: Oxford University Press, 2016.

Jolles, André. *Einfache Formen.* Tübingen: Niemeyer, 1930.

Jones, Geraint. *The Art and Truth of the Parables: A Study in Their Literary Form and Modern Interpretation.* London: SPCK, 1964.

Jülicher, Adolf. *Die Gleichnisreden Jesu.* 2 vols. Tübingen: Mohr Siebeck, 1888–99.

Kaltner, John, and Steven L. McKenzie, eds. *New Meanings for Ancient Texts: Recent Approaches to Biblical Criticisms and Their Applications.* Louisville: Westminster John Knox, 2013.

Kant, Immanuel. *Critique of Judgment.* Translated by W. Pluhar. Indianapolis: Hackett, 1987.

Kaufman, Robert. "Everybody Hates Kant: Blakean Formalism and the Symmetries of Laura Moriarty." *MLQ* 61, no. 1 (2000): 131–155.

———. "Negatively Capable Dialectics: Keats, Vendler, Adorno, and the Theory of the Avant-Garde." *CI* 27, no. 2 (2001): 354–384.

———. "'Red Kant,' or The Persistence of the Third 'Critique' in Adorno and Jameson." *CI* 26, no. 4 (2000): 682–724.

Kavanagh, James. "Ideology." In *Critical Terms for Literary Study,* 2nd ed., edited by Frank Lentricchia and Thomas McLaughlin, 306–320. Chicago: University of Chicago Press, 1995.

Keith, Chris. "The Narratives of the Gospels and the Historical Jesus: Current Debates, Prior Debates and the Goal of Historical Jesus Research." *JSNT* 38 (2016): 426–455.

Kelley, Shawn. "Race, Aesthetics, and Gospel Scholarship: Embracing and Subverting the Aesthetic Ideology." In *Prejudice and Christian Beginnings: Investigating*

Race, Gender, and Ethnicity in Early Christian Studies, edited by Laura Nasrallah and Elisabeth Schüssler Fiorenza, 191–209. Minneapolis: Fortress, 2009.

———. *Racializing Jesus: Race, Ideology, and the Formation of Modern Biblical Scholarship.* New York: Routledge, 2002.

Kelly, Gordon P. *A History of Exile in the Roman Republic.* Cambridge, UK: Cambridge University Press, 2006.

Kennedy, George A. *The Art of Rhetoric in the Roman World, 300 B.C.–A.D. 300.* Princeton: Princeton University Press, 1972.

———. *A New History of Classical Rhetoric.* Princeton: Princeton University Press, 1994.

———. *New Testament Interpretation through Rhetorical Criticism.* Chapel Hill: University of North Carolina Press, 1984.

Kilgallen, John J. "Luke 2.41–50: Foreshadowing of Jesus, Teacher." *Biblica* 66 (1985): 553–559.

Kim, Chan-Hie. *Form and Function of the Familiar Letter of Recommendation.* Missoula, MT: Scholars Press, 1972.

Kingsbury, Jack Dean. "Ernst Fuchs' Existentialist Interpretation of the Parables." *LQ* 22 (1970): 380–395.

———. "Major Trends in Parable Interpretation." *Concordia Theological Monthly* 42 (1971): 579–596.

———. *Matthew as Story.* Philadelphia: Fortress, 1986.

Kinukawa, Hisako. "The Story of the Hemorrhaging Woman (Mark 5:25–34) Read from a Japanese Feminist Context." *BibInt* 2 (1994): 283–293.

Kitzberger, Ingrid Rosa, ed. *Autobiographical Biblical Criticism: Learning to Read between Text and Self.* Leiden: Deo, 2002.

Kjärgaard, Mogens Stiller. *Metaphor and Parable: A Systematic Analysis of the Specific Structure and Cognitive Function of the Synoptic Similes and Parables qua Metaphors.* Leiden: Brill, 1986.

Klauck, Hans-Josef. "Adolf Jülicher: Leben, Werk und Wirkung." In *Historische Kritik in der Theologie: Beiträge zu ihrer Geschichte*, edited by Georg Schwaiger, 99–150. Göttingen: Vandenhoeck & Ruprecht, 1980.

Klausner, Joseph. *The Messianic Idea in Israel, from Its Beginning to the Completion of the Mishnah.* Translated by W. F. Stinespring. New York: Macmillan, 1955.

Klein, William W., Craig L. Blomberg, and Robert L. Hubbard Jr. *Introduction to Biblical Interpretation.* Rev. ed. Nashville: Thomas Nelson, 2004.

Kloppenborg, John S. "Literate Media in Early Christ Groups: The Creation of a Christian Book Culture." *JECS* 22, no. 1 (2014): 21–59.

Knust, Jennifer. "Who's Afraid of Canaan's Curse? Genesis 9:18–29 and the Challenge of Reparative Reading." *BibInt* 22 (2014): 388–413.

Koch, Dietrich-Alex. *Die Bedeutung der Wundererzählungen für die Christologie des Markusevangeliums.* New York: de Gruyter, 1975.

Koch, Klaus. *The Growth of the Biblical Tradition: The Form-Critical Method.* New York: Scribner, 1969.

Koosed, Jennifer L., ed. *The Bible and Posthumanism.* Atlanta: Society of Biblical Literature Press, 2014.

Koosed, Jennifer L., and Stephen Moore, eds. "Introduction: From Affect to Exegesis." *BibInt* 22 (2014): 381–387.

Kotrosits, Maia. *How Things Feel: Biblical Studies, Affect Theory, and the (Im)personal.* Leiden: Brill, 2016.

———. *Rethinking Early Christian Identity: Affect, Violence, and Belonging.* Minneapolis: Fortress, 2015.

———. "The Rhetoric of Intimate Spaces: Affect and Performance in the Corinthian Correspondence." *USQR* 62 (2011): 134–151.

Kraus, Christina S. "Historiography and Biography." In *The Oxford Handbook of Roman Studies,* edited by Alessandro Barchiesi and Walter Scheidel, 403–410. Oxford: Oxford University Press, 2010.

Kreitzer, Larry. *The New Testament in Fiction and Film: On Reversing the Hermeneutical Flow.* Sheffield: Sheffield Academic, 1993.

Krueger, Derek. *Writing and Holiness: The Practice of Authorship in the Early Christian East.* Philadelphia: University of Pennsylvania Press, 2013.

Kugel, James L. "On the Bible and Literary Criticism." *Prooftexts* 1 (1981): 217–236.

Kuhn, Thomas. *The Copernican Revolution.* Cambridge: Harvard University Press, 1957.

Kukkonen, Karin. "Form as a Pattern of Thinking: Cognitive Poetics and New Formalism." In *New Formalisms and Literary Theory,* edited by Verena Theile and Linda Tredennick, 159–176. New York: Palgrave Macmillan, 2013.

Kümmel, Werner Georg. *The New Testament: The History of the Investigation of Its Problems.* Translated by S. Mclean Gilmour and Howard C. Kee. Nashville: Abingdon, 1972.

Kurz, William S. *Reading Luke-Acts: Dynamics of Biblical Narrative.* Louisville: Westminster John Knox, 1993.

Kwok, Pui-lan. *Introducing Asian Feminist Theology.* Sheffield: Sheffield Academic, 2000.

———. *Postcolonial Imagination and Feminist Theology.* Louisville: Westminster John Knox, 2005.

Lacan, Jacques. "The Agency of the Letter in the Unconscious or Reason Since Freud." In *Écrits: A Selection,* translated by B. Fink, 146–178. New York: Norton, 1977.

———. *The Ego in Freud's Theory and in the Technique of Psychoanalysis, 1944–1955.* Translated by Sylvana Tomaselli. New York: Norton, 1988.

Lakoff, George. *Women, Fire, and Dangerous Things: What Categories Reveal about the Mind.* Chicago: University of Chicago Press, 1987.

Lane, William L. *The Gospel of Mark.* NICNT. Grand Rapids, MI: Eerdmans, 1974.

Lawrence, Louise J. "Emotions in Protest in Mark 11–13: Responding to an Affective Turn in Social-Scientific Discourse." In *Matthew and Mark across Perspectives: Essays in Honour of Stephen C. Barton and William R. Telford,* edited by Kristian A. Bendoraitis and Nijay K. Gupta, 83–107. New York: Bloomsbury T&T Clark, 2016.

Lawson, Andrew, ed. *Class and the Making of American Literature: Created Unequal.* New York: Routledge, 2014.

Lazarus, Neil. *The Postcolonial Unconscious.* Cambridge, UK: Cambridge University Press, 2011.

Ledbetter, Mark. "Telling the Other Story: A Literary Response to Socio-Rhetorical Criticism of the New Testament." *Semeia* 64 (1993): 289–301.

Legaspi, Michael. *The Death of Scripture and the Rise of Biblical Studies.* Oxford: Oxford University Press, 2010.

Leitch, Vincent B. *American Literary Criticism Since the 1930s.* 2nd ed. London: Routledge, 2009.

———. *Literary Criticism in the Twenty-First Century: Theory Renaissance.* New York: Bloomsbury Academic, 2014.

———. *Living with Theory.* Malden, MA: Blackwell, 2008.

———. "A Primer of Recent Critical Theories." *College English* 39 (1977): 138–152.

Lentricchia, Frank. *After the New Criticism.* Chicago: University of Chicago Press, 1980.

———. "Last Will and Testament of an Ex-Literary Critic." *Lingua Franca* 6 (1996): 59–67.

Léon-Dufour, Xavier. *Exégèse et herméneutique.* Paris: Seuil, 1971.

Lesjak, Carolyn. "Reading Dialectically." *Criticism* 55, no. 2 (2013): 233–277.

Lévi-Strauss, Claude. *Myth and Meaning.* New York: Schocken Books, 1995.

———. *Structural Anthropology.* New York: Basic Books, 1963.

Levine, Amy-Jill. "Discharging Responsibility: Matthean Jesus, Biblical Law, and Hemorrhaging Woman." In *Treasures New and Old: Contributions to Matthean Studies,* edited by David R. Bauer and Mark Allan Powell, 379–397. Atlanta: Scholars Press, 1996.

———. "Feminist Criticism." In *The Blackwell Companion to the New Testament,* edited by David E. Aune, 156–165. Malden, MA: Blackwell, 2010.

———. Foreword/Preface/Introduction/Preamble/Exordium to *The Bible in Theory: Critical and Postcritical Essays,* xi–xiv. Atlanta: Society of Biblical Literature, 2010.

———. *Short Stories by Jesus: The Enigmatic Parables of a Controversial Rabbi.* New York: Harper Collins, 2014.

Levinson, Marjorie. "What Is New Formalism?" *PMLA* 122, no. 2 (2007): 558–569.

Lewis, Thomas. *Why Philosophy Matters for the Study of Religion—and Vice Versa.* Oxford: Oxford University Press, 2015.

Leys, Ruth. "The Turn to Affect: A Critique." *CI* 37, no. 3 (2011): 434–472.

Lieb, Michael, Emma Mason, and Jonathan Roberts, eds. *The Oxford Handbook of the Reception History of the Bible.* Oxford: Oxford University Press, 2011.

Lieu, Judith. *Christian Identity in the Jewish and Graeco-Roman World.* Oxford: Oxford University Press, 2004.

———. *Neither Jew nor Greek? Constructing Early Christianity.* London: T&T Clark, 2002.

Liew, Tat-siong Benny. "Postcolonial Criticism: Echoes of a Subaltern's Contribution and Exclusion." In *Mark and Method: New Approaches in Biblical Studies.* 2nd ed., edited by Janice Capel Anderson and Stephen D. Moore, 211–231. Minneapolis: Fortress, 2008.

———. "Queering Closets and Perverting Desires: CrossExamining John's Engendering and Transgendering Word across Different Worlds." In *They Were All Together in One Place? Toward Minority Biblical Criticism,* edited by Randall C. Bailey, Tat-siong Benny Liew, and Fernando F. Segovia, 251–288. Atlanta: Society of Biblical Literature, 2009.

———. *What Is Asian American Hermeneutics? Reading the New Testament.* Honolulu: University of Hawai'i Press, 2008.

Lin, Yii-Jan. *The Erotic Life of Manuscripts: New Testament Textual Criticism and the Biological Sciences.* New York: Oxford University Press, 2016.

Lindbeck, George. "The Story-Shaped Church: Critical Exegesis and Theological Interpretation." In *Scriptural Authority and Narrative Interpretation,* edited by Garrett Green, 161–178. Philadelphia: Fortress, 1987.

Long, F. J. *Ancient Rhetoric and Paul's Apology: The Compositional Unity of 2 Corinthians.* Cambridge, UK: Cambridge University Press, 2005.

Longman, Tremper, III. *Literary Approaches to Biblical Interpretation.* Minneapolis: Zondervan, 1987.

Lowden, John. "The Word Made Visible: The Exterior of the Early Christian Book as Visual Argument." In *The Early Christian Book,* edited by William E. Klingshirn and Linda Safran, 13–47. Washington, DC: Catholic University of America Press, 2007.

Luijendijk, Anne Marie. *Greetings in the Lord: Early Christians and the Oxyrhynchus Papyri.* Cambridge, MA: Harvard University Press, 2008.

Luther, Susanne, Jörg Röder, and Eckhart D. Schmidt, eds. *Wie Geschichten Geschichte schreiben: Frühchristliche Literatur zwischen Faktualität und Fiktionalität.* Tübingen: Mohr Siebeck, 2015.

Luz, Ulrich. "The Secrecy Motif and Marcan Christology." In *The Messianic Secret,* edited by Christopher Tuckett, 75–96. Philadelphia: Fortress, 1983.

Lyons, William John. "Hope for a Troubled Discipline? Contributions to New Testament Studies from Reception History." *JSNT* 33, no. 2 (2010): 207–220.

Lyotard, Jean-François. *The Postmodern Condition: A Report on Knowledge.* Translated by G. Bennington and B. Massumi. Minneapolis: University of Minnesota Press, 1984.

MacDonald, Dennis R. *Mimesis and Intertextuality in Antiquity and Christianity.* Harrisburg: Trinity, 2001.

Mack, Burton L. *Rhetoric and the New Testament.* Minneapolis: Fortress, 1990.

MacLeish, Archibald. "Ars Poetica." In *Collected Poems, 1917–1982,* 106–107. Boston: Houghton Mifflin, 1985.

Maier, John, and Vincent Tollers. "Introduction: The Bible and Its Literary Milieu." In *The Bible and Its Literary Milieu: Contemporary Essays,* edited by John Maier and Vincent Tollers, 1–23. Grand Rapids, MI: Eerdmans, 1979.

Malbon, Elizabeth Struthers. *Mark's Jesus: Characterization as Narrative Christology.* Waco, TX: Baylor University Press, 2009.

———. "Narrative Criticism: How Does the Story Mean?" In *Mark and Method: New Approaches in Biblical Studies,* edited by Janice Capel Anderson and Stephen D. Moore, 24–49. Minneapolis: Fortress, 1992.

Malbon, Elizabeth Struthers, and Adele Berlin, eds. *Characterization in Biblical Literature, Semeia* 63. Atlanta: Scholars Press, 1993.

Malherbe, Abraham J. *Ancient Epistolary Theorists.* Atlanta: Scholars Press, 1988.

Malina, Bruce. *The New Testament World: Insights from Cultural Anthropology.* 3rd ed. Louisville: Westminster John Knox, 2001.

Mandler, Jean Matter. *Stories, Scripts, and Scenes: Aspects of Schema Theory.* Hillsdale, NJ: Erlbaum, 1984.

Mangum, Douglas, and Douglas Estes, eds. *Literary Approaches to the Bible.* Vol. 4, Lexham Methods Series. Bellingham: Lexham, 2017.

Manly, J. M. "Literary Form and the Origin of Species." *Modern Philology* 4 (1907): 577–595.

Marchal, Joseph. "Female Masculinity in Corinth? Bodily Citations and the Drag of History." *Neot* 48, no. 1 (2014): 93–113.

Marcus, Joel. *Mark 1–8.* AB 27. New York: Doubleday, 2000.

Marcus Manilius. *The Astronomica of Marcus Manilius.* Translated by G. P. Goold. Cambridge, MA: Harvard University Press, 2014.

Marguerat, Daniel. *The First Christian Historian: Writing the "Acts of the Apostles."* Cambridge, UK: Cambridge University Press, 2002.

———. "Luc, metteur en scène des personnages." In *Analyse narrative et Bible: Deuxième colloque international du PRENAB,* edited by C. Focant and A. Wènin, 281–295. Leuven: Peeters, 2005.

Marguerat, Daniel, and Yvan Bourquin. *Pour lire les récits bibliques.* Paris: Cerf, 1998.

Marquis, Timothy Luckritz. *Transient Apostle: Paul, Travel, and the Rhetoric of Empire.* New Haven: Yale University Press, 2013.

Martin, Dale B. *The Corinthian Body.* New Haven: Yale University Press, 1995.

———. "Introduction: The Myth of Textual Agency." In *Sex and the Single Savior,* 1–16. Louisville: Westminster John Knox, 2006.

———. "Jesus in Jerusalem: Armed and Not Dangerous." *JSNT* 37, no. 1 (2014): 3–24.

———. "Response to Downing and Fredriksen." *JSNT* 37, no. 3 (2015): 334–345.

———. "Review of Stephen D. Moore, *God's Gym: Divine Male Bodies of the Bible.*" *JBL* 117, no. 4 (1998): 736–738.

———. *Slavery as Salvation: The Metaphor of Slavery in Pauline Christianity.* New Haven: Yale University Press, 1990.

Martin, J. *Antike Rhetorik: Technik und Methode.* Munich: Verlag C. H. Beck, 1974.

Martin, Luther H. "The Anti-Individualistic Ideology of Hellenistic Culture." *Numen* 41 (1994): 117–140.

Marx, Karl, and Frederick Engels, *The German Ideology*. Pt. 1. Edited by C. J. Arthur. New York: International Publishers, 1970.

Massumi, Brian. "The Autonomy of Affect." *Cultural Critique* 31 (1995): 83–109.

———. *Parables for the Virtual: Movement, Affect, Sensation*. Durham, NC: Duke University Press, 2002.

Matera, Frank. *New Testament Theology: Exploring Diversity and Unity*. Louisville: Westminster John Knox, 2007.

Matterson, Stephen. "The New Criticism." In *Literary Theory and Criticism: An Oxford Guide*, edited by Patricia Waugh, 166–176. New York: Oxford University Press, 2006.

Matthews, Shelly. "The Weeping Jesus and the Daughters of Jerusalem: Gender and Conquest in Lukan Lament." In *Doing Gender—Doing Religion: Fallstudien zur Intersektionalität im frühen Judentum, Christentum und Islam*, edited by Ute E. Eisen, Christine Gerber, and Angela Standhartinger, 381–403. Tübingen: Mohr Siebeck, 2013.

Maxwell, Kathy Reiko. *Hearing between the Lines: The Audience as Fellow-Worker in Luke-Acts and Its Literary Milieu*. New York: T&T Clark, 2010.

McCall, Leslie. "The Complexity of Intersectionality." *Journal of Women in Culture and Society* 30 (2005): 1771–1800.

McCutcheon, Russell T. *Manufacturing Religion: The Discourse on Sui Generis Religion and the Politics of Nostalgia*. New York: Oxford University Press, 1997.

Mcguire, M. R. P. "Letters and Letter Carriers in Ancient Antiquity." *Classical World* 53 (1960): 148–199.

McPhillips, Robert. *The New Formalism: A Critical Introduction*. 2nd ed. Cincinnati: Textos, 2005.

McQuillan, Martin, Graeme MacDonald, Robin Purves, and Steven Thomson, eds. *Post-Theory: New Directions in Criticism*. Edinburgh: University of Edinburgh Press, 1999.

Medvedev, P. N. *The Formal Method in Literary Scholarship: A Critical Introduction to Sociological Poetics*. Translated by A. G. Weherl. Baltimore: Johns Hopkins University Press, 1978.

Meeks, Wayne A. *The First Urban Christians: The Social Word of the Apostle Paul*. New Haven: Yale University Press, 1983.

Meier, John P. *A Marginal Jew: Rethinking the Historical Jesus*. 5 vols. New York: Doubleday, 1991–2016.

———. *Roots of the Problem and the Person*. Vol. 1 of *A Marginal Jew: Rethinking the Historical Jesus*. New York: Doubleday, 1991.

Melick, R. R., Jr. "Literary Criticism of the New Testament." In *Foundations for Biblical Interpretation: A Complete Library of Tools and Resources*, ed. S. Dockery, K. A. Mathews, and R. B. Sloan, 434–453. Nashville: Broadman & Holman, 1994.

Mercer, Calvin. *Norman Perrin's Interpretation of the New Testament: "Exegetical Method" to "Hermeneutical Process."* Macon, GA: Mercer University Press, 1986.

Merenlahti, Petri. *Poetics for the Gospels? Rethinking Narrative Criticism.* London: T&T Clark, 2002.

Metzger, Bruce M. *A Textual Commentary on the Greek New Testament.* 2nd ed. Stuttgart: Deutsche Bibelgesellschaft, 1994.

Meyer, Ben F. *The Aims of Jesus.* Eugene, OR: Pickwick Publications, 2002.

Meynet, Roland. *L'Évangile selon saint Luc: Analyse rhétorique.* 2 vols. Paris: Cerf, 1988.

Michalowski, Piotr. *Letters from Early Mesopotamia.* Edited by Erica Reiner. Translated by Piotr Michalowski. Atlanta: Scholars Press, 1993.

Miguez-Bonino, José. "Marxist Critical Tools: Are They Helpful in Breaking the Stranglehold of Idealist Hermeneutics?" In *Voices from the Margins: Interpreting the Bible in the Third Word,* edited by R. S. Sugirtharajah, 58–68. London: Orbis, 1995.

Miller, Anna. "Not with Eloquent Wisdom: Democratic Ekklēsia Discourse in 1 Corinthians 1–4." *JSNT* 35, no. 4 (2013): 323–354.

Miller, Joseph M., Michael H. Prosser, and Thomas W. Benson, eds. *Readings in Medieval Rhetoric.* Bloomington: Indiana University Press, 1973.

Mitchell, Christine. "Power, *Eros,* and Biblical Genres." In *Bakhtin and Genre Theory in Biblical Studies,* edited by Roland Boer, 31–42. Atlanta: Society of Biblical Literature, 2007.

Mitchell, Margaret M. "New Testament Envoys in the Context of Greco-Roman Diplomatic and Epistolary Conventions: The Example of Timothy and Titus." *JBL* III, no. 4 (1992): 641–662.

———. *Paul and the Rhetoric of Reconciliation: An Exegetical Investigation of the Language and Composition of 1 Corinthians.* Tübingen: Mohr Siebeck, 1991.

———. *Paul, the Corinthians, and the Birth of Christian Hermeneutics.* New York: Cambridge University Press, 2010.

Moessner, David P. "Luke as Tradent and Hermeneut: 'As One Who Has a Thoroughly Informed Familiarity with All the Events from the Top' (παρηκολουθηκότι ἄνωθεν πᾶσιν ἀκριβῶς, Luke 1:3)." *NovT* 58 (2016): 259–300.

Möller, Karl. "Renewing Historical Criticism." In *Renewing Biblical Interpretation,* edited by Craig Bartholomew, Colin Greene, and Karl Möller, 145–171. Grand Rapids, MI: Zondervan, 2000.

Montrose, Louis A. "Professing the Renaissance: The Poetics and Politics of Culture." In *The New Historicism,* edited by Harold Aram Veeser, 15–36. London: Routledge, 1989.

Moore, Stephen D. *The Bible in Theory: Critical and Postcritical Essays.* Atlanta: Society of Biblical Literature Press, 2010.

———. *Empire and Apocalypse: Postcolonialism and the New Testament.* Sheffield: Sheffield Phoenix, 2006.

———. *God's Beauty Parlor and Other Queer Spaces in and around the Bible.* Stanford, CA: Stanford University Press, 2001.

———. *God's Gym: Divine Male Bodies of the Bible.* New York: Routledge, 1996.

———. *Gospel Jesuses and Other Nonhumans: Biblical Criticism Post-poststructuralism.* *Semeia* 89. Atlanta: Society of Biblical Literature Press, 2017.

———. "History after Theory? Biblical Studies and the New Historicism." *BibInt* 5 (1997): 289–299.

———. *Literary Criticism and the Gospels: The Theoretical Challenge.* New Haven: Yale University Press, 1989.

———. *Mark and Luke in Poststructuralist Perspectives: Jesus Begins to Write.* New Haven: Yale University Press, 1992.

———. "A Modest Manifesto for New Testament Literary Criticism: How to Interface with a Literary Studies Field That Is Post-Literary, Post-Theoretical, and Post-Methodological." *BibInt* 15 (2007): 1–25.

———. *Poststructuralism and the New Testament: Derrida and Foucault at the Foot of the Cross.* Minneapolis: Fortress, 1994.

———. "True Confessions and Weird Obsessions: Autobiographical Interventions in Literary and Biblical Studies." *Semeia* 72 (1995): 19–51.

Moore, Stephen D., and L. Kearns, eds. *Divinanimality: Animal Theory, Creaturely Theology.* New York: Fordham University Press, 2014.

Moore, Stephen D., and Fernando F. Segovia. "Postcolonial Biblical Criticism: Beginnings, Trajectories, Intersections." In *Postcolonial Biblical Criticism: Interdisciplinary Intersections,* edited by Stephen D. Moore and Fernando F. Segovia, 1–22. London: T&T Clark, 2005.

Moore, Stephen D., and Yvonne Sherwood. "Biblical Studies 'after' Theory: Onwards towards the Past, Part Three: Theory in the First and Second Waves." *BibInt* 18 (2010): 191–225.

———. *The Invention of the Biblical Scholar: A Critical Manifesto.* Minneapolis: Fortress, 2011.

Morrison, Susan Signe. *The Literature of Waste: Material Ecopoetics and Ethical Matter.* New York: Palgrave Macmillan, 2015.

Morrison, Toni. *Playing in the Dark: Whiteness and the Literary Imagination.* Cambridge, MA: Harvard University Press, 1992.

Moss, Candida R. "The Man with the Flow of Power: Porous Bodies in Mark 5:25–34." *JBL* 129, no. 3 (2010): 507–519.

Muilenburg, James. "Form Criticism and Beyond." *JBL* 88, no. 1 (1969): 1–18.

———. "Literary Forms in the Fourth Gospel." *JBL* 51, no. 1 (1932): 40–53.

Murphy-O'Connor, Jerome. "Co-Authorship in the Corinthian Correspondence." *Revue Biblique* 100 (1993): 562–579.

———. *Paul the Letter-Writer: His World, His Options, His Skills.* Collegeville, MN: Liturgical, 1995.

Nadella, Raj. *Dialogue Not Dogma: Many Voices in the Gospel of Luke.* New York: T&T Clark, 2011.

Najman, Hindy. "The Idea of Biblical Genre: From Discourse to Constellation." In *Prayer and Poetry in the Dead Sea Scrolls and Related Literature: Essays in Honor of Eileen Schuller on the Occasion of Her 65th Birthday*, edited by Jeremy Penner, Ken M. Penner, and Cecilia Wassen, 307–321. Leiden: Brill, 2011.

Nandy, Ashis. *The Intimate Enemy: Loss and Recovery of Self under Colonialism*. New Delhi: Oxford University Press, 1983.

Nasrallah, Laura. "'Out of Love for Paul': History and Fiction and the Afterlife of the Apostle Paul." In *Early Christian and Jewish Narrative*, edited by Ilaria Ramelli and Judith Perkins, 73–96. Tübingen: Mohr Siebeck, 2015.

————. "'You Were Bought with a Price': Freedpersons and Things in 1 Corinthians." In *Corinth in Contrast: Studies in Inequality*, edited by Steven J. Friesen, Sarah A. James, and Daniel N. Schowalter, 54–73. Leiden: Brill, 2014.

Nasrallah, Laura, and Elisabeth Schüssler Fiorenza, eds. *Prejudice and Christian Beginnings: Investigating Race, Gender, and Ethnicity in Early Christian Studies*. Minneapolis: Fortress, 2009.

Neumann, Birgit, and Ansgar Nünning. "Einleitung: Probleme, Aufgaben und Perspektiven der Gattungstheorie und Gattungsgeschichte." In *Gattungstheorie und Gattungsgeschichte*, edited by Marion Gymnich, Birgit Neumann, and Ansgar Nünning, 1–28. Trier: Wissenschatflicher Verlag, 2007.

Newmyer, Stephen Thomas. *Animals, Rights, and Reason in Plutarch and Modern Ethics*. New York: Routledge, 2006.

Neyrey, Jerome. "Miracles, in Other Words: Social Science Perspectives on Healings." In *Miracles in Jewish and Christian Antiquity: Imagining Truth*, edited by John C. Cavadini, 19–56. Notre Dame, IN: University of Notre Dame Press, 1999.

Ngai, Sianne. *Ugly Feelings*. Cambridge, MA: Harvard University Press, 2005.

Nicolet-Anderson, Valérie. *Constructing the Self: Thinking with Paul and Michel Foucault*. Tübingen: Mohr Siebeck, 2012.

Nietzsche, Friedrich. "Description of Ancient Rhetoric (1872–73)." In *Friedrich Nietzsche on Rhetoric and Language*, edited and translated by Sander Gilman, Carole Blair, and David J. Parent, 2–206. New York: Oxford University Press, 1989.

Nilges, Mathias, and Emilio Sauri, eds. *Literary Materialisms*. New York: Palgrave Macmillan, 2013.

Nongbri, Brent. "2 Corinthians and Possible Material Evidence for Composite Letters in Antiquity." In *Collecting Early Christian Letters: From the Apostle Paul to Late Antiquity*, ed. Bronwen Neil and Pauline Allen, 54–67. Cambridge, UK: Cambridge University Press, 2015.

Norden, Eduard. *Agnostos Theos: Untersuchungen zur Formengeschichte religiöser Rede*. 2nd ed. Leipzig: Teubner, 1923.

————. *Die antike Kunstprosa vom VI. Jahrhundert v. Chr. bis in die Zeit der Renaissance*. 2 vols. Leipzig: Teubner, 1898.

Norton, David. *A History of the English Bible as Literature*. Cambridge, UK: Cambridge University Press, 2000.

O'Brien, Kelli S. *The Use of Scripture in the Markan Passion Narrative.* London: T&T Clark, 2010.

Olender, Maurice. *The Languages of Paradise: Race, Religion, and Philology in the Nineteenth Century.* Cambridge, MA: Harvard University Press, 1992.

O'Neill, Patrick. *Fictions of Discourse: Reading Narrative Theory.* Toronto: University of Toronto Press, 1994.

Osiek, Carolyn. "Female Slaves, *Porneia,* and the Limits of Obedience." In *Early Christian Families in Context: An Interdisciplinary Dialogue,* edited by David L. Balch and Carolyn Osiek, 253–274. Grand Rapids, MI: Eerdmans, 2003.

O'Toole, Robert. F. *The Unity of Luke's Theology: An Analysis of Luke-Acts.* Wilmington, DE: Glazier, 1984.

Overbeck, Franz. "Über die Anfänge der patristischen Literatur." *Historischen Zeitschrift* 48 (1882): 417–472.

Parsons, Mikeal C. *Body and Character in Luke-Acts: The Subversion of Physiognomy in Early Christianity.* Grand Rapids, MI: Baker Academic, 2006.

Parsons, Mikeal C., and Richard I. Pervo. *Rethinking the Unity of Luke and Acts.* Minneapolis: Fortress, 1993.

Patai, Daphne, and Will H. Corral, eds. *Theory's Empire: An Anthology of Dissent.* New York: Columbia University Press, 2005.

Patte, Daniel. *Ethics of Biblical Interpretation.* Louisville: Westminster John Knox, 1995.

———. *The Gospel according to Matthew: A Structural Commentary on Matthew's Gospel.* Philadelphia: Fortress, 1987.

———. *Paul's Faith and the Power of the Gospel: A Structural Introduction to the Pauline Letters.* Philadelphia: Fortress, 1983.

———. *Structural Exegesis for New Testament Critics.* Minneapolis: Fortress, 1990.

———. *What Is Structural Exegesis?* Minneapolis: Fortress, 1976.

Pearson, Brook W. R. "New Testament Literary Criticism." In *A Handbook to the Exegesis of the New Testament,* edited by Stanley E. Porter, 241–266. Boston: Brill, 1997.

Pease, Donald E. "Author." In *Critical Terms for Literary Study,* edited by Frank Lentricchia and Thomas McLaughlin, 105–117. Chicago: University of Chicago Press, 1995.

Penner, Todd, and Davina Lopez. *De-Introducing the New Testament: Texts, Worlds, Methods, Stories.* Malden, MA: Wiley Blackwell, 2015.

Peppard, Michael. "'Poetry, 'Hymns,' and 'Traditional Material' in New Testament Epistles, or How to Do Things with Indentations." *JSNT* 30, no. 3 (2008): 319–342.

Perrin, Norman. *Jesus and the Language of the Kingdom: Symbol and Metaphor in New Testament Interpretation.* Philadelphia: Fortress, 1976.

———. *What Is Redaction Criticism?* Philadelphia: Fortress, 1969.

Perry, Menakhem. "Literary Dynamics: How the Order of a Text Creates Its Meanings [With an Analysis of Faulkner's 'A Rose for Emily']." *Poetics Today* 1 (1979): 35–64, 311–361.

Petersen, Norman R. *Literary Criticism for New Testament Critics.* Philadelphia: Fortress, 1978.

———. "Literary Criticism in Biblical Studies." In *Orientation by Disorientation: Studies in Literary Criticism and Biblical Literary Criticism,* edited by Richard Spencer, 25–50. Pittsburgh: Pickwick, 1980.

———. *Rediscovering Paul: Philemon and the Sociology of Paul's Narrative World.* Philadelphia: Fortress, 1985.

Petitfils, James. *Mos Christianorum: The Roman Discourse of Exemplarity and the Jewish and Christian Language of Leadership.* Tübingen: Mohr Siebeck, 2016.

Petracca, Vincenzo. *Gott oder das Geld: Die Besitzethik des Lukas.* Tübingen: Francke, 2003.

Phillips, Gary A. "Exegesis as Critical Praxis: Reclaiming History and Text from a Postmodern Perspective." *Semeia* 51 (1990): 7–49.

———. "History and Text: The Reader in Context in Matthew's Parables Discourse." *Semeia* 31 (1985): 111–138.

Pinnock, Clark H. *The Scripture Principle: Reclaiming the Full Authority of the Bible.* Grand Rapids, MI: Baker Academic, 2006.

Pokorný, Petr. *Colossians.* Peabody, MA: Hendrickson, 1991.

Poland, Lynn M. *Literary Criticism and Biblical Hermeneutics: A Critique of Formalist Approaches.* Chicago: Scholars Press, 1985.

———. "The New Criticism, Neoorthodoxy, and the New Testament." *JR* 65 (1985): 459–477.

Polischuk, Pablo. "A Metacognitive Perspective on Internal Dialogues and Rhetoric: Derived from the Prodigal Son's Parable." *Journal of Psychology and Theology* 43, no. 1 (2015): 60–72.

Pollock, Edward. "The Golden Gate." In *Poems of America,* edited by Henry Wadsworth Longfellow, 194–195. Boston: Houghton, Mifflin, 1882.

Porter, Stanley E. "Literary Approaches to the New Testament: From Formalism to Deconstruction and Back." In *Approaches to New Testament Study,* edited by Stanley E. Porter and David Tombs, 77–128. Sheffield: Sheffield Academic, 1995.

Porter, Stanley E., and Bryan R. Dyer, eds. *Paul and Ancient Rhetoric: Theory and Practice in the Hellenistic Context.* New York: Cambridge University Press, 2016.

Poster, Carol. "The Economy of Letter-Writing in Graeco-Roman Antiquity." In *Rhetorical Argumentation in Biblical Texts: Papers from the Lund 2000 Conference,* edited by Tom Olbricht, Walter Ubelacker, and Anders Eriksson, 112–124. Harrisburg: Trinity, 2002.

Poster, Carol, and Linda Mitchell, eds. *Letter-Writing Manuals and Instruction from Antiquity to the Present: Historical and Bibliographic Studies.* Columbia, SC: University of South Carolina Press, 2007.

Powell, Charles. "The 'Passivity' of Jesus in Mark 5:25–34." *BSac* 162 (2005): 66–75.

Powell, Mark Allan. *Chasing the Eastern Star: Adventures in Biblical Reader-Response Criticism.* Louisville: Westminster John Knox, 2001.

———. "Expected and Unexpected Readings of Matthew: What the Reader Knows." *AsTJ* 48 (1993): 41–51.

———. "The Magi as Kings: An Adventure in Reader-Response Criticism." *CBQ* 62 (2000): 459–80.

———. *What Is Narrative Criticism?* Minneapolis: Fortress, 1990.

Probyn, Elspeth. *Blush: Faces of Shame.* Minneapolis: University of Minnesota Press, 2005.

Putnam, Hilary. *The Collapse of the Fact/Value Dichotomy and Other Essays.* Cambridge, MA: Harvard University Press, 2002.

Pyrhönen, Heta. "Genre." In *The Cambridge Companion to Narrative,* edited by David Herman, 109–124. Cambridge, UK: Cambridge University Press, 2007.

Räisänen, Heikki. *The "Messianic Secret" in Mark.* Translated by Christopher Tuckett. Edinburgh: T&T Clark, 1990.

Ransom, John Crowe. "Criticism, Inc." In *The World's Body,* 2nd ed., 327–350. Baton Rouge: Louisiana State University Press, 1968.

———. *The New Criticism.* Norfolk, CT: New Directions, 1941.

———. "Poetry: A Note in Ontology." In *The World's Body,* 2nd ed., 111–142. Baton Rouge: Louisiana State University Press, 1968.

Reed, Walter. *Dialogues of the Word: The Bible as Literature according to Bakhtin.* New York: Oxford University Press, 1993.

Regev, Eyal. *Sectarianism in Qumran: A Cross-Cultural Perspective.* Berlin: de Gruyter, 2007.

Reinfandt, Christoph. "Reading Texts after the Linguistic Turn: Approaches from Literary Studies and Their Implications." In *Reading Primary Sources: The Interpretation of Texts from Nineteenth- and Twentieth-Century History,* edited by Miriam Dobson and Benjamin Ziemann, 37–54. New York: Routledge, 2009.

Reinhartz, Adele. "Building Skyscrapers on Toothpicks: The Literary-Critical Challenge to Historical Criticism." In *Anatomies of Narrative Criticism: The Past, Present, and Futures of the Fourth Gospel as Literature,* edited by Tom Thatcher and Stephen D. Moore, 55–76. Leiden: Brill, 2008.

———. "Editor's Foreword: *The Journal of Biblical Literature* and the Critical Investigation of the Bible." *JBL* 134, no. 3 (2015): 457–470.

———. *Why Ask My Name? Anonymity and Identity in the Biblical Narrative.* New York: Oxford University Press, 1998.

Renan, Ernest. *History of the People of Israel till the Time of King David.* Vol. 1. Translated by C. B. Pitman and D. Bingham. London: Chapman and Hall, 1888.

Resseguie, James L. "Defamiliarization and the Gospels." *Biblical Theology Bulletin* 20, no. 4 (1990): 147–153.

———. *Narrative Criticism of the New Testament: An Introduction.* Grand Rapids, MI: Baker Academic, 2005.

———. "Reader-Response Criticism and the Synoptic Gospels." *JAAR* 52 (1984): 307–324.

Rhoads, David. "Narrative Criticism and the Gospel of Mark." *JAAR* 50 (1982): 411–434.

———. "The Syrophoenician Woman in Mark: A Narrative-Critical Study." *JAAR* 62 (1992): 342–375.

Rhoads, David, and Donald Michie. *Mark as Story: An Introduction to the Narrative of a Gospel.* Philadelphia: Fortress, 1982.

Richards, E. Randolph. *Paul and First-Century Letter Writing: Secretaries, Composition and Collection.* Downers Grove, IL: InterVarsity, 2004.

Richards, I. A. *Practical Criticism: A Study of Literary Judgment.* London: Paul, Trench, Trubner, 1929.

———. *Principles of Literary Criticism.* London: Paul, Trench, Trubner, 1925.

Ricoeur, Paul. *Freud and Philosophy: An Essay on Interpretation.* Translated by Denis Savage. New Haven: Yale University Press, 1970.

———. *From Text to Action.* Translated by Kathleen Blamey and John B. Thompson. Evanston, IL: Northwestern University Press, 1991.

Robbins, Vernon K. "The Claims of the Prologues and Greco-Roman Rhetoric: The Prefaces to Luke and Acts in Light of Greco-Roman Rhetorical Strategies." In *Jesus and the Heritage of Israel: Luke's Narrative Claim upon Israel's Legacy,* edited by David P. Moessner, 63–83. Harrisburg: Trinity, 1999.

———. *The Invention of Christian Discourse.* Vol. 1. Blandford Forum, UK: Deo Publishing, 2009.

Roberts, Sasha. "Feminist Criticism and the New Formalism: Early Modern Women and Literary Engagement." In *The Impact of Feminism in English Renaissance Studies,* edited by Dympna Callaghan, 67–91. New York: Palgrave Macmillan, 2007.

Robinson, W. C. "Theological Context for Interpreting Luke's Travel Narrative (9:51ff.)." *JBL* 79, no. 1 (1960): 20–31.

Rogerson, John. "Recent Literary Structuralist Approaches to Biblical Interpretation." *Churchman* 90 (1976): 165–177.

Rooney, Ellen. "Form and Contentment." *MLQ* 61 (2000): 17–40.

Rosch, Eleanor. "Cognitive Representations of Semantic Categories." *Journal of Experimental Psychology* 104 (1975): 192–233.

Rosen, David. "Terry Eagleton's Republic of Letters." *Raritan: A Quarterly Review* 33 (2014): 147–161.

Rowe, C. Kavin. *Early Narrative Christology: The Lord in the Gospel of Luke.* Berlin: de Gruyter, 2006.

Rowlett, Lori. *Joshua and the Rhetoric of Violence: A New Historicist Analysis.* Sheffield: Sheffield Academic, 1996.

Royalty, Robert. *The Origin of Heresy: A History of Discourse in Second Temple Judaism and Early Christianity.* New York: Routledge, 2013.

Rueckert, William. "Literature and Ecology: An Experiment in Ecocriticism." In *The Ecocriticism Reader: Landmarks in Literary Ecology,* edited by Cheryll Glotfelty and Harold Fromm, 105–123. Athens: University of Georgia Press, 1996.

Rumelhart, D. E. "Schemata: The Building Blocks of Cognition." In *Theoretical Issues in Reading Comprehension*, edited by R. Spiro, B. Bruce, and W. Brewer, 33–58. Hillsdale, NJ: Erlbaum, 1980.

Runions, Erin. "From Disgust to Humor: Rahab's Queer Affect." In *Bible Trouble: Queer Reading at the Boundaries of Biblical Scholarship*, edited by Teresa J. Hornsby and Ken Stone, 45–74. Atlanta: Society of Biblical Literature Press, 2011.

Ryan, Michael, ed. "Introduction to the Encyclopedia of Literary and Cultural Theory." In *The Encyclopedia of Literary and Cultural Theory*, vol. 1, xiii-xx. Chichester, UK: Wiley-Blackwell, 2011.

Ryken, Leland. *How to Read the Bible as Literature . . . and Get More out of It*. Grand Rapids, MI: Zondervan, 1984.

———. *Words of Life: A Literary Introduction to the New Testament*. Grand Rapids, MI: Baker Book House, 1987.

Ryken, Leland, and Tremper Longman III. "Introduction." In *A Complete Literary Guide to the Bible*, edited by Leland Ryken and Tremper Longman III, 15–39. Grand Rapids, MI: Zondervan, 1993.

Said, Edward. *Orientalism*. New York: Pantheon, 1978.

Schenke, Ludger. *Die Wundererzählungen des Markusevangeliums*. Stuttgart: Verlag Katholisches Bibelwerk, 1974.

Schleiermacher, Friedrich. *Hermeneutics: The Handwritten Manuscripts*. Edited by Heinz Kimmerle. Translated by James Duke and Jack Forstman. Missoula, MT: Scholars Press, 1977.

Schliephake, Christopher, ed. *Ecocriticism, Ecology, and the Cultures of Antiquity*. Lanham, MD: Lexington, 2017.

Schmidt, Darryl D. "Rhetorical Influences and Genre: Luke's Preface and the Rhetoric of Hellenistic Historiography." In *Jesus and the Heritage of Israel: Luke's Narrative Claim upon Israel's Legacy*, edited by David P. Moessner, 27–60. Harrisburg: Trinity, 1999.

Schmidt, Karl Ludwig. *Der Rahmen der Geschichte Jesu. Literarkrit: Untersuchungen zur Ältesten Jesusüberlieferung*. Berlin: Trowitzsch & Sohn, 1919.

———. "Die Stellung der Evangelien in der allgemeinen Literaturgeschichte." In *Eucharisterion: Hermann Gunkel zum 60. Geburtstag*, edited by H. Schmidt, 50–134. Göttingen: Vandenhoeck & Ruprecht, 1923.

Schmithals, W. "Die Korintherbriefe als Briefsammlung." *ZNW* 64 (1973): 263–288.

Schniedewind, William. *How the Bible Became a Book: The Textualization of Ancient Israel*. Cambridge, UK: Cambridge University Press, 2005.

Schüssler Fiorenza, Elisabeth. *Bread Not Stone: The Challenge of Feminist Biblical Interpretation*. Boston: Beacon, 1984.

———. *But She Said: Feminist Practices of Biblical Interpretation*. Boston: Beacon, 1992.

———. *Discipleship of Equals: A Critical Feminist Ekklesia-logy of Liberation*. London: SCM, 1993.

———. "The Ethics of Biblical Interpretation: Decentering Biblical Scholarship." *JBL* 107, no. 1 (1988): 3–17.

————. *Rhetoric and Ethic: The Politics of Biblical Studies*. Minneapolis: Fortress, 1999.

————. "Rhetorical Situation and Historical Reconstruction in 1 Corinthians." *NTS* 33, no. 3 (1987): 386–403.

Schwáb, Zoltán. "Mind the Gap: The Impact of Wolfgang Iser's Reader-Response Criticism on Biblical Studies—A Critical Assessment." *Literature and Theology* 17 (2003): 170–181.

Schwarz, Daniel. *In Defense of Reading*. Malden, MA: Blackwell, 2008.

Schweickart, Patrocinio. "Reading Ourselves: Toward a Feminist Theory of Reading." In *Gender and Reading: Essays on Readers, Texts, and Contexts*, edited by Patrocinio Schweickart and Elizabeth Flynn, 31–62. Baltimore: Johns Hopkins University Press, 1986.

Scott, Bernard Brandon. *Hear Then the Parable: A Commentary on the Parables of Jesus*. Minneapolis: Fortress, 1989.

————. *Jesus, Symbol-Maker for the Kingdom*. Philadelphia: Fortress, 1983.

Scott-Baumann, Elizabeth. *Forms of Engagement: Women, Poetry and Culture, 1640–1680*. Oxford: Oxford University Press, 2013.

Searle, J. R. *Expression and Meaning: Studies in the Theory of Speech Acts*. Cambridge, UK: Cambridge University Press, 1979.

————. *Speech Acts: An Essay in the Philosophy of Language*. Cambridge, UK: Cambridge University Press, 1969.

Seccombe, D. P. *Possessions and the Poor in Luke-Acts*. Linz: A. Fuchs, 1982.

Sedgwick, Eve Kosofsky. "Paranoid Reading and Reparative Reading, or, You're So Paranoid, You Probably Think This Essay Is about You." In *Touching Feeling: Affect, Pedagogy, Performativity*, 123–151. Durham, NC: Duke University Press, 2003.

————. *Touching Feeling: Affect, Pedagogy, Performativity*. Durham, NC: Duke University Press, 2003.

Sedgwick, Eve Kosofsky, and Adam Frank. "Shame and the Cybernetic Fold: Reading Silvan Tomkins." In *Shame and Its Sisters: A Silvan Tomkins Reader*, edited by Eve Kosofsky Sedgwick and Adam Frank, 1–28. Durham, NC: Duke University Press, 1995.

Seeberg, Alfred. *Die Didache des Judentums und der Urchristenheit*. Leipzig: Deichert, 1908.

Seeley, David. *Deconstructing the New Testament*. Leiden: Brill, 1994.

Segovia, Fernando F. *Decolonizing Biblical Studies: A View from the Margins*. Maryknoll, NY: Orbis, 2000.

Segovia, Fernando F., and R. S. Sugirtharajah, eds. *A Postcolonial Commentary on New Testament Writings*. New York: Continuum, 2007.

Seim, Turid Karlsen. *The Double Message: Patterns of Gender in Luke-Acts*. Edinburgh: T&T Clark, 1994.

Selden, Raman, ed. *The Theory of Criticism from Plato to the Present: A Reader*. New York: Routledge, 2014.

Selinger, Reinhard. *The Mid-Third Century Persecutions of Decius and Valerian*. 2nd ed. Frankfurt: Peter Lang, 2004.

Selvidge, Marla. "Mark 5:25–34 and Leviticus 15:19–20: A Reaction to Restrictive Purity Regulations." *JBL* 103, no. 4 (1984): 619–623.

Shaner, Katherine. *Enslaved Leadership in Early Christianity*. Oxford: Oxford University Press, 2017.

Sheehan, Jonathan. *The Enlightenment Bible: Translation, Scholarship, Culture*. Princeton: Princeton University Press, 2005.

Shelton, James B. *Mighty in Word and Deed: The Role of the Holy Spirit in Luke-Acts*. Peabody, MA: Hendrickson, 1991.

Shepherd, Tom. "The Narrative Function of Markan Intercalation." *NTS* 41, no. 4 (1995): 522–540.

Shepherd, William H., Jr. *The Narrative Function of the Holy Spirit as a Character in Luke-Acts*. Atlanta: Scholars Press, 1994.

Shillingsburg, Peter. "Text as Communication." In *Textuality and Knowledge: Essays*, 83–93. University Park, PA: Pennsylvania State University Press, 2017.

Shiner, Whitney. "Creating Plot in Episodic Narratives: The Life of Aesop and the Gospel of Mark." In *Ancient Fiction and Early Christian Narrative*, edited by J. B. Chance and J. Perkins, 155–176. Atlanta: Scholars Press, 1998.

Shively, Elizabeth. *Apocalyptic Imagination in the Gospel of Mark: The Literary and Theological Role of Mark 3:22–30*. Berlin: de Gruyter, 2012.

———. "Intentionality and Narrative Worldmaking in the Gospel of Mark: Rethinking Narrative Communication." In *Reading the Gospel of Mark in the Twenty-First Century*, edited by Geert Van Oyen, 297–348. Leuven: Peeters, 2019.

Shklovsky, Viktor. "Art as Technique." In *Russian Formalist Criticism: Four Essays*, edited and translated by Lee T. Lemon and Marion J. Reis, 3–24. Omaha: University of Nebraska Press, 1965.

———. "The Connection between Devices of *Syuzhet* Construction and General Stylistic Devices." In *Russian Formalism: A Collection of Articles and Texts in Translation*, edited by Stephen Bann and John E. Bowlt, 48–72. Edinburgh: Scottish Academic Press, 1973.

Showalter, Elaine. "Toward a Feminist Poetics." In *New Feminist Criticism: Essays on Women, Literature, and Theory*, edited by Elaine Showalter, 125–142. New York: Pantheon, 1985.

Sidney, Sir Philip. "An Apology for Poetry." In *Critical Theory Since Plato*, edited by Hazard Adams and Leroy Searle, 143–162. Boston: Wadsworth, 2005.

Siegert, Folker. *Argumentation bei Paulus: Gezeigt an Rom 9–11*. Tübingen: Mohr Siebeck, 1985.

Sinding, Michael. "After Definitions: Genre, Categories, and Cognitive Science." *Genre* 35 (2002): 181–220.

Skinner, Christopher, ed. *Characters and Characterization in the Gospel of John*. London: Bloomsbury, 2013.

Skinner, Christopher, and Matthew Hauge, eds. *Character Studies and the Gospel of Mark.* London: Bloomsbury T&T Clark, 2015.

Smith, Dennis E. "Table Fellowship as a Literary Motif in the Gospel of Luke." *JBL* 106, no. 4 (1987): 613–638.

Soulen, Richard N., and R. Kendell Soulen. *Handbook of Biblical Criticism.* 4th ed. Louisville: Westminster John Knox, 2011.

Spencer, F. Scott. "Acts and Modern Literary Approaches." In *The Book of Acts in Its Ancient Literary Setting*, vol. 1, edited by Bruce W. Winter and Andrew D. Clarke, 381–414. Grand Rapids, MI: Eerdmans, 1993.

———. *Salty Wives, Spirited Mothers, and Savvy Widows: Capable Women of Purpose and Persistence in Luke's Gospel.* Grand Rapids, MI: Eerdmans, 2012.

Spingarn, Joel E. "The New Criticism." In *Creative Criticism: Essays on the Unity of Genius and Taste*, 3–44. New York: Henry Holt, 1917.

Spinks, Lee. "Thinking the Post-Human: Literature, Affect, and the Politics of Style." *Textual Practice* 15 (2001): 23–46.

Spivak, Gayatri Chakravorty. "Can the Subaltern Speak?" In *Marxism and the Interpretation of Culture*, edited by Cary Nelson and Lawrence Grossberg, 271–313. Urbana, IL: University of Illinois Press, 1988.

———. *In Other Worlds: Essays in Cultural Politics.* New York: Methuen, 1987.

Squires, John T. *The Plan of God in Luke-Acts.* Cambridge, UK: Cambridge University Press, 1993.

Staley, Jeffrey. *Reading with a Passion: Rhetoric, Autobiography, and the American West in the Gospel of John.* New York: Continuum, 1995.

Steele, E. Springs. "Luke 11:37–54—A Modified Hellenistic Symposium?" *JBL* 103, no. 3 (1984): 379–394.

Stein, Robert H. *An Introduction to the Parables of Jesus.* Philadelphia: Westminster, 1981.

Steiner, Peter. *Russian Formalism: A Metapoetics.* Ithaca, NY: Cornell University Press, 1984.

———. "Russian Formalism." In *The Cambridge History of Literary Criticism: From Formalism to Poststructuralism*, vol. 8, edited by Raman Selden, 11–29. Cambridge, UK: Cambridge University Press, 1995.

Stendahl, Krister. "The Apostle Paul and the Introspective Conscience of the West." *Harvard Theological Review* 56 (1963): 199–215.

———. "Biblical Theology, Contemporary." In *The Interpreter's Dictionary of the Bible*, vol. 1, edited by Keith Crim, 418–432. Nashville: Abingdon, 1962.

Sterling, Gregory E. *Historiography and Self-Definition: Josephos, Luke-Acts, and Apologetic Historiography.* Leiden: Brill, 1992.

Sternberg, Meir. *The Poetics of Biblical Narrative: Ideological Literature and the Drama of Reading.* Bloomington: Indiana University Press, 1985.

Stevenson, Robert Louis. *The Strange Case of Dr. Jekyll and Mr. Hyde.* London: Longmans, Green, 1886.

Stewart-Sykes, Alistair. "Ancient Editors and Copyists and Modern Parti-tion Theories: The Case of the Corinthian Correspondence." *JSNT* 61 (1996): 53–64.

Stone, Lawrence. "History and Post-Modernism." *Past & Present* 131 (1991): 217–218.

Stowers, Stanley Kent. *The Diatribe and Paul's Letter to the Romans.* Chico, CA: Scholars Press, 1981.

———. *Letter Writing in Greco-Roman Antiquity.* Philadelphia: Westminster, 1986.

———. *A Rereading of Romans: Justice, Jews and Gentiles.* New Haven: Yale University Press, 1994.

Strachan, R. H. *The Second Epistle of Paul to the Corinthians.* Moffatt New Testament Commentary. London: Hodder and Stoughton, 1935.

Strier, Richard. "How Formalism Became a Dirty Word, and Why We Can't Do without It." In *Renaissance Literature and Its Formal Engagements,* edited by Mark David Rasmussen, 207–215. New York: Palgrave, 2002.

Sugg, Richard. *Jungian Literary Criticism.* Evanston, IL: Northwestern University Press, 1992.

Sundberg, Walter. "The Social Effect of Biblical Criticism." In *Renewing Biblical Interpretation,* edited by Craig G. Bartholomew, Colin J. D. Greene, and Karl Möller, 66–81. Grand Rapids, MI: Zondervan, 2000.

Swales, John. *Genre Analysis: English in Academic and Research Settings.* Cambridge, UK: Cambridge University Press, 1990.

Talbert, Charles H. *Reading Luke: A Literary and Theological Commentary.* Macon, GA: Smyth & Helwys, 2002.

Tannehill, Robert C. "Beginning to Study 'How Gospels Begin.'" *Semeia* 52 (1991): 185–192.

———. "The Disciples in Mark: The Function of a Narrative Role." *JR* 57 (1977): 386–405.

———. "The Gospel of Mark as Narrative Christology." *Semeia* 16 (1979): 57–95.

———. *The Narrative Unity of Luke-Acts: A Literary Interpretation.* 2 vols. Philadelphia: Fortress, 1986, 1990.

———. *The Sword of His Mouth.* Philadelphia: Fortress, 1975.

Taylor, Joan, ed. *Jesus and Brian: Exploring the Historical Jesus and His Times via Monty Python's "Life of Brian."* New York: Bloomsbury, 2015.

Theissen, Gerd. *The Miracle Stories of the Early Christian Tradition.* Translated by Francis McDonagh. Philadelphia: Fortress, 1983.

Thiele, Verena. "New Formalism(s): A Prologue." In *New Formalisms and Literary Theory,* edited by Verena Thiele and Linda Tredennick, 3–26. Basingstoke: Palgrave, 2013.

Thiele, Verena, and Linda Tredennick, eds. *New Formalisms and Literary Theory.* Basingstoke: Palgrave, 2013.

Thiselton, Anthony. "Christology in Luke, Speech-Act Theory, and the Problem of Dualism in Christology after Kant." In *Jesus of Nazareth, Lord and Christ: Essays* on the Historical Jesus and New Testament Theology, edited by Joel B. Green and Max Turner, 453–472. Grand Rapids, MI: Eerdmans, 1994.

Thompson, John B. *Ideology and Modern Culture: Critical Theory in the Era of Mass Communication*. Stanford, CA: Stanford University Press, 1990.

Thorsteinsson, Runar M. *Roman Christianity and Roman Stoicism: A Comparative Study of Ancient Morality*. Oxford: Oxford University Press, 2010.

Tischleder, Babette Bärbel. *The Literary Life of Things: Case Studies in American Fiction*. Frankfurt: Campus Verlag, 2014.

Tissol, Garth, and William Wendell Batstone, eds. *Defining Genre and Gender in Latin Literature: Essays Presented to William S. Anderson on His Seventy-Fifth Birthday*. New York: Peter Lang, 2005.

Todorov, Tzvetan. *Genres in Discourse*. Translated by Catherine Porter. Cambridge, UK: Cambridge University Press, 1990.

Tolbert, Mary Ann. "How the Gospel of Mark Builds Character." *Int* 47 (1993): 347–357.

———. *Sowing the Gospel: Mark's World in Literary-Historical Perspective*. Minneapolis: Fortress, 1989.

Tolmie, François. *Narratology and Biblical Narratives: A Practical Guide*. Eugene, OR: Wipf & Stock, 1999.

Tomkins, Silvan. *Affect, Imagery, Consciousness*. 2 vols. New York: Springer, 1962–63.

Too, Yun Lee. *The Idea of Ancient Criticism*. Oxford: Oxford University Press, 1998.

Trebilco, Paul. *The Early Christians in Ephesus from Paul to Ignatius*. Tübingen: Mohr Siebeck, 2004.

Treier, Daniel. *Introducing Theological Interpretation of Scripture: Recovering a Christian Practice*. Grand Rapids, MI: Baker Academic, 2008.

Trotsky, Leon. *Literature and Revolution*. Translated by Rose Strunksy. Chicago: Haymarket, 2005.

Twelftree, Graham H. *Jesus the Miracle Worker: A Historical and Theological Study*. Downers Grove, IL: InterVarsity, 1999.

Tynyanov, Yury. "The Literary Fact." In *Modern Genre Theory*, edited by David Duff, 29–49. London: Routledge, 2014.

———. "On Literary Evolution." In *Twentieth Century Literary Theory*, edited by Vassilis Lambropoulos and David Neal Miller, 152–162. Albany: State University of New York Press, 1987.

Usher, Stephen. *Dionysius of Halicarnassus: The Critical Essays*. Vol. 1. Cambridge, MA: Harvard University Press, 1974.

VanderKam, James C. "1 Enoch, Enochic Motifs, and Enoch in Early Christian Literature." In *The Jewish Apocalyptic Heritage in Early Christianity*, edited by James C. VanderKam and William Adler, 33–101. Assen: Van Gorcum, 1996.

Vanhoozer, Kevin J. *Is There a Meaning in This Text? The Bible, the Reader, and the Morality of Literary Knowledge*. Grand Rapids, MI: Zondervan, 1998.

van Seters, John. "A Response to G. Aichele, P. Miscall and R. Walsh, 'An Elephant in the Room: Historical-Critical and Postmodern Interpretations of the Bible.'" *Journal of Hebrew Scriptures* 9 (2009): 2–13.

van Unnik, W. C. "Luke's Second Book and the Rules of Hellenistic Historiography." In *Les Actes des Apôtres: Traditions, rédaction, théologie*, edited by J. Kremer, 37–60. Leuven: Leuven University Press, 1979.

———. "Once More St. Luke's Prologue." *Neot* 7 (1973): 7–26.

Vásquez, Víctor Manuel Morales. *Contours of a Biblical Reception Theory: Studies in the Rezeptionsgeschichte of Romans 13.1–17*. Göttingen: V & R Unipress, 2012.

Verheyden, Joseph, ed. *The Unity of Luke-Acts*. Leuven: Leuven University Press, 1999.

Via, Dan Otto. *Kerygma and Comedy in the New Testament Parables*. Philadelphia: Fortress, 1975.

———. *The Parables: Their Literary and Existential Dimension*. Philadelphia: Fortress, 1967.

Vitruvius. *Vitruvius: Ten Books on Architecture*. Edited by Ingrid Rowland and Thomas Noble Howe. Translated by Ingrid Rowland. New York: Cambridge University Press, 1999.

Vlahogiannis, Nicholas. "Disabling Bodies." In *Changing Bodies, Changing Meanings: Studies on the Human Body in Antiquity*, edited by Dominic Montserrat, 13–36. London: Routledge, 1998.

von Dobschütz, Ernst. "Zur Erzählerkunst des Markus." *ZNW* 27 (1928): 193–198.

von Harnack, Adolf. "Fifteen Questions to Those among the Theologians Who Are Contemptuous of the Scientific Theology." *Die Christliche Welt* (January 11, 1923); reprinted in *The Beginning of Dialectic Theology*, edited by James M. Robinson, translated by Keith R. Crim, 165–166. Richmond, VA: John Knox, 1968.

von Ranke, Leopold. *Geschichten der romanischen und germanischen Völker von 1494 bis 1514*. 3rd ed. Leipzig: Duncker & Humblot, 1885.

Wainwright, Elaine M. "'Hear Then, the Parable of the Seed': Reading the Agrarian Parables of Matthew 13 Ecologically." In *The One Who Reads May Run: Essays in Honour of Edgar W. Conrad*, edited by Roland Boer, Michael Carden, and Julie Kelso, 125–141. New York: T&T Clark, 2012.

———. "Images, Words, and Stories: Exploring Their Transformative Power in Reading Biblical Texts Ecologically." *BibInt* 20, no. 3 (2010): 280–304.

———. "Place, Power, and Potentiality: Reading Matthew 2:1–12 Ecologically." *Expository Times* 121, no. 4 (2010): 159–163.

———. "Reading Matt 21:12–22 Ecologically." *Australian Biblical Review* 60 (2012): 67–79.

Walaskay, Paul W. *And So We Came to Rome: The Political Perspective of St. Paul*. New York: Cambridge University Press, 1983.

Walters, Patricia. *The Assumed Authorial Unity of Luke and Acts: A Reassessment of the Evidence*. Cambridge, UK: Cambridge University Press, 2009.

Walzer, Kevin. "Dana Gioia and Expansive Poetry." *Italian Americana* 16 (1998): 24–40.

———. *The Ghost of Tradition: Expansive Poetry and Postmodernism*. Ashland, OR: Story Line Press, 2000.

Watson, Francis. *Text and Truth: Redefining Biblical Theology*. Edinburgh: T&T Clark, 1997.

Waugh, Patricia. "Introduction: Criticism, Theory, and Anti-Theory." In *Literary Theory and Criticism: An Oxford Guide,* edited by Patricia Waugh, 1–33. Oxford: Oxford University Press, 2006.

Webb, Ruth. *Ekphrasis, Imagination and Persuasion in Ancient Rhetorical Theory and Practice*. Burlington, VT: Ashgate, 2009.

Weinsheimer, Joel. Foreword to *Introduction to Literary Hermeneutics,* by Peter Szondi, xi–xxiii. Cambridge, UK: Cambridge University Press, 1995.

Welborn, Lawrence L. "Marxism and Capitalism in Pauline Studies." In *Paul and Economics,* edited by Thomas R. Blanton IV and Raymond Pickett, 361–396. Minneapolis: Fortress, 2017.

———. "Paul's Appeal to the Emotions in 2 Corinthians 1.1–2.13; 7.5–16." *JSNT* 82 (2001): 31–60.

———. "'That There May Be Equality': The Contexts and Consequences of a Pauline Ideal." *NTS* 59, no. 1 (2013): 73–90.

———. "Towards Structural Marxism as a Hermeneutic of Early Christian Literature, Illustrated by Reference to Paul's Spectacle Metaphor in 1 Corinthians 15:30–32." *B&CT* 8 (2012): 27–35.

Wellek, René. "The Concept of Evolution in Literary History." In *Concepts of Criticism,* edited by Stephen G. Nichols Jr., 37–53. New Haven: Yale University Press, 1963.

———. *A History of Modern Criticism, 1750–1950*. New Haven: Yale University Press, 1955.

———. "Literary Theory, Criticism, and History." In *Concepts of Criticism,* edited by Stephen G. Nichols, Jr., 1–20. New Haven: Yale University Press, 1963.

Wellek, René, and Austin Warren. *Theory of Literature*. 2nd ed. New York: Harcourt, Brace, and World, 1956.

Wenk, Matthias. *Community-Forming Power: The Socio-Ethical Role of the Spirit in Luke-Acts*. Sheffield: Sheffield Academic, 2000.

Werbner, Pnina. "Essentialising Essentialism, Essentialising Silence: Ambivalence and Multiplicity in the Construction of Racism and Ethnicity." In *Debating Cultural Hybridity: Multicultural Identities and the Politics of Anti-Racism,* edited by Pnina Werbner and Tariq Modood, 226–254. London: Zed, 1997.

Whitaker, Robyn J. *Ekphrasis, Vision, and Persuasion in the Book of Revelation*. Tübingen: Mohr Siebeck, 2015.

White, Lynn. "The Historical Roots of Our Ecological Crisis." *Science* 155 (1967): 1203–1207.

Wilder, Amos N. *Early Christian Rhetoric: The Language of the Gospel.* Cambridge, MA: Harvard University Press, 1971.

———. "Scholars, Theologians, and Ancient Rhetoric." *JBL* 75, no. 1 (1956): 1–11.

Williams, James G. *Gospel against Parable: Mark's Language of Mystery.* Sheffield: JSOT, 1985.

Williams, Jeffrey. "The Posttheory Generation." In *Day Late, Dollar Short: The Next Generation and the New Academy,* edited by Peter C. Herman, 25–44. Albany: State University of New York Press, 2000.

Williams, Raymond. *Marxism and Literature.* Oxford: Oxford University Press, 1977.

Wilson, Brittany. *Unmanly Men: Refigurations of Masculinity in Luke-Acts.* Oxford: Oxford University Press, 2015.

Wimbush, Vincent, ed. *African Americans and the Bible: Sacred Texts and Social Textures.* New York: Continuum, 2000.

Wimsatt, W. K., and M. C. Beardsley. "The Affective Fallacy." In *The Verbal Icon: Studies in the Meaning of Poetry,* 21–39. Lexington: University of Kentucky Press, 1954.

———. "The Intentional Fallacy." In *The Verbal Icon: Studies in the Meaning of Poetry,* 3–18. Lexington: University of Kentucky Press, 1954.

Windisch, H. *Die katholischen Briefe. HNT* 15. Tübingen: Mohr Siebeck, 1951.

Windschuttle, Keith. *The Killing of History: How Literary Critics and Social Theorists Are Murdering Our Past.* New York: Free Press, 1997.

Winter, Irene. "Agency Marked, Agency Ascribed: The Affective Object in Ancient Mesopotamia." In *On Art in the Ancient Near East,* vol. 2, *From the Third Millennium B.C.E.,* edited by Irene Winter, 307–331. Leiden: Brill, 2010.

Wire, Antoinette Clark. *The Corinthian Women Prophets: A Reconstruction through Paul's Rhetoric.* Minneapolis: Fortress, 1990.

———. "The Structure of the Gospel Miracle Stories and Their Tellers." *Semeia* 11 (1978): 83–113.

Witherington, Ben, III. *New Testament Rhetoric: An Introductory Guide to the Art of Persuasion in and of the New Testament.* Eugene, OR: Cascade, 2009.

———. *Women in the Ministry of Jesus.* Cambridge, UK: Cambridge University Press, 1984.

Wittgenstein, Ludwig. *Philosophical Investigations.* Edited by G. E. M. Anscombe and Rush Rhees. Translated by G. E. M. Anscombe. Oxford: Blackwell, 1958.

Wolfson, Susan J. *Formal Charges: The Shaping of Poetry in British Romanticism.* Stanford, CA: Stanford University Press, 1997.

———. "Reading for Form." *MLQ* 61 (2000): 1–16.

Woloch, Alex. *The One vs. the Many: Minor Characters and the Space of the Protagonist in the Novel.* Princeton: Princeton University Press, 2003.

Wordsworth, William. "Preface to the Second Edition of *Lyrical Ballads.*" In *Critical Theory Since Plato,* edited by Hazard Adams and Leroy Searle. Boston: Wadsworth, 2005.

Wrede, William. *Das Messiasgeheimnis in den Evangelien: Zugleich ein Beitrag zum Verständnis des Markusevangeliums.* Göttingen: Vandenhoeck & Ruprecht, 1901.

Wright, Benjamin G., III. "Joining the Club: A Suggestion about Genre in Early Jewish Texts." *Dead Sea Discoveries* 17 (2010): 289–314.

Wuellner, W. H. "Greek Rhetoric and Pauline Argumentation." In *Early Christian Literature and the Classical Intellectual Tradition: In Honorem Robert M. Grant,* edited by William R. Schoedel and Robert L. Wilken, 177–188. Paris: Beauchesne, 1979.

Yamada, Kota. "A Rhetorical History: The Literary Genre of the Acts of the Apostles." In *Rhetoric, Scripture and Theology: Essays from the 1994 Pretoria Conference,* edited by Stanley E. Porter and Thomas H. Olbricht, 230–250. Sheffield: Sheffield Academic, 1996.

Yamasaki, Gary. *Point of View and Evaluative Guidance in Biblical Narrative.* Eugene, OR: Cascade, 2012.

Yee, Gale. "'Fraught with Background': Literary Ambiguity in II Samuel 11." *Int* 42 (1988): 240–253.

Yeo, Khiok-khng. *Rhetorical Interaction in 1 Corinthians 8 and 10: A Formal Analysis with Preliminary Suggestions for a Chinese, Cross-Cultural Hermeneutic.* Leiden: Brill, 1995.

Young, Robert. *Colonial Desire: Hybridity in Theory, Culture, and Race.* New York: Routledge, 1995.

Zimmermann, Ruben. *Puzzling the Parables of Jesus: Methods and Interpretation.* Minneapolis: Fortress, 2015.

Ancient Sources Index

Other Ancient Writings

General Index

Abrams, Meyer, 14, 22, 23–26, 27–31, 40, 43, 44, 191–192
Adam, A. K. M., 2, 127, 139
Adorno, Theodor, 85, 211n38
affective fallacy, 53–54, 178
affect theory, 11, 189, 192; emphases of, 106, 132, 163, 175; literary criticism and, 176–178, 182, 214n8
"After Theory" movements, 22–23, 106, 130–131, 132–134
Ahmed, Sara, 177–178, 229n66
Aichele, George, 130, 214n7
Allan, Rutger, 183
Allen, Amy, 133–134
Alter, Robert, 18, 153
Althusser, Louis, 6, 87
Anderson, Paul, 128
animal studies, 132
Ankersmit, Frank, 76
Aschcroft, Bill, Garet Griffiths, and Helen Tiffin, 134
Ashton, John, 12, 42
Auerbach, Erich, 24, 27–28, 210n126
Aune, David, 20, 58
authorial intent, 25, 37, 53–54, 66, 88, 111, 118, 122, 128, 173, 184, 186, 188, 203n75, 206n39. See also intentional fallacy

Bailey, James, 225n88
Bailey, Mark, 73

Bailey, Randall, 128
Bakhtin, Mikhail, 50–52, 115
Bal, Mieke, 12, 156, 191, 225n25
Baldick, Chris, 46
Barreto, John, 124
Barthes, Roland, 75, 76, 105, 113, 116, 189, 205n9, 216n35, 217n54
Barton, John, 34, 35–36, 123, 204n90
Bazzana, Giovanni, 94–95, 172
Beardslee, William, 17, 68
Beebee, Thomas, 82, 207n70
Benjamin, Walter, 78, 85, 211n18
Bennett, Jane, 178, 180
Berlant, Lauren, 177
Bernstein, R. J., 95–96, 121
Betz, Hans Dieter, 18
Bhabha, Homi, 109–110
Blomberg, Craig, 117, 141
Blount, Brian, 128
Bockmuehl, Markus, 8, 65–66, 94, 100, 117, 123, 126, 217n59
Boer, Roland, 91, 92, 97
Bogel, Frederic, 148, 158
Borg, Michell and Graeme Miles, 113–114
Bornkamm, Günther, 188
Bourdieu, Pierre, 86, 120, 227n35
Briggs, Sheila, 125
Brooks, Cleanth, 53, 54, 58
Brooks, Peter, 177, 212n56
Brooten, Bernadette, 124–125